PRAISE FOR *APRIL 1945*

"This newest book by Craig Shirley propels him into the first rank of American historians. In *April 1945*, Shirley tells well a story that has never been told before, and he does so with the same verve, energy, and detail as he did with his books on Ronald Reagan, his biography of me, and his book on Mary Ball Washington. *April 1945*, his companion book to his bestseller *December 1941*, is a must-read."

—NEWT GINGRICH, FORMER SPEAKER OF THE HOUSE OF REPRESENTATIVES AND BESTSELLING AUTHOR

"April 1945 was a turning point in history. Nobody tells the real story and drama of that time better than Craig Shirley."

—CHRISTOPHER RUDDY, CEO OF NEWSMAX MEDIA, INC.

"Craig Shirley's great talent for taking us back to key inflection points in our history is on full and vigorous display in this book. So much of the way we live now can be traced to the end of World War II, and Shirley recaptures that epochal time with brio and insight. A terrific book!"

—JON MEACHAM, PULITZER PRIZE WINNER AND BESTSELLING AUTHOR OF *AMERICAN LION*

"With the advent of *April 1945*, Craig Shirley must be considered among the first rank of American historians. He tells well one of the most important months in American history. This book is sensational. A must-read!"

—MARK LEVIN, NATIONALLY SYNDICATED RADIO HOST AND BESTSELLING AUTHOR

"Craig Shirley has become such a solid go-to historian, and a prolific one. His books stand out as not just compelling, well written, and thoroughly researched, but unique. He is so adept at identifying pivotal people and pivotal points in history, and this is one of them. This book's focus on the pivot points of April 1945 is fascinating. It's a really engaging and really important work. April 1945 was truly a hinge of history, and this is truly a significant historical work."

—PAUL KENGOR, PROFESSOR OF POLITICAL SCIENCE, GROVE CITY COLLEGE

"Craig Shirley has produced the fitting bookend to his previous *December 1941*, for it is falling out of focus today how much America had changed during our four-year involvement in the world war. Even with victory in sight in the spring of 1945, it was not yet clear where America's place in the world might settle once the shooting ended. Shirley's fine-grained narrative captures both the details of everyday life on the ground along with the larger strategic questions that overwhelmed the world's leaders."

—STEVEN F. HAYWARD, AUTHOR OF *THE AGE OF REAGAN*

"As always, Craig Shirley reminds us why real history is elegantly written, thoroughly researched, and painstakingly defended."

—LAURA INGRAHAM, HOST OF *THE INGRAHAM ANGLE*
AND BESTSELLING AUTHOR

"Craig Shirley's *December 1941* was a veritable time machine, one that placed us so precisely in the moment when a startled nation awakes to find itself at war. His *April 1945* skillfully transports us once again, this time to a world at war's end. It's an account of history as exacting and rigorous as you will find, events worthy of this careful look by one of our nation's most talented historians."

—JOHN HEUBUSCH, EXECUTIVE DIRECTOR OF THE RONALD REAGAN
PRESIDENTIAL FOUNDATION AND INSTITUTE

"Craig Shirley gives you compelling new stories of the events and people that shaped 1945, a year that fundamentally transformed the United States and the world. His gripping account of the fall of Germany, rise of the Cold War, and the political leaders who shaped that period is riveting. He documents what shaped the second half of the twentieth century in a way only Craig Shirley can do."

—STEVEN SCULLY, C-SPAN HOST AND LECTURER

"*April 1945* transports readers through the last days of World War II. It's as if we're reading multiple social-media feeds from Hitler, FDR, average Americans, reporters, and generals in real time. Once again, Craig Shirley delivers an important must-read."

—JANE HAMPTON COOK, AUTHOR OF *RESILIENCE ON PARADE*

APRIL
1945

ALSO BY CRAIG SHIRLEY

*Reagan's Revolution: The Untold Story of
the Campaign That Started It All*

*Rendezvous with Destiny: Ronald Reagan and
the Campaign That Changed America*

December 1941: 31 Days That Changed America and Saved the World

Last Act: The Final Years and Emerging Legacy of Ronald Reagan

Reagan Rising: The Decisive Years, 1976–1980

Citizen Newt: The Making of a Reagan Conservative

*Mary Ball Washington: The Untold Story
of George Washington's Mother*

APRIL
1945

The Hinge of History

CRAIG SHIRLEY

NEW YORK TIMES BESTSELLING
AUTHOR OF *DECEMBER 1941*

NELSON
BOOKS

An Imprint of Thomas Nelson

Published in Nashville, Tennessee, by Nelson Books, an imprint of Thomas Nelson. Nelson Books and Thomas Nelson are registered trademarks of HarperCollins Christian Publishing, Inc.

Thomas Nelson titles may be purchased in bulk for educational, business, fundraising, or sales promotional use. For information, please e-mail SpecialMarkets@ ThomasNelson.com.

Any internet addresses, phone numbers, or company or product information printed in this book are offered as a resource and are not intended in any way to be or to imply an endorsement by Thomas Nelson, nor does Thomas Nelson vouch for the existence, content, or services of these sites, phone numbers, companies, or products beyond the life of this book.

ISBN 978-1-4002-1714-4 (Audiobook)

Library of Congress Cataloging-in-Publication Data

Names: Shirley, Craig, author.
Title: April 1945: the hinge of history / Craig Shirley, New York Times bestselling author of December 1941.
Description: Nashville, Tennessee: Thomas Nelson, [2022] | Summary: "Acclaimed historian and New York Times bestselling author Craig Shirley delivers a compelling account of 1945, particularly the watershed events in the month of April, that details how America emerged from World War II as a leading superpower"—Provided by publisher.
Identifiers: LCCN 2021037040 (print) | LCCN 2021037041 (ebook) | ISBN 9781400217083 (hardcover) | ISBN 9781400217113 (ebook)
Subjects: LCSH: World War, 1939–1945—United States—Chronology. | United States—History—1933–1945.
Classification: LCC D769 .S542 2022 (print) | LCC D769 (ebook) | DDC 940.53/73—dc23
LC record available at https://lccn.loc.gov/2021037040
LC ebook record available at https://lccn.loc.gov/2021037041

Printed in the United States of America

22 23 24 25 26   LSC   10 9 8 7 6 5 4 3 2 1

As with everything, this book is dedicated to my beloved wife,
Zorine, who has made forty years seem like forty minutes.

CONTENTS

PROLOGUE

"Hitler in Radio Talk Predicts Nazi Victory"
Boston Daily Globe

"American Captives Starved by Nazis"
New York Times

"Washington the City Is Overcrowded, Badly Housed,
Expensive, Crime-Ridden, Intolerant"
Harper's

In April 1945, life-altering events happened. The old order was dying, and a new America was being built.

And many people died, including world leaders.

April, they say, is the cruelest month.

In 1945, Americans were still reeling from the attack on Pearl Harbor, where many men remained unidentified four years later. Hawaii had once been a peaceful and idyllic island chain in the Pacific. One resident, Gene Paterson Ames, wrote to her mother immediately after the attack of hearing the tinkling of Japanese shell casings falling from their planes as they flew overhead, looking for anything to shoot. "At first, I just went to pieces—all of us did," she wrote frankly.[1] She also wrote of the carnage there, of trenches being dug around houses, and of her husband being deployed to help guard the beach against a possible invasion. She was shortly evacuated to the mainland. Her husband, Major Alan Strock, later became a much-decorated soldier, fighting for four years in the Pacific.

ON DECEMBER 7, 1941, PEARL Harbor was a sitting duck. Now, in 1945, it was the Gibraltar of the Central Pacific.

WHEN HE FIRST BECAME president years earlier, Franklin Delano Roosevelt had traveled to Hawaii, taking two of his sons, Franklin Jr. and John. While there, he toured the island and attended a Harvard reunion. That island was no longer the paradise he had once savored.

IN THE FIRST MONTHS of 1945, the great war correspondent Ernie Pyle was killed in the Pacific. Auschwitz and Buchenwald were discovered, as were their horrors. And then, Franklin Roosevelt, on the verge of victory over the Axis powers, died suddenly at the age of sixty-three. He died in April 1945, just as Abraham Lincoln died in April 1865. Harry Truman became president of the United States. British leader Winston Churchill had once called FDR the "best friend" to England. Churchill once dubbed Roosevelt "the greatest man I have ever known." Churchill and FDR were part of the "Big Three" along with Soviet dictator Joseph Stalin. Of the Big Three, Churchill and Roosevelt never completely trusted each other, definitely not Stalin; but all were united in their desire to defeat Nazism.

IN THE EARLIER YEARS of the 1940s, young women had inundated Washington looking for work. So had minorities. Washington, before the war, had been a sleepy Southern town that flooded often and then frequently reeked as the Potomac spilled over its shallow banks while mosquitoes buzzed everywhere. Charles Dickens once visited Washington and was appalled at the filthy conditions. After the New Deal, and then during the war, it grew exponentially as well as bureaucratically. Washington had quickly become the capital of the world. "If the war lasts much longer, Washington is going to bust right out of its pants," wrote *Life* magazine in January 1943.[2]

EVEN IN THE THICK of the war, movies continued. Disney launched their new feature, *The Three Caballeros*. Many movies had a war theme, but some were focused on suspense, as with Alfred Hitchcock's *Spellbound* starring Ingrid Bergman and Gregory Peck, produced by David O. Selznick.

ELEANOR ROOSEVELT, FDR'S WIFE and fifth cousin, had reshaped the office of the First Lady into a newly powerful position, unlike other women who had preceded her. She was a force to be reckoned with. Even so, FDR practically died in the arms of his lover, Lucy Mercer Rutherfurd, far from Eleanor. FDR was vacationing in his beloved Warm Springs, Georgia, when he died of an intracerebral hemorrhage. In the following days, a national magazine featured on its last page a picture of the lonely dog Fala waiting in vain for his master, FDR.

Still, the war was nearly won by FDR and Churchill, despite their flaws. The phrase "April in Paris" took on a whole new meaning while jet planes flew overhead in Europe continuously. Night after night, Allied planes bombed German cities.

In April, the despicable monster Adolf Hitler, half-crazed and trapped in his bunker, finally committed suicide. So did his longtime mistress, Eva Braun. They left behind the many Germans and Europeans who participated in the so-called Final Solution as a means of exterminating millions of Jews, political opponents, Poles, Russians, homosexuals, and other human beings. All told, he was responsible for the deaths of millions of people and had destroyed many countries. Hitler's mission had also been to change the face of Europe by destroying the existing culture and replacing it with a Germanic culture.

Hitler may not have changed the face of Europe, but the war did change the face of the home front and the world. Two of his last orders included "Clausewitz," which was the final defense of Berlin, and the

"Nero Decree," which was an order to destroy as much matériel as possible to prevent it from falling into Allied hands. He was a monster right to the end.

PLEXIGLAS WAS DEVELOPED FOR wartime and peacetime use. Americans debated Alexis de Tocqueville's *Democracy in America* while simultaneously debating *Can Democracy Recover?* by Louis Marlio. Liberty ships dotted the oceans. Future presidents Dwight David "Ike" Eisenhower, John Kennedy, Lyndon Johnson, Richard Nixon, Gerald Ford, Ronald Reagan, and George H. W. Bush all served in uniform in the war, as did millions of other young Americans.

Under the cover of secrecy, engineers developed giant bombs while Americans drove cars, sparingly because of gas rationing, that included Fords, Plymouths, Chryslers, LaSalles, Mercurys, and Nashes, although they also traveled by planes, trains, and buses.

Women's hats were a trend, and the "Eisenhower jacket" kicked off a fad in women's fashion that ran to chic, slim pantsuits, wide lapels, and pleated pants. Men's fashion had not changed—and would not change even years later. A suit was a suit. A haircut was a haircut.

John Steinbeck's *Cannery Row* had been released to mostly critical praise and Bob Hope was everywhere. Lifebuoy soap was popular as were Jell-O puddings and hard liquor. Denture breath was often a problem. Professional baseball players—because of military service—were often too young or too old. So, women played the game and played it well.

In Buchenwald, thousands of German civilians were forced by US Army officials to bear witness to the Nazi atrocities committed in that city alone. Many fainted and more cried. George Patton, who had seen so much in war and peace, threw up at the spectacle of the human carnage by the Germans. In the news often, Patton was due for his fourth star.

The old Confederacy buried a ninety-six-year-old general, Homer Atkinson, in Petersburg, Virginia. *Life* magazine did a profile of the leaders who lost. Drew Pearson continued to write his error-filled Washington Merry-Go-Round column. A profile was written about

Herb Brownell, leader of the perpetually failing Republican Party. The Republicans always fell to the titanic Democratic Party.

Just a few months earlier, FDR had voted for himself at Hyde Park for an unprecedented fourth term. When asked his occupation, he inscribed "tree planter."

Hitler ally Benito Mussolini was dragged down by the mob, as was his mistress, and they were both shot by a firing squad, then hung upside down for public display and ridicule in Milan. And POWs hated the Nazis. With good reason, too, as they were horribly treated. Same for the Japanese, who were ghastly in dealing with American POWs.

THE BATTLE FOR OKINAWA was initially thought to be "very light," at least according to the *Washington Post*, but it turned out to be one of the bloodiest battles of the entire war. Millions of men went to war in Europe and the Pacific and to other parts of the world as military personnel, but so did millions of civilians, especially women. In the thick of the war years, Americans everywhere were volunteering for the war effort, giving blood, saving scrap metal, growing Victory gardens. Propaganda posters were in heavy use. Australia suffered a drought, but women's stockings and silk lingerie ads were ubiquitous as the war was winding down and silk was no longer needed for military parachutes.

FAR AND WIDE WAR bonds, known as Liberty Bonds in World War I, were for sale, and civilians bought more than $1 billion worth of them. The bonds were used to pay for the war effort. Bonds were advertised, put on promotional posters, and written about in magazines such as *Life*, *Look*, *Harper's*, *Saturday Evening Post*, and *Reader's Digest*. Each week *Life* magazine featured human-interest stories, ads galore of all types, the news, and lots of actors, including Humphrey Bogart and Lauren Bacall touting their first movie together, *To Have and Have Not*. They would go on to film several more movies together and to marry, despite their big age difference.

Beautiful Rita Hayworth still graced the cover of many magazines.

Helpful articles on movie etiquette and stories about religion were printed alongside advertising for military equipment. An issue of *Life* magazine featured an article titled "The Nine Young Men" about the Supreme Court. It also contained a sponsored article on pneumonia and how a new drug, penicillin, was saving millions of lives. An ad for Welch's fudge and a cartoon of a man striking a woman after the woman struck the man appeared in print. Old Gold cigarettes advertised that they could cure dryness, and Philip Morris touted the health benefits of smoking their brand.

MILLIONS—PERHAPS BILLIONS—IN PLUNDERED GOLD, money, jewelry, and paintings were discovered in secret Nazi caches in Europe, stolen mostly from the Jews of Europe.

RAMESES WERE BEING ADVERTISED, but they were not what you think; these were cigarettes. The war and war news changed America. "There's a war on!" was a repeated phrase and headline, delivered both sarcastically and seriously. The *Washington Post* reported in big black letters "Report Nazi Surrender" on April 29. (The actual date was May 7.) The next day it was reported, "Mussolini, Mistress Slain by Patriots."

As of the end of December 1944, nearly two million men had separated from the army through all forms of discharge: honorable and otherwise, killed in action, wounded and missing, and POWs.

To fight the war, Roosevelt had essentially created a new government and laid it on top of the old government. The once middle-class town of Washington was changed by the patrician from the Hudson Valley in New York. Government intervened in every aspect of the American economy and culture, right down to the price of diapers and a bottle of ketchup. Though it had failed to defeat the Great Depression, it had succeeded in defeating Nazi Germany and the Empire of Japan.

The military depended on Campbell's Tomato Soup, and cigarettes were in high demand. Chesterfield cigarettes were advertised featuring women fetching slippers for a man and his smokes. Makeup ads also sometimes depicted women as men's pets. They wore hose for their legs, and the Andrews Sisters were still thrilling crowds with their crooning while Fred Astaire and Ginger Rogers were still entertaining movie audiences.

THE CONTRAST WAS UNAVOIDABLE: Slavish falsehoods about the Soviets' "workers' paradise" appeared in all the magazines and newsreels while a hotel room in Miami was going for around $37 a day with two hundred thousand visitors expected—there were plenty of steaks too.

IN THIS BOOK, THE reader will journey through the waning days of World War II and experience the everyday events of what Americans were thinking and feeling in those heady days, much like in my previous book *December 1941*. This is a companion book to that one, the alpha and the omega. Many were experiencing bittersweet feelings as they were happy with the victory yet devastated at the loss of a son in uniform.

The reader cannot fully appreciate the significance of April 1945 without learning about the preceding months. These months were a horrible prelude to the horrors of April 1945.

IT WAS A MEANNESS of times, but it was also a kindness of times. It was a blending. It was an ending. And it was a beginning. The great Winston Churchill was famous for saying, "Now this is not the end. It is not even the beginning of the end. But it is, perhaps, the end of the beginning."

Such was April 1945.

Craig Shirley
Ben Lomond
Dunnsville, Virginia
2021

CHAPTER 1

JANUARY 1945

"Nazis Will Never Give Up, Hitler"
WASHINGTON POST

"Patton's Army Launches Full-Scale Offensive"
LOS ANGELES TIMES

"Prisoners Slain"
HONOLULU STAR-BULLETIN

The Second World War continued unabated in January 1945 as it had for the previous six years. German chancellor Adolf Hitler took to the airwaves for the first time in over five months, proclaiming that the Fatherland would never give up, even as the Russians were closing in on his thousand-year Reich from the east and the Americans, British, French, and Canadians were marching steadily toward Berlin from the west.

The German leader, in his midnight broadcast as reported by the Associated Press, also oddly announced the deaths of General Field Marshal Albert Kesselring, along with a host of other "Nazi party members and state personalities,"[1] but in fact, Kesselring was alive (and lived until 1960). Hitler also made several references to the failed assassination attempt against him back in July 1944, seeing his survival as vindication for his dictatorship.

Hitler lengthened his comments to denounce Winston Churchill for the bombing campaign against Germany; French general Charles de Gaulle, whom he called Winston Churchill's protégé due to his supposed desire to include Germany in a new French Order; and, significantly, Stalin's Jewish colleague Ilya Ehrenburg, who he said "goes further and announces that the German people must be smashed and destroyed." To the bitter end, the evil man was virulently anti-Semitic. He predicted that the war would not end until 1946 unless the Germans defeated the Allies earlier: "We know the democratic statesmen, the Bolshevists and Jews want to bring Germany to slavery, despoil our youth and let millions starve."[2]

Hitler also threatened the German people: "We are going to destroy everybody who does not take part in the common effort for the country or who makes himself a tool of the enemy."[3]

Hitler's delusion stretched through his senior leadership. Air Marshal Hermann Goering went on radio also to proclaim his smashed Luftwaffe had been rebuilt, and said, "We look to the future full of hope and confidence. We have new squadrons in the air, our parachutist troops are exemplary, our flak gunners eager for battle."[4] In reality, the last major offensive of the Luftwaffe was over by the time Hitler spoke. Operation Bodenplatte, a last-ditch effort of the once-mighty German Air Force to achieve air superiority in the Low Countries of Europe, had failed. The air belonged to the Allies.

Minister of Propaganda Paul Joseph Goebbels likewise went on radio, calling the war pointless, but only because the Allies were fighting it, not because Germany had started it: "We have no idea what sense enemies see in this war. We see in it an embodiment of a bad universal principle."[5] The war was going badly for the Nazis, but at propaganda and lies, they excelled.

Fortress Europe had been breached. Almost every German territorial gain on the Western Front had been erased. What took the Germans years to conquer took the Allies months to liberate. General George S. Patton had "unleashed a full-scale offensive" on the European continent across Belgium, racing toward the neck of the German "bulge."[6] His forces were pushing back against the German army's surprise winter counteroffensive "in an apparent attempt to split Field Marshal Karl von Rundstedt's three armies."[7]

THE BATTLE OF THE Bulge was the last major German offensive of World War II. The German offensive had begun the prior month, in December, attacking a weak spot in the Allied lines and pushing out into the shape of a "bulge." The Third Reich threw everything into the desperate battle, and as a result was showing signs of success when they first waged this counteroffensive in mid-December 1944. The battle raged on, and although blunted just after Christmas, the Germans would not give up easily. Contributing to the Allies' problems was bad weather, which made air reconnaissance difficult. Also, frankly, the Allies had become over-confident. The liberation of Europe was moving at a speed unexpected by all but the most optimistic of generals. Supply lines were struggling to keep pace with the Allied advance. In effect, the Allies were at risk of being defeated by their own victories. The Germans deployed four hundred thousand troops into the battle, fourteen hundred tanks, two thousand artillery pieces, and it all shaped up, by some estimates, as the largest and bloodiest battle of the war for the Americans.

It was also unbearably cold and wintry. The Associated Press reported that "blizzard conditions made this campaign the most difficult yet faced by the Americans on either side of the Western or Italian Fronts."[8] The American fight had been waged in part by the 4th Cavalry Regiment, formerly a horse outfit but now mechanized. An early press estimate suggested, "Civilians suffered heavily from bombing and shelling, with 300 buried under debris. Emaciated women and children emerging from cellars and nearby woods when American jeeps rolled in found their homes in ruins."[9] In reality, more than three thousand civilians were killed during the battle, but not all were incidental. At least two hundred fifty civilians were executed by Nazi SS.

Giant maps of the world adorned many newspapers, helpfully reminding readers of all that had been accomplished by the Allies in 1944, from General Dwight D. Eisenhower's amphibious, successful, and historic invasion of the French coast across the twenty-one miles of the English Channel—D-Day—to General Douglas MacArthur's brilliant strategy of island-hopping in the Pacific, jumping over Japanese strongholds from Australia to New Guinea and eventually retaking the Philippines. MacArthur was already making plans for the invasion of the Japanese home islands.

Meanwhile, the US Navy's campaign across the Central and Western Pacific was bearing fruit as well. Islands long held by the Japanese such as the Marianas—including Guam, Tinian, and Saipan—were being taken. For thousands of years, these islands had been paradises for the native Polynesian people, with wide beaches, roaring oceans, coconuts, and peace and quiet. Now, the crashing of guns from the decks of American and Japanese battleships was heard as often as the crashing of the blue Pacific Ocean on the shores of these small slices of Eden.

With the Allied capture of these small islands formerly held by the Japanese, the wondrous Seabees—the construction battalion—moved in quickly. It was important for the Americans to take these islands and atolls in their drive across the Central and Western Pacific, which allowed the Navy Seabees to move in and create rough airfields and landing strips from where navy and marine planes could further prosecute the war against the Japanese.

The Seabees, often comprised of men too old to fight, were scattered across the Pacific. A syndicated columnist Hamilton W. Faron wrote, "From Pearl Harbor . . . to the Aleutian Islands to New Caledonia, these men . . . have gone with their construction equipment to convert waste lands into modern naval bases. Buildings of all types rise literally overnight under the energetic drive of the Seabees."[10]

Their work was difficult in these steaming jungles, filled with poisonous snakes, thick underbrush, plant life, and more than occasionally a Japanese sniper shooting at them as they labored to construct coarse air bases out of the jungles. Their unofficial motto was "Can do. Will do. Did." Stories popped up about the ongoing struggles and successes of the indefatigable Seabees, including fighting "hand to hand combat with the Japs while bulldozing a vital airfield. A total of 320 Japs were slaughtered. Yet, Seabees prepared the airfield for use in seven days."[11]

Still, the Japanese were fighting on, relentlessly. On January 1, the Japanese news agency Domei claimed that Japan had sunk ten American ships, including a cruiser and five transports. Reports from the propaganda machine were confused as to exactly how many US Navy ships had actually been sunk or damaged, but there was no doubt the liberation of the Philippines was a ferocious campaign. The Americans were fighting back, hard. General MacArthur's headquarters reported that fourteen of thirty-two attacking Japanese planes had been shot down and Japanese troops had been killed on Leyte Island in a "mopping up" action, a phrase by MacArthur that infuriated some army men as sounding too casual about war. An International News Service story was more brutal, headlined "117,997 Japs Join Ancestors in Bruising Leyte Campaign."[12]

Indeed, Fleet Admiral Chester W. Nimitz predicted 1945 would be the bloodiest year of the Pacific war. "The war to come will consist of obtaining bases closer and closer to the Japanese Empire from which we can reach the enemy with all the weapons we have. But the war will be far from won even when we cross the Pacific. At that time the war enters its toughest phase for us."[13]

Each engagement in the Pacific—just as it was in Europe—was bloody and hard-fought, and many young men sacrificed themselves on the altar of victory and freedom. The Japanese propagandists had once told their people that Americans were soft, too interested only in good food and good times. The German propagandists had also told their people much the same. They said the Americans couldn't fight. The Japanese, and later the Germans, found out after Pearl Harbor the

American fighting men were in fact the best in the world—brave, resolute, and strong. "Our armies have demonstrated that they can take it as well as dish it out. It has been discovered again that American troops do not panic, even when relatively green, when confronted by the unexpected; but that they rally and take swift and appropriate action. . . . We are facing tough and resourceful enemies, whose reserves of men and material have been greatly underestimated, whose will to fight has been little impaired and whom it will take all we can muster to defeat."[14]

THE UNITED STATES OF America had changed radically and significantly in the four years since the unprovoked attack by the Japanese on Pearl Harbor in December 1941. On the sixth of December, the United States was decidedly an isolationist country, trying desperately to stay out of the conflict that had engulfed all of Europe, the African coast, and much of the Far East—indeed, most of the world.

From the end of the Great War in 1919 until late 1941, Americans had forlornly asked of the First World War, "What did we get out of the first world war but death, debt and George M. Cohan?"[15] Americans were foursquare against getting involved in another world war. Americans were sending "Bundles for Britain" and had "loaned" old World War I naval destroyers to the British, along with other matériel. Franklin Delano Roosevelt and Winston Churchill had signed the Atlantic Charter, a statement of general agreement on trade and other such matters. But because the American people remained steadfastly opposed to any direct American involvement in the European war, on this crucial matter the charter was silent, and many claimed it was not a formally ratified treaty and therefore unenforceable.

The isolationist America First Movement was a potent political force, as it was bipartisan in opposition to another war. Both Democrats and Republicans were prominent members and, in 1941, had vowed to field candidates in all the federal races if the incumbent Republican or Democrat was not sufficiently anti-war.

America would stay out of the world war until December 8, 1941.

Twenty-four hours after the attack on Pearl Harbor, America became forever an internationalist country. Faraway names of countries, towns, and battlefields, which no one really paid attention to in hundreds of daily newspapers, now could be rattled off with familiarity and regularity by American citizens. Everybody was an expert on the war, and why not? All were invested in the war through military service, civil defense work, war industries, rationings, Victory gardens, scrap drives, and a thousand other examples of sacrifice and effort. "Hard fighting in Europe and hard work at home will do more to end the war favorably. . . . The armies will fight. Will we work?" editorialized the *Los Angeles Times*.[16]

Much overlooked by the rest of the world was the role of the Soviet Union in not only ridding their country of the German invaders but pushing them back to their own native soil. The British Air Corps got high marks for taking the fight to the Axis powers in the skies over Western Europe, and both the American infantry in the Pacific Southwest and the American navy's island-hopping campaign across the Central and Western Pacific were reviewed glowingly. All in all, the area over which the Axis powers ruled was shrinking, sometimes by the day. China also got high marks for taking the fight to the Japanese. But so, too, were the Americans. On New Year's Day, American B-29s pounded the Japanese homeland. The Federal Communications Commission intercepted Tokyo radio's attack warnings to her citizens as incendiary bombs fell from the skies. "The first New Year's sleep of tens of millions of Japanese was interrupted by the drone of high flying United States Super fortresses."[17]

WORLD WAR II WAS NOT just fought in the fields of Europe or the jungles of Asia but also on the American home front. In Montana, a balloon was discovered and thought to be of Japanese origin. The Federal Bureau of Investigation was investigating.[18] For some time, it had been known the Japanese, using friendly westerly winds, attached incendiary devices to balloons to float across the Pacific and hopefully find targets in North America. Several fires over the years had been started as a result.

A "war footing" in America manifested itself in many ways. For over four years, almost everything from gas to milk to coffee to meat had been rationed for the war effort. Blackouts, brownouts, searches, internment camps, and a thousand other signs everywhere in America indicated that a world war took center stage and that civilians had to make many sacrifices, big and small. New Year's Eve in Los Angeles was ordered halted in the bars and clubs at midnight. Drinks were ordered to be off all bars "by the Board of Equalization [and the mahogany wiped clean] at the stroke of midnight."[19] Later, the mandate to close was overruled as the board was not a legislative body and, thus, had no power to arbitrarily close the bars at midnight.

Partygoers in Southern California may have had good reason to stay indoors on New Year's Eve as the evening temperatures dipped to a frigid thirty-seven degrees, glacier-like for the normally balmy town of actors, actresses, celebrities, and hangers-on.

In Boston, it was just the opposite. Partiers were allowed to dance but not until after midnight, and even then the public celebrations were allowed for only one hour. In New York City, celebrants were even freer to celebrate, and "theatres and nightclubs, despite shortages, did a record business." The iconic Times Square, "national symbol of year-end gayety," was crowded, despite being covered in a heavy fog, and a little less noisy due to fewer "tin horns" available. The sidewalk hawkers selling New Year regalia were now scarce.[20]

In Washington, the president of the United States, Franklin Roosevelt, having won an unprecedented fourth term of office, was hosting a White House party to ring in the New Year. Some guests had been invited, and the president offered a toast to America.[21]

The years in a wheelchair certainly did nothing to help his circulation, but now he looked haggard and "drawn."[22] Smoking two packs of Camel filterless cigarettes did nothing to help either, nor did his erratic diet or his "fivesies," as Eleanor called his afternoon Manhattan and old-fashioned adult beverages. FDR often called the five o'clock drinking time his favorite hour of the day. The war years, the Great Depression, and twelve years in office had finally caught up with him. Long days and nights of meeting with the military brass, reading untold number of war dispatches, despairing and worrying over young boys in combat (including his own four boys in uniform), and directing a far-flung war had taken a terrible toll on the now frail man with permanent dark circles under his eyes—who looked much older than his sixty-three years.

One young journalist remarked on his surprise when he had his first up-close look at Franklin Roosevelt during a White House press conference.

> It was a shock, unnerving. Here was the most famous face in the world, one he had seen a thousand times. In newspaper and magazine and newsreel pictures it was the face of a handsome man with strong, well-formed features displaying a smiling, good-natured manner, chin tilted high, ivory cigarette holder pointed to the sky. Those were the pictures. Here was the reality—a man who looked terribly old and tired. No doubt youth was too quick to notice the effects of age, but this man's face was more gray than pink, his hands shook, his eyes were hazy and wandering, his neck drooped in stringy, sagging folds accentuated by a shirt collar that must have fit at one time but now was two or three sizes too large.[23]

This was in 1943, when the young journalist, David Brinkley, was appalled at the FDR he beheld.

> In private, Press Secretary Stephen Early was asked why the president didn't buy shirts that fit. Collars hanging so loosely made the president look even more shrunken and drawn.
>
> "That damn Dutchman is so tight he won't buy new shirts until the old ones are ready to use for cleaning rags."
>
> "What's the matter with him?"
>
> "He's just tired. Running a world war is a hell of a job."[24]

And that was two years earlier.

Still, as always, he was boundlessly optimistic. Winston Churchill once said meeting FDR was like opening a bottle of champagne. The man was naturally bubbly, effervescent. A first-class temperament, indeed.

Nineteen forty-four was now in the history books, but Americans did reflect on the most momentous war year in their history. The rest of the world was focused on the events at hand, not dwelling on the past year. Of course, the D-Day invasion of Europe, gaining a toehold for the Allied forces, was a hard-fought success, though a bloody one.

IN 1945, AMERICAN NEWSPAPERS, as they had been for over four years, were crammed with war news. An ad in the *Los Angeles Times*, placed by the Los Angeles Railway, proclaimed, "Hail! 1945! The New Year calls for sterner measures, greater sacrifices and a more steadfast faith in a just God. . . . May Americans emerge from this torment of strife, stalwart, true and worthy, before God, to take its place as the first nation among all nations."[25] American attitudes about isolation and internationalism had changed fundamentally and profoundly.

After all the years of war, many papers had become franker about the fighting and the atrocities. In one paper, a photograph was featured of a boy killed at the hands of the Nazis as an American GI looked somberly at the small corpse.[26]

The brutality of the Nazis was evident everywhere, in every way. On January 1, it was revealed that one month earlier the German army gunned down 115 "helpless prisoners" of war "before the flaming guns of German tanks" near Malmedy, Belgium. The slain soldiers were all Americans, including two GIs who were simply driving an ambulance truck. The Americans were lined up six deep and machine-gunned at a range of only seventy-five feet. Then "the German soldiers walked through deliberately shooting those who showed signs of life."[27] The Allied Supreme Headquarters protested loudly, saying the murders were a violation of the Geneva Conventions, but the Third Reich had trampled all over this document for years. It became known as the "Malmedy

Massacre." All American newspapers decried this newest atrocity by the Third Reich, but there would be more to come.

The Germans were inventive if also vile. They dressed up their soldiers as the Allies, complete with papers and impeccable English, to try to infiltrate the American troops. On January 30, they dropped elite parachute assassins into Luxembourg in an attempt to murder high-ranking American officers and government officials.[28]

One GI saw the brutality of the Germans up close. After a battle when some of his platoon lay in the snow, wounded and dead, the Nazis methodically shot and bayoneted the fallen Americans, but not before going through their pockets, petty-thief style.[29]

Berlin radio claimed its U-boats had sunk six Allied transports, but the Germans were masters of propaganda and disinformation.

Even the tawdrier stories from early 1945 were wrapped in war news. An American war bride, unfaithful to her soldier husband who had just returned from twenty-eight months overseas, was murdered by her lover, who then took his own life. The husband was quoted as saying he forgave his wayward bride but to no avail. Such were the fortunes of love and war.[30]

WAR WASN'T THE ONLY event causing Americans grief. A terrible train accident, operated by the Southern Pacific, occurred in Odgen, Utah, on New Year's Eve. Possibly as many as fifty passengers were killed after the engineer reportedly fell asleep at the switch.[31] Major train accidents were nearly a way of life for Americans, as three others had occurred in 1944.

Bottled water was being hyped in the *Los Angeles Times*: "From Hot Springs, Arkansas. The natural mineral water aids in conditions of ARTHRITIS, KIDNEY, STOMACH, BLADDER. Free delivery" could be arranged.[32] Theatergoers were enjoying the new movie *Together Again* starring Irene Dunne and Charles Boyer. Grocery shoppers were picking up a pound of Washington State apples for 10 cents, a three-pound can of Maxwell House coffee for 64 cents, and a thirty-ounce box of Grape Nuts for 21 cents.

Syndicated columnists in the major papers included the scandal-mongering Drew Pearson, Hollywood gossip maven Hedda Hopper, Walter Lippmann, and others. Advice columns included tips for dealing with creaky joints and people who wrote in asking why they hated their mothers.

THE B-29 WAS A significant development for the Boeing Company and the Allies, as it flew too high for Japanese fighter planes to attack and, because of its long range, could take off from airfields on tiny islands in the Western Pacific and bomb Japan with impunity.

Of the thirteen stories on the front page of the *Washington Post* on January 1, 1945, ten were about the war. One was about a horrible fire that injured five firefighters, and another was about the horrible train wreck in Utah that included "victims [who] were servicemen returning from overseas."[33] The thirteenth story was about the instability of the Greek government caused by the war.[34]

The most recent tally of Washington's young men killed in combat reached numbers far outstretching the number killed in World War I.

While American B-29s were pounding Japan, British and American bombers in Europe were doing likewise to Germany. On January 1, the *Chicago Tribune* reported, "American Flying Fortresses and British Halifaxes and Lancasters, with their escorts of Mustangs, Spitfires and Thunderbolts hit German oil refineries, communications and troop concentrations in support of the Allied ground armies."[35] Also, a fleet of Royal Air Force (RAF) bombers was reported to have laid waste to "vital Nazi communication lines" in a nighttime raid while American bombers, in daytime raids, launched a three-thousand-plane attack on German armies.

China was taking the fight to the Japanese invaders successfully, but Generalissimo Chiang Kai-shek also promised to bring constitutional government to the mainland before the end of the war instead of within one year after the end of hostilities. "We must prepare for the convening of Peoples' Congress within the year," the Generalissimo said.[36] Chiang had been a loyal ally of the United States in the fight against Japan, slowly but inexorably pushing back against the invasion of the mainland, where Japanese troops committed genocide and rape with exculpation.

THE NEW CONGRESS WAS facing a heavy legislative schedule at the onset of 1945. "Universal military training, social security expansion, taxes, wartime financing, price control, congressional reorganization and international treaties" were just a few of the many items on their collective plates.[37] They also had to formally count the Electoral College votes from the 1944 election. FDR had won another smashing victory over the Republicans and their sacrificial lamb, New York governor Thomas E. Dewey, 432 to Dewey's paltry 99 electoral votes. The popular vote was somewhat more competitive, with the president winning 53.4 percent to Dewey's 45.9 percent. But in terms of states it was a massacre, with FDR taking 36 to only 12 for Dewey. Roosevelt won in the East, the South (never in doubt), and the West. Dewey took only a few states in the Republican Midwest. In Texas, Roosevelt won with the help of the young and reputable congressman Lyndon Johnson, 821,605 to 191,425! Texas had a long and time-honored tradition of running clean elections.

FDR, in 1940, had already broken the unwritten but observed two-term limit set forth by the first president, George Washington, in 1797. But now, with a victory over the Axis powers within his grasp, it was impossible to think FDR would be turned out of office.

The only significant development in the 1944 campaign had been Roosevelt's unceremonious dumping of Vice President Henry Wallace, an embarrassing pacifist in the face of Axis aggression, and replacing him with Senator Harry S. Truman of Missouri. Truman was no lightweight, despite what some around FDR thought. He was a respected veteran of the First World War, and although he had associated with the shady Thomas Pendergast political machine in Missouri, he had emerged as a combative legislator, heading a task force investigating corruption in the War Department. So far the task force had uncovered billions in waste, fraud, and abuse in the military-industrial complex that also included some tawdry and suspicious defense contracts involving Roosevelt cronies, including the president's old buddy Tommy "the Cork" Corcoran. FDR loved Corcoran. Truman despised him. Some whispered that Truman was put on the ticket as a means of getting him off his anticorruption crusade and controlling him, as he was getting too close to the powers that be.

On the minds of many politicians and bureaucrats in Washington, especially the Director of the Office of War Mobilization and Reconversion James F. Byrnes, was what to do with men classified as 4-F. The government estimated that there were over four million young men designated 4-F for physical or mental reasons, thus they never served in uniform. Still, the government reasoned, they could perform "war work" in essential industries, and the debate centered on how to compel these 4-Fers to leave their jobs in nonessential industries for national service.[38] Even so, the war industry suffered greatly over the Christmas and New Year's holidays, with rampant absenteeism. "Although some war plant areas demonstrated shining examples of patriotic duty throughout the holidays, the overall picture was a dark one." Plants, especially near big cities, had the greatest drop-off in civilians showing up for work. Indeed, in New York City, a survey revealed that only 15 percent of the workforce had shown up on New Year's Day.[39]

The Congress was nearing a debate about compulsory peacetime military service for America's youth, a matter FDR had already indicated his support. They also were scheduled to take up the issue of creating sixty million peacetime jobs and a tax cut, despite a war that had already cost, by all estimates, billions of dollars.[40] The *Washington Post* editorialized against any cut in taxes as "ill-timed" but did call for more donations to the Russian Relief Effort and a more unified postwar world. "The concept of one world may be lost again to the peril of all mankind," it warned.[41]

The fear of a renewed isolationism was part of the backdrop of 1945, and, indeed, the Roosevelt administration was already making plans for postwar international conferences to work out arrangements between

Great Britain, Russia, and America. A new world organization was being bandied about, where nations of the world could settle their differences.

THE WAR EFFORT AND the New Deal comingled in intent and control. The War Manpower Commission (WMC) issued a briar patch of regulations on work in essential war industries that included this one: "Under the Stabilization Program, a worker leaving essential employment without a statement of availability is not eligible for further employment for 60 days."[42]

New calendars for 1945 were on the market featuring not pastoral scenes or leggy women but military airplanes.

Housing in Washington had been a problem since the New Deal and continued unabated throughout the war. There were simply too many bureaucrats and "Government Girls" (aka "the Lipstick Brigade") and military personnel in the nation's capital to accommodate. Even cabinet secretaries faced problems with leaky roofs and plumbing. Cabs were also often impossible to find or flag down, and the bars and restaurants were jammed at all hours.

Pravda hit Pope Pius XII hard for not being tougher on Nazi Germany, accusing the pontiff of being an "apologist" for fascism and holding "a policy to help Germany escape full responsibility for her war crimes." The newspaper pointed out, "It is very significant that in his message you cannot find a single word about the unprecedented monstrous crimes of Hitlerite bandits."[43] Over the course of the war, going back to the concordat signed between the Vatican and Nazi Germany, the loyalties of the Catholic Church had been questioned from time to time. Overlooked, of course, were the monstrous crimes committed by the communist state against her own people in the 1930s.

Catholic leaders in America came to the pope's defense while other denominations touted their religious and missionary work. The president of the Washington City Bible Society said 250,000 Bibles had been distributed to military personnel, and "the United States government also expended large sums on chapels and service equipment."[44]

CURIOUSLY, THE WEATHER IN both Washington, DC, and Los Angeles was cold and blustery on the first of January 1945. But unlike the City of Angels, the city of lobbyists was also covered in snow and ice. Several injuries were reported in the *Washington Post*, including "Evelyn Lewis, Negro, of 1018 Whittingham Pl. NE, and Paul Hanbury, Negro, 18, of 4623 Minnesota Ave. NE." They "were injured yesterday morning when the sled on which they were riding collided with a taxi at the intersection of 44th and Gault Sts. NE." The taxi was operated by "Thomas Barnes, Negro, 53," police said.[45]

The college Orange Bowl was being played, pitting the Tulsa Golden Hurricane against the Georgia Tech Yellow Jackets. Tulsa put the screws over the favored engineers, 26–12, before a crowd of twenty-three thousand in Miami, Florida. Georgia fumbled away the ball three times. Other collegiate bowl games this day included the Rose Bowl, the Cotton Bowl, the Sugar Bowl, and the Spaghetti Bowl featuring the Fifth Army squad versus the Twelfth Air Force.[46] The coming end of the war had loosened up many sporting events, including the dog and horse tracks.

Many newspaper cartoons, as of the end of 1944, had a military theme, including *Terry and the Pirates*, *Mary Worth*, *Mickey Finn*, and *Don Winslow of the Navy*. Indeed, there was little that was funny about the funny pages.

Sportswriters were already predicting better bowl games in the future with the return of GIs from overseas. The play of college bowls was thought to be inferior during the war, but "there is little reason to think there won't be an ever-increasing trend toward more of them in that bright beautiful postwar world."[47] Bowl games, in addition to the well-known Rose, Sugar, and Orange, also included the Vulcan and Lily bowl games.

The radio stations and radio networks were more popular than ever and were listened to by millions each day. Gabriel Heatter, famed for his dulcet tones and opening refrain "There's good news tonight!" broadcast the latest war news as did other announcers, but there was also plenty for followers of the daily soap operas such as *Guiding Light* and those performed on the program *Lux Radio Theater.* There were also popular action and adventure shows like *Dick Tracy, Jack Armstrong* ("the All-American Boy"), *Captain Midnight, Our Gal Sunday,* and *Stella Dallas.*[48] The shows were listed daily in the newspapers, and at the top was the curious title "Eastern War Time."[49]

"2 SPIES LANDED BY Submarine Seized by FBI," screamed a headline in the *Washington Post* on January 2, 1945.[50] The new year was only a day old, but there was no ducking the reality of war, especially when it appeared on American shores.

Nineteen forty-five brought fresh news of two German spies apprehended near Frenchman's Bay, Maine, after being dropped off by a submarine the previous November. FBI director J. Edgar Hoover made the announcement: "The landing of these two men and of the two Japanese balloons in the Northwest and other matters I cannot disclose at the moment for reasons of security, indicate that the German government has a very intensified program of training and sending agents into the Western Hemisphere." The two men, one a German and the other an American who had previously served in the US Navy, were eventually caught, but only after residing a month in the United States spending money lavishly, hanging around expensive bars, and obtaining parts for a shortwave radio. To boot, they had in their possession "secret ink" for written messages to German officials but apparently had not established contact yet.[51]

The two men were caught by happenstance by a teenager on his way home from a dance during a snowstorm. Harvard Merrill Hodges had borrowed his father's car to go to a dance, but upon his return, he noticed two lightly dressed men walking alongside the road. Dressed in such a manner in the deep Maine winter caught the teenager's eye, and he followed them. Later he told his father, who happened to be the local deputy sheriff, who notified the FBI, who picked up the two spies.[52]

Hoover also warned of the Nazis undertaking an "intensified effort" of spying and sabotage against America. The headline in the *Honolulu Advertiser* shouted, "Sabotage Menace Seen."[53]

And it was reported that a downed third balloon was found in Oregon and being investigated by the FBI and army officials. The large balloon could have conceivably held several men, but this one apparently carried "incendiary devices."[54]

In London, it was reported that the German Luftwaffe lost "at least 241 planes" in one fell swoop to the Allied fighters and antiaircraft fire from the ground. It was thought by some that rebuilding London would take ten to twenty years. Britain's high taxes would help finance it. In 1945, for an Englishman to have a $20,000-a-year income meant he had to make around $250,000 a year.

The German air forces had attempted a daring counteroffensive against Allied air bases in France, but it was successfully repulsed. It was reported that part of the German air offensive included capturing American and British planes and repainting them with German markings. This was the work of the Kampfgeschwader 200, a German Luftwaffe Special Operations unit that had, among other missions, recovered, repaired, and repainted dozens of Allied planes. With thousands of ditched and wrecked planes littering Europe, spare parts were not in short supply. Committing these planes to the fray was a Klaxon that rang desperation on the part of the Luftwaffe. The feeble and failed attempt did nothing to slow the onslaught of American and British bombers, which on New Year's Day alone totaled over six thousand heavy airplanes.[55]

The same day, thousands of miles away, American bombers pounded the island of Iwo Jima, a tiny speck of land in the Western Pacific. Iwo Jima was one of two Japanese Volcano Islands and part of the larger Ogasawara Archipelago. Japanese forces had heavily garrisoned the island, and the Americans knew they had to dislodge the enemy before moving on to other islands.

The war was far from ending—hopefully, victoriously for the Allies—but that did not stop the squabbling between the Soviets and the Americans over Polish rule. The Soviets recognized the pro-Soviet puppet government already taking shape, while the Americans and the British favored the Polish government in exile in London. Another fight over who would rule Greece was emerging as well. No one knew it yet, but it was the early stirrings of the Cold War.

The Soviet army continued its advance on Budapest, and the fall of the Hungarian capital city was thought to be imminent. Soviet forces had moved to encircle the city in late November 1944. By January 1, 1945, over one hundred thousand German soldiers and more than eight hundred thousand civilians were surrounded. Taking the city wouldn't be easy, though. It was reported that "hand-to-hand fighting narrowed the enemy-held zone," but "the enemy dead were running into the thousands for the last 48 hours alone." Then, almost as an afterthought, "there was no estimate of the number of civilian casualties."[56] The Russians, like the Germans, were hesitant to let out any news reports of failures on the part of their troops to the rest of the world, and consequently news of the Soviet advances in Austria and Czechoslovakia was sparse.

But the advance on Budapest was quite specific as "almost 900 blocks of buildings in battered Budapest were in Russians hands." Day by day, the Red Army blasted their way into the capital, house by house, with the goal of total annihilation of enemy forces on both sides of the Danube. Russian artillery commanders were firing over open sights, and, with German resistance weakening rapidly, frontline dispatches broadcast from Moscow indicated the bloody siege was probably over. Except "the Germans were [reportedly] linking the below-street-level chambers by chopping holes through cellar walls."[57] The Soviets had taken most of the western section of Buda and the eastern quarter of Pest.

"THOUSANDS OF RUSSIAN CANNON and rocket guns began levelling Budapest, block by block today as the Reds, inflamed by the murder of two emissaries proclaimed 'no quarter' for the cornered Nazi Elite Guard. . . . 'Death to the last man' was the Soviet war cry."[58] The bloody and dangerous reality of the world war was evident around the world.

In China, a P-51 American pilot, Captain John Meyer of Birmingham, Alabama, was fired on by Japanese artillery, hitting the canopy of his plane, shattering it. His eyes bleeding from the shrapnel, Meyer was blinded but was safely talked down by another pilot, Lieutenant John Egan of Fort Lauderdale, Florida. "Wing to wing, Egan and Meyer raced back to their base from a Yangtze River strafing mission." After Meyer landed, Egan peeled off. A flight surgeon, who was waiting at the airfield when Meyer landed safely, proceeded to pluck from his bloody face "six metal slivers out of the corneal area of his right eye and nine out of the left eye. . . . 'Egan did a swell job of navigating. We talked about the possibility of bailing out over the home field, but I couldn't see washing out a perfectly good airplane like that,'" Meyer said. In retrospect, he said, "I guess I was lucky."[59]

IN VIRGINIA, THE RATIONING of wine and alcohol continued, as it had for years now. "The amount of port, sherry, muscatel and tokay wines—all above the 14 percent which places them in the fortified class—which may be purchased in one day will be reduced to two-fifths. It has been five-fifths. Gin, if it can still be found on store shelves, will be sold at the maximum limit of a fifth or one quart per day."[60]

Despite the rationing, the newspapers were filled with cheery ads touting all sorts of adult beverages: Old Overholt rye whiskey, Senate beer and ale, Hunter blended whiskey, and Philadelphia whiskey. Also found were ads touting anthracite coal for home heating, calling it "the modern fuel."[61] Even so, coal was rationed, along with most everything else. And the government asked homes and businesses to keep thermostats to sixty-eight degrees or lower. The Office of War Mobilization and Reconversion director, James F. Byrnes, also banned outdoor advertising, along with other mandated cuts in electricity usage. Government regulation, intrusion, and infringement was an accepted part of the culture of America in World War II.

Also, the government was preparing to launch a census of America's six million farmers using about twenty-six thousand enumerators. The cost of the farm census was estimated to be around $5.5 million and questions asked included "the location . . . how many live on it, how many houses they live in . . . the value of the lands, buildings and machinery, and the amount of the mortgage debt." The nosy government questioners also asked farmers about their income "and the number of days on which the farm operator may have worked off the farm for pay or profit."[62] In the metropolis of Danville, Virginia, local government officials wanted to know why local cabbies were continuing to operate, despite the decision to refuse "to renew their licenses for 1945" following reports questioning the "character and adequateness of service rendered."[63] Warrants were served on the rebellious cabbies.

A POLL OF IOWANS reported their belief that the reason FDR was reelected in 1944 was the war. "Unwillingness to change leadership during the war was given as the reason for the president's re-election by 54% of a cross section of the state's population."[64]

The retooling of the American economy into an "arsenal for democracy" was evidenced everywhere and not just in Detroit. American forces had just successfully navigated "amphibious tanks" for 125 miles around the isthmus of Leyte in the Philippines. The odd-looking tanks had been made by the Food Machinery Corporation, known before the war for making hardware for America's farmers.[65]

The draft was still going on and young men across the country were still reporting for induction ceremonies. No one knew for sure how much longer the war would continue, especially in the Pacific, where General MacArthur was making plans for a massive invasion of the Japanese home islands. Even so, a new federal agency was created to help returning veterans find jobs. Because of the wartime draft, many state guard outfits were lacking manpower.

The entertainment industry mixed easily with the all-war, all-politics, all-the-time culture. Actor Eddie Bracken had campaigned for Tom Dewey the previous year and now complained "that an entertainer jeopardized his career by taking sides in a political campaign," though he had just signed a contract with Warner Brothers for a new movie.[66]

Director Alfred Hitchcock met with longtime Democratic operative Jim Farley, and both agreed they had to get on diets. Farley had once been a Roosevelt confidant. The three-hundred-pound Hitchcock realized he had to lose weight while he was in Rome for an audience with the pope. The portly director had no suit that fit, so he quickly went to a men's store that specialized in extra-large suits. "The proprietor took one quick appraising look at me and went straight to the very last suit in the very last row," he said.[67]

The movies, still popular in January 1945, included *Lost in a Harem*, *Hollywood Canteen*, and *Thirty Seconds over Tokyo*, which was based on a 1943 bestselling book by the same name. It was written by Captain Ted W. Lawson, who participated in the historic US Army air raid of Japan. The movie starred Van Johnson, who ironically was 4-F because of a metal plate in his head resulting from a car accident. Johnson was also one of many gay actors compelled to hide their sexual identity from the public. It also starred Spencer Tracy as the redoubtable Jimmy Doolittle, who conceived and led the raid; Don DeFore (later famous for the TV show *Hazel*); and Phyllis Thaxter (who years later portrayed Superman's earthly mother, Martha Kent). It was directed by the famed Mervyn LeRoy, and the screenwriter was Dalton Trumbo, who, several years later, would be one of the "Hollywood Ten," the accused Soviet sympathizers. Other movies included *Pack Up Your Troubles* and *Top Hat*. Also popular were the newsreels and short films. They aired across the country at such edifices like the Palace, the Metropolitan, and the Hippodrome. Films would premiere in major theaters and then, if popular enough, find a second life at smaller venues. Films like *Meet Me in St. Louis*, starring Judy Garland and Margaret O'Brien, and *Lost in a Harem*, both released in 1944, could still be seen well into 1945.

A longtime popular radio show *Inner Sanctum* was still running on the CBS Radio Network. Meanwhile, a pure wartime movie *Winged Victory* was taking off in theaters across the country. Each Wednesday over the CBS Radio Network was heard "Old Blue Eyes," a song by the "Chairman of the Board," Frank Sinatra, who made teenyboppers' hearts go pitter-patter. Making men's hearts go pitter-patter was the young torch singer Dinah Shore, who had terrific pipes and beautiful gams. A striking blonde, she came across as kind and modest.

A radio station in Washington placed a novel ad for an on-air employee: "The management is seeking a negro announcer. This, the station believes, will help break the Jim Crow . . . which heretofore has barred members of the race from this field."[68] Though Jim Crow would persist beyond 1945, the gallantry and heroism of black Americans throughout World War II would be a major catalyst for the changes to come.

FOR THE MOST PART, corporate America had gone along with the demands and edicts from Washington. Rationing meant foodstuff and textile products. All sorts of manufacturers and growers and distributors of products understood the war effort came first. None squawked, at least not publicly.

But Montgomery Ward, the well-known retailer and manufacturer, took the unusual (and risky) step of taking out newspaper ads pushing back against the Roosevelt administration for wage mandates. "The order of the President to effect the seizure of the property and business of Montgomery Ward is a violation of the Constitution of the United States. . . . The purpose of the President's order is to enforce, by an exercise of arbitrary power, orders of the War Labor Board which the courts have declared to be merely advisory and legally unenforceable."[69]

As later recorded, on December 27, 1944, as World War II dragged on, President Roosevelt ordered his secretary of war to seize properties belonging to Montgomery Ward because the company refused to comply with a labor agreement. In 1942, in an attempt to avert strikes in vital war-support industries, Roosevelt created the National War Labor Board. The board exchanged agreements between management and labor to avoid shutdowns in construction that might cripple the war effort. During the war, Montgomery Ward had supplied the Allies with everything from tractors to auto parts to workmen's clothing—items deemed as important to the war effort as bullets and ships. However,

Montgomery Ward chairman, Sewell Avery, refused to comply with the terms of agreement with the United Retail, Wholesale and Department Store Union hammered out between 1943 and 1944. In April 1944, after Sewell refused another order, FDR called out the Army National Guard to seize the firm's primary plant in Chicago. Sewell himself had to be carried out of his office by National Guard troops. By the end of the year, Roosevelt was sick and tired of Sewell's intransigence and disrespect for the government's power. (The uber-capitalist Sewell's favorite insult was to call someone a "New Dealer"—a direct reference to Roosevelt's Depression-era policies.) On December 27, Roosevelt ordered the secretary of war to seize Montgomery Ward's plants and facilities in six major states. Roosevelt emphasized that the government would "not tolerate any interference with war production in this critical hour." He issued a stern warning to labor unions and industry management alike: "Strikes in wartime cannot be condoned, whether they are strikes by workers against their employers or strikes by employers against their Government."[70] Sewell took the fight to federal court but lost.

Sewell had a legitimate beef. The War Labor Board's authority was very limited, and the "courts have declared [it] to be merely advisory and legally unenforceable . . . and no government official has the right to impose punishments on those who do not comply."[71]

FDR was not the first president to interpret the powers of the executive branch to be limited only by his imagination, nor would he be the last.

The saga of the government takeover of Montgomery Ward took on a darker tone as the US Army moved in to take over the massive department store over federal wage and union directives. Eleven top management officials were summarily dismissed and a grand jury began an investigation. "The Army's crackdown came during a day of renewed activity in the controversy, with orders and charges coming thick and fast from Chicago headquarters of Maj. Gen. Joseph W. Byron, military manager who took over . . . under Presidential seizure order. The 11 company officials [were] discharged because they refused to cooperate and accept Army appointment to continue their jobs under Uncle Sam." But Sewell said the seizure order was "unconstitutional and [he] could not accept or obey it." Ominously, posters were put up in the department stores that stated, "You are now working for the United States and you have no other employer. The seizure, developing from Ward's refusal to comply with War Labor Board directives for union maintenance of membership and wages increases, will be up for judicial determination in a Federal Court hearing January 8."[72]

SPECULATION WAS RAMPANT THAT Hitler's January broadcast was not him but a clever imposter. Rumors had swept the Allies for years that the Führer had several body doubles supposedly seen in different locations. "The fact that Hitler's voice has been heard again after a silence of almost six months [did] not end the long-continued speculation regarding his whereabouts, his physical and mental state. Whether it was the Führer or not, all who heard the speech could not help but note that it was delivered in a listless and apathetic manner with the shrieking and table-pounding and hysterical outbursts that were so characteristic of Hitler's past utterances conspicuously absent from this latest effort."[73] Clearly, the pressure of the Allied onslaught was getting to the leader of the Third Reich as his generals were bringing him increasingly bad news about the war.

Hitler did mention Germany's former allies, but only in terms of calling them cowards with a "lack of resolve." He did inveigh against "the Jews" and the "pluto-democracies" and the "bolshevists" while blaming the war on the Allies, not himself. "And, with fantastic effrontery, he passed over Germany's abysmal record of savagery and barbarianism to denounce the Allies." He also took note of the Allied bombing campaign, saying, "By destroying our cities, [the Allies] hope not only to kill our women and children, but also to efface any trace of documents of our culture which is thousands of years old—because they have no equal accomplishments to set against this culture."[74] As always, the ultimate Master Race proponent was extolling his so-called master race, even as his master-race culture was coming down around his ears. War correspondents traveling along with American troops as they raced toward the heart of Germany were taken aback to learn, when speaking with local Germans, that they felt "no sense of personal guilt for the endless atrocities perpetrated by the Nazi regime."[75]

Plans were already moving forward to create the United Nations, a second attempt at Woodrow Wilson's League of Nations made in the aftermath of World War I. In a State Department ceremony, France became the thirty-sixth nation to join the United Nations. At this time, France lacked a functioning and legitimized government, so their formal membership would not be recognized until October. President Roosevelt hailed the historic event by calling France "the first ally of our country in our own war of liberation."[76]

However, Undersecretary of State Joseph Grew cautioned that the new United Nations would not be the ultimate salve to the world's problems. "We must realize that whatever peace structure is erected, it will not satisfy everyone," he said. Grew knew all too well about satisfying the desires of other countries, as he'd been the US ambassador to Japan in the days leading up to their attack on Pearl Harbor. Grew and the embassy staff went through an ordeal to get out of Japan and back to the United States after December 7, 1941.[77] Still, a postwar Europe and how it would take shape after Hitler had been defeated was on everyone's minds, most especially Winston Churchill's. He worried about the Soviets and Joseph Stalin's "power politics" and "sphere of influence."[78]

The *Washington Post*, on January 2, weighed in with a harsh editorial dealing with the plight of a young conscientious objector, Charles DeVault, who had been sentenced to three and a half years in prison "because his conscience forbade him to enter the Army or to waste his abilities on the punitive type of leaf-raking civilian work to which Selective Service reluctantly assigned him."[79]

The essence of the editorial essentially said there must be better ways to put to use the skills of conscientious objectors. It was a debate that had raged for the last four years but with no resolution in sight, except for, of course, the end of the war.

IN LONDON, AN ARMY bishop warned unfaithful wives their behavior was lessening the morale of British troops away in combat.

> The morale of British soldiers in the Far East and Mediterranean is being increasing lowered by unfaithfulness of wives at home, Dr. P. N. Herbert, Bishop of Norwich, reported today after receipts of letters from that area. He quoted a letter from a colonel in the Far East: "In the last two days, two fresh cases of wives having illegitimate children have been reported to me." The colonel asked the Bishop whether the government was aware of the situation and whether it was doing anything to "impose restraining influence on men who are seducing wives of soldiers serving away from home."[80]

According to some sources, as many as one in ten wives of overseas servicemen had been "unfaithful."[81]

Back in America, a black market selling illegitimate babies to parents for as much as $2,000 was also being discussed. Fewer than half of the United States had laws on the books forbidding such practices, so there was little authorities could do except warn prospective mothers to place their infants with acceptable adoption agencies.[82]

Major cities were well stocked with women's clubs for books, gardening, golf, dinner, and of course war work. The women's pages of the major newspapers continued unabated throughout the war, though they took on a more utilitarian tone; many focused on war work and some discussed the three new female members of Congress elected in November 1944. Under the heading "The Gentler Sex" was announced, "The three new women Representatives who will sit in the Congress convening tomorrow are prophetic of both the future of women and of Congress. They are examples of the steady enlargement of women's lives and of the growing demand for specially equipped legislators. All will bring to Congress the viewpoints of wives and mothers, plus other specialized knowledge and attainment. All have felt the noblesse oblige to reach beyond their homes and hobbies to give service to society."[83]

One of those newly elected members, Helen Gahagan Douglas, would go on to be a sad footnote in history, losing the 1950 US Senate contest to Richard Nixon in California as he stepped over her to eventually become vice president, president, and then the only president to resign. Nixon smeared Douglas as "the pink lady" for supposedly being soft on communism, just as the McCarthy era began to take full wing in America. A well-known actor in Hollywood, Ronald Reagan, had campaigned vociferously for the beautiful Douglas, wife of another popular actor, Melvyn Douglas, but to no avail. Nixon won, though he also lost because Douglas hung the hated moniker on him for the rest of his life: Tricky Dick.

These newly elected Democratic women would be joining the beautiful and talented Renaissance woman Clare Boothe Luce, a Republican from Connecticut already in Congress. Roosevelt took a dislike to Luce and attempted, in 1944, to prevent her reelection with the help of Vice President Wallace, who publicly called her "a sharp-tongued glamour girl of forty."[84] Luce retaliated by scorching Roosevelt, calling him "the only American president who ever lied us into a war because he did not have the political courage to lead us into it."[85] Luce was rich society. Roosevelt was rich society. It might as well have been the Episcopal country club versus the Lutheran country club. Luce was also married to the famed publisher Henry Luce, whose *Life* and *Time* magazines generally favored FDR policies.

Other women's page stories inevitably announced the marriages of men in uniform to soon-to-be war brides and who was up and who was down in society circles. Asked a columnist Carolyn Bell, "In the 'fabulous hostess' title, what about Mrs. Robert Low Bacon—or is she just too Republican?"[86] According to another columnist Drew Pearson, these new women in Congress would be joining "two negros," William L. Dawson of Chicago and "rip snorting colored preacher, Adam Clayton Powell."[87] A recent exit from the new Congress was Texas Democrat "Cousin" Nat Patton, who, when once meeting King George and Queen Elizabeth, called them "cousin."[88]

VICE PRESIDENT HENRY WALLACE, soon to be out of a job, was on Capitol Hill to swear in the new senators, and the galleries were filled with the curious but also with men and women in uniform, wearing "khaki, blue and olive."[89] By Wednesday, January 3, it was announced that the German army had mounted an impressive counterattack against General Patton's army in Belgium. One dispatch reported, "Beaten back in their bulge in Belgium, German armies have lashed out again in furious attacks farther south and have made a sizable dent in the United States Seventh Army front south of the Maginot Line . . . close to the Reich's border field dispatches disclosed tonight."[90] Yet another war dispatch stated, "The Germans counterattacked the Third Army 21 times in 36 hours."[91]

Other reports said the Allies were making a "gallant stand" at Bastogne, while the Germans claimed to have destroyed 479 Allied planes at airfields in Holland and Belgium. Additional updates said the Germans were making impressive stands against Patton's onslaught. "American airmen reported columns of German troops, tanks and armored vehicles were moving eastward . . . from the German frontier," according to one report.[92]

FDR, having thought about it, endorsed the "work or fight" legislation being debated in Congress.[93] In the DC area alone, more than thirty-six thousand men would be affected by the legislation should it pass. James F. Byrnes, director of War Mobilization and Reconversion, was pressing hard for its passage. Famed columnist Walter Lippmann weighed in supporting the bill. "The need for universal service, that is to say the power to keep men and women at necessary war jobs will be the greatest precisely when the end of the German war is in sight and the Japanese war has still to be won," he wrote. "That was proven last summer when the prospects of an early victory in Europe caused so many men and women to look for post-war jobs, even at lower wages, rather than remain in their war jobs, which they believed would soon shut down."[94]

A new survey by the Gallup polling company showed that, by a wide margin, Americans expected their income to drop precipitously after the war. The end of the war was welcomed by all, even if it meant hard times ahead.[95] Further, Gallup asked the American people how best to create new jobs in a postwar world, and surprisingly a quarter said private industries should be encouraged to create jobs. After that, government was suggested. After all the years of the New Deal, many Americans still preferred private-sector jobs to public-sector jobs.[96]

On the other hand, worrying FDR and the War Department was the shortage of aluminum for many types of airplanes. But the shortage was due "to a lack of labor, not lack of producing facilities."[97] Roosevelt had more than a full dance card. He was contemplating a postwar world and presciently said the Allies would have plenty of disagreements and squabbles among themselves in a new, peaceful world. In a January 3 press conference, Roosevelt said he hoped differences could be settled in the planned conferences with British prime minister Winston Churchill and Soviet premier Joseph Stalin. "Sparring with reporters on questions of foreign policy, the President commented that persons who write sometimes lose sight of the difference between details and principles."[98]

Roosevelt fared well in the press conference even as he answered sometimes disjointedly. While the extent of his health problems was not widely known, the war years had done their fair share of damage. Before a lifetime of captivity in a wheelchair, Roosevelt had been a tall and athletic young man.

Gasoline shortages were reported for Washington-area doctors and nurses, who were supposed to get priority service of the limited liquid commodity. Agencies that had jurisdiction over such matters included the District Medical Society, the District Office of Price Administration (OPA), and the office of the Petroleum Administration for War, among others.[99] Meanwhile, cabbies and other nonemergency vehicles found gasoline plentiful.

The Seventy-Ninth Congress convened that January 3 morning for the first time since the November elections. Having staged a slow but sure offensive in 1938 and 1942, the GOP slipped backward in the 1944 races, going from a very competitive 209 members to 189 seats. The

Democrats formally nominated Sam Rayburn of Texas as Speaker, as he'd been since 1940.[100] Rayburn had a time-honored tenet: "To get along, go along." A new proposal to raise members' pay from $10,000 a year to $25,000 was bandied about.

New members were sworn in and old members were ushered out. However, those departing Congress rarely left Washington. The adage "How ya gonna keep 'em down on the farm after they've seen Paree?" was actually a song from World War I, but it also applied to outgoing members of Congress. "Washington itself is an insidious habit. Those who stay long enough rarely go back home. You can see around Washington any number of ghosts of past Congresses. They hardly ever go back to Pocatello. Worth Clark, who came from that town in Idaho, is staying on in defeat to practice law. Staying on, they feel they're still part of the big show under the Capitol dome. And, what with all the friendships they've made and the positions they've helped to fill, it often pays handsomely to stay on."[101]

SAD NEWS WAS REPORTED when Americans learned of the loss of the submarine *Harder*, holder of five Presidential Unit Citations. Its keel had been laid on December 1, 1941. The 1,525-ton submersible, named after the fish, was listed as lost, along with three other navy vessels in December, though it had actually been sunk the previous August with all hands. The *Harder*, with a crew of sixty-five men, was commanded by Samuel D. Dealey of Dallas, Texas. So far, in this war, the Americans had lost thirty-five submarines and 243 vessels, all told.[102] Dealey received the Congressional Medal of Honor posthumously. He was the son of George P. Dealey, publisher of the *Dallas News* and after whom Dealey Plaza was named, where President John F. Kennedy would be assassinated years later in November 1963. In an irony of ironies, Kennedy had been a heroic skipper commanding a navy PT boat in the Western Pacific and, like Dealey, had lost his boat to the Japanese.

The total American army and navy casualties as of 1944 had been tallied and announced by the War Department. All told, 644,037 men had been reported killed, wounded, missing, or taken prisoner, not including the recent battle on the Western Front of Europe. All parents or wives had received telegrams from Uncle Sam often saying, "We regret to inform you . . ." These missives "bore the sad news that a son, a husband, a brother had been killed, or was wounded, missing . . . or a prisoner."[103] Official army and navy casualty figures as of December 14 disclosed that 82,634 Americans lost their lives in combat during that year. Of these, 70,676 were in the army and 11,958 were in the navy, marine corps, and coast guard.[104]

Of the young men fighting—some really still boys, to be frank: "soda jerks and grocery clerks"—the future of the free world hung in the balance.[105] All services, across the board, suffered casualties.

Patton's army kept rolling on through the first week of the new year, taking Bourcy, just northeast of Bastogne, the deepest penetration into the German bulge. The Germans fought on, though "there was no clear indication of the Germans' plans. The terrain east of Bastogne is favorable for defense, and it was thought possible that Nazis might try to establish a line running northwestward from that American-held traffic hub and fall back slowly in their Siegfried Line defenses 15 to 20 miles to the east."[106] The Americans also gained some ground previously lost, and German POWs told of the heavy damage the Allied bombers and artillery had inflicted, by some accounts 50 percent of German units. But then winter weather rolled in, undermining the Allied campaign.[107]

IN VIRGINIA, TWO GERMAN POWs escaped from a prisoner-of-war facility at the Cumberland branch. Dogs, local volunteers, and the state police worked with the military police to recapture the two men named Adolf Jost and Ewald Grabosch.[108] From Chicago, it was reported by United Press International that Americans would face another meat shortage, but due only in part to the war. "You and your family may have to learn the red point way to like boiled beef, pork chops or lamb stew as well as porterhouse, but not all meat, from the lowly frankfurter to the more snobbish steaks and chop will be drastically reduced this year, whether the war ends or not," it said.[109]

Ads across the nation placed by Philip Morris warned of a cigarette shortage due to overseas shipments to GIs. According to one ad, "The War Department has recently called for greatly *increased* shipments of Philip Morris Cigarettes—to our Armed Forces in the various war the-atres throughout the world. This inevitably results in a further shortage of Philip Morris for civilian consumption. . . . We genuinely regret that you must, therefore, sometimes do without—we also know you would never want one of our fighting sons or daughters deprived of this slight extra relaxation and enjoyment."[110] Cigarettes had been included in military rations since World War I. As always, the ads featured a bellhop yelling, "Call for Philip Morris!"[111]

In Washington, the major radio stations announced their program-ming each morning, filled with war news, local news, community news, "News of the World," and sports news, but also "Morning Devotional" and a segment hosted by Martin Agronsky, a political commentator. They also featured national programming from Morton Downey and *Breakfast at Sardis.* As with nearly all stations across the country, radio stations signed off at midnight and then resumed broadcasting at six or seven o'clock in the morning.

Again, long print ads running across the country touted the success of "brand advertising," this time telling the successful story of a par-ticular soap and how, in 1837, a candle maker by the name of Proctor got together with a soap maker named Gamble to come up with a new kind of soap. This soap was different in that it was nearly white and, as a bonus, it floated. It was christened Ivory Soap.[112] Whether or not it was "99 44/100% pure" was another question, but it was wildly successful and had been for years.

Coca-Cola was prominent in the advertising game, as always. One print ad on January 12 featured two American sailors singing along with a Panamanian mandolin player: "being ambassadors of good will. *Qué gran vida, amigos!* . . . Have a Coke."[113] It was part of a national theme depicting soldiers and sailors in exotic ports of call, always enjoying a Coke. Of course, newspapers would not be complete without the venerable "Uncle Ben" hawking Cream of Wheat.

Successful radio telegraph transmissions to the United States from the "European War Zone" in Holland were announced. Now Americans could get updated reports from the advancing Allied lines. Previously, radio telegraph transmissions had been set up on Normandy Beach one week after June 6, 1944, under the call sign "Station PX." Radio broadcasts had commenced on Leyte Beach in the Philippines immediately following the successful landing there by General MacArthur's Allied forces.[114]

Authorities, as of early January, had not solved the mystery of the "balls of fire balloons" that had landed in Oregon, and what the balloons carried was not reported. The Japanese were prime suspects for launching the assumed incendiary devices, but the FBI could not be sure. The FBI thought it was "highly improbable" that the balloons were launched from Japan; it was just too great a distance, though it was possible they were launched from a sub. Theories abounded explaining how the balloons lit up the sky, from "St. Elmo's fire" to "gremlins" to mysterious searchlights.

The US government was making plans to announce a new lend-lease program, this time with Russia. Lend-lease with Great Britain was one of the cunning ways the old master, FDR, had gotten around the various Neutrality Acts of the 1930s—passed by Congress and signed by, ironically, FDR—to "lend" much-needed aid to England as she bore the brunt of the battle with Nazi Germany. Roosevelt made the case for lend-lease by using the allegory: if your neighbor's house were on fire, you'd lend him your garden hose to put it out and keep your own house from catching fire; then he'd give the hose back to you. It was, legally, a specious argument, but it worked, and America sent her old ally as well as Free France and the Republic of China foodstuffs, oil, military hardware, and used naval destroyers. Senator Robert Taft, Republican of Ohio, had the last word on lend-lease when he quipped, "There are two things you don't want back. Used military equipment and used chewing gum."[115] FDR artfully slipped around the opposition by saying how important it was to America's defense.

The voting for new entries in the Baseball Hall of Fame was beginning to stir controversy in the "hot-stove league" as it did every year. Who would join Ty Cobb, Babe Ruth, Tris Speaker, Walter Johnson, Lou Gehrig, John McGraw, and others in the hallowed hall? A consensus was forming around Miller Huggins, the great manager of the New York Yankees. From Brooklyn came a suggestion to a radio call-in show for Mel Ott, the terrific New York Giant. But when asked by a sportswriter to identify himself, the caller said, "If anybody over here in Brooklyn knew I was plugging for a Giant, I'd be kilt."[116] Also making the list of the "great mentioner" was famed St. Louis pitcher Dizzy Dean, the "Ol' Diz."

The long-losing Washington Senators reelected Clark Griffith as president of the team (easy since he owned the team). Also reelected as vice president was Calvin Griffith, his son. The team was suffering from a loss of fans, and Clark Griffith said, "Night baseball is the answer." He also disclosed that the team had spent the princely sum of $49,500 "for playing talent last year."[117] The elder Griffith had once been a fine pitcher in the major leagues for teams including the St. Louis Browns and the Chicago Orphans. Despite a tough reputation, he was credited with urging FDR to keep baseball going during the "national emergency," something that did not apply to all sporting events, such as thoroughbred horse racing. "A 'request' from the War Mobilization and Reconversion director that racetracks cease operation for the duration of the war" went into effect in January 1945.[118]

The Washington Redskins never seemed to escape controversy, on and off the field. "Slingin' Sammy Baugh," the Redskins quarterback, was scrutinized for extensive travel between his home in Texas and Washington as officials generally frowned on frivolous travel. George P. Marshall, the owner of the team, always tone-deaf but never in doubt, sent his entire team three thousand miles to California in '42, '43, and

'44. "It wasn't at all smart."[119] More importantly, though, how could this big and tough Texan be classified as 4-F by his local draft board in the Lone Star State? Washington vowed to look deeply into the matter of able-bodied young men getting medical deferments to play pro football. Even so, a group of major league baseball players had just returned from a six-week journey entertaining the troops overseas. The ballplayers were mostly platoon players, second stringers.

IN CHICAGO, THE SUPERIOR Court ordered the dissolving of the corporate charter of the "Gentile Cooperative Association," charging it with being "absolutely contrary to the ideals of our form of government." The ruling judge, Joseph A. Graber, called the group "one of those subversive organizations the same as the Ku Klux Klan, the Silver Shirts, the Know-Nothings and all the rest of them . . . arranging one class against another, building up prejudice and intolerance of one group against another."[120] The group got the attention of the court and the state attorney general's office when it published a "Gentile Business Directory."

THE WAR NEWS CONTINUED to report American and Allied advances and Axis defeats. On January 4, in the Pacific, General MacArthur's headquarters announced losses of Japanese ships: "American bombers sank or set afire 25 enemy ships in a strike west of Luzon, Monday (Philippine Time)."[121] The Americans had taken out of action a seven-thousand-ton transport, a six-thousand-ton freighter, and two dozen smaller craft. In addition, Allied troops had landed ashore on several islands in the Philippines. Slowly but inexorably, MacArthur was working to achieve his goal and return to the islands he loved so much. "Continuing the neutralization of Japanese facilities in southern Luzon, Corsairs hit railroad installations, reservoirs, barracks and barges in that part of the island, just north of Mindoro."[122] Also, planes from aircraft carriers, including Avengers, Helldivers, and Hellcats, heavily bombed Japanese redoubts on Formosa and Okinawa Island, but "the communique said details of the strike were not available."[123] Additional information was provided later in the *Honolulu Advertiser*, which screamed "95 Jap Ships Blasted"[124] and "China Coast Battered."[125] The dateline was from the Pacific Fleet headquarters at Pearl Harbor. "American carrier pilots destroyed or damaged 331 enemy aircraft and 95 ships in a shattering, 48-hour offensive against the Japanese island fortresses of Formosa and Okinawa Jima Jan. 2 and 3, Fleet Admiral Chester W. Nimitz revealed in a communique."[126]

In a dispatch from "Superfortress Headquarters" on Guam, it was announced that a squadron of the new B-29 bombers had opened a new front with the massive bombing of the Japanese homeland. "American aerial invasion of the Japanese homeland, designed to knock out Nippon's war industries, entered a new phase today with a Superfortress raid directed for the first time from the new Twenty-First Bomber Command headquarters on Guam Island. The mammoths of the sky, taking off from Saipan, lashed Nagoya, a key aircraft center less than 220 miles west by south of Tokyo. The sizable force of B-29s sent against Japan's main Honshu Island, hit the Japanese with a bomb load that probably exceeded the explosive tonnage dropped on Nagoya in three previous attacks and equaled the heaviest unloaded on Tokyo in five earlier raids."[127] For once, Japanese radio confirmed the attack but also claimed to have damaged and shot down some of the B-29s.

Because of the great distances involved in fighting a Pacific air war, the B-17, so reliable in compact Europe, was of limited use in the vast distances of the Western Pacific. Some years earlier, at the urging of famed flier Charles Lindbergh, Hap Arnold, chief of the Army Air Corps, began talking to airplane manufacturers about creating a "super fortress" plane that could carry heavy bomb loads thousands of miles at high altitudes, where few fighter planes could reach. The development of the B-29 was not smooth, however. Boeing, which won the contract, experienced multiple problems, glitches, fires, and crashes before the plane was deemed airworthy. Even so, the plane needed airfields on tiny islands in the Pacific from which to launch bombing raids on the Japanese main islands. The fight was on from 1942 into 1945 to secure these bits of land jutting up into the vast ocean from the occupying Japanese.

They were taken through the combined bloody efforts of the navy, the army, and the marine corps, and then turned over to the Seabees and the Corps of Engineers to eke out airfields from which the B-29s could be launched. The B-29 was a revolution in aircraft engineering, capable of flying thousands of miles without refueling. The cockpit was pressurized, allowing the plane to reach high altitudes. But it wasn't all smooth sailing; one mission of B-29s had to confront 265-mile-per-hour headwinds in a flight from Guam to the Japanese mainland and back. An intrepid pilot landed his giant bomber just as his fuel ran out. The plane was also damaged, missing a propeller.

The Army Air Forces was moving ahead with an even bigger bomber, the XBLR-2 (later changed to XB-19), with an incredible 212-foot wingspan, a range of over five thousand miles, and a weight capacity that could carry an eighteen-ton bomb!

A highly decorated and much-esteemed pilot, the American ace Major Richard I. Bong, made a short trip back to the United States to brief officials on the Pacific air campaign and to get married before returning to duties. He had two pieces of advice while flying: look behind you "because it's the one you don't see that gets you" and "the Japs are a soft touch." By early January 1945, Bong had already shot down forty Japanese planes.[128] Bong was 5 feet, 6½ inches tall, blond, stocky, twenty-four, and all-American. He'd been a farmer, exempt from the war, before joining the fight. Bong had already been on two tours of duty and was raring to go for his third.

FARMERS AND THEIR SONS had been exempted from the military draft starting in December 1941, but by 1945, that policy had changed as "Uncle Sam . . . tapped that poll of able-bodied farm manpower under 26 years to meet increasing military demands for combat replacements."[129] Some 364,000 youth from ages eighteen to twenty-six were available for the draft, while young men ages twenty-six to twenty-nine—800,000—were "deferred to industry." But Roosevelt felt that "in view of existing conditions, agriculture, like other war industries, can, with few exceptions, be carried on by those in the older age groups."[130]

Back in Washington, it was the same old, same new. The Dies Committee, named for Democratic congressman Martin Dies of Texas, was revived by the House on a bipartisan vote over the objections of the Roosevelt White House. The Dies Committee was charged with investigating un-American activities in the country. The committee had originally been created by the Democratic Congress in the late 1930s to investigate communist activities in government, businesses, political committees, the media, and the like. The committee had recommended, shortly after the outbreak of war with Japan, the internment of thousands of Japanese Americans in a document known as "The Yellow Report."

The Federal Communications Commission (FCC) came in for some scrutiny by Congress, as some members charged it with "political favoritism" and endangering the public "by refusing to give the Department of Justice the fingerprint files of ship radio operators." The FCC was also accused of seeking "to punish newspapers politically opposed to the administration."[131] Washington was, as always, awash in politics, paranoia, and pseudopatriotism.

THE WINTER IN EUROPE ground on with snow piled high and temperatures low and winds strong. It was a terrible time to fight a war. "German casualties for the winter offensive were estimated unofficially . . . at 60,000," and the number of German prisoners at 20,000.[132] The enemy at the same time said American casualties surpassed 50,000, of whom 24,000 were prisoners.[133] The German troops on the front lines were looting Belgian houses for food as their supply lines became an increasing problem. Since December, Patton's Third Army had decimated five German divisions. A German division contained 10,000 to 20,000 men, traditionally. But another twenty German divisions lay between Patton and the heart of Germany, and half of those were Panzer grenadiers.

Again, maps of the German bulge and Patton's counteroffensive filled the nation's newspapers. Pictures of the winter campaign ran in magazines and newspapers, showing images of soldiers dressed in cold-weather garb while headlines signaled hope and victory ahead. At home, it was as if Anton Chekhov's winter was drawing near: "The snow has not yet left the earth but spring is already asking to enter your heart."[134] They knew not the darkness to come.

It was reported in several American newspapers that the first of the Nazi death camps had been discovered, initially by the British.

> Twenty-first Army Group Headquarters—The British army, in its first official account of German atrocities, today published a document disclosing that Belgian civilians were subjected to tortures rivaling the Spanish Inquisition. Six methods of torture included: Blows across the face or body, particularly below the belt with a truncheon or cat-o-nine tails: The victim was bound across a table and thrashed: The prisoner was hoisted to the ceiling by a pulley and lashed in midair, or released to fall on sharp pointed wooden blocks: The victim's body was burned with cigar ends: His fingers were crushed in a medieval-style screw press: His body was burned with a four-pointed electrical needle instrument. . . .
>
> Women prisoners were also tortured, and one witness said she was completely nude while these devices were applied in an attempt to wrest information from her. . . .
>
> Forty-eight prisoners jammed into rooms 42 feet long, 21 feet wide, and 13 feet high . . . there were also iron-barred cell 6 feet, 8 inches by 4 feet, 5 inches equipped with wall shackles. "More dangerous" type prisoners were kept in handcuffs or shackles night and day, and forced to eat dog fashion on all fours. Black hoods were thrown over their heads when they were taken out for four or five minutes daily.[135]

It was just the beginning. Within months, other Nazi death camps, even more horrifying than Breendonk, were discovered by the Allies. The Nazis, at the direction of Adolf Hitler, had created factories for the murder of Jews, gypsies, homosexuals, political prisoners, and anyone who stood in the way of the Master Race. Ten million living souls were wiped from the face of the earth, all because the monster Hitler had become chancellor in 1933 with less than 40 percent of the German vote.[136]

Of the German last-ditch campaign, Nazi commentator Ludwig Sertorius said, "It seems that the battle of the Ardennes has not yet reached a climax and the resumption of a big German offensive is not impossible, but it is also likely that the Allies will extend their counterattacks."[137] Nazi forces claimed to have destroyed 400 American big guns and more than 1,200 tanks and armored vehicles while taking 24,000 American POWs.

From the American side, the news was not good.

> It was disclosed that American troops had withdrawn from a seven-mile strip of German soil on the Third Army front east of Sarreguemines, after being subjected to steady enemy pressure. . . . American troops now appear to have no important foothold on German soil. . . . American troops made two attacks yesterday . . . but ran into stiff resistance and gained little ground. On the Luxembourg portion of the front to the southeast, Yank forces came under heavy artillery fire near Lutrebois. . . . There was bitter fighting for high ground between Tillet and Bonnerue. American patrols pushed into St. Hubert, ran into German armor, and withdrew.[138]

Still, Patton started the new year with a hopeful message to his troops on January 3, 1945: "The speed and brilliancy of your achievements is unsurpassed in military history."[139] General Dwight D. Eisenhower also was hopeful, but British general Bernard Montgomery simply sent a message to Ike saying his troops would follow him anywhere.[140] That same day, American and British bombers dropped three thousand tons of bombs, mostly along the roads and supply lines leading to the German bulge. Their usual fighter escort was grounded, according to reports.

IN FORT MEADE, MARYLAND, cigarette rations were cut from two packs a day to one pack a day for soldiers and civilians stationed there, due to the shortage.[141] A London paper carried a small inaccurate item saying that FDR had "created" new ways of playing poker, much to the chagrin of his fellow players. FDR did not play poker, at least literally. But he was unparalleled at the high-stakes game of world poker.

A Senate committee urged the creation of a "vast federal-state health plan" for the country "centered . . . on post-war . . . construction of hospitals and health centers." The proposal called for "fulltime public health departments in all communities as soon as needed personnel becomes available with increased Federal grants to State department agencies." It also called for "medical men with training in psychiatry 'with a view to providing child-guidance and mental hygiene clinics on a far wider scale.'" The motive for the proposal was an interesting one, though. "The report to the agency noted that about 4,500,000 men have been rejected by the Army and the Navy because of physical and mental defects, and said it is estimated that 22 million men of military age in the country, at least 40 percent, are unfit for general military duty." However, the final report would not take a position on "fee-for-service versus taxpayer supported medicine."[142] The government was already thinking about the next war and how to get more men physically and mentally healthy so as to get more young men into war.

Ration stamps for shoes would continue, even the fashionable ones, despite rumors to the contrary. The food rationing-stamp program would also continue, as would stamps for other consumer items, including gasoline, "to protect the American public against scarce supplies and inflationary prices," according to Chester Bowles, price administrator.[143]

However, the Series E bonds, raising money for the war effort, continued to sell like hotcakes. The Series E was the sixth bond issued by the government, and this one alone raised $32,650,000 and exceeded its quotas, reaching 108.8 percent. Perhaps sensing victory, Americans wanted to make sure their government would have enough to finish the job. Bonds were even used as prizes in professional golf tournaments.

Celebrities spent untold time pushing bonds and war loans. Ads featured the pretty actress Ann Rutherford help sell the "Third War Loan."[144] Rutherford sometimes made movies with the journeyman actor Ronald Reagan.

But on the manufacture of war planes, the government missed its target by 12,631 planes. Various companies had built 96,369 planes for the year 1944, and the factory output was clocked at 98 percent. Still, in terms of total weight of all planes of all sorts, there had been a 50 percent increase over 1943.

Congress announced to the American people that there would be no change in tax policy, up or down, until the war was over. But Treasury Secretary Henry Morgenthau went one step further and said taxes would have to remain high after the war to pay for the national debt. "I think people of my generation . . . should realize that for the rest of our lives we will be paying high taxes . . . and I think we should," said Morgenthau.[145] He was fifty-three years old.

From Chungking, the Free Chinese announced on January 4 the retaking of Wanting, a town on the Burma Road that had been captured by the Japanese in 1942: "The town . . . fell yesterday and enemy dead and war trophies were being counted while enemy remnants were fleeing southward with our troops in pursuit. The fight was long and bitter with the Japanese fanatically contesting every strong point. American-trained Chinese troops finally drove the invaders out in savage no-quarter fighting."[146]

The relatively new FM broadcasting spectrum was being hotly debated. While AM—amplitude modulation—had been around for years, and millions enjoyed listening each day on their Philco radios, FM—frequency modulation—was relatively new, and there were discussions as to what its potential would be. The *Washington Post* weighed in: "Frequency modulation seems destined to bring something like a new birth of freedom in the broadcasting industry. Diversification of control and of program content are essential if radio is to fulfill its public service potentialities."[147]

Again, the debate over Hitler appearing on radio several days before was still being kicked around. "Most of the experts who listened to the speech were convinced the speaker they heard was really Hitler." But "there was not that curious blending of Austrian and Hanoverian dialects which were so characteristic of [Hitler's] earlier speeches." More important, though, "If it was Hitler, [it] was a weary and worried individual whose volcanic fire had somehow been dampened by defeat and diversity. The Hitler who spoke this time was a man very much on the defensive."[148]

THE AMERICA OF 1945 was a "nation of joiners," as Alexis de Tocqueville had written one hundred years earlier in *Democracy in America*. Americans went to church each Sunday and joined in scrap metal drives, rubber drives, paper drives. They saved old cooking grease and old stockings used for the war effort and joined Civil Defense and learned about blackouts and brownouts and drove slowly to save on gas in addition to using gas rationing coupons. They joined bowling leagues, the Grange, the American Legion, the Veterans of Foreign Wars, sewing circles, the Masons, the Knights of Columbus, Daughters of the Nile, DeMolay, the Rainbows, the Boy Scouts, the Cub Scouts, the Girl Scouts, Blue Birds, Brownies, 4-H Clubs, and Future Farmers of America. Americans gave up butter for oleo (along with the dye to make it look more appealing); they skimped on meat and milk and extra clothing; they joined gardening clubs and antique clubs and hunt clubs; and they planted Victory gardens, accounting for much of the produce grown in America.

And, of course, women took to the factories while the men served overseas. Women welded, women built armaments, women built tanks and jeeps and troop transports, women tested machine guns and inspected bombs, women flew and delivered planes, women rolled bandages, women volunteered for the USO (United Service Organizations) and in hospital wards, women in every imaginable way replaced the men in the factories and on the farms. As much as any GI in a foxhole or navy shipboard, women won the war. It was one of the greatest experiences of their lives; they did so cheerfully and cherished their work and the memories for the rest of their lives. And American families simply gave up their husbands, sons, grandsons, and uncles to frontline duty, in many instances never seeing them alive again.

A group of WAVES (Women Accepted for Volunteer Emergency Service) arrived in Honolulu. They arrived dressed for work detail, but as they came down the gangplank, "sailors in whites jammed the pier, shouting and waving their caps while craning for a glimpse of their Navy sisters." A subhead to the story read, "New Caps Top Blonde, Brunette, Red Heads."[149]

THE SUBJECT OF THE two German spies apprehended after coming ashore in Maine would not go away. It was learned they had in their possession a cache of ninety-nine small diamonds, to be cashed in when needed. The men, after being interrogated personally by FBI director J. Edgar Hoover, were somewhat surprised to learn they would be tried rather than shot immediately. They also carried an extraordinary amount of cash—$56,574.61—which was confiscated, as were the diamonds, which would later be auctioned off, according to the FBI.[150]

Drew Pearson was chortling in a column about a fuming Winston Churchill, who was angry about an embarrassing leak to the famed fault-finder. Churchill wasn't the first to scream bloody murder about Pearson, nor would he be the last. The *Indianapolis News* trumpeted a story: "The Pugnacious Drew Pearson. As candid and as revealing as is his own key-hole reporting . . . feared and hated by Capital bigwig . . . the man whose predictions come out only 60% right."[151]

Another new movie was premiering at the end of the month, *The Thin Man Goes Home*. The wildly popular Thin Man comedies, starring the suave William Powell and the elegant Myrna Loy, had been based on *The Thin Man* novel by Dashiell Hammett about a private detective and his witty wife. Powell and Loy played wealthy Manhattanites Nick and Nora Charles, who drank and smoked their way across the silver screen, and Americans who could barely scrape two nickels together found enough money to attend these movies. Class warfare, if it existed in America, did not extend to movie stars. Sure, the rich were taxed at sometimes 90 percent of their income, but the American people never reached for their pitchforks and torches to hang the rich and famous; instead, they wanted to be like them.

On January 5, the *Washington Post* reported, "US First Army armor and infantry struck through a raging blizzard today on a 17-mile front, grinding out gains up to 3½ miles, which put them scarcely 12 miles from where the Third Army was hammering back an enemy onslaught led by 100 tanks."[152] One dispatch described the battle as taking place "in a blinding blizzard that cut visibility to 100 yards." All in all, the Americans were winning, but it was slow going, and the Germans threw everything into the desperate battle to prevent the Allies from marching into Germany. One news report described the winter weather in Belgium as a "white hell."[153]

Gas rationing in America continued unabated. In one report, it was said that cars could not be filled up if the gas gauge indicated less than a quarter filled. "A" cardholders could get four gallons of gasoline at a time. "B" and "C" cardholders could purchase additional gallons of the precious liquid. This included doctors, ministers, construction workers, and military personnel, among others, who needed the additional fuel to complete their jobs. The directive was "self-enforcing" and, indeed, there were but a few incidences reported of gas stations or motorists gaming the system. Even with these new, stricter regulations, the phrase "There's a war on!" was on all Americans' lips and had been for over four years.[154]

Regulations were everywhere. President Roosevelt was reportedly about to sign a bill banning "big conventions" as a means of lessening the travel on railroads. The head of the American Transit Association sent a telegram to James F. Byrnes, director of War Mobilization and Reconversion, stating, "We are prepared to bow to the judgement of those who command the facts and knowledge of the urgency in behalf of the war effort which such an act on your part surely represents."[155]

The government was also issuing new regulations on textiles and lumber. And "a lethal blow was struck at the Nation's poolrooms and bookmaking establishments late yesterday when the Government cracked down on the use of private wires and telephones for dissemination of racing news. The Federal Communications Commission, acting on the recommendation of Board of War Communications, has asked the telegraph and telephone industries to voluntarily discontinue the use of public communications information from foreign tracks."[156] US tracks had been closed for the war, and one in Santa Anita, California, was converted into a Japanese internment camp.

A Mustang pilot over Europe, Lieutenant Edward Hyman, was at twenty thousand feet when he saw, whooshing by him, a German V-2 rocket. "It looked like a big .50-caliber bullet, as long as a telephone pole."[157] The Germans were not going to surrender without a fight.

The Dies Committee had been re-formed, but now a fight ensued over who would control it. Allies of the Roosevelt White House fought with southern Democratic conservatives and allied with Republican hardliners, who took a more hardline approach when it came to ferreting out communists in American society. Nevertheless, it was announced the Soviet ambassador Andrei Gromyko and his wife would attend the National Symphony concert.

A captured photo of a despondent Adolf Hitler walking among the ruins of a bombed-out German city was released for newspaper publication.

The pounding administered by the US Navy on Luzon and Formosa continued, morning and night. A landing by US troops on Luzon, the main island of the Philippines, was anticipated within days, and Japanese troops were rushed to the area to repel the invasion. The first landings would begin on January 9.

Irish radio was accused of giving weather information to the Germans, so the Office of the Irish High Commissioner went public and denied the charges that Radio Dublin was broadcasting any "weather news."[158]

Nazi propaganda minister Joseph Goebbels went on radio again to issue a warning to the Allies: Though Germany was at her "hour of greatest trial. We might lose all our belongings; we might lose our lives but we will never lose sight of this deadly danger. We must, under no circumstances, repeat the mistake of our enemies—namely underestimate our opponent." And the little man then went on to accuse the Allies of making "a disastrous mistake" by "making public their plans for destroying us."[159]

PRESIDENT ROOSEVELT WAS HARD at work on his State of the Union address to the Congress, scheduled for January 6. Still being bandied about was a bill to make "national service" compulsory for men registered as 4-F. The Selective Service announced that all men classified as 4-F at local draft boards have their records stamped "Reject-Temporary" if they were deemed to be temporarily unfit for military service.[160]

General Kuehne in Hitler's brownshirts, of the SA, was killed. The SA and the SS were particularly gruesome as the authors of German purity. Kuehne said he would fight to the death for the Führer, the Fatherland, and National Socialism.

The US Navy, in advance of FDR's speech, asked for $1.5 billion in additional funding "to keep pace with a vastly expanding operation program."[161] The money would go for new bases, ships, planes, repairs, equipment, ordnance, and radios.

After all, the Nazi threat was not over, not by a long shot, at least according to Secretary of War Henry Stimson. He noted the slow advances in Europe and the setbacks by the US Army, saying "the Germans have not been willing to retire from temporary advantages."[162] Stimson, a realist, also remarked, "No hope is held for an immediate breakthrough by Lt. General George S. Patton's Third Army columns."[163] Stimson was a mixture of noblesse oblige and realpolitik. He was born wealthy, married wealth, but devoted his life to public service, including serving as secretary of war under Republican president Howard Taft and again under Democrat Franklin Roosevelt. But he'd also served in the front lines of World War I. Stimson was like so many other men of his era: patriotic, principled, and public spirited.

Congressional Medals of Honor were handed out to 134 veterans of the army, navy, marine corps, and one coast guardsman. The Medal of Honor, which was actually awarded by the President of the United States and not Congress, was and remains the highest honor a president could bestow on a military man or woman.

Despite the war, life went on in America, and ads for Mrs. Morrison's Pudding, Enriched Washington Flour, Duff's Waffle Mix, Breyer's Ice Cream, Tetley Tea, and of course Pepsi and Coke littered the nation's magazines and newspapers. As always, the newspapers of America listed dead, wounded, and missing men in action from across the globe. It was just another daily reminder of the reality of a world at war. Before the public announcements, the government went to great pains to notify the next of kin. But the papers also conveniently listed local USO troops and their routines.

The *American Magazine* was touting, in their January issue, a front-page story on "Streamlining Congress. Why and How Our Creaking Legislative Machinery Should Be Overhauled." In later years, the reputation of the *American Magazine* would suffer heavily for penning a 1934 story praising Alger Hiss. During that period, the famed government official was a Soviet spy, though this revelation would not come out until 1948.

Drew Pearson wrote a column about the importance of military intelligence, noting that the campaign in Belgium was going poorly in part because the Allies did not know the extent to which the Germans would launch their counteroffensive in the Battle of the Bulge, whereas in Italy, "military intelligence spotted Nazi preparations against the All-Negro Ninety-second division in advance. So, when the enemy attacked, the Ninety-second was prepared."[164] Also in Italy, American troops had donned white camouflage and skis to further press the war. "Ghostly, white-garbed American Fifth Army patrols—some operating on snow-shoes or skis—stalked enemy outposts in the Apennine Mountains below

Bologna today," said a news report.[165] But in snow-covered Luxembourg, US troops covered themselves in bedsheets to conceal themselves.

Back at home, in the papers, not all the comics had a military premise or backdrop. Superman, when not fighting bad guys, was fighting off the amorous affections of *Daily Planet* reporter Lois Lane, despite the fact that in the January '45 strip she'd received a $3 million inheritance and was fighting off gold-digging suitors. Superman often found himself in strange love triangles. In one strip, he was trying to give advice to a young woman who couldn't decide between two servicemen, until one of them won a combat medal.[166]

But many daily comics had a soap-opera-type theme, well-drawn and written more for adults than children. Women were often depicted with ample cleavage. The serious strips like *Dick Tracy, Mary Worth, Mickey Finn, The Sea Hound*, and *Don Winslow of the Navy* far outnumbered the comical ones like *Winnie Winkle*. One very serious cartoon strip was *The Sea Wolf*, which featured sexy women in plunging evening gowns with a strong wartime theme of fighting Nazis.

In Virginia, seven hundred coal miners went on strike "over the dispersal of cigarettes at the company store."[167] Kool cigarettes were hyped as a cure for the common cold. Sometimes ads featuring women's fashion would depict a model holding a smoking cigarette.

THE MASSIVE INVASION OF Luzon was in the works, or so the Japanese assumed. Tokyo reported that "Gen. Douglas MacArthur's forces were preparing to invade the Philippine Island of Luzon and that one of the three great invasion fleets already had reached the Lingayen Gulf area, where the main Japanese force landed more than three years ago."[168]

On January 9, the Blue Network announced, "General Douglas MacArthur's latest communique told of aerial assaults. . . . Japanese broadcasters forecast with an increasing note of urgency today an imminent American invasion of Luzon."[169]

President Roosevelt's 1945 State of the Union address was read to the Congress gathered in the House chamber on January 6. It was not all that unusual. George Washington and John Adams delivered the annual speech in person, but Thomas Jefferson started the practice in 1801 by sending a message to be read to the Congress, and this practice remained until Woodrow Wilson delivered the speech in person in 1913. Until 1946, the annual message from the president was known simply as the "Annual Message." After 1946, it became known officially as the State of the Union Address. (As of 2020, there have been ninety-seven total in-person addresses.)[170] For almost an hour, senators and House members who were assembled in a joint session listened to the "president's comprehensive (8,000 word) review of his war and peace policies and his repeated call for those prompt home front steps to make 1945 'the greatest year of achievement in human history.'"[171]

In his written speech, FDR asked Congress to pass his proposed legislation mandating "work or fight" for all remaining eighteen- to forty-five-year-old men in the country, especially since the army was lowering physical standards to allow more men in any draft. Roosevelt again cautioned against baseless rumors, as he did in December 1941, saying, "Every little rumor which is intended to weaken our faith in our allies is like an actual enemy agent in our midst—seeking to sabotage our war effort. When you examine these rumors closely, you will observe that every one of them bears that same trademark—'Made in Germany.'" He also quoted Emerson: "To have a friend, be a friend."[172]

FDR, in his prepared remarks, covered German U-boats still operating in the Atlantic, the progress of the war in the Pacific, and the relationship with England and Russia; he proposed a National Service Act; and he shared a healthy dollop of motivational talk to the American people about hope and the future. National service was popular with the American people. Indeed, according to Gallup, 70 percent favored regular military service following the war.[173] It was also being debated whether to continue the draft if and when the war ended. Not surprisingly, both labor and business interests appeared before Congress to voice their opposition to compulsory national service.

FDR went on radio for half an hour to summarize his annual message for Americans to hear. As always, his voice was resonant, eloquent: "Let's join the ranks against the foe. Let the bugles of battle be heard above the bickering. That's the demand of our fighting men. We cannot fail to heed it. . . . This is no time to quit or change to less essential jobs. There is an old and true saying that the Lord hates a quitter. . . . We must never make the mistake."[174]

The sports world reacted as if the world was coming to an end as the new proposed edict would force all 4-Fers into some sort of service. According to Shirley Povich, a sports columnist, "The blackest day for professional sports since Pearl Harbor was recorded yesterday, when President Roosevelt, in his message to Congress, recommended that all 4-Fs be funneled into essential war work."[175]

In major league baseball alone, some 261 healthy players otherwise classified as 4-F were on the various rosters of the teams. Almost half of all major league baseball players were classified as 4-F, and in pro football the percentage was "even higher." As it turned out, the whole infield of the St. Louis Browns, the improbable winners of the 1944 American League pennant, carried 4-F cards, and the manager of the Cleveland Indians, Lou Boudreau, was also 4-F.[176] Boudreau was already working in the off-season at a war plant near Chicago.

No reason was given as to why Roosevelt did not deliver the speech in person, but that did not stop Washington from being awash in rumors about his health.

A NUMBER OF AMERICAN women descended on Capitol Hill to protest the diaper deficiency. The *Washington Post* reported, "Something new in marches on the Capitol . . . at a definite toddle . . . will be conducted by irate babies of servicemen and workers (convoyed by their mothers, of course) to complain about the diaper shortage. Protesting that diapers are not reaching the public despite a War Production Board declaration that production is adequate," the mothers wanted the shortage investigated. "The National Institute of Diaper Services of New York last week stated that during the past week, diaper services have not received sufficient

JANUARY 1945 | 53

dydies. . . . Mothers . . . hope to get to the bottom. . . . The situation is hitting their young'uns below the belt."[177] The rash of complaints fell on deaf ears, however, as the government said the allotment would have to suffice for the time being. The diaper deficiency had bottomed out.

Meanwhile, the Associated Press reported that the rumors that some American generals had been "sacked" as a result of not better anticipating the German counteroffensive in the Battle of the Bulge were false, although "admittedly, somewhere the Allied command guessed wrong. Correspondents were told a counterattack was expected, but not a counteroffensive."[178] The Nazis had made a gain. The Atlantic Coast Line Railroad was offering new services for civilians, even though FDR and the government were worried that commercial railroads were already too crowded with civilians to meet the needs of the military.

In a speech to the National Geographic Society, Lieutenant Commander Samuel F. Harby revealed that 85 percent of the men who had ships shot out from underneath them returned to active duty. Credit was given to the rigorous navy training, which included "how to leave their ship, how to swim in the sea, how to maintain themselves . . . on the open sea by means of raft, chemical filters and sun stills for drinking water, and how to live on strange lands."[179] Harby also told of sailors adrift for days on end, including Ensign J. H. Carroum, who treaded water and swam for "73 hours," while another, Lieutenant George H. Smith, floated in a one-man raft for twenty days. Then there was the unbelievable story of a mess steward, Poon Lim, "who kept afloat and alive for 133 days in a raft in the South Atlantic."[180]

The growing optimism in the country over the belief that the Allies were winning and peace was in sight, plus the explosion of jobs and war work, led many Americans to boost department store sales by a phenomenal 11 percent. And, in the Christmas season, sales had popped a whopping 17 percent.[181]

A REPORTER WROTE A whimsical story about flying across the Atlantic and told of how pleasant his fellow passengers were, including "a very lovely girl" who was going to work in the American embassy in Paris. The flight took almost a day but was made agreeable by the "plush" plane, the comfortable seats that could recline so one could take a decent nap, the good food and coffee, and the interesting passengers, including a dozen stevedores from the West Coast hired to help supervise the loading of ships. When the reporter commented on their healthy appetite to one of the dockworkers, he replied, "Hell, man, this is nothing. You ought to see my wife eat."[182]

FLEET ADMIRAL CHESTER W. Nimitz predicted that the Japanese would have a "very unhappy 1945," and in fact called 1945 the "most critical year." Nimitz let it be known that America had over one thousand combat vessels engaged in the Pacific. "This year of 1945 is a critical year in our war against Japan," he said. "The allied nations are closing in on the enemy from all sides. His cities are being blasted from the air." He continued, "What remains of his stolen empire is in peril. Now we may expect our desperate enemy to fight back bitterly in order to stave off final defeat."[183] American newspapers announced "jittery reports of battles given over Radio Tokyo"; indeed, for the first time in the Pacific war, the Japanese were now faced with the real prospect of an invasion of their home islands.

Inexorably, the navy had been moving steadily across the Pacific as MacArthur and his army moved up the Asian coast. By early 1945, the Japanese fleet had been nearly obliterated, with no aircraft carriers left. According to the navy's estimates, they were down to only 14 battleships, 11 cruisers, 34 destroyers, and 63 submarines. Meanwhile, the US Navy boasted 23 battleships, 10 carriers (plus 9 converted cruiser carriers), 63 "baby flattops," 59 cruisers, 425 destroyers, 494 destroyer-escorts, and 247 submarines.[184] This large navy was also intended to invade the main Japanese island. The debate now was whether to actually invade or enact a tight blockade of the island and slowly strangle it to death.

As happened every two years since the beginning of the Republic, it seemed, columns and articles appeared on how to "modernize" Congress.

The supercilious *Washington Post*, by virtue of being one of several papers
in the national capital, had cornered the market on such smug and puerile
proclamations. The paper editorialized on its coverage of sensitive war
news and how it could give vital information to the enemy, but naturally,
the paper came down on the side of "the need of the people to know."
Yet the paper somehow failed to mention how much more profit it made
reporting on such sensitive war news, not to mention the blood and gore
of war, which really sold papers and, thus, advertising. War profiteers?
You bet.

A postwar world was being contemplated, not just for governments but for private citizens as well. New products envisioned for
the future included "cigarettes that burn without ash," baby carriages
weighing less than the baby, "books that will read themselves to you,"
processed foods, machines that "answer the phone while you are
away and repeat the message to you later," along with cheap family
airplanes ($1,000 to $3,000) and helicopters and radio receivers that
incorporated a television function. Also forecast for the future was
"fluorescent lighting."[185]

Another part of that postwar time included the radical changes to
the South's agrarian economy. It was reported that "from 800,000 to
2,500,000 negroes and whites will be leaving the Southland in the first
six years after the war."[186] This was technological dislocation, as mechanized cotton pickers, along with much-improved cotton gins, would
take the place of farm workers, picking cotton day in and day out. Also,
thirty-eight different airline companies filed applications with the Civil
Aeronautics Board for routes in the South. These included National Air
Lines, Eastern Air Lines, Carolina Air Lines, Piedmont, and many others
like Consolidated Bus Lines and All Virginia Air Feeder Lines. One
woman, Miss Angeline Harris, applied for an air permit and proposed
"autogiro, helicopter and aerocoup service over three routes in North and
South Carolina, Tennessee and Virginia."[187]

The timeless blue bottle of Phillips' Milk of Magnesia was gracing
the daily newspapers, a timeless cure for a timeless problem. According to

one ad, "As a laxative, Phillips is so mild it can be taken any time without thought of embarrassing urgency."[188]

The brilliant novelist John Steinbeck, author of such classics as *The Grapes of Wrath* and *Of Mice and Men*, released his new novel, *Cannery Row*, to many good and some poor reviews. Wrote Sterling North, "I am fed up, disgusted and nauseated with Mr. Steinbeck's sentimentalized bums. The arthropodal illiterates who steal, lie, refuse to work, smash windows, phonograph records, and remain in a rosy alcoholic haze 24 hours of the day are no more 'philosophers' than Steinbeck."[189]

As this was January 1945, the newspapers were also filled with ads for hotels and motels in Florida—Orlando, St. Petersburg, Boca Raton, and of course Daytona Beach—all promising a healthy and happy stay.

The news of the war and the exploits of the American fighting men were not always heroic and filled with brave deeds. Human nature was sometimes base. From France came the tawdry story of five American deserters operating a black-market operation selling stolen food rations to the local civilian population. When discovered by US military police, a firefight broke out, and one military policeman was killed, before the criminal operation was shut down.[190] All the GIs involved were quickly tried and convicted and sentenced to long terms of "40 to 45 years at hard labor," and one was quickly sentenced to life in prison.[191]

As of mid-January, headlines in America's newspapers suggested a back-and-forth stalemate in Europe. "Germans Hit Back . . ." said one headline, while another said "Nazis Seize Town Above Budapest," and yet another shouted, "Teamwork, Yank Skill Credited by Montgomery for Nazi Halt."[192]

However, according to one news report, "the full consequences of the German offensive are being withheld from the American public by something like a news blackout. This may be necessary to keep vital information from the enemy. The War Department fosters the illusion that nothing has been altered by the German offensive. That may be one reason why scare rumors have begun to gain currency."[193]

In addition to the new draft bill the FDR administration was pushing, some around Roosevelt were also, incredibly, calling for the drafting of nurses as the number of volunteers had not met the demands of the war. But it was still just a trial balloon, and opposition began to form immediately. There were forty-one thousand nurses serving, many of them in the war zone, but the administration felt that twenty thousand more were needed. In a press conference, Mrs. Roosevelt let it be known she favored the drafting of nurses. Indeed, she said she wished such a draft had been imposed from the beginning of the war. Shortly thereafter, a bill drafting nurses, ages eighteen to forty-five, was introduced.

The new Congress organized a seminar for "homeless" congressmen, designed to help them find adequate housing for themselves and their families.

Supreme Commander Dwight D. Eisenhower was taking a beating in the British press, and British general Bernard Montgomery called for restraint: "And so I ask all of you to lend a hand and stop that sort of thing."[194]

Pensions were already being paid out to wounded American veterans, rising by over $40 million from 1943 to 1944. These amounts, as much as $30.76 a month, were going to 208,509 veterans. But it was not just wounded veterans of World War II receiving government pensions. There was, as of January 1945, a daughter of a War of 1812 soldier receiving a monthly check. Mrs. Esther Ann Hill Morgan was eighty-seven years old. She was the daughter of John Hill, a private in that war from 130 years earlier. Incredibly, two veterans of the Civil War were in veteran hospitals and another 383 were still alive and receiving pensions![195] Of course, there were still thousands of men from World War I who were hospitalized and receiving pensions.

Rumors were also spreading that Americans were prepared to land in China and that the Japanese were using "some kind of flying bomb" for the aerial defense of mainland China.

Sometimes items appeared in newspapers speculating that FDR would run for another term in 1948. "If you get back by 1948, you'll be in time to see President Roosevelt inaugurated," wrote Drew Pearson.[196] The president was busy and in the nation's newspapers all the time. He proposed a budget of $83 billion, he called for a "sound labor policy" to handle returning GIs, and he urged an increase in the wages of civilian government workers. FDR and Winston Churchill jointly announced that U-boat activity had recently stepped up in the North Atlantic. Of course, FDR was constantly meeting with his generals and reading military memos and war dispatches, including the still troublesome ones about the Battle of the Bulge. FDR also read about the Bronze Star awarded to Lieutenant General Omar Bradley by General Eisenhower, right in the middle of the battle.

BY JANUARY 10 IT WAS official. MacArthur's troops had landed on Luzon, the first step in retaking the Philippines. It had been predicted that the invading force of sixty thousand was going to have great difficulty against the Japanese, but the first wave arrived with "surprisingly weak opposition," and the second wave, "upright—no opposition."[197] They quickly established four beachheads. It was noted later that Franklin D. Roosevelt Jr. had commanded a destroyer escort during the Luzon invasion. Indeed, all four Roosevelt boys saw real action during World War II: James was a marine colonel, Elliot was a colonel in the Army Air Corps and had already won the Distinguished Flying Cross and the Air Medal, and Franklin Jr. and John were also in the Pacific as a navy lieutenant.

It was then that MacArthur, watching the battle from a navy ship, ordered his personal landing craft to take him ashore. Close in, he stepped off the bow of the craft and waded the rest of the way through calf-deep water, making for one of the most inspirational and iconic photos of the Pacific war. The photo flashed across the world press, and the road to Manila lay ahead for the general and his troops. The *Los Angeles Times* reported that a signalman on the beach bellowed, "Get that boat outa here!" until he saw MacArthur when the ramp dropped; then, in a different tone, he said to the general, "Good morning. How are things going?"[198]

At the same time, the *Honolulu Advertiser* ran an ad: "Filipinos Win with MacArthur. . . . On the waterfront, at Pearl Harbor and in the cane fields Filipinos are performing war work."[199] More importantly, Filipino guerrillas had been working in the jungles for three years to help pave the way for the Allied invasion.

The city-state of Washington, DC, was considering building yet another airfield in Arlington as the facilities at the National Airport had become overwhelmed with commercial activity.

Three US destroyers and several smaller craft were lost in a Pacific typhoon, and several hundred men died at sea. Only eighty-four seamen were rescued.[200] In Europe, the US Troop Carrier Command ambulance flew one hundred thousand wounded GIs back to England for treatment.[201]

Anticipation was building for the forthcoming meeting of the Big Three—Churchill, Stalin, and FDR. The location was not announced publicly but speculation centered on the Mediterranean. In anticipation of a postwar world, there would be much for the three leaders to discuss. The debate was ongoing over what penalties and punishments to impose on Germany. A consensus was forming not to enact another Versailles Treaty, which meted out very harsh sentences on Germany after World War I, because it was now widely believed to have led to the rise of Adolf Hitler and National Socialism.

Oddly, a less committed Nazi officer helped the Allies capture his entire unit in the Alsace. The officer called roll of his men in the middle of the battle, then went looking for those who did not answer so he could hand them over personally—all 120 of them—to the Allies.[202]

The army's psychological warfare branch set up huge speakers and broadcast to a group of German soldiers, offering them a "trial surrender" behind the battle lines in France: "Try it out for three days. If you don't like being a prisoner with us, you can return to your units." Eight Nazi soldiers surrendered; four then returned to their units but then came back "a few hours later, bringing more than 50 of their tired Nazi comrades to join them in the comparatively luxurious prison camp surroundings."[203]

The duties of office had become great for Roosevelt, but the tradition of handing out the Congressional Medal of Honor was one of the most time-honored, and five army soldiers and two navy men went to the White House to receive the awards.

As of January 11, a meeting had been organized by Representative Mary Norton, Democrat of New Jersey and dean of the nine women in Congress, to address the aforementioned diaper crisis. Officials of the Office of Price Administration (OPA) and the War Production Board (WPB) had been fingered as the culprits and, as such, were also invited to attend to clean up the mess. The WPB ordered an increase in the production of "critically needed" baby shoes of a certain size (4½ to 8) but also ordered a slowdown in the production of another sized baby shoe (0 to 4).

The coming liberation of the Philippines carried some immediate benefits. Since the Japanese occupation—three years—the supplies of hemp (for high-grade rope), sugar, coconut oil, rice, gold, silver, copper, and other materials had been cut off to the United States. The Philippines also over the years had sent a large shipment of tobacco to the United States. When restored, it was seen as a coming boon to America's smokers, relieving the cigarette shortage. In December 1944 alone, Americans smoked 17.8 billion coffin nails, but that was down from 22.8 billion just one year earlier.[204] Smoke 'em if you got 'em? You bet.

The Red Cross, responding to new demands for surgical dressings in the European theater, shipped forty-three million of the desperately needed clinical gauzes. As of 1945, the Red Cross had produced two billion wraps for wounded soldiers.

On a sad note, a train engineer and his fireman were killed instantly when the boiler exploded on their troop transport, just outside of Washington.

According to the Associated Press and the French Press Agency, a young French woman was lynched by Parisians when she was fingered for identifying and turning in seventeen patriots to the Gestapo. Infuriated when the judge decided to remand Jeannette Davinot, 27, to doctors for a mental examination, "the crowd burst in, seized her from guards, and hanged her from a tree outside the courthouse."[205]

The extent of the brutality of the Gestapo was just beginning to come to light. In Belgium, the bodies of thirty-four civilian men and boys were discovered brutally murdered and "frozen in grotesque shapes on the floor of a flimsy shanty here. Townsfolk [said] they were victims of a Christmas Eve atrocity." One Gestapo officer shot them as they were led through the doorway, one by one. One witness escaped alive to tell the tale. Even more ghastly, the Germans had used the innocent as human shields. According to the Associated Press, "Hundreds of bodies of civilians already have been dug up by Soviet sappers under the ruins of a building blown up by the Germans. During the past two days, the Germans have been resorting to their old trick of advancing behind groups of women and children."[206]

A smitten young woman met an Italian POW interned in Pennsylvania and became engaged to the prisoner, but the War Department said the wedding would have to wait until after the war. Meanwhile, the matter of life and death was always present in civilian life. An article on January 11 reported, "From blackened military insignia and other identifying marks, Army and airline officials today sought to identify the burned bodies of 24 persons killed when an American Airlines passenger plane crashed in the foothills after turning away from the fog-shrouded Burbank airport early yesterday. The victims included 18 Army men, three sailors and three crew members. All apparently were killed instantly, when the plane plowed into the slope and exploded, investigators said."[207]

By January 12, Patton's offensive was now rolling along through Belgium and Luxembourg toward Berlin. "On the south, Lt. Gen. George S. Patton's Third Army in heavy attacks from three sides, cut the size of the Harlange box in half in eleven hours, took 400 prisoners, slaughtered a retreating convoy and sent survivors floundering through snowdrifts into the woods," reported the Associated Press. But resistance was still stiff, and the bulk of the German army had eluded an Allied vise, though the Germans admitted they were quitting the Belgium bulge. "It seems clear that the western phase of the battle of the Belgium bulge was in its last stage and the rest would be fought in the wider eastern sector of the Ardennes where the German holding will be little more than a fourth the size it was at the high tide of conquest."[208]

Manpower was still a problem. Secretary of War Henry Stimson held a press conference in which he said, for the remainder of the war, "the armed forces must take every able-bodied man under thirty years of age," while "older men, women and 4-F's must fill the gaps on farms and war production lines. Nazi determination to fight to the finish and the unexpected speed of the war against the Japanese make it essential to increase monthly draft calls for the Army by 20,000."[209] It was estimated that 900,000 men out of a pool of 1.8 million were suitable. Officials expected 40 percent would be rejected for physical deferments. "The needs of the armed services are so great, with the Army now actually under strength because of battle casualties, that passage of a National Service Act is needed to solve manpower problems," Stimson said.[210] Actually, the government had decided to delay for a time the announcement of casualties as a result of the war in Europe.

The first month of 1945 was quickly speeding by, but the US Postal Service still had not decided which commemorative stamps to issue for the year, though there were plenty of things worthy of celebrating. Some centennial celebrations coming up that year included the anniversaries of the entrance of Texas and Florida into the Union, the formation of the US Naval Academy, and the birthday of John Jay, the first chief justice of the Supreme Court. Anxious stamp collectors, who met in clubs all over America, were eager to know.

The debate over professional athletes and the war was still unresolved after four years. As of January 1945, it seemed as if a resolution was finally at hand. One reporter noted, "There were indications yesterday that War Mobilizer Jimmy Byrnes will soon be asked to make a definitive overall decision on what to do with wartime sports."[211] A "general shutdown" of all sports—professional and amateur—was in fact discussed.

As of the afternoon of January 12, the Germans gave up the Bastogne offensive, "abandoning nearly 100 square miles of Belgium and Luxembourg to the Allies. All organized enemy resistance ceased . . . at the western end of the Ardennes . . . and the Germans were falling back to the east." Patton's Third Army "crushed the German box position southeast of Bastogne . . . and seized 3,400 prisoners. The Germans were in flight."[212] German losses in the Ardennes were estimated at one hundred thousand men in early 1945.

MacArthur's forces had demolished an astonishing forty-six Japanese ships, mostly freighters and coast vessels, while his armies had advanced twelve miles inland on Luzon. Some fighting was heavy, while other beachheads reported only token resistance. Meanwhile, one thousand miles away, the Pacific Fleet headquarters in Pearl Harbor reported that flights from carriers had sunk twelve Japanese ships and badly damaged thirteen more. It happened during an attack off French Indochina. The American fleet suffered no damages. Within a short time, US forces were twenty miles into Luzon, less than ninety miles from Manila. Japan radio was monitored to hear them say relief was on the way for Luzon. There was no relief.

One month later, on February 21, Bataan would be liberated and the brutality of the Japanese would be on display for all to see. Of the 16,327 American and Filipino defenders of the archipelago, "fewer than 2,000" remained, having been essentially beaten and starved to death by the monstrous Japanese army. Another 14,933 American and Filipino captives had been taken to forced labor camps in Japan. Also, some 5,200 Allied soldiers died during the Bataan "death march" as a result of "starvation and other barbaric treatment."[213] Before it was all over, grisly stories of the tortures of the horrifying death march would surface.

A casual inspection of German POW letters showed how low their morale was as well as their morals. Both the prisoners and their apparent many lovers seemed to be obsessed only with losing the war and losing their scruples. The letters revealed that "the morals of Nazi Germany have deteriorated to an all-time low and unmarried girls [were] having babies at an unprecedented rate. . . . Many letters suggested extreme promiscuity among soldiers away from home while their wives often were having illicit relations with other soldiers, civilians and even with foreign slave laborers."[214]

The German POWs also carried an extreme amount of pornography and love letters from several different women. One soldier had letters from fifteen different women, all professing their undying devotion to him. Also, a German mailbag had been captured by the American 84th Infantry Division, and it only confirmed the letters of the POWs. In one all-too-frank missive, a woman mentioned that a friend had just had a baby son and how "it would be interesting to know who the father is."[215]

An American sailor who had escaped a Japanese prison camp went on to elude his captors for two years in the Philippines, moving from island to island. Aviation machinist Mate Charles O. Watkins had escaped in 1942 and was rescued in 1944, but his story did not come to light until 1945. He lived off rice and sometimes killed wild animals, including monkeys. Of the monkey meat, he said, "It tastes pretty good—anything tastes good when you get hungry."[216]

IN MID-JANUARY, MRS. ROOSEVELT INITIATED the annual March of Dimes campaign. The campaign to raise money to find a cure for polio had been launched by her husband in 1938. Of course, FDR had suffered for years from infantile paralysis, or polio, leaving him confined to a wheelchair, paralyzed from the waist down, for the rest of his life. He'd been a big, athletic man before contracting polio at their summer home at Campobello Island in New Brunswick, Canada, in 1921.

Again, looking toward a postwar country, chairman of the Cincinnati Planning Commission, Alfred Bettman, addressed a Senate subcommittee. He estimated and recommended that $15 billion would be necessary to eliminate all the slums in the country. The plan was to cover the cost through the leasing and selling of the bulldozed lands.[217]

COMMANDER WILLIAM F. "BULL" Halsey's Third Fleet was running amok in the South China Sea area. His fleet had already sunk or disabled dozens of ships—an estimated thirty-eight vessels—and downed or destroyed several dozen planes. And "between 15,000 and 20,000 Jap troops were believed to have been crowded aboard six transports sunk at Saigon by carrier planes" from Halsey's aircraft carriers.[218] Reports varied, and at one point there was a news blackout, but one thing was clear: the American fleet was laying waste to the Japanese navy and air force.

THE NAZIS WERE RETREATING again, and it looked as if they "might be forced to fall back to the Siegfried Line inside Germany." The Siegfried Line was a series of emplacements or pillboxes along Germany's western border, stretching almost four hundred miles, opposite the French Maginot Line. Allied tanks and infantry "battered south through the treacherous, snow-bound Belgian forests. . . . An enemy counterblow in two-company strength . . . was warded off."[219] German soldiers were also transferred from Norway to Italy to help bolster the Italian defense there. Again, the Nazis used prisoners as protective shields against the Allies.

American soldiers sometimes struggled with the harsh winter, as did others. "Their eyes were red, their faces drawn. They hadn't shaved for several days," said the Associated Press. Their boots were wet and cold, their gloves were wet and cold, their pants were wet and cold, and their jackets were wet and cold. But the cold was also cruel to the enemy. A photograph was taken showing some crude crosses with German helmets hanging from them in a field of snow in Belgium with the caption "These Germans Will Remain in Belgium."[220] And the Soviet offensive continued unabated, powerfully, racing through southern Poland toward Germany. "Stalin's aim is to shatter the entire German east front, the Russians are staking all on one card for quick decision," said Berlin radio. The Red Army consisted of 250 divisions—2.5 million men—"supported by great forces of artillery, tanks and planes."[221] German soldiers, as they retreated, laid waste to small towns and homes.

The war news came fast and furious. In Virginia, a young brother shot his older brother who'd gone AWOL (absent without leave), wounding him. In France, an American GI killed one hundred Germans using his machine gun in a six-day firefight. Also in France, a German saboteur, dressed up as an American GI, changed his mind and tried to surrender—to another German dressed as an American. "I am a member of a German sabotage group too. You are a traitor," the second said. Then both were picked up by real American troops, who had overheard the entire conversation.[222]

A large group of American veterans returned to the United States for thirty-day furloughs after three years overseas and were greeted by "Red Cross Gray Ladies." The first thing one returning vet wanted was a glass of milk, and he got it after two years in combat. "I sneaked up on a cow in Normandy once. But this is American milk!" he said. All "wearing . . . from 1 to 12 decorations . . . they crowded the decks of their troop transport. . . . They waved captured swastika flags. They whistled at pretty girls, plain girls, any girls. They yelled at the band for jive music."[223]

The cost of war was measured in many ways, including taxes. It was estimated that the United States had financed the war effort with 40 percent in taxes. The rest was through bonds and deficit spending. The British, on the other hand, had paid for their effort with 50 percent in taxes.[224] Also, a fight was brewing over the FBI's budget. The Roosevelt administration was recommending huge cuts to the bureau's budget since it was expected that war work—including investigating suspected espionage—would soon come to a halt.

The Republican National Committee made plans to create an organization designed to fight the power of labor unions, specifically their political committees. It was a fool's errand. The Congress of Industrial Organizations (CIO) had more financial resources than the Democrats and the Republicans combined. The GOP was also studying ways to make the tax code simpler, but few were paying mind to the tiny minority party, nor was anybody listening to the GOP leader who said they needed to rebuild the party from the ground up.

Fashion was a constant, even with the war in full tilt. A popular lipstick for sophisticated women was the Dorothy Gray brand. It came in "Fuchsia Hat, a deep throbbing, blue-blue red" and "Fashion Red, a gay, heart-tickling pink." They were "creamy, smooth, softening, indelible."[225] Also popular with women were Pacquins Hand Cream, Halo Shampoo, and Barbizon slips, gowns, and "bed jackets." Women were sporting a new look in apparel, the stylish "Lilli Ann" suits, complete with a chic Magnin sailor hat and synthetic elastic girdle.

Women's fashion featured both the glamorous business attire and everyday outfits, including tapered slacks. They were uniformly slim, chic, and stylish. Elegant hats were also popular. Women, even Rosie the Riveter, did not go out unkempt with dirty hair or no makeup, and heaven forbid a woman goes out with no lipstick. Not every woman in America in 1945 was a fashion model or a Hollywood star, but almost all wanted to look like one. Bullock's Wilshire, a high-end women's department store, was pushing the "Liberated Look."[226] And Max Factor cosmetics, headquartered in Los Angeles, were everywhere as the makeup to the stars. Lipstick, foundation, mascara, you name it—if women put it on their faces, Max Factor put it in their hands. Revlon was also a popular makeup for women. Fashions for young men were, well, interesting, looking oddly like a pre-zoot suit, with wide lapels and squared-off shoulders. An ad for Silverwood's clothing store proclaimed, "Your boy . . . knows clothes! He knows his Levis, Cords, loud shirts."[227]

Whereas in the early days of the war newspapers were reluctant to feature photographs of the dead, it was now common to see depictions of dead soldiers, especially German, but not exclusively. Sometimes the daily death notices in American papers were of fathers who left behind orphans and widows.

Meanwhile, on January 15, one Honolulu paper reported that "Allied planes flying an estimated 4,000 sorties outfought an aggressive Luftwaffe from Denmark to the Swiss border yesterday and destroyed 215 enemy planes in a day of blazing air battles featured by the greatest American fighter victory of the war."[228] British Spitfires and American Mustangs swarmed the skies, attacking planes, V-2 rocket storage facilities, and

Nazi living quarters. As a sign of things to come, the American Export Airline Company began advertising commercial flights to Europe.

THE TEN BEST MOVIES of 1944 were announced. The first, starring Bing Crosby, was about a new, young priest replacing an old priest in New York City. The movie was *Going My Way*, and it was a hit, as was the accompanying song "Would You Like to Swing on a Star?" Many of the movies had a war theme, like *The White Cliffs of Dover*, *Lifeboat*, and *A Guy Named Joe*, but not all. Also on the list was the thriller *Gaslight*. One of the year's bestselling books was *Forever Amber*, a racy novel about a young woman who slept to the top of nineteenth-century English society, the first woman to ever contemplate such a thing.

But going to the movie theater on a biweekly basis was about to become a thing of the past. Television was being touted as the next best thing in home entertainment. "One day you'll sit in your living room while world events form an endless caravan before your eyes. Television will have 'arrived,'" said one ad. It was placed by the Nickel Company, makers of "barium and strontium" oxide tubes for the coming TV sets.[229]

Speaking of the movies, the retrial of "the Little Tramp," Charlie Chaplin, was about to begin in Hollywood. Chaplin was being tried in a paternity suit over a little girl, brought by Joan Barry, a sometimes actress, sometimes vagrant, often unstable woman thirty years his junior.

Kennesaw Mountain Landis, baseball's commissioner for life—since 1920—had passed away of a heart attack in 1944 at age seventy-eight, and it was time to pick a successor. Landis was slow on the issue of race, but he was credited with cleaning up baseball after the "Black Sox Scandal," which almost ruined the game in 1919. The leading candidate to replace Judge Landis was Ford Frick, a former newspaper reporter who had become president of baseball's National League.

The movies and entertainment in Hawaii were, well, somewhat racier than what was featured on the mainland. Features included *The Child Bride*—with the ads telling panting readers of "innocent youth sacrificed on the altar of man's desire" and "a land where lust was just!"—along with *The Foolish Virgin* and *Bathing Beauty*. One drinking establishment, the Florentine Garden, warned "Civilians Only." The movie theaters in Hawaii included the Aala, the Kaimuki, the Kalihi, the Kapahulu, the Kewalo, the Liliha, and the Varsity.[230]

A young Hawaiian soldier with nine campaign stars was on furlough to his island paradise after fighting in Europe. Private First Class Mikio Tamane had been drafted in November 1941, miraculously one month before the Japanese surprise attack. He reminded reporters, despite the booming entertainment industry and the country's general shift toward thinking about the future, the war in Europe against the strategic Germans was still being hard fought. "The Germans are smart men, hard to beat. They're tops at strategy but when our ammunition got short and it was hand-to-hand fighting, they weren't so good. . . . They still think they are winning. We talked to some prisoners who bragged they had invaded New York," he said.[231]

As of 1945, thirty-nine million people were collecting Social Security. The system had been established only ten years earlier. The average retired male worker in 1945 was receiving $25.71 per month, but plans were being considered by the administration and some in Congress to fashion "cradle to grave" security payments. The proposal was earning the ire of the American Medical Association and various drug manufacturers as "socialized medicine." But a prime sponsor of the legislation, congressman Charlie Dingell of Michigan, said, "Take my word for it, there is not one word in the bill which would in any way impair or violate the . . . relationship of doctor and patient."[232]

SUPREME COMMANDER DWIGHT D. Eisenhower had made clear he wanted an "unconditional surrender" by the Germans. But some in Congress objected, favoring a negotiated surrender, including the former isolationist Democratic senator Burton K. Wheeler of Montana, who'd been a thorn in the side of the Roosevelt administration for years. Those favoring a negotiated surrender feared the unconditional approach would make the Germans fight longer and harder. "The Roosevelt-Wheeler feud is deep and bitter. . . . His open break with the President came in Mr. Roosevelt's so-called Supreme Court 'packing' bill in 1937. In the fight, he attracted . . . conservative interests which previously had considered him beyond the pale, and that alienated some of his liberal support. The 'New Deal' guard did not forgive him," wrote *Honolulu Advertiser* columnist Thomas L. Stokes.[233]

Wheeler also got in hot water by discussing postwar foreign policy in Europe after the Roosevelt administration specifically asked the Congress to refrain from any such discussion until after the war. But Winston Churchill also wanted an unconditional surrender and said so. Loudly. He told a group of reporters in London that Germany would be forced to her knees. He also noted that all the other Allies were in agreement on the matter. No negotiated surrender would do. The FDR administration also asked all not to speculate on the end of the war, fearing it would relax American will. As if. Besides, as one paper opined, "now if someone would only muzzle Drew Pearson."[234] Pearson was the notorious muckraking syndicated columnist and radio commentator.

The science of war sometimes took a bizarre turn. Sure, new medicines such as penicillin had been invented, rocket technology was being perfected, and new, more deadly planes and ammo were being fashioned, but the plan to create earthquakes in Japan left some scratching their heads. In the early days of the war, "military and scientific authorities" looked into creating earthquakes on the mainland by "the explosion of millions of pounds of dynamite to be dumped into the sea . . . at certain 'trigger points' on the earth's crust. It was never adopted; but it was never wholly rejected. Rather, the idea was put aside while more prosaic methods of warfare were employed."[235] Also in the bizarre category were rumors the Germans had developed "human torpedoes."

In Los Angeles, a street panhandler was selling "picture postcards" and making good money—about $87 a day—with the extra he received from sympathetic pedestrians passing by. The panhandler held a card that said, "I am deaf and dumb." But when he went before a judge who told him to get a job, he heard perfectly and spoke perfectly. He asked the judge, "Why can't you give me a license to beg? I make more money that way." The judge said no.[236]

A GI was photographed sitting at a desk in a sixth-grade grammar school in Florida. He'd been mustered out of the army and now wanted to get an education.[237] Meanwhile, a psychologist said the mental age of an average GI was thirteen years old. One GI, he said, "suffered from a constitutional psychopathic condition of emotional instability and explosive and primitive sadistic aggressiveness."[238]

In combat, friendly fire was not unusual. Major G. E. Preddy, a P-51 pilot who'd shot down twenty-six enemy planes, was accidentally killed by an Allied antiaircraft battery. He'd won the Distinguished Service Cross, the Silver Star with oak clusters, and the Air Medal with five clusters. Several nights before his death, he'd won $1,200 in a dice game and put all his winnings into war bonds. He'd called his many victories "luck," but on Christmas Day 1944, Preddy's luck ran out.[239] It was also reported that B-17s flying over small towns accidentally dropped five-hundred-pound bombs on American troops in Europe. A day did not go by in America in which readers did not learn of military men-in-training also dying in accidents, often student pilots dying in plane crashes. Over the Atlantic, two army planes, a B-26 and a P-47, collided and all on board were killed.

Ads were running in the *Los Angeles Times* telling men to "Get into railroading—*now*! Plenty of work ahead, helping us run the war trains through for the Pacific offensive. Good wages, friendly people, fine opportunities. Big, progressive company."[240]

The Russian army, advancing in Poland, was now quickly closing on Berlin, attacking on three fronts. They were advancing at a rate of a mile an hour. Whatever newspaper you read, whatever radio you listened to, one thing was clear: the Allies were advancing on all fronts and the Axis powers were retreating on all fronts. The war was not over, and the enemy could be counted on to attempt some more counteroffensives, but everybody could see victory in sight. "The casualty lists announced late yesterday show American losses to have been lighter than expected, and only about half those of the Germans," reported the *Los Angeles Times*.[241] The best that Berlin radio could muster was against the Russian army, which said the Germans had scored "spectacular defensive successes."[242]

A man who attempted suicide by trying to set fire to his boat in Los Angeles Harbor was sentenced to eighteen months in a federal prison; he had quarreled with his wife.

Mrs. Martha Elizabeth Downey of Chattanooga, Tennessee, turned herself in for being married to four men, three in uniform overseas, and collecting dependent checks from all. She realized the "jig was up" when two of her husbands were stationed at Camp Cooke. "They apparently met and compared notes . . . because allotment checks from No. 1 stopped coming six months ago."[243]

A Hollywood hairdresser, Mrs. Melba Darling, whose husband was overseas, was charged with harboring a young man who was a draft dodger. She of course denied a "close friendship" with the young man who was not her husband.[244] David Brinkley, while a young reporter in Washington, DC, when housing was nearly impossible to find, miraculously found a room in a private home occupied only by a very attractive middle-aged woman. The woman told Brinkley her husband had been overseas for many years, and the steady flow of letters trickled down to nothing. She offered to rent a room to Brinkley with an adjoining door to her bedroom. And, if he agreed to leaving the door open, his monthly rent would be far less.[245]

British radio was under orders not to make fun of Americans anymore to promote Allied harmony.[246] Warner movie houses in the Los Angeles area were still running *To Have and Have Not*, starring Humphrey Bogart and a steamy new actress, nineteen-year-old Lauren Bacall. The movie was loosely based on a novel by Ernest Hemingway. Amusingly, a headline of a small newspaper article noted that "Firearms Play Important Part in Bogart Films." Bogie said he could not remember making a movie without "firearms and shooting."[247]

On a more somber note, the British announced their casualties for the duration of the war, from September 1939 right up to November 1944. It was a chilling, mind-numbing 1,043,554, with the United Kingdom suffering 635,107; Canada, 78,985; Australia, 84,861; New Zealand, 34,115; South Africa, 28,943; India, 152,597; and various colonies, 28,946.[248] No wonder Churchill wanted unconditional surrender.

THE "ARSENAL OF DEMOCRACY" had met the needs of America and the world in more ways than one. General Motors alone had sent over 450,000 men in service.[249] Still, it was not unusual to read of civilians injured or killed in war-industry jobs. Toxic fumes, accidentally exploding bombs, being run over by trains, and airplane crashes were just a few of the many ways in which war workers were maimed and killed. Airplane plants caught on fire, rubber factories erupted in flames, oil refineries detonated, and many civilians died.

As of January 17, the Allies had regained the offensive in Europe from the west. The Russian army was gaining steadily from the east, in three thrusts, forming a giant vise that was squeezing Germany. A Ukrainian army was advancing through southern Poland, also heading for Berlin. Hitler's thousand-year Reich was now quickly disappearing. An important figure who saw the significance of the Russian drive was Captain Eddie Rickenbacker, America's "Ace of Aces" in World War I. According to Rickenbacker, "The Russian drive in Poland, if it continues until the east wall of Germany is assaulted, will shorten the war in Europe by months."[250]

The matter of getting more and better work out of 4-F men and others not in service was finally settled, despite some calls to draft men as old as sixty. Those classified as "essential activities" were reclassified as "critical" and "essential." These 4-F men were still needed in the "critical" production and maintenance of "airplanes . . . mines, bombs, grenades . . . meat production, slaughtering . . . forestry, logging . . . mining of copper, iron, lead, mercury." However, many of the young men who had previously been deferred because they worked on farms were now pressed into service. The list of duties for young men to be inducted by July 1, 1945, went on and on.[251]

A Hungarian diplomat who had met with Hitler in September 1944 described, in no uncertain terms, that Hitler was "mad." Colonel Janos Voros said Hitler was prepared to "fling the last man, the last drop of blood" to defend the Fatherland. He told of how Gestapo agents killed many Hungarian officials in a last-ditch effort to keep the beleaguered country in the war. "I still wince when I think of the last time I saw Hitler . . . such lies, such hysteria, such crafty ruthlessness," he said. He met with Hitler for two hours, listening to his lunatic-like yelling, ranting, and raving, and described him as looking "like a pig who had been fed too much. . . . Plainly he was sick in mind and body."[252]

The largest prisoner exchange of the war took place, involving thousands of Americans and Germans. The exchange was arranged by the Swiss government.

William McGaffin, *Chicago Daily News* war correspondent, took an, ahem, entertaining pass at how to describe war: "For once, the 'vivid verb' school of communique writers seems to be correct in pulling out all the stops to describe our carrier plane attacks on the China and French Indo-China coasts. These attacks—the first to me made on either coast— are 'smashing, daring, pregnant with portent, terribly significant' . . . the words have been used so often they have become clichés." He did get serious, though, when he pointed out the average aircraft carrier cost $70 million and they had gone deeper into enemy territory than ever before, not losing one carrier and only "16 planes around Saigon."[253] Commanding the Third Fleet were Admiral Halsey and Vice Admiral John McCain. All now knew carriers had replaced battleships as the workhorses of naval engagements.

Generalissimo Michinomiya Hirohito was said to be "unperturbed" by the American bombing of Japan, according to Domei news, the official propaganda agency of the Empire.[254] But rumors swept Washington that the Japanese vowed to "lynch" any American airman who was forced down on Japanese soil. The Gallup polling company asked Americans their attitudes about this and if America should retaliate with gas. The results were surprising, given the hatred of Japan going back to

December 7, 1941. While 43 percent said yes, America should retaliate with gas attacks, a plurality of 47 percent said no.[255]

ONE WOULD NOT KNOW that there were any limitations on goods and produce if you read the Safeway ad. By the pound, carrots were going for 5 cents, celery for 10 cents, sliced liver for 24 cents, wieners for 33 cents, and chopped ham for 31 cents. Also available were macaroni loaf, Heinz tomato soup, banana squash, Kraft cheese, and many other assorted consumer goods.

Ads in papers also touted doctors and cure-all medicines for "glands," "bronchial coughing," "asthma," and "eyes [that] don't work for war workers." They also cautioned "don't use eyes unnecessarily."[256] There were also ads for losing weight "in the right places." Stage shows often pushed strip clubs, also known as "follies": "Hot as a robot bomb. A honey in the hay."[257] The stock market was going through a small boom, and as of January 1945, the average Dow stocks stood at 152.58.[258] Yet investors also saw a downturn ahead as the world changed from a wartime economy to a peacetime economy.

Popular actress Joan Crawford's home in Los Angles was the scene of a bizarre melee. A strange woman broke into the actress's home claiming that Crawford's adopted son, Christopher, was really hers. Mrs. Rebecca Kullberg said "an angel of the Lord" told her she could find her son in Crawford's home. Lucky little Christopher had two Mommies Dearest.[259] Meanwhile, a resolution was being debated in Inglewood, California, on whether to draft Andrew V. Hahn. Apparently, he was a cherished garbage collector. According to sources, he was "worth more to his country than one more man in uniform."[260]

AS THE BATTLE OF the Bulge—as it was becoming known—was settling in the Allies' favor, the casualties were being released. "Considering the type of action and background against which it was waged, the ratio of killing to wounded is remarkable. . . . The over-all American losses as shown in the preliminary report . . . included 4,083 killed and 27,645 wounded. . . . The proportion of killed to wounded, about one in seven, is unusually low, compared with some previous ratios of 1 to 2 in this war and with World War I overall ratio of one killed to four wounded."[261]

Warsaw fell, but the Russian army quickly moved on. The beleaguered city was swiftly encircled, and the German army continued to retreat in the face of Stalin's two-million-man juggernaut. It was only 304 miles from Warsaw to Berlin. The fall of the Polish capital was a huge blow to German morale, though Warsaw could hardly be called a city now, having been bombed by the Germans in 1939. Parts of the city devolved into an infamous ghetto where the Nazis herded Jews in preparation for the depraved "Final Solution."

Hitler told the Reichstag in September 1939 that he did not "wage war against women and children." Then he waged war against Polish women and children, killing sixty thousand during the siege of Warsaw. The Germans had detailed maps of the old city, clearly showing where churches, hospitals, and ancient markers were. No matter. The Germans blasted anything and everything they could, destroying ten thousand of the twenty thousand buildings in Warsaw. This remarkable story was filed on Thursday, January 18, by the United Press International:

> From that day began a reign of terror during which men either fought from the underground or became slaves; when a piece of bread was more precious than jewels and the remnants of Warsaw's prewar population of 1,300,000 lived amid ruins. Death from starvation was common: carts rumbled through the streets at night to pick up the dead.
>
> For Jews, the city became a living hell. The Nazi conquerors packed more than 500,000 into a dismal, 100-block section in the northern part of Warsaw—surrounded by an eight-foot wall with broken glass on the top. Rations were about half those allotted to Poles outside the ghetto. On April 10, 1943, the battle of the ghetto began. Using arms smuggled in by the Polish underground, the Jews opened fire on the Nazis and for six weeks held off the German army. But they

finally succumbed to the massed fire of tanks and heavy guns. Then began the systematic execution of Jews, numbered in the hundreds of thousands, until the only ones left were those in hiding under assumed Aryan names.[262]

This story, buried on page seven of the *Los Angeles Times*, was one of the first to report on the Nazi war atrocities on the Jewish population of Europe. It was just the beginning.

The United Press International published a story from Cairo where Arab women no longer wanted to wear the veil, that their place was no longer in a harem, and that "polygamy be limited to men who can financially afford it." These women also demanded the right to vote and to run for office.[263]

The Office of Price Administration rationed grapefruit and "blended juice," and stockpiles were "held for armed forces."[264] Bob Hope was awarded by Poor Richard's Club for his tireless work in boosting the morale of America's GIs. Hope, by 1945, was a national treasure, committing countless hours traveling the world on behalf of the USO to entertain the troops, from freezing Aleutian Islands to the Far East and throughout Western Europe. It was not unusual for Hope to be entertaining troops—often with ribald humor not heard on the radio—within earshot of enemy artillery fire.

The US Postal Service reported a profit of $47 million for 1944. A discussion took place in Los Angeles on whether to implement a temporary two-hour daylight-saving-time mandate to reduce electricity usage.

A SAILOR, SEAMAN LEON LeRoy, was bumped off an army cargo plane to make room for a large dog. The dog's owner was Elliott Roosevelt, FDR's son. According to news reports, the dog had a "higher priority rating."[265] Elliott Roosevelt was later promoted to the rank of general but not without merit. He was in charge of the 325th Reconnaissance Wing and had under his command some five thousand soldiers. He had recorded eleven hundred flying hours, including three hundred in combat, and flew thirty missions himself. Elliott had also won "the Distinguished Flying Cross, the Air Medal, the Legion of Merit and has numerous citations. Both his superiors and his junior officers [praised] his abilities."[266] Elliott was also married to a glamorous movie actress, Faye Emerson Roosevelt.

The Roosevelt White House later had to wipe the egg from its face over the embarrassing, if also true, story of what had happened to LeRoy. Press Secretary Stephen Early denied anyone in the administration had anything to do with it, and one bureaucrat after another called it a "regrettable combination of errors" to "an error in judgement." But no one thought to offer to reimburse the $87 LeRoy had to shell out to get to his duty station after getting bumped from the military plane. Congress naturally called for an investigation, and the newspapers had a ball spoofing the whole mess. The newspapers were now in the hunt for examples of Roosevelt privilege. They found one story in which a Chicago train was held for over an hour waiting for another FDR son, Colonel James Roosevelt.

MacArthur's daily war bulletins reported a steady advance on Bataan while killing Japanese soldiers by the bushel, an astonishing 6-to-1 ratio. He also reported that navy planes destroyed another sixty-one Japanese planes. A later report said the five-star general's air forces had shot down or damaged several hundred planes in the air and on the ground. American submarines, no slacker in the Pacific war, updated their kills, and it was impressive. The "Silent Service" was anything but silent in sinking twenty-four more Japanese ships, adding handsomely to their total of 958 Nipponese ships of all types and models, all sunk to the bottom. The Japanese news agency, Domei, announced that the Americans had killed eighty-three admirals as of January 1945.

Enemy planes were falling from the skies like autumn leaves. Toward the end of the war, the Japanese were sending up inexperienced pilots and inferior aircraft, and it showed. One report said two American pilots downed ten Japanese planes in fifteen minutes. Another American pilot, in the Philippines, downed four planes in one night. Another, Lieutenant

Alex Vraclu, had shot down nineteen planes and twenty-one on the ground in what he called "a turkey shoot" before he himself was shot down. Alone in the jungle, he organized his own guerrilla operation against the Japanese. Vraclu had once turned down the chance to go home, opting to stay and continue the fight. When his guerrilla outfit was discovered, his first thought was of his wife. He asked that word get through to his wife that he was alive so she would not worry. He made it back with a Japanese saber.[267] Yet another American fighting man, Sergeant Clyde McHenry, popped up—three years after disappearing in the Philippines.[268] An American pilot was not shot down but was recalled to the United States after it was learned he flew two women, Lady Cecilia Johnstone and Lady Diana Nixon, from England to Brussels without authorization.

THE NAZIS HAD ONCE controlled dozens of major European cities. With the fall of Warsaw, and before that, Rome, only a handful such as Vienna, Oslo, the Hague, and Copenhagen were still in the clutches of the Germans. In their siege against the Germans in Warsaw, the Russians had employed "their new Joseph Stalin super tank," reportedly the "most powerfully gunned . . . armored vehicle in the world."[269] News reports varied on how far the Russian army was from Berlin, but one thing was for sure: it was only a matter of time before the capital of the Third Reich was under assault. Berlin radio, usually only good for propaganda and mythologizing the Aryan Nation and hatred for its enemies, for once got it right when they broadcast, "This is it. The Bolsheviks are out for a decision. Our soldiers are going through hell. They no longer are fighting for positions but for the existence of the entire nation."[270]

The actress Marlene Dietrich, once falsely rumored to be a German sympathizer, was apparently "unrumored" as news reports said she had not been taken prisoner by the Germans after all and was spotted in Paris, getting ready for a USO show. In fact, Dietrich was an early and strong supporter of the war effort, selling bonds and participating in numerous wartime shows. She loved her adopted country, America, and proved it many times, given her number of American lovers. Another family that loved America were Mr. and Mrs. Tarquino Salmon of San Diego, California. They had seven sons, all in uniform, with an eighth about to join their ranks.

The drinking life was very much a part of American culture and society, even during Prohibition and even more so in 1945, with the ban on drinking just a long-forgotten hangover. To prove it, Americans in 1944 consumed $7 billion in booze, up $1 billion from just one year before. Americans may have been drinking over the cost of this war. All told, according to Uncle Sam, World War II had cost a whopping $244.5 billion from July 1, 1940, forward.[271]

Heinrich Himmler, a weak-chinned, pasty-faced, potbellied, vile weakling of a bureaucrat with a shabby little mustache, was the head of the hated and feared Gestapo and, among other things, the *Einsatzgruppen*, the paramilitary responsible for mass assassinations and the rounding up and extermination of millions of Jews and others hated by the Nazi state in dozens of concentration camps, which were literally factories for killing. By mid-January, he attempted to use Jews as hostages and offered to the Allies three hundred thousand "political deportees," mostly Jews, for the tidy sum of $5 million.[272]

Winston Churchill had had enough. As the Allies marched toward victory at the Battle of the Bulge, the outcome of the war was apparent to all, save Berlin and Tokyo. Churchill told the Germans to surrender. Now. Unconditionally. "If you surrender now, nothing you will have to endure after the war will be comparable to what you otherwise are going to suffer during the year 1945," he said.[273] Churchill made his remarks as part of a broader speech to Parliament on January 18 to brief them on the overall effort.

Security for the American GI who was stateside had been a cause of concern since the beginning of the war. These men could be trusted to fly airplanes, steer ships, and launch ground assaults against the enemy, but they were still young men—even boys—many of whom were still just a few months off the farm or from small towns, naive and unschooled in the ways of the darker world. "Crime against the personnel of the armed forces . . . has become a flourishing business that runs into profits of thousands of dollars annually for the perpetrators and which is coming dangerously close to impeding the progress of the prosecution of the war effort. . . . Offenses including murder, robbery, shootings, bunko games, drunk 'rollings,' the spread of venereal diseases among combatant servicemen . . . and general hooliganism . . . women on the loose, careless talk of ship movements . . . feminine 'bar flies,' thieves, degenerates and habitual criminals are all having their innings."[274]

Despite the war and rationing and other distractions, the party scene in the nation's capital went on uninterrupted. Transportation was often a problem, and it wasn't unusual to see eight or more people exit one car, regardless of rain or snow. Topic du jour was FDR's recent snub of the Gridiron Dinner because he didn't like the skits several years earlier, but he planned to attend both the Correspondents' Dinner and the Radio Correspondents' Dinner. As always, Washingtonians loved to talk about themselves.

JUST WHEN ANGELENOS THOUGHT it might be safe to go back into the water, it was announced "Jap Sub Sinks Ship off Coast." Though it had happened months earlier in October 1944, it was not reported until January 20, 1945. A Japanese sub sank the Liberty ship *John A. Johnson* sailing between Hawaii and the West Coast. Reportedly, the sinking was another scene of Japanese atrocities as the Rising Sun sailors "shouted in glee, machine-gunned and rammed the survivors." The Japanese sailors yelled "You Yankee sons of—" and "Banzai" at the helpless men floating in the frigid, oil-covered ocean.[275] At least ten men died and only two survived. The American public had, since December 7, 1941, developed a healthy hatred of the Japanese, and news of the sinking and behavior would only inflame it further. The Japanese later claimed to have sunk two more American ships operating in the general vicinity. Meanwhile, British subs announced they'd sunk an incredible number of Japanese ships in the home waters of the Rising Sun Empire. True, the ships were small, but over the past six months, British subs had sent over two hundred Japanese ships to the bottom.[276] The Germans once again mounted a counteroffensive across the Rhine River in France and "assumed ominous proportions today as . . . enemy troops broke from their bridgehead and joined up with other forces on a solid 75-mile front."[277] It was clear the Germans were attempting to outflank the American position.

JANUARY 20, 1945, WAS UNUSUAL for the *Los Angeles Times*. On its front page, there was almost no war news for the first time in years. There was a tiny item about a navy commander listed as missing and another item about a Gold Star mother "splashing" a naval vessel. But January 20 was also the date prescribed by the government to inaugurate the president, and on that Saturday, at noon, Franklin Delano Roosevelt, thirty-second president of the United States, was sworn in on the south portico of the White House—and not the US Capitol—for his fourth term. He stood at a simple lectern with an American flag draped across the balcony. Standing beside FDR was Harry Truman, now the new vice president, and US Marine colonel James Roosevelt, his son. Roosevelt promised a "just and durable peace" as part of "the human community." He closed with a prayer that the country would find "a better life for ourselves and our fellow man."[278] After the opening prayer and the playing of "Hail to the Chief," he spoke, but only for five minutes. According to the *Los Angeles Times*, his speech was only 551 words long, and he looked gaunt and drawn. The white stuff covered the south lawn and Roosevelt children engaged in snowball fights as five thousand invited guests (including wounded vets) inside the fence and another few thousand outside the fence watched. All the Roosevelt women were dressed tastefully but understatedly. "The gravity of the event was emphasized by the presence of scores of men and women in uniform."[279]

Gray skies were overhead, and it resembled nothing like the pomp and circumstance of 1941 when five hundred thousand lined the streets and military planes flew overhead. Newspapers across the country offered prayers for the president and the men and women in uniform. FDR was "wheeled to the railing of the South Portico and assisted to his feet by his son James and a Secret Service agent."[280] A rare hint of his affliction. He was the "first president to be inaugurated in wartime since the Civil War."[281] FDR was presented with his now familiar cape but refused to wear it. He was sworn in by Chief Justice Harlan Stone. Truman was sworn in by his predecessor, Henry Wallace. The whole ceremony was over in a matter of minutes. Truman later called his ninety-one-year-old mother, who admonished him to "behave yourself." [282] The dutiful son promised his mother he would, and later told reporters he hoped to return to the Senate after his term as vice president was done.

On the day before his swearing-in, FDR had held a press conference in which he was jocular and upbeat. FDR's navy doctor, Admiral Ross T. McIntire, as much as said the president was the picture of health and compared him "favorably" to other sixty-three-year-old men. FDR joked to reporters that the first twelve years were the hardest. He was asked if his fourth term would be his last, but the president demurred. When asked what would happen to Henry Wallace now that he'd been booted from the ticket, FDR jokingly said, "He won't starve."[283] FDR's feelings for Wallace—which were not high—were an open secret. Once, Wallace got into an argument with Commerce Secretary Jesse Jones, and Roosevelt "slapped Wallace down."[284] Still, FDR later forced Jones out and replaced him with Wallace.

UNBELIEVABLE STORIES ABOUT NAZI atrocities and concentration camps were beginning to surface. One, from the Russian army, was the story of a German camp commandant having children tossed into the air for him to shoot with a machine gun for the amusement of his family, as "his daughter applauded and cried 'Papa, do it again. Papa, do it again.'" The Soviets reported "the most inhumane deeds . . . were committed . . . where a savage system of extermination was perfected" by the German SS.[285] The United Press International report did not say whether the children or the camp inmates were Jews.

Attempted violence against some "returning Japanese-Americans" in California was reported as "several carloads of persons" were said to have tried to employ dynamite and gunfire after driving onto a farm owned by Japanese Americans. The report was sketchy and did not say where they had returned from or whether the assault was successful, but authorities did not hesitate erecting barriers for protection, and the state attorney general said that Japanese Americans are not to be judged as "fair game." Ironically, of three Japanese Americans in residence at the farm, one had a deferment for farm work, but his two brothers were in the army.[286] The governor, Earl Warren, proclaimed, "I can't conceive of people who claim to be good Americans trying to further the war effort doing a thing of that kind."[287]

In between losing the war, the Germans had time to put fifty officers of the Luftwaffe on trial for cowardice, disobeying orders, and "defeatist remarks on German war aviation."[288] Twenty of the officers were convicted and sentenced to death.

A vote of confidence had been forced in Parliament, but Winston Churchill won easily, 310–7, in part because of his rousing three-hour speech.

New reports from Eastern Europe and the Western Pacific continued to show Allied advances, more quickly now. In the west, the Russians reported capturing or killing an additional 94,000 German troops, while in the east, MacArthur's troops had divided in two the remaining Japanese army, which was "crumbling and breaking into disorganized groups."[289]

The newly organized United Nations War Crimes Commission announced their war criminal charges against Adolf Hitler and twenty-four other Nazi gangsters for sentencing to death three thousand Czech citizens for their involvement in the death of Reich-protector Reinhard "the Hangman" Heydrich. If possible, Heydrich was even more of a monster than Hitler. As part of Hitler's last desperate attempt to hold on, he stepped up the use of V-2 rockets being launched toward London from Holland and other locations to defend the "fortress of Germany." V-1 rockets—flying bombs launched from airplanes—were also employed. German radio was frank about the war and broadcast that reversals had to be expected, but that "we would not be good Nazis if we were not convinced that, in the end, spirit will win over numbers."[290] The Allies signed a peace agreement with Hungary, and Hitler lost yet another ally, along with Rumania (spelling was changed to Romania around 1975) and Bulgaria.

Mail was one of the most important forms of communication, along with newspapers, magazines, and radio—not including the spoken word, which was guarded. Mail was especially important for servicemen. One ad had a man in uniform saying, "Mail is a great thing. When we don't have mail for long periods, the morale becomes very low . . . but just as soon as mail is brought aboard, the entire ship brightens."[291] People were urged to use V-mail, which applied "standardized stationary and micro-film processing to produce lighter, smaller cargo."[292] According to the National Postal Museum, "V-mail ensured that thousands of tons of shipping space could be reserved for war materials. The 37 mail bags required to carry 150,000 one-page letters could be replaced by a single mail sack. The weight of that same amount of mail was reduced dramatically from 2,575 pounds to a mere 45." This saved considerable weight and bulk at a time when both were hard to manage in a combat zone. "In addition to postal censorship, V-mail also deterred espionage communications by foiling the use of invisible ink, microdots, and microprinting, none of which would be reproduced in a photocopy."[293]

The Soviet army moved into the "heart of Germany," overtaking Silesia, and Patton's army was close to doing the same from the west. The Soviet newspaper *Pravda* reported, "Allied operations have brought Hitlerite Germany to ruin."[294] Meanwhile, the Allied psychological division began leafleting Berlin, telling the citizens there that continued fighting was hopeless, that the German army was being smashed, and that surrender was the only option. The psychological warfare must have worked because within hours it was reported that residents were bolting from Berlin. "German radio appealed for help against 'this bestial, overwhelming mass onslaught,'" but that did not stop "women and children" from "streaming out."[295]

Hitler convened yet another meeting with his generals to discuss the worsening war situation. It was later reported by the BBC that the chancellor went to the Eastern Front to "take personal command of the German defense against the Russians."[296] But the Russian armies continued and were now reported to be just 150 miles from Berlin. In the west, the German bulge finally collapsed "as Allied warplanes knocked out nearly 3,000 enemy motor vehicles and tanks—enough to equip almost an entire panzer division." The Associated Press called it an "aerial slaughter."[297] Civilians were leaving border towns to get out of the path of the coming Russian army. They were also beginning to leave Berlin, again, fearful of the Russians. "Hitler is no good!" some children were heard saying.[298] A news report flashed across the world that Hitler suffered a nervous breakdown, morose over the Russian advance. It was said he canceled an address to his generals in Berchtesgaden because of his mental state.[299]

The Americans in the west were closing in on the Siegfried Line, a nearly four-hundred-mile-long defensive emplacement running between Germany and France. At approximately the same time, the British Second Army tanks breached the Siegfried Line and marched on German soil. Germany was stripping what meager defenses they still had in the west and reassigning them to fight the Russians on the Eastern Front. British pilots also reported a "steady stream of filled trains moving east and empties returning for new loads."[300] In that period, a second RAF report revealed that planes had "destroyed or damaged more than 210 locomotives and 700 railway cars."[301] Germans began digging trenches around Berlin for the final defense of the city, not that there was much to defend; American and British bombers, after bombing the city night and day for months on end, had flattened it. All Berliners were under orders from Gestapo chief Heinrich Himmler to join in the effort. Himmler later dodged an assassination attempt, announced Berlin radio. He then beefed up his personal guard and had some members of the *Volkssturm* (the home guard) arrested. Plans were also underway to move the capital of Germany to Berchtesgaden.

More quickly now, things were falling apart in the once gleaming symbol of Aryan supremacy. Nazis were making plans to blow up what was left of Berlin's industrial plant and "key war facilities. While the first women and children evacuees began leaving Berlin . . . sources said Volkssturm units, directed by army demolition engineers, had begun mining . . . bridges, gas and electricity plants."[302] And Moscow radio reported that planes were being readied at Berlin airport to whisk away "high Nazi officials at a given moment."[303]

On January 27, the American army, over the American Broadcasting Station, broadcast a call on German soldiers to give up the ghost and surrender, "explaining that unconditional surrender did not mean individual Germans would 'ever be treated to arbitrary treatment.'" Moreover, "the Allies [were] of the opinion that the German surrender must be unconditional in order to avoid repetition of German claims that Germany had been tricked by enemy promises." Therefore, the Allies had to say, "no promises and no negotiations with the Nazis." The message elaborated to say that if the ordinary soldier was not involved in war crimes, then the rules of the Geneva Conventions would apply, and that "mass retaliation is one of the things we are fighting against." The message concluded, saying that President Roosevelt looked forward to the day when Germany could rejoin the "European family of nations."[304]

Things were getting bad, though, when a local woman was spotted "beating" a Nazi party official over evacuation policy.[305]

Patton's army was moving and "reached the German frontier . . . as the harassed Germans withdrew behind the natural barriers in Germany all along the Western Front. The 3rd Army, in pushing . . . in several places emulated the US 9th Army and the British 2nd Army, which have reached the west banks of the Roer River system. . . . Thus, the three Allied armies [were] poised on the banks of river barriers to the Reich."[306] The Allies also resumed air raids on Berlin, which had paused momentarily without explanation. It was rumored that Germany was pulling its forces out of Italy in order to better garrison itself. Later, it was reported that the Germans were cannibalizing their forces in the west to send those troops to repel the Russians.

The Burma Road was finally opened for the first time in years. No longer could the Japanese stop the Allies from using that strategically important highway from supplying the Free Chinese. As the navy continued across the Pacific, their planes destroyed or badly damaged 240 Japanese planes on the ground in Formosa. A Bataan "death march" survivor described his three-year captivity in the most hellish terms. Corporal Gerald Wade had surrendered in April 1942 and was forced to march eighty-five miles to a prison camp. Along the way, he said, they got no food or water from the Japanese, who frequently beat the American prisoners with bamboo poles. The Japanese would also eat the American C-rations, including chocolate, in front of the Americans and then discard the empty containers to prevent their prisoners from scavenging the cans for meager sustenance.[307]

President Roosevelt renewed a call for Americans "in the cities, towns and villages" to plant Victory gardens, from picket fence to picket fence: "During the past three years every American who has played a part in the job of growing, conserving, harvesting, distributing and processing of our food supply has done a magnificent job. I call upon the millions of Victory gardeners who have done so much to swell the nation's food supply in these war years to continue their good works."[308]

American servicemen for years had shipped back from overseas souvenirs of every imaginable shape and size: swords, pistols, Nazi flags, Japanese flags, ribbons and pins off dead officers, and hula skirts, but also dangerous ordnance, including bombs. One Los Angeles collector of customs, William Jennings Bryan Jr., took matters into his own hands and ordered a roundup of such hazardous items like a lamp "made from shell casings" with enough "powder in the base to blow the receiver into the next state."[309]

Staff Sergeant Joe Louis, also a former heavyweight champion of the world, told reporters that the rumors were not true that he was hanging up his gloves. But he did say he'd like to fight Billy Conn and then see what happened. "A lot of things can happen to make a fella change his mind," he said. Conn, for his part, was cocky, predicting he would "lick Louis."[310] (They fought in 1946, and Louis knocked out Conn in the eighth round. Before the fight, Louis famously said of the faster Conn, "He can run but he can't hide."[311])

ROOSEVELT, IN A RARE Senate rebuke, saw his nominee for secretary of commerce and his former vice president, Henry Wallace, suffer a 10–2 vote to have his nomination "sidelined." He was later confirmed in a 56–32 vote, but only after the Reconstruction Finance Department, an agency with "multi-billion dollar lending power," was removed from his jurisdiction. Additionally, FDR's longest-serving cabinet member, Francis Perkins, the secretary of labor, tried to resign, but FDR would not accept her tender.

Roosevelt also got a setback when a federal judge ruled that his army invasion of the peaceful Montgomery Ward department store was unconstitutional. "Judge Phillip L. Sullivan ruled that President Roosevelt had neither statutory authority nor constitutional authority to order Army seizure of 16 company properties."[312] The Roosevelt administration was preparing an appeal and Congress looked to create a law enabling FDR to mediate all labor and contract disputes, though the Constitution clearly states the national government has no right to interfere in private contracts.

MacArthur's drive for Manila was proceeding apace. Heading toward the capital city, his forces liberated the infamous Camp O'Donnell, a POW prison, but instead found mostly graves: the graves of "several thousand American and Filipino war prisoners who died of disease, starvation and malnutrition." Only after Bataan, "Camp O'Donnell was one of the most notorious pestholes maintained by the Japanese for war prisoners."[313] To conceal their crimes, the Japanese had attempted to burn the camp and destroy the evidence. Farther north, Admiral Halsey's Third Fleet hit Okinawa for the third time. Taking Okinawa would help to sever Japan's supply line, running from the main island of Japan along an island chain all the way to the Philippines. At the same time, several members of Congress raised the idea of taking the islands in the Western Pacific permanently as a means of "the future defense and protection of the United States."[314] A political cartoon depicted an angry American eagle herding along a Japanese soldier with the caption "The New March of Death."[315]

IT WASN'T ONLY THE military that came in for horrible treatment at the hands of the Japanese. So, too, did civilians on the island of Luzon. One American woman, a mother of two, who lived under Japanese rule said, "They would rip off fingernails of victims one by one and then break each finger. They stabbed victims with bamboo poles and bayonets and beat their bodies until nothing was left but pulp, but there was still life in the bodies. There were hundreds of these cases of torture. They (the Japanese) are the most gruesome, cruel and barbarous people on the face of the earth. They should be annihilated."[316]

Japanese resistance stiffened on Luzon for a moment, holding off the Allies. In America, the head of the Council Against Intolerance in America, James Waterman Wise, called for tolerance of the Japanese, but the story was buried, after the financial pages. Instead, America answered by hitting Iwo Jima, again, from the air; bombs rained down on the tiny but strategically important island. The Superfortresses also, again, hit the Japanese mainland.

American dogfaces, or army foot soldiers, also received more than their fair share of torture. A civilian witness, an elderly Belgian woman, said she saw German troops "murder eight captured American tankmen, one by one," and also saw an armored SS division "slaughter some 100 other Americans in an open field." She witnessed, while milking cows, Germans "marching 24 prisoners before them," she said. "The Germans, all of whom were young and loud, were shouting at the Americans and knocking them about. About 20 yards from our house, they halted the Americans and ordered eight of them to dig graves" for some dead German soldiers. And "after the Americans finished digging the graves the eight were lined up. . . . The German officer . . . then stepped out and shot them in the face one at a time. The Germans then kicked the bodies over the hill and into a ditch." The dead Americans were later discovered with their arms still over their heads "stiffly in surrender."[317]

It wasn't all that unusual to read of messy marriages and even messier divorces, nor was it all that uncommon to read of men being married to more than one woman or one woman being married to more than one man. In one example, a train engineer managed the feat of being married to eleven women—all at the same time. Frances H. Van Wie, San Francisco's "Carline Casanova," was a full-time cable car driver and an overtime con man. One of his wives said, "There was something demonical about the man." Another said he was a perfect gentleman, even in church, except when they got home he turned into a wife beater.[318] In another example, a woman in Los Angeles was under police investigation for being married to two men at the same time, though she claimed she'd paid a lawyer for a divorce from the first. Both men had been in uniform.[319] Also, a Pasadena "drugstore waitress" was arrested for contributing to the delinquency of a minor for allowing her sixteen-year-old sister to meet a twenty-one-year-old sailor for trysts at her apartment. The younger sister was later removed and "turned over to juvenile authorities."[320]

MOST AMERICANS EXPECTED FRANKLIN Roosevelt to seek a fifth term as president and see the war through to its final victory and then build a new peace. When Democrats were asked in an informal poll about their preference of presidential candidates that included Vice President Truman and former vice president Henry Wallace, a large plurality of 30 percent (better than 3–1 over the next name) said Wallace. Truman was at a paltry 6 percent.

Along with American men serving honorably in war, being injured, and dying, there were also thousands of American GIs who had gone AWOL. In the European theater alone, some twelve to thirteen thousand American men per day went missing. Not too surprisingly, many were found loitering around Paris, where they were promptly arrested. And there were the ongoing black-market problems; these involved not only GIs but some officers and even a brigadier general, who was ordered back home by Eisenhower himself.[321]

Back home, Americans were smoking up a storm and drinking coffee by the gallons. The year prior, 1944, Americans ground down and then drank up 18,812,071 bags of coffee beans, up by almost 20 percent from 1943.[322] There were inevitable and widespread sleepless nights. The government was also moving ahead with plans for the auction of surplus government matériel and war goods to the general public. Up for auction included "jeeps, saddles, spurs, gasoline tanks, machinery, assault boats and thousands of other articles."[323] Katharine Hepburn, once a film ingenue then box-office poison, was back on top of the film industry with hits that were released nearer the beginning of the war, *The Philadelphia Story* and *Woman of the Year.*

In preparation for the end of the war, on January 26, the Office of Price Administration (OPA) announced the coming end of the food coupon program in about six weeks. It was an impossible system of coupons, regulations, stashing, tokens, and quotas; and now, the poor housewife who had hoarded her precious coupons might find herself stuck with the useless pieces of paper in less than two months. As one example, "In December, many consumers had saved stamps for year-end holiday buying and were incensed when OPA canceled them without advance notice because of reduced supplies."[324] Fraud was rampant in the multicoupon economy, and it was not unusual to read of people being arrested for trafficking in illegal coupons.

A big part of the premeeting dance of the Big Three was what to do with Germany. One early proposal was to annex it into three parts, with the Big Three countries having jurisdiction over each. But France was squawking, wanting their piece of *la tarte* too.

THE BELOVED NEW YORK Yankees were sold for $2.8 million on January 25. Along with the equipment, almost four hundred major league and minor league players came with the deal, although two hundred of the players were playing away, in khaki and navy uniforms, for the most important home team of their lives.

At about this same time, the poor little rich girl Gloria Vanderbilt was in the news again. Gloria was a professional inheritor and full-time handful. Her mother and an aunt had battled over Gloria's custody and who would handle little Gloria's large inheritance. Her father, who was also a professional inheritor, was the subject of newspaper scandal sheets for years and had died at a young age from alcoholism. In 1941, at the age of seventeen, Gloria married a man much older—part-time gangster and full-time scoundrel Pasquale DiCicco—but divorced him within a few years at the advanced age of twenty-one. The *Los Angeles Times* described their marriage as "once perfect."[325] It certainly was not perfect, but it was once. Gloria and her marriage to the wrong men would quickly become a habit for the empty jet-setter, who slept with men like she was eating breakfast.

A political cartoon in the *Los Angeles Times* featured a very nervous Hitler and a very scared Tojo looking at movie posters of MacArthur and the Russian bear, the American eagle, and the British lion. The Tojo caricature was short and bucktoothed, in every way America's image of the Japanese in 1945.[326] Hollywood was also hyping the new movie *National Velvet*, along with the pretty and talented actress Elizabeth Taylor. As the story went, put out by the publicity mills of Tinseltown, young Taylor had a way with animals.

THE DEPUTY MAYOR OF Breslau was executed by firing squad by the German home guard, the *Volkssturm*, for being a "coward devoid of honor."[327] On January 28, the German press began telling the citizens of Berlin that the next eight days would determine the outcome of the war, saying "panic is sweeping the nation from east to west. Our officers, the quality of our weapons and our Fuehrer (spirit of leadership) has been worn out during these years."[328] Refugees now swarmed across Germany; by some estimates two million European citizens were wandering, homeless. An American political cartoon depicted a giant hammer and scythe floating over Berlin. No one in America batted an eye.[329] A French editor, Charles Maurras, was sentenced to life imprisonment and hard labor for "treasonable intelligence with the enemy."[330] Maurras was seventy years old.

It wasn't unusual to see General MacArthur at the scene of the fight, with bullets whizzing by and pillboxes exploding. According to one news report, "The General and his five-star jeep rolled into the ruined main street of San Manuel, a half hour after American forces had been pinned down by heavy enemy mortar and artillery fire. . . . In three days the Yanks have prodded through fanatical Japanese last-man resistance. . . . MacArthur watched intently as the doughboys continued their bloody job."[331]

By January 30, MacArthur was within sight of Manila. The Russians had crossed the Obra River and were a little more than ninety miles from Berlin. At the same time, General Patton's forces crossed the Our River and were also heading for Berlin, where there was bedlam. The Associated Press reported, "Serious riots have broken out in the eastern and southern districts of Berlin and police and S.S. [Elite Guard] troops were called out to quell rising waves of unrest in the Reich capital. . . . Hitler had been told by his generals that it was 'useless to continue the war.'"[332] Later, armed Berliners fired on law enforcement. And "long columns of trucks laden with official Berlin archives, furniture and other effects continued to stream in the direction of Munich in the exodus of government departments."[333]

Yet, the next day, Hitler went on radio to call on the German people to fight to the end. With "his creaking Reich invaded from the east and teeming with war-crossed refugees, [Hitler] called on the German people . . . 'to fight on no matter where and no matter under what circumstances until final victory crowns our efforts.'" The half-crazed dictator, on the twelfth anniversary of his ascendancy to the German chancellorship, said, "Whoever stabs us in the back will die an ignominious death.

In this hour, I appeal to the whole people and above all to my old comrades and all soldiers to arm themselves with an even greater and tougher spirit of resistance."[334] He claimed he'd been spared assassination in 1944 by the "Almighty," while calling himself a "ruthless National Socialist."

> If the spirit of Versailles still prevailed in Germany today, Europe would have been swept away by the Asiatic springtide long ago. . . . I do not want to leave any doubt about another matter on this day; my present life is being determined solely by the duties which lie upon me . . . to work for my people and fight for them. Germany will never go down before the Bolshevists . . . therefore, continue on my path of uncompromising representation of the interests of my people . . . imbued with the sacred conviction that in the end the Almighty will not let down a man who wanted nothing else throughout his life but to save his people. . . . The Almighty has created our nation and by defending our existence we are defending his works. We will do our duty in the most critical times. I can only be absolved from my duty by Him (God) who called me to my work and fight for my people.[335]

The Russians also called on the German people to rise up—against the Nazis: "The twilight of the Nazi God has begun in the shrine of the flaming German cities. . . . Let your slogan be, 'No soldiers, no weapons, no food for the Hitlerite regime.'"[336]

American women had been going to war for nearly five years, and that included women in prison. A January 29 story in the *Los Angeles Times* detailed how over 150 female inmates had joined the war effort. They sewed mosquito netting, pillowcases, and baby clothing for the children of men in uniform. "In the past, the inmates have co-operated with every military suggestion and precaution . . . for many months, [they] operated a 24-hour aircraft warning post," it said.[337]

A reporter who escaped Japanese imprisonment in the city of Manila told of the atrocities there. Almost one million people had been suffering in starvation and deprivation for four years. Their only hope was for the coming liberation by the Americans. "The children of Manila poke through the garbage cans for their food; scores die each day; the dead are buried naked, and their clothing sold to buy a meal for the living. Cats and dogs already had been eaten," he said.[338] The poverty was appalling. Graves were robbed for clothing. Just as these new indignities were being revealed, Japan's foreign minister, Mamoru Shigemitsu, went before the Japanese Diet and appallingly told the gathered that the "Allies were hell bent to destroy Japan and Germany" as they had "groundless fears that we are not human beings and will menace them in the future." He went even further: "Japan's just war aims are to construct a world free from menace and aggression. We have no desire other than to be kind to all mankind."[339]

January 30 was President Franklin Roosevelt's birthday. As with each of his birthdays, he paid tribute to the March of Dimes and the ongoing fight against paralysis. Bob Hope arrived in Florida—by train—unharmed. It had been rumored that he'd been hurt in an airplane accident.[340] New rations of canned fruits and vegetables were ordered by the government; 61 percent of canned vegetables were ordered to be set aside for "war requirements."[341]

Errol Flynn, famed swashbuckling and B-movie actor, was the subject of rumors and in the scandal sheets far more than he ever was in the movies. On January 31, a new rumor popped up that the thirty-five-year-old actor had married—and had a child—with twenty-year-old cigarette salesgirl and candy counter clerk Nora Eddington. He'd met Eddington two years earlier when he was in court to answer charges made against him by two teenage girls. Flynn was cavalier, telling reporters, "No comment except to observe that this makes the third or fourth time I've been reported married in the last couple of years."[342]

THE RUSSIAN ARMY LIBERATED yet another death camp, Oswiecim, south of Krakow in Poland. Initial reports said that some 12,500 survivors of the Warsaw Uprising had been captured and shipped off to Oswiecim for extermination. "The Moscow accounts said gaunt mothers with sick children in their arms and enfeebled middle-aged persons were herded into airtight rooms and while guards watched through windows, they were killed by gas."[343]

As with most stories about death camps, they did not tell the reader that the defenseless inmates were mostly Jews, nor did they tell of the millions of Jews exterminated by the Nazis. Not yet.

Herman Wouk wrote in *War and Remembrance*, "The Germans are using an old name . . . from . . . when Oswiecim was Austrian. Not only is it harsher, as German names tend to be; Auschwitz hardly even sounds like Oswiecim."[344]

CHAPTER 2

FEBRUARY 1945

"Reds Closing in on Berlin"
Boston Daily Globe

"Bataan Veterans Freed in Jap Prison Raid"
Evening Star

"'Big 3' Agree on Disarming of Reich"
Washington Post

British sources said that George Bernard Shaw "has admitted he hasn't the foggiest notion what is going to happen in 1945. The old gentleman must really be slipping."[1] Shaw may not have known what was going on in 1945, but everybody else in the world did.

"A Federal Communications Commission investigator who spent some time checking on the leased wires of bookies and racetrack publications won $1,200 betting on the horses during that period," wrote columnist Louis M. Lyons.[2]

The army and the navy announced that casualties—including dead, injured, missing, and POWs—were closing in on 1,000,000, especially with the fierce fighting in the Pacific and Europe. However, it was estimated that over 16,350,000 had died at the hands of the Nazis, including 10,000,000 Russians, 5,000,000 Poles, 1,000,000 Jugoslavs, 145,000 Dutch, 83,000 Greeks, 60,000 Czechs, 50,000 French, 15,000 Belgians, 750 Norwegians, and 75 Danes. Nowhere did they mention that 6,000,000 were Jews and another 4,000,000 were assorted gypsies, homosexuals, communists, political dissidents, and others considered to be enemies of the state.

The government's plan to auction off surplus military supplies ran into an immediate snag when New York City mayor Fiorello La Guardia denounced the president of Surplus Liquidators as "unfair and unethical" and "stupid and arrogant."[3] Jacob Goldberg's company had won the bid to handle the auction and, by contract, the city was not allowed to make a bid.

A charge was made that Goldberg had offered a $20,000-a-year job to an employee of the Defense Plant Corporation, the company in possession of the surplus matériel, as a means of influencing the decision to award the contact to Surplus Liquidators, which La Guardia called a "scandalous proceeding."[4] It was later reported that Goldberg would lose the contract due to "irregularities."[5] As an example, life rafts were sold to the auction company for 50 cents apiece, which was no doubt reselling them for $50 apiece.

Some $8.5 million in surplus goods was also going to be auctioned off in New England. Purchasing for the war effort had been an ongoing scandal as war profiteers sold to the government at often rip-off prices. One plumbing supplier told a Senate investigating committee that the government had repurchased floor strainers for $12 after having sold them at auction for only $3.25.[6] Such stories were legion.

Of much greater importance was the liberation of a Japanese internment camp on Luzon, where eventually 3,700 prisoners, mostly American and British, were released. They were rescued by American Rangers and Filipino guerrillas. According to one news report, "A convoy of ambulances and trucks transported the rescued captives back to safety and freedom—except for two of 513 who died en route. No men ever received more sincere homage than these lean, ragged captives who had come back from death."[7] Stories continued to fill the papers of Japan's terrible treatment of Allied POWs. "The Japs always liked to slap us, and sometimes they'd give us a real stiff beating," recalled one soldier. Another POW recounted how the Japanese guards would lure the Americans to a perimeter fence with candy and tobacco only to be then whipped or shot. One of those Americans not liberated was General Jonathan Wainwright, who'd been sent to a POW camp on Formosa, where some seventeen other generals were also imprisoned.[8] Along about the same time, a starving Japanese soldier dressed in rags wandered into a US Army officers' mess, struck his flag, and surrendered.[9]

The Filipino guerrillas deserved much of the credit for the quick advance of General Douglas MacArthur's forces. For three years, they had lived in the jungles, bombing bridges and harassing Japanese supply lines. They'd dug up roads and done whatever they could to badger and hound and weaken the Japanese invaders.

Harry Hopkins, FDR's closest aide, popped up in Rome at a forty-minute meeting with Pope Pius XII. Rumor held that Hopkins was soon headed to Moscow on a fact-finding mission in preparation for the meeting of the Big Three—Roosevelt, Churchill, and Stalin—at the Yalta Conference on February 4, 1945. Hopkins ventured his opinion that postwar Europe should go left in its politics "provided it does not go to the extreme of totalitarianism."[10] He was one of the last of the original New Dealers. His secret meetings with Churchill, Stalin, and the pope were in all the newspapers. It was also rumored the British prime minister was spotted on Gibraltar. Churchill was planning his own way of dealing with the Germans and postwar Europe. He was operating on the belief that Germany's remaining political system had broken down, spiraling down to deep decay and anarchy. The Americans also had some ideas on how to deal with the Axis war criminals, but on this matter there would be no dissension from the British or the Russians. All had their legitimate reasons to despise the Germans.

Stories appeared wondering if the Russians had gone faster than their supply lines in the assault on Berlin. The Associated Press reported, "It is quite possible the Red Army surge may stop short of Berlin, but if it does it may well be because of their logistic problem."[11] If the Russians were temporarily waylaid, General George S. Patton's army was unrelenting, pushing the last Germans out of Belgium. They were within several miles of piercing the Siegfried Line. However, for the Russians, failing to take Berlin was not an option. Supply line shortages were not an acceptable excuse for "Uncle Joe." Stalin would not be denied his conquest. Soviet forces gained eight miles to take the cities of Frankfurt and Krustin and were now only forty miles from Berlin. Along the way, they killed or captured an additional seventeen thousand German troops. The resistance was still tough, however, as the Germans were not going to give up without a fight. Thousands of miles away, MacArthur was closing in on another enemy-held city: Manila. Again, Japanese resistance was tough but, like the Germans', was faltering in the face of superior Allied numbers.

Readers of newspapers saw a series of photographs rarely seen by civilians. For example, a Grumman F6F Hellcat cracked up upon landing on an unnamed carrier, then the badly damaged plane was pushed overboard. The censors for the US military, however, often did not let pictures slip through of unfortunate incidents involving military personnel.

A columnist, Barnet Nover, saw clearly what the last days of Germany meant to the delusional Hitler. He wrote on February 1, "The Hitler who spoke last Thursday, on the twelfth anniversary of his accession to power, was a man who, witnessing the death agony of his nation, sought to revive it with a hypodermic of oratory. This is not surprising. Oratory was Hitler's stock in trade when he first emerged on the German scene. Oratory is his last resort now. But the situation confronting the Reich is beyond the capacity of words to alter."[12] The famed syndicated columnist Walter Lippmann foresaw very bad times ahead for Hitler and the German people, far worse than after 1918. According to Lippmann, Nazism had destroyed everything but Nazism. There was nothing left of civil society: no civilian government, no independent courts, no free expression, no place for any decent person to turn. Except Nazism. "The suffering which this will impose on the German people, the guilty and the innocent alike, is incalculable. There is no precedent in history for what is going to happen when 70 or 80 million people living in a complicated modern economy find themselves without a general government of their own which can provide the elementary necessities of life. But, thanks to Hitler, that will be the condition of Germany, and what the allies can do about it in view of their own necessities, and the commitment of the Japanese war, is not clear at all."[13]

Much attention had been focused on Germany's rocket program, especially the V-2. But the Americans had their own rocket program, though not as sophisticated. Small rockets had been developed for use in the Philippines to fire on the Japanese infantry. But back in Europe, the Americans captured huge German rocket launch installations "for rockets aimed at the United States," according to General Eisenhower himself.[14] Also, the Russians were using their own rocket guns to great effect. In January alone, Hitler's V-2—the "revenge weapon"—killed 585 Britons and wounded another 1,629. All told, some three thousand Britons were eventually killed by the one thousand V-2 rockets that Germans aimed at England.

What they heard or read in the news on Saturday was a preview of the sermons at various churches on Sundays: "One Blood" at Mt. Vernon Church, "Morals Afloat" at Old South Church, "Transfiguration Beauty" at Copley Church in Boston.

WASHINGTONIANS ALWAYS ENJOYED NIGHTCLUBS and evening entertainment, but one of the most popular was the "Copacabana Review" at the Deo Rio nightclub downtown. That was the good news. The somber news was that Chambers Undertakers—reputedly "the largest undertaker in the world"—was offering funerals for as low as $95. At the upscale Mayflower Hotel on Connecticut Avenue, plans were going forward to celebrate their twentieth anniversary, and the festivities would be held in the Chinese Room as the advertising said.

MEXICO ANNOUNCED IT WAS sending the 201st Fighter Squadron to the Far East to aid in the Allies' fight.

The Works Progress Administration (WPA), one of the first of the New Deal programs, suddenly appeared in the news. What was it doing now, ten years later? It was trying to find people whom other people were looking for, people who used to be associated with the WPA.[15] It was a long way down from its gigantic mission of the early and heady days of the New Deal that included building streets, housing by the thousands, and providing work for millions of unemployed men.

An American dogface who refused to fight, Henry Weber, was sentenced to hang. His wife, Grace Weber, pleaded for clemency, telling the military brass he was deeply opposed to "killing his fellow man." She told the newspapers the US Army had "known that all along." Henry Weber later said it was his "revolutionary mind" that led him to refuse to march or fight.[16] The War Department announced that five hundred thousand other dogfaces were going to be reassigned from army bases in the United States to overseas combat assignments. They were part of the three million men in uniform in the country, many of whom were assigned to "housekeeping units."[17] American infantrymen in the army were occasionally known as "doughfoots."

In Washington, the *Evening Star* trumpeted the creation of a second all-colored fire company: "Seven colored firemen . . . will be transferred to the new unit. There are 27 colored firemen in the department."[18] All were making salaries of just over $2,000 a year, equivalent to just over $30,000 today. The DC police stuck to the spirit and letter of the law and auctioned off thousands of dollars' worth of contraband liquor. Shoppers in the downtown area were warned that DC would go through its first brownout, designed to save coal used for power plants to create electricity. Commercial lights and marquees would be turned off, but that did not stop Bostonians in early February from gathering on the streets to collect bags and buckets of the "black diamonds."[19]

More charges circulated that "certain very sinister Germans had been escaping from the Reich on false passports."[20] At the same time, an editorial in a Moscow paper charged that "Argentina was 'swarming with Hitler agents.' . . . Every day from Stuttgart there arrive in Barcelona planes with Hitlerites who then proceed to Argentina."[21]

Twin radio reports told of how General Patton's army was close to crossing the Siegfried Line from the west. They were capturing German POWs by the bushelful now. Also, "Allied planes spotted heavy German rail movements eastward."[22] Again, the stories about trains heading east out of Germany did not contain many details.

In Massachusetts, a military plane accidentally dropped a five-hundred-pound bomb, hitting a house and killing a woman instantly. Her son was in the house at the time and was also killed.[23] But the story of the tragedy was buried. In Yuma, Arizona, a B-17 crashed and all four servicemen on board were killed.

In Georgia, both branches of the legislature voted overwhelmingly to repeal their one-dollar-a-year "poll tax." The poll tax had been an important weapon in Jim Crow laws throughout the South as a means of preventing blacks from voting. "Repeal of the poll tax in Georgia [left] seven with the levy—Alabama, Arkansas, Mississippi, South Carolina, Texas, Virginia and Tennessee."[24] In Maryland, there was also a move to abolish the Jim Crow laws, but first there came a commission to study the "problems affecting the colored population . . . the inconsistency of denying 'basic rights and equalities at home while many thousands of our colored citizens are engaged patriotically in this world-wide battle.'"[25]

A member of Congress John Edward Fogarty of Rhode Island, Democrat, returned from his assignment in the Seabees in the Pacific. Fogarty was a carpenter's mate. He was one of a small handful of elected officials who served in the war. Lyndon Johnson of Texas joined so he could be photographed in uniform by professional Hollywood photographers (after getting his officer's uniform professionally tailored), and then went on a very brief tour of duty in the Pacific. Governor Harold Stassen, the "boy governor" of Minnesota, resigned his office and served honorably in the US Navy in the Pacific, including serving on the staff of Admiral William "Bull" Halsey. Stassen was later chosen by FDR to serve as a delegate to the first conference of the United Nations at Dumbarton Oaks. Stassen, like Wendell Willkie and Tom Dewey, was among the first neoconservatives, openly advocating one world government and "strong world policy."[26] Two-thirds of US senators favored mandating that Germany and Japan never be allowed to arm again.

Americans had gotten used to seeing women in the workplace for the previous four plus years, but now, at war's end, some began to question the effect it had on the family. An article in DC's *Evening Star* noted, "The wartime industrialization of married women may become a permanent post-war institution menacing family life."[27] Brendan Brown, acting dean of Catholic University, asserted that many present-day problems of easier divorces and juvenile delinquency stem from the employment of married women. Brown elaborated, saying the whole situation was leading to the breakdown of the family and of marriage as an institution. But the classified ads in the papers were filled with positions for women—girl elevator operator, women for light industry work, bakery salesgirls—and many noted that married women were preferred.[28] The female job listings in the newspapers were far longer than the male listings in the want ads. Keeping up morale was important for the women in industry. For example, the Firestone Tire and Rubber company in Akron invested $2.5 million creating an athletic center for the thirty thousand employees, including a bowling alley, an archery range, Ping-Pong tables, horseshoes, badminton, swimming, and other assorted recreational games and events.

On the society pages were the usual marriage announcements and society parties but also an item about the meeting of the "Jewish Juniors."[29] Some culture pages, often featuring pictures of women announcing their engagements, were called "War Time Society," and the Junior Leaguers had gone to war as well, stating, "If you think the Junior Leaguers are mere social butterflies flitting away time, you're dead wrong."[30] Junior Leaguers were working with the Red Cross, in military motor pools, as nurses' aides, and in officers' clubs and servicemen's clubs. At the end of the war, there would be many a thank-you note to send.

THE ARMY WAS PLANNING for the prompt return of soldiers imprisoned in Bataan. One reporter captured the sentiments of those who had survived the ordeal: "They want their health back. They want to see their folks. Then they want to come back and fight the Japanese."[31] These were the sentiments of the American prisoners who'd survived the awfulness of Bataan. "They have bitter memories of surrender at Bataan and Corregidor. Many had to undergo the 'death march' from Bataan." They had memories of dozens being forced into small cells and some being shipped off to Japan to work as slave laborers. During the death march, they weren't given water for days and some drank from mud puddles. Even then, the bayonets were ever present, always threatening. They didn't eat for days on end, and even when they did, it was always rice. When some Filipinos tried to sneak some of the men food and were caught, they were beaten, and some died.

One headline shouted of the freed men: "Hysterical with Happiness over Freedom, Flag, Food." A famished prisoner looked at the delectables brought to him by MacArthur's army and exclaimed, "This probably will make me as sick as hell, but I don't care." Another was a one-armed American prisoner. "The haggard, one-armed young soldier—he lost his limb at Bataan, ate six eggs, a large helping of meat, seven biscuits with jam and a can of grapefruit. He washed it down with five cups of coffee." Meanwhile, a British officer yelled, "White bread! Blimey, this is better than I got in peacetime!"[32] It was the first major rescue of Allied POWs in the Pacific. At another death camp, seventy-three Japanese guards were killed in five minutes, "shot, bayonetted or knifed" by American troops.[33]

The War Manpower Commission said some fifty thousand nurses were available for duty should the need arise. A draft of nurses had run into several roadblocks, including the argument that if eligible nurses were drafted then why not all eligible women? Some considered that a good question.

At a Boston rally for seven hundred nurses, a speaker exclaimed, "Don't wait to be drafted! Let history say . . . not one of its members waited to be drafted." Another speaker, the lieutenant governor of the Bay State, Massachusetts, told the women, "[Nursing] is one of the proudest professions known to mankind."[34]

While the European newspapers were filled with detailed stories about the forthcoming meeting of the Big Three, White House reporters were under a gag rule and not allowed to write about what they knew; they were not a happy lot. They knew FDR's aide Harry Hopkins was in Europe but were not supposed to write about that either. The White House blamed the British for the clampdown.

Hopkins later wrote a thoughtful article for the *American Magazine* in which he called for the permanent occupation of Germany and Japan "to prevent their rearmament." He also called for a compulsory drafting of all American boys, beginning at the age of eighteen, and mandatory service of one year "to discourage all future aggressors."[35] He was in good company as 70 percent of Americans favored compulsory service. Hopkins said, "I have no doubt that powerful forces in Germany and Japan are preparing even now for their next attempt to conquer us. We will try to keep them impotent, but only a perpetual army of occupation would be able to prevent them from rearming eventually." And he went even further, saying "mentally or physically handicapped boys should be included [in the draft]."[36] His opinion held public significance because he had enjoyed FDR's confidence for years, was an important adviser, and for a time lived in the Roosevelt White House.

More rumors appeared that the Big Three were already in meetings, deep in discussion. And being bandied about was the matter of the Soviets and the Japanese. As of February's end, Russia had still not declared war against the Empire of the Rising Sun. Secondhand reports said Roosevelt and Churchill would not pressure but presumed Stalin would join the fight against Japan.[37]

Another item was how and how soon to redeploy British and American men and matériel from Europe to the Pacific theater to finish the fight against the Japanese once the fight against the Germans had been won. But there was also concern about weariness among the troops.

One news report said, "By keeping the units so long in the line, the veterans had become more tired and less able to keep their combat efficiency. They see no future except the dangerous drudgery of battle and a few of them get into a frame of mind in which they actually welcome a wound that takes them to a hospital."[38]

"Schluss. Schluss" was heard over Berlin radio during a massive American daylight bombing. It meant, "That's enough. That's enough." No one was sure if the terrified broadcaster was reacting to the massive bombing campaign or simply, and accidentally, broadcasting the end of a program.

BERLIN HAD BEEN NEARLY flattened by the relentless Allied bombing, but on February 4, American bombers really let the city have it. Terrified Berliners looked up to see one thousand B-17 bombers blackening the smoke-filled skies. The bombers were escorted by more than nine hundred fighters and dropped over three thousand tons of explosive bombs on Berlin over forty-five minutes on a day when the weather was clear. For the first time, no German fighters rose to meet the Allied challenge. Even if they had, they would have come up against the superior American fighter planes, such as the P-51 Mustang. The German planes were now obsolete, as were those of their Axis counterparts. The only German airplanes receiving good reviews were their experimental jets, which, reportedly, could travel over ten miles a minute.

The once-feared Luftwaffe was now nearly destroyed as well as aircraft factories and ball-bearing factories, and its oil capacity had been reduced by 70 percent. German roads and communications systems had been all but destroyed, and German currency was useless. The morale of the Allies was soaring. They believed the end was in sight. There was talk of a brave new world once the war was over.

In the Pacific, American pilots and planes were now vastly superior to the Japanese models, and by 1945, the Americans had shot down 9,819 enemy planes while losing only 1,882, a better than 5:1 ratio. Also, 65 percent of downed American navy pilots were rescued, only to see action again. There were no statistics available on downed Japanese pilots, but since the advent of the kamikaze pilots and their treatment of POWs and torture of civilians, all knew about the low regard the Japanese had for life.

The next day, the Allies launched an even larger armada, this time 2,220 planes to bomb various locations. One of the air leaders was Lieutenant General James "Jimmy" Doolittle, hero of the air attack on Japan just months after the savage sneak attack on helpless American sailors and soldiers at Pearl Harbor. He'd devised the idea of launching sixteen B-25 bombers from the decks of American aircraft carriers hundreds of miles from Japan and flying at treetop level over Tokyo and several other cities, bombing them, and then flying on to China. Once there, the plan was to land and get back to American forces as best they could despite the heavy presence of Japanese patrols in occupied China. Some of the pilots died on this extremely hazardous mission, but most made it back to America, including Doolittle, who was secreted out of China by several Chinese citizens and American missionaries, including John Birch. Doolittle was lauded and became a national celebrity. The "Doolittle Raid" was just the tonic demoralized Americans needed. America had just punched the Japanese in the nose. But this newfound celebrity did not turn Doolittle's head, except skyward, and he was back to the war in a matter of months.

American fliers had their own prayer: "God of the evening, God of the dawn, . . . / God of the morning, God of the light, / Keep our engines strong in flight, / And then Lord, let it be thy will, / That there will come a day when we need not kill."[39]

Men who resisted combat weren't new, but a news story of an AWOL (absent without leave) serviceman—one for the books—came out of Atlanta on February 4. Henry Bembnowski had disappeared in August 1943 after being assigned to an artillery unit. The bearded, disheveled, long-haired man emerged sixteen months later when a fire burned down the service club he'd been hiding under. He was immediately hospitalized to determine his physical and mental health.[40] AWOL—aka "goldbrick neurosis"—was the subject of a battery of psychological tests at Fort Belvoir in Virginia. It seemed some men resented authority, especially while being shot at. Another poor, distraught woman from a Boston boarding house was pleading for clemency for her twenty-two-year-old son. She said her son was not a bad boy. Karl Hulten, a private in the army, was convicted of stabbing a London cabbie to death and sentenced to be hanged.

An American pilot and former news writer declared, "there are no atheists in combat planes." Sergeant William Umstead had landed his plane in Italy, had "cracked up," and was nursed back to health at a "reassignment center on the West Coast."[41] Yet another pilot, Lieutenant Richard Chapman, had put in fifty long missions over Italy when he was reassigned to the China-Burma-India theater, which he described as a "vacation."[42]

The signs and sights of the terrors of war were evident all over America. At Walter Reed General Hospital, maimed men missing arms and legs were going through rehabilitation, including learning how to drive again.

The radio fare of America, of course, continued to feature war news, but there was also plenty of local and network programming. *The Life of Riley*, a comedy, was aired nationally, as was the *Philco Radio Hall of Fame*, which showcased such talents as Hedy Lamarr and Marjorie Main of *Ma and Pa Kettle* fame. And on any given station, you could always, it seemed, hear the Andrews Sisters.

Four divisions from Patton's Third Army crossed the Our and Sûre Rivers by boat and bridge, closing the gap to Berlin. Later, the First Army "drove through the last barriers of the double Siegfried Line," capturing reservoirs and dams along the way. "The dam system is capable of sending an 18-foot wall of water down the 36-miles of the Roer."[43] They also encountered Nazi minefields along the way. Patton was "pushing a full-scale offensive along a 40-mile section."[44] One February 4 report said the First Army was already eleven miles inside Germany.

Each day, the *Evening Star* featured on the second page a "Roll of

Honor," which displayed the pictures of boys and men from the Greater DC area who had been killed, wounded, or taken prisoner. The photographs often depicted young men in aviator caps complete with goggles, overseas caps, or officer's hats, handsome all. The ages of the deceased were listed too: twenty-one, twenty-two, twenty-six. . . .

The boys and men who did come home often had their minds on the friends they left behind in the jungles of the Philippines, in the waters of the North Atlantic and the Pacific, in the muddy battlefields of Europe, and on the sands of North Africa. "You can't help remembering the guys you left over there," said one forlorn corporal. Even so, even from a train, these wounded men "still [whistled] from their white hospital berths if a pretty girl [crossed] the platform in one of these southern towns."[45] Sharp-eyed *Boston Daily Globe* reporter Francis Burns, writing about a train full of wounded veterans, poetically said, "But you know that a soldier with a boy's face didn't have that bewildered, frightened look in the eyes when he went away."[46] A wounded paratrooper, involved in three in-combat jumps, pulled out a large piece of his parachute from his duffle bag, and the nurse mirthfully said, "Those are my nylons." On his last jump into Holland, "he was wounded in the arms" and saw that all his fellow soldiers had been "knocked out"; he was eighty miles behind enemy lines. He eventually made his way back and hooked up with a British outfit.[47]

Brownouts to save on fuel now extended to Boston and Portland, Maine, as directed by the War Production Board (WPB). There were some griping and complaining, but the decision went ahead. Later reports said that, although inconvenient and odd to see Boston darkened at night with no commercial lighting, some eighty tons of coal had been saved. Movie marquees had been turned off, and the only lighting allowed were streetlamps. Stores that did not comply were sent telegrams from the WPB, telling them to comply with the orders or their electricity would be shut off.

There might be a war going on, but it was still cold in the Northeast and women still wanted to look smart and fashionable when they went out on the town. Crawford's Furriers in Boston was offering muskrat, Persian, raccoon, skunk, and fox fur coats, priced from as low as $128 all the way up to $695. Men's winter coats, worsted and tweed, were more reasonably priced at $27.50. And, new dress shirts were going for as much as $1.35.

The Russian army was moving again, now apparently unchecked by Nazi opposition, and, depending on which news report one read, it was only forty-five miles from Berlin. In one day, it had advanced ten miles under the command of General Georgy Zhukov, a career military man who was well regarded for his on-field command.[48] The Americans, the British, and the Russians got the lion's share of the press coverage about the advance on Germany and Berlin, but Canadian and French troops were also involved in massive offensives, including some American troops under the command of the French army.

More and more stories speculating on Hitler were appearing. Most everybody knew he was a madman, and nearly everybody believed he was evil (though not everybody knew how evil he truly was in February 1945), but no one could explain his hold over the German people. There was no doubt he and his minions were fascinating to some. Some stories examined how long he might last, while others, the state of his mind. Goebbels, propaganda minister and "gauleiter dictator," was said to be in charge of the defense of Berlin, and as such, he said the city would be "scorched" rather than surrendered to the Allies. Many buildings, including the zoo, had been converted into rudimentary battle emplacements in and around Berlin.[49]

The war was not even over, but that did not stop some from engaging in finger-pointing over how it started. One charge and target came from an unusual source: the president of Dartmouth, Dr. Ernest Hopkins. He blamed colleges and universities in America and Great Britain for being irresponsible in the face of fascism. He leveled the academy, saying, "In spite of their high intelligence, no people have been more completely misunderstood than those of the United States. There was an over-abundance of ignorance until December 1941 when we came to the first realization that this was one world, and that affects all. Although our first allegiance is to the principles of this government, still the melting pot has not worked fast enough for us not to engage in racial thinking, and to be influenced by our backgrounds. We are still not completely a united or realistic people." Hopkins delivered his ground-trembling remarks before a group of two thousand academics at Tufts University.[50]

Meanwhile, New England Telephone and Telegraph was admonishing customers not to place long-distance calls to keep the lines clear for servicemen calling home, especially between the hours of 7:00 p.m. to 10:00 p.m. The winter of 1945 was especially hard in the land of the bean and the cod. A meeting was convened in Boston, attended by all the governors of the New England states, to discuss how to handle the severe fuel shortage.

The National Service Act was still being debated in Congress. An amendment was offered in the House, which proposed that workers did not need to join a union. That was voted down. An amendment was offered "that race, creed or color should not be a condition of employment." That was voted down too.

The world war was not over, but fighting had ceased in some countries, sparking many to ponder the future of a new world and new world problems. A writer for the *Christian Science Monitor*, Reuben Markham, who had been a Balkan correspondent, warned a small group in Boston of the dangers of a communist Yugoslavia and Greece. Even as the war continued to destroy, in its wake people began to rebuild in war-torn France; an army unit was already putting up telephone lines.

Boy Scout Week, February 8 through 14, was coming up and already it was being written about and photographed.[51] In early February, the owners and leaders of Major League Baseball were meeting again to determine once and for all if the 1945 season would proceed. They also had to elect a new commissioner to replace Kenesaw Mountain Landis, who'd ruled baseball with an iron fist for nearly twenty-five years. After these "important meetings of the American and National leagues . . . it may be known whether there will be any professional league ball this year, or any other year until the end of World War II," wrote Melville Webb of the *Boston Daily Globe*.[52] One big question was whether players classified as 4-F would be pulled into working in essential war industries under the legislation being debated in Congress. The War Department said it would "not counsel against" baseball in the spring of 1945.

Americans feasted on the daily newspaper cartoons. Some were funny and some were serious, but *Race Riley and the Commandos* was noteworthy, as it depicted Japanese as the worst racial stereotypes: slanted eyes and big, buck teeth.[53]

The newspaper advertising in the early days of February was extensive, if also "interesting." Colgate "ribbon dental cream" cleaned your breath while it cleaned your teeth. There was Serutan for the thirty-five and over crowd for relief from constipation and to restore "regularity." Also, one ad featured a woman telling the reader "how to keep your husband happy after 35." The solution, she said, was to "get real relief from constipation." Her husband, after taking Serutan, was a "changed man. He feels better—looks better. And we're both enjoying life again."[54] And to help create the constipation, Betty Crocker was pushing a "corn sausage pie." Welch's jams were pushing "Grapelade." Sometimes helpful stories were written guiding the reader on how to fill out the seven questions on their 1945 federal tax return.

A female war correspondent working for the *Boston Daily Globe* sent daily dispatches from the front in Europe while traveling with the First Army. Iris Carpenter's writing was clean and businesslike. "Despite stubborn resistance, which increased as the day wore on, we made gains all along the front today," she wrote on February 3.[55] The advance of the American First Army was now ten miles inside of Germany. The Associated Press reported, "The United States 3rd Army along the southern sector of the 40-mile front likewise was beating at the Rhineland's western defenses, widening its foothold inside the Reich."[56]

The Americans were broadcasting to the German people to rise up against the Nazis, the Russians were broadcasting to the German people to rise up against the Nazis, and now the "Free German Committee" in Moscow was broadcasting to their fellow Germans to rise up against the Nazis: "Use your weapons—turn them against the true enemy of Germany. Persuade the soldiers and men of the Volkssturm that they should not continue to fight for Hitler. Germans, rise! Overthrow Hitler. The hour has struck."[57] A theme for all broadcasts was "Hitler has lost the war. Five million Germans are dead. Today, Hitler is throwing 15 and 14-year-old children into the futile fight. Old men and cripples have to save Germany. Refugees stream into Berlin, but Hitler welcomes them with hunting squads, and Volkssturm battalions."[58] Elaborating, they said the Nazi leaders are only prolonging the war now "so that the bloody skins of the Nazi henchmen survive one more week or one more month. . . . The rescue from total catastrophe lies in surrender."[59]

Hitler was so desperate to defend Berlin, he resorted to drafting women into the fight. "The Nazis conscripted all German women and girls for the Volkssturm," and then Hitler made some vague comments that Germany would still prevail. Women aged from sixteen to sixty were conscripted for duty "by a decree from Heinrich Himmler."[60]

Berlin radio half threatened, half exhorted the people of the city to come to the defense of the Reich. Berlin radio tried to blame their predicament on two old propaganda enemies. They denounced "Bolshevik terror and Jewish revenge," and said their "terms will be made public only after we have laid down our arms."[61] Citizens were accused by broadcasters of hoarding needed goods. It was not a way to boost morale, nor was the strict rationing of everything, including soap and fake laundry soap, which Berliners were told had to last from "February 5 to April 1."[62] No matter. Much of Berlin had no running water anyway. It was rumored that anti-Hitler groups had finally sprung up in various German cities, although this came twelve years too late for some. When a Nazi film crew tried to escape to Switzerland, along with sixty rogue party members, the Gestapo shot them. And then nine party members were shot for cowardice in the Sudetenland. Germans were shooting Germans, doing the Allies' work for them.

Among other things, the Big Three would be considering the

treatment of the Nazi war criminals, as they were now called. One thing was for sure: the Allies already said that if and when the war was won, first, the Nazis would be subject to the laws of the country where they committed their crimes; and second, in "the case of the major criminals whose offenses have no particular geographic location," like Hitler and Goebbels, they would face their judgment by a "joint decision" of the Allied governments. Another agenda item was the forced and permanent disarmament of Germany and Japan.

William Shirer was more perceptive than most writers alive in 1945. He'd been a CBS correspondent in Berlin until he'd had his fill of the German government censors some years earlier. In 1941, he wrote the landmark book *Berlin Diary*, a huge bestseller about the rise of Nazi Germany. Now, in February 1945, Shirer wrote, "It is now clear from Hitler's [recent] broadcast and from the outbursts of his henchmen in print and on the air that the fanatical German Fuehrer is determined—to go down fighting and in doing so to pull Germany and all the Germans down with him. There has always been a strange and weird fascination in the German mind at the prospect of mass, self-willed annihilation. Hitler, steeped as he is in the Wagnerian world of pagan gods, undoubtedly sees himself as Wotan, who in Wagner's version atones for his guilt by setting Valhalla in flames."[63] Still, this did not stop Shirer from writing a column complaining about the censorship coming from the War Department.[64]

Harvard professor Perry G. Miller had somewhat of a different take on the German people, writing, "These men, a lot of them, keep on fighting out of sheer ignorance. Some of these prisoners thought they were within a few miles of Paris. They hadn't had anything to eat for two days, they'd been melting snow for drinking water, and still they believed they were on their way to victory! . . . They felt like victors because they were wearing several layers of captured G. I. underwear and eating K rations."[65] He also understatedly delved into the effect on his own students, saying, "All of the kids I get right after the war will have been soldiers or will have been in some way affected by the war."[66] Harvard, as always, was about Harvard. They announced plans to improve their medical school after the war. But the plan itself was complicated.

The Russian army had pierced the last line of defense between itself and Berlin. Still, the Germans were "throwing in heavy reinforcements." Berlin was the key. All knew if it fell, Nazi Germany would fall. On February 4, *Boston Daily Globe* reported, "The 4,000,000 people of the German capital live in an area of 339 square miles. . . . It cannot be taken until it is encircled. Soviet progress to the northeast has been steady but against strong resistance. So far, the Germans had a lack of sufficient power to deliver a counter offensive in the north, but they still hold many positions from which heavy drives could be successfully launched."[67]

Longtime Kansas City political boss Thomas Pendergast had passed away in January at the age of seventy-two, but his impact was lasting. Many a Democratic politician had been helped along by Pendergast's generous donation of thousands of ballots, tipping many elections. In return, "Boss Pendergast" got and cashed in political favors. One of his favored politicians was Harry Truman, whose first election to the US Senate was always clouded in some doubt over ballot box stuffing. It didn't matter. The buck did not pass by Truman, who flew back to Missouri to attend the funeral of his old friend and sponsor. Columnist M. E. Hennessy wrote, "Pendergast made no attempt to regain his lost prestige in politics once he had paid his penalty for his crime. Most of those he had befriended in politics avoided him, but Harry Truman was not among them. Ingratitude is not part of his nature and Pendergast had no more sincere mourner in the congregation that filled the church than the Vice President of the United States."[68]

Truman was later photographed playing an upright piano while the seductive, green-eyed film star, Lauren Bacall, was perched sexily atop it at the National Press Club's canteen. "Wow," exclaimed a marine. "She is really a sizzler!"[69] Truman may have been an afterthought in the FDR White House, but he was often a hit in the DC social scene. It wasn't unusual for the Trumans to be feted at some society wingding with senators, congressmen, and assorted other hangers-on. Indeed, the society pages of the Washington, Los Angeles, and New York papers were as avidly read as the front sections and the sports pages.

"Nazis Slaughtered on Oder" screamed headlines across the country.[70] But even as the German army was failing in the field, Nazi U-boats were still doing a great deal of damage. A tanker, the H.D. *Collier*, owned by the Standard Oil Company, was transporting 102,000 gallons of high-test gasoline when three U-boat submarines slammed into it as it made passage through the Arabian Sea. Thirty-three hands were lost. In fact, U-boat action was reported to be greater in January 1945. Indeed, seven ships were torpedoed off Nova Scotia, and seventy-three seamen lost their lives. Some of the attacks were within sight of the shoreline and in daylight hours too.

The war, so thought, was close to being won, but who really knew? Death notices for young men continued to fill the papers, such as "Bomber Crash Kills Medford Corporal."[71] Part of the War Department's effort to keep the American people involved and motivated in the war was by sending lecture groups far and wide. One such group was comprised of former German and Japanese POWs, who were off on a thirty-city tour to tell their tales of Axis abuses. This tour was sponsored by the Red Cross and the US Army Air Forces.

Periodically, the Manpower Priorities Committee would release a list of job openings in essential war industries. There were openings for set-up men, draw press operators, tool grinders, machine operators, foundry laborers, radio engineers, plumbers, carpenters, and dozens of other opportunities. Jobs not listed by the War Manpower Commission included major league baseball players. But the good news was the league decided to go ahead with the 1945 season, although they did consider asking the government for some sort of aid. However, baseball's mandarins did say they would "continue its policy of full co-operation with the country's all-out war effort."[72] No less a figure than FBI director J. Edgar Hoover paid tribute to the importance of baseball, and Washington was ready to hear it. "Baseball has the same right as many other groups to come to Washington and tell its story, and it will find that every official door opens readily to its knock," Hoover said.[73] Still, the navy was unmoved by the personal needs of professional athletes and announced they would guard against any premature discharge from the blue water service.

What was remarkable was how life in America continued unabated but also affected by the war. High school, college, and professional athletes played. People went to work, went to movies, traveled, shopped at clothing and grocery stores, went to church, went to social functions, went to book lectures, played golf, drove cars, traveled on trains and planes as the war raged on. The resiliency of the American people was in some ways astonishing. Politicians and poets and writers and philosophers all noted how remarkably calm Americans were. They believed they were going to win the war, they prayed they would win the war, but they also took the victories and defeats in stride, all of it a testament to the American people.

"US FLAG [FLIES] OVER Manila" trumpeted many newspapers in America the first week of February 1945. According to the Associated Press, "Just 26 days after their initial Luzon invasion, American troops speared to the heart of Manila yesterday, freed thousands of civilian war prisoners, seized the government palace and pressed against little more than sniper fire toward complete control of the Philippine capital. The Stars and Stripes was raised over the palace even though Americans had only captured half the city. Veteran 1st Cavalry Division forces made an encircling drive in darkness to seize the Santo Tomas internment camp from the east. About 3000 civilians, mainly American women and children, have been held at Santo Tomas since May 1, 1942."[74] Many of the civilian prisoners had festering wounds with nothing available to treat them.

Manila was referred to as the "Pearl of the Orient." It had one of the best harbors in all of the Far East. The city was founded in 1571, six years after the Philippines were conquered for Spain. "The Spaniards followed trail-blazing Fernando Magellan, the Portuguese explorer . . . in 1571. It was in Manila Bay that Admiral George Dewey destroyed the Spanish fleet in the Spanish-American War in 1898. The Americans acquired the islands by virtue of the Treaty of Paris which ended the war. Manila underwent extensive modernization under United States rule of the islands. Americans assisted in the modernization of the harbor, effected sanitary improvements, built bridges, boulevards and installed the city's famous open-air electric trolley system."[75] America governed the Philippines benevolently, but plans were going forward for self-rule of the 7,083 islands, as Roosevelt had promised, as soon as the Japanese were defeated. The Japanese had installed a puppet government to administer the control and demise of the islands.

For MacArthur, it was a signal day, fulfilling his famous pledge, "I shall return!" He made the pledge in March 1942 after he arrived in Australia following a hazardous trip in a worn-out PT boat, hundreds of miles from Corregidor to Australia, along with his wife and young son. Now, having returned with a mighty army, navy, and air corps, he didn't pause his efforts. Rather, he issued a bold but also frank statement:

> The fall of Manila was the end of one great phase of the Pacific struggle and set the stage for another. We shall not rest until our enemy is completely overthrown. We do not count anything done as long as anything remains to be done. We are well on the way but Japan itself is our final goal. With Australia saved, the Philippines liberated, and the ultimate redemption of the East Indies and Malaya thereby made a certainty, our motto becomes "On to Tokyo!" We are ready in this veteran and proven command when called upon. May God speed the day![76]

MacArthur's forces also liberated "800 prisoners of war and 550 civilian internees at filthy, torture-chambered Bilibid Penitentiary. Released from the vermin-infested prison by the 37th division Yanks, they made a total of about 5,500 when added to others liberated earlier at Santo Tomas by the 1st Cavalry Division."[77] As the Japanese withdrew from Manila, they put some of the city to the torch. Manila had once been a proud city of people—over six hundred thousand as of 1939—from all walks of life and all places, a mixture of the "Orient and the Occident." When it had been an American city, the city gleamed, the health care and education systems were excellent, the streets wide and clean and businesses thrived, and the Filipinos were reverent. Under the three-year Japanese rule, it had rotted and decayed, becoming a place in which only rats and starvation and brutality thrived. But in one almost destroyed home, American troops were pleased to discover a Filipino guerrilla playing the "Star-Spangled Banner . . . in swing time." It was reported the pianist was "hot on the keys."[78]

Just because MacArthur had retaken the city didn't mean the Japanese gave up without a fight. In addition to setting parts of the city ablaze, there also occurred house-to-house fighting. "The Japanese [had] artillery employed in the area to aid them in their last stand."[79] They also destroyed buildings and installations that might prove useful to the advancing Allies.

Liberated were other American POWs being held on Japanese prison ships, described as a "hell-hole." When tough marines were handed new uniforms to replace the rags they had been wearing, some sobbed. Similarly to the men who had been prisoners in Bataan, they had endured "hunger, sickness and Japanese brutality for three years without a whimper," which was why they wept when they "were handed the uniforms with glittering insignia."[80] Other Japanese tortures and abuses included looting Red Cross packages and stealing watches, jewelry, pictures, anything they could take from the prisoners. One freed prisoner said whatever you heard about the Japanese tortures, it was worse. Another joked the prison campaign should have been called "Dysentery Flats."[81]

IN EUROPE, IT WAS reported on February 5 that the Soviets were thirty-eight miles from Berlin and the Americans were closing in on the bombed-out city from the west. But in China, the recently reinforced Japanese drove thirty-two miles and took a city near China's wolfram mines. The Americans knew the Japanese were not going to give up and

lay down their arms, even after the last several years of reversals in the
Pacific. Even so, just a few days later, the fortunes of the Japanese changed
radically, and now they were losing their grip on the mainland. "Japan's
once powerful position on the mainland [was] deteriorating rapidly,"[82]
while the morale of the Chinese troops was rising.

BABE RUTH CELEBRATED HIS fifty-first birthday. "'I'm just having a little
birthday party tonight,' he wheezed, punctuating the words with hoarse
barks."[83] A war movie about an aircraft carrier, *The Fighting Lady*, starring
Robert Taylor, was popular, as was *This Man's Navy*, starring Wallace
Beery. Errol Flynn was about to make his premiere as a paratrooper in
Operation Burma, which was sure to be a hit. Legislation was introduced
to deport actor Charlie Chaplin as an undesirable. He claimed it was over
his movie *The Great Dictator*, a parody of Hitler, but everybody knew it
was really about his pro-Soviet views and his morals, or lack thereof,
including a taste for underage girls.

Siroil Laboratories was pushing their anti-psoriasis medication
in blunt advertisements: "Often attractive women are unable to wear
'revealing gowns' because such costumes would expose their psoriasis
lesions. If you suffer such dress handicaps—try SIROIL. . . . [It] tends
to remove the crusts and scales of psoriasis. . . . It might mark a new
day for you."[84] Hair tonics for balding men filled the newspapers as they
had for years. Still, men lost their hair. A winter storm was blasting the
Northeast. Buffalo alone got hit with an astonishing ninety-two inches
of the white stuff. Cars were stuck, lines were downed, and the region
was in a deep freeze. In Batavia, New York, men on skis delivered food
to families.

The famed advice columnist, Dorothy Dix, had her hands full with
the problems of women who wrote for frank advice. Take, for example,
this entry: "Dear Dorothy Dix—Before my husband and I were married
I wanted so much to have a husband who would cuff me around a bit
and show me who was really boss. Well, I got my wish. My husband
orders me around as if I were a slave. What can I do to make him change

his attitude towards me? I hate to admit I am a beaten woman." Dix's long, long, long advice began, "You seem to illustrate the truth of the old axiom that a woman never knows what she wants in a man." And, finally, "Still the longer you put off making a strike for freedom, the harder it will be to do it and you had best put on your fighting clothes and go for it."[85]

A harsh report emerged highly critical of the inadequate uniforms and woeful preparation for the European winter by the US Army. It said jackets were ineffective and boots not up to snuff: "It shows, beyond any doubt, that hundreds of thousands of American combat troops fought through the first months of this winter with inadequate clothing, clothing [that was] definitely inferior."[86] Later, the clothing improved dramatically. Another story of another uniform, this one with a funny edge, surfaced. A member of the Royal Air Force thought he'd play a joke when he happened upon a cache of German uniforms. Putting one on, he paraded around London. He asked a bobby (policeman), "Pliss vich las der vay to London?" He was basically unmolested and ignored until two American GIs grabbed him. But instead of turning him in to authorities, the three retired to a local pub.[87]

Finally, the Third Army broke through the Siegfried Line. They'd been on the brink for several days and broke through, but now resistance was "stiffening."[88] General Patton's army had found an effective way of dealing with the many German pillboxes along the line. They would sneak around to the backside and weld the Germans inside. As of late February, his armies had punched through the German line in at least two points. Patton was widely regarded as difficult and hard on his men but also a brilliant leader. His adversary in the Allied ranks, British general Bernard Montgomery, was also regarded as difficult but not nearly the military leader Patton was. Patton's Third Army continued to seize German towns and cities in its drive across the Third Reich. In one report, his army captured forty towns in a matter of only a few days.

The United Service Organizations celebrated its fourth anniversary on February 4 by hosting events in three thousand "clubs and canteens" across America.[89]

AFTER MUCH ANTICIPATION AND ballyhoo, a formal announcement in February said the Big Three were in conference in Yalta and already talking about how to put the brakes on future aggression. The Soviets were advocating the defeat of Hitler first before turning to Japan. A story circulating was that Russia was going to push for several million Germans to be dispatched to Russia to aid in the rebuilding efforts there. As always, the Russians were the doctors of hidden and not so hidden agendas. Just a day later, the Russian Orthodox Church, over Moscow radio, broadcast troubling propaganda, saying the Vatican was trying to keep the Nazis from facing any punishment.[90] Churchill had once proclaimed Russia to be "a riddle, wrapped in a mystery, inside an enigma." But German propagandists warned of "trickery" by the Big Three in this "decisive round of the war." The official Nazi newspaper ran the headline, "New Gigantic Swindle Planned."[91] Rumors also circulated that Goebbels had abandoned Berlin while strict rationing was imposed and orders were sent to defend Berlin. Threats of "victory or Siberia" were made.[92] But it was a bluster. Germany was near ruin.

The Big Three "were planning their final blows and means of controlling the disorganized German homeland once victory is won."[93] But none could predict when the Third Reich would actually fall. The end was in sight and paralysis had gripped the Nazis with "the shortage of oil and trucks and locomotive and rail cars" as a result of the heavy bombing campaign by the British and Americans. Germans, having lost the means to fight, were now losing the will to fight.

At that time, Paris "was in a state of high excitement, all the way from the girl who sells violets near the Madeleine to the top layer of French officialdom. The newspapers were saying that the Russians were rolling down on Berlin in an avalanche. Marshal Zhukov was fifty miles away, he was forty miles away, he was across the Oder!"[94] However, not everything was coming up roses in the City of Lights. A handful of soldiers were killed or blinded when they drank a concoction of wood alcohol and a flavoring element that amounted to bootleg alcohol at Parisian bars.[95] All bars and nightclubs were closed or severely cut back in France, not as a result of the poison alcohol but a lack of coal and electricity. Also, an anti-alcohol campaign, promoted by the government, was initiated. "France, with the exuberance of liberation long past, [appeared] to be heading toward post-war Puritan-like sobriety." The government's plan was to promote the drinking of fruit juices, and also to move toward the "suppression of legalized prostitution."[96] Americans, however, if the newspaper ads were any indication, were in no mood for abstinence. They were drinking Old Overholt rye and Kinsey whiskey and Fleischmann's blended whiskey and PM whiskey and Paul Jones whiskey and Distaff dry gin and Gold Medal dry gin and Kentucky Tavern bonded whiskey and Old Thompson whiskey and Johnnie Walker and Jack Daniels and Landsdowne Reserve and Hunter and Robert Morris; the choices went on and on, a veritable overserving of alcohol.

Along the road to Berlin, Zhukov's men found abandoned German equipment, including tanks, guns, transports, and "thousands of corpses in snow drifts." The Russian army moved on, and many of their tanks featured graffiti: "On to Berlin."[97] All along the way, young girls rushed out to greet the Russians while "political, labor and war prisoners of all nationalities [emerged] from behind barbed-wire fences looking like human shadows."[98]

Some twenty-seven American servicemen were rescued by the Soviets from a labor camp in Poland, but only after these servicemen had intermingled with German refugees and others fleeing from somewhere and going nowhere. Of the refugees, it was reported, "This strange column of frightened, fat German housewives, perspiring male civilians, minor members of the Nazi party, Polish slaves" had crossed paths with "several hundred US officers in uniform."[99] A cross section of humanity.

FDR's 1944 opponent, Governor Tom Dewey of New York, pledged his support for the Yalta Conference, provided the three "be in accordance with American ideals of liberty and justice and be neither concealing nor devious."[100] Stalin, Churchill, and FDR all agreed to quickly occupy Germany should its government and military suddenly collapse. A bigger matter under discussion was how and to what extent Germany should be allowed to rejoin the community of nations. There was a deep concern about the German people's willingness to go along so easily with Hitler's policies of racial purity, racial hatred, and the anti-Semitism that was the glue that held together the Aryan Nation. Outsiders wondered about the psyche of the German people. As millions of Jews, Poles, gypsies, and political dissidents were sent off to the factories for murder, the German people pretended they didn't know. They knew and, with only a very few lonely exceptions, did nothing. The adage that the German people were either at your feet or at your throat had its basis in fact. For thirteen years, they'd been at the feet of Hitler and at the throats of Jews. And just because they were beaten, humiliated, hated, and their country destroyed didn't mean they would stop worshiping at the altar of the former paper hanger and failed watercolorist. The question was not just whether to allow Germany to rejoin the family of nations, but whether any of the family of nations wanted Germany's membership. Plans were going ahead, quickly, for tribunals for the Nazi elite. "The United States has prepared plans to punish German leaders and their henchmen for their crimes against German Jews, regardless of where they were committed."[101] Still, there was opposition from the State Department. "'Legalistically minded' officials in the State Department [contended] that punishment of crimes by Germans against their own nationals was an internal German question that could not be dealt with under international law."[102] Some British agreed with the American bureaucrats.

It was easy to see the first decision made by the conferees was the permanent disarmament of Germany—forever. Also, they decided the new United Nations would meet in San Francisco to organize its charter on April 25. The Big Three agreed to "split Germany into zones of military occupation after the war; France to occupy one zone, the United States, Great Britain, and Russia to each occupy their own German zone." And that a commission would take place in Moscow to determine reparations owed by Germany to the world. Winston Churchill, Joseph Stalin, and Franklin Roosevelt met at the summer palace of Tsar Nicholas II for the Yalta Conference and "reached full accord on a program to crush Germany's armies, to impose a peace tough enough to make Hitler howl, to make a quick start on establishing a world security organization and set up a new government for Poland."[103] The matter of Poland was an important one for Russia. Twice in the twentieth century Germany had invaded Russia by marching through Poland.

All official announcements and communications from the conference were released simultaneously from Washington, London, and Moscow. The Big Three were planning for a springtime of peace for the world but only winter for Hitler and Germany. Editorial comment around much of the world was universally favorable, and even Herbert Hoover, the Republican defeated by FDR in a landslide twelve years earlier, proclaimed the document to his liking.

At maybe the worst possible time, with a war going on and soldiers sacrificing their lives for their countries, the Republican Party held a big, fancy dinner—$4 a plate—and announced it would seek an end to the New Deal. The tone-deaf GOP said the New Deal "was never dead, just playing possum." The Republicans dug themselves a further hole when the principal speaker, Congressman Charlie Halleck of Indiana, said that the party "will not permit this war to be made an excuse for the distorting of the American way of life. It will not tolerate New Deal intentions to make permanent the temporary tyrannies under which we cheerfully suffer because war demands it of us."[104] Since the rise of the New Deal in 1933, the Republican Party had been reduced to a menagerie of nonstarters, naysayers, and wannabes. It was completely incoherent. And, with FDR in Yalta putting the finishing touches on the successful world war America had waged, the contrast could not have been worse for the Republicans.

Despite rumors to the contrary, French general Charles de Gaulle had not been invited to Yalta—and he was furious. "French pride mixed with French disappointment over the failure of the 'Big Three' to invite de

Gaulle to the Yalta sessions."[105] It led de Gaulle to retaliate by rebuffing FDR's subsequent request to meet in Algiers. The French leader objected to this location as it was the site of "French humiliation" prior to its liberation.[106] The fact that Roosevelt sent the invitation to the French general *from* Yalta did nothing to assuage de Gaulle. It was an open secret that Roosevelt could not stand de Gaulle. Same for Churchill, who had little use for the French, as he told the Canadian Parliament back in 1941. While FDR was in Casablanca, de Gaulle had to be prodded and cajoled to leave his gilded cage in London and fly thirteen hundred miles to meet with the president of the United States, who had flown thousands of miles out of his way.

FDR and Churchill also met alone in Alexandria, Egypt, for four hours to discuss Japan. The Soviets did not want to debate the war in the Pacific, of which they had little involvement.

IT HAD BEEN FOUR months since the famed war correspondent Ernie Pyle had filed a column. He'd been on furlough back in America. He was blunt when he finally banged out his column, writing, "In four months of non-production a writer gets out of the habit. He forgets the rhythm of words; falls into the easy habit of not making himself think or feel in self-expression." Pyle was now in the Pacific. "Friends warn me of all kinds of horrible diseases in the Pacific. About dysentery, and malaria, and fungus that gets into your ears and your intestines, and that horrible swelling disease known as elephantiasis. All I can say is, I am God's gift to germs. Those fungi will shout and leap for joy when I show up."[107] Pyle had won the Pulitzer in 1944 for his "you are there" war dispatches. He also had a new bestselling book flying off the shelves, *Brave Men*.

A writer of plays (and other assorted talents), the famed platinum blond sex symbol Mae West was debuting a new one. West was famous for so many quips and one-liners such as "Too much of a good thing is wonderful," and when someone beheld her many diamonds draped around her neck and exclaimed, "My goodness!" West replied, "Goodness had nothing to do with it."

By the second half of the 1930s, West's popularity was affected by her dialogue being severely censored. In December 1937, West appeared in two separate sketches on ventriloquist Edgar Bergen's radio show *The Chase and Sanborn Hour*. She went on the show eager to promote her latest movie, *Every Day's a Holiday*. Appearing as herself, West flirted with Charlie McCarthy, Bergen's dummy, using her usual brand of wit and risqué sexual references. West referred to Charlie as "all wood and a yard long" and commented, "Charles, I remember our last date, and have the splinters to prove it!"[108] She once remarked, "I believe in censorship. I made a fortune out of it."

Her racy play was appropriately titled *Catherine Was Great*, in which she starred with approximately fifty men. (However, legend has it that Catherine the Great numbered her lovers in the hundreds.) Other plays she had written and starred in included *Sex* and *Pleasure Man*, to name a couple. West was such a cultural icon, even navy life preservers were nicknamed "Mae Wests" because of the fulsome chest it created.

Of less distinction was *Cosmopolitan* magazine, full of the tawdry, tasteless, and lacking in humor ads, such as "How many women could have stood the shock that came to Mimi Foster? Newlywed and madly in love, she found that her husband was her mother's former lover . . . revenge!"[109]

OF THE WAR-TORN COUNTRIES left behind in the wake of the Nazi onslaught, there was obviously resentment and tremendous anger. The Germans took what they wanted, looted, maimed, murdered, exterminated, and destroyed the once beautiful and lush landscape of Europe. "This is Europe's outraged sense of justice. And an outraged sense of justice is one of humanity's most dangerous emotions . . . especially so, when millions of people in the depths of want and hunger and suffering share it with a common feeling of smoldering anger and revulsion," one reporter wrote.[110] An old French lady, threadbare, freezing, sitting in Paris with little to do, said bitterly, "Oh, this war—that it may finish quickly. That filthy wretch—that monster of a Hitler—that murderer."

The unidentified madam, disheveled, lamented the loss of so many young French and couldn't understand why Nazi sympathizers still roamed the streets of Paris. "And there's been no purge. There is a man, right in this street. He used to be with the Boches every night. He's still there. Why doesn't somebody get him?" she asked.[111]

The French wheels of justice, in fact, were moving more quickly than in other countries. "There [were] thousands of untouched collaborators still circulating in Paris. Even so, de Gaulle's government has done far more to punish notorious traitors than has yet been done by the government or Allies in any other liberated country. French courts of justice have imposed 350 death sentences and 200 of these found guilty have been executed." Still, "when you consider the great number who helped sell France to the Nazis, the restraint and extreme legality exercised by the de Gaulle government [was] truly remarkable."[112]

The matter of the US government's planned auction of surplus war matériel and how and who to handle the auctions evolved into a full-time scandal. The Senate was facing increasing charges of "witness lied" and "discrepancy" and "stormy." A "barrage of questions" of the witnesses, including civilians and elected officials, now filled stories about the growing imbroglio. The hearing was at times contentious.

FRANK SINATRA'S NUMBER WAS up, and he was about to join the army. He'd lose his $1-million-a-year income, but he seemed eager to get on with it. He'd already had one physical, and a second, then was sent to Governor's Island for "further observation." Old Blue Eyes said, "I want to go into the armed forces and if I don't go in, I don't want to sing. I want combat service. In the Army, I would prefer the tank or anti-tank services. In the Navy, I would like to serve on P-T boats."[113] The navy was planning an expansion of the fleet by an additional twenty-four thousand ships, so Sinatra might get his chance. If these were added, the size of the US Navy would total eighty-five thousand ships of all sizes and varieties, but the vast majority would be landing craft for the Pacific.

The US Navy had come a long way from the meager fleet John

Paul Jones had at his disposal in the Revolutionary War. The navy was also asking for an additional twenty-eight thousand planes to add to the thirty-seven thousand of various sorts all across the world. The navy's ordnance budget for 1944 was $3.3 billion, but it was slated to increase by another $200 million for 1945.[114] The firepower of the navy in World War II was awesome. At the time, they possessed enough armaments to fire "24,000 tons an hour. Thus, in 1500 hours these warships would have a firing rate of 36 million tons, or equal to the estimated total annual steel production capacity of Germany as of the end of 1944."[115]

SHYSTERS AND CON MEN saw the returning vets as easy prey. Get-rich-quick schemes and other grifter designs often left the poor GI with nothing in his pockets except lint. GIs who applied for farm loans were especially susceptible. It was such a problem that government officials contemplated getting involved. Theft of military hats, especially foreign, was sometimes a problem when they were set down in a restaurant or bar or at a reception.

Kellogg's All-Bran cereal came up with a unique way to sell their product. It claimed to "keep proper iron level in blood," and as proof, part of the ad featured Miss Dorothy D. Ficker of Old Greenwich, Connecticut, who had already donated seven pints of blood, apparently due to her heavy regimen of eating Kellogg's All-Bran.[116] Oh yes, it was also good as a laxative, calling it "naturally regulating." Breakfast cereal was an important part of American culture in 1945, and the variety proved it. From Nabisco's Shredded Wheat to Quaker Quick Oats to General Mills' CheeriOats (changed to Cheerios later in 1945), Americans had a wide variety to choose from in the morning.

A terrible winter storm swept across the Northeast. Small towns were isolated, roads were closed everywhere, food shortages resulted, and telephone lines were down. Scores died. Women, assisted by the police, arrived at area hospitals in the nick of time to have babies. In Maryland, three spinster sisters were all found dead; at least one was believed to have frozen to death.

Government officials predicted that meat could virtually disappear for the summer of 1945 for civilians. Under various government agencies, meat was diverted to the military and the lend-lease countries including Great Britain and Russia. Civilians were still being urged to save fats for the war effort. Recycled fats were used for everything, some of which people would find astonishing. According to one ad, "We must save more used fats as long as our fighters need . . . medicines . . . new miraculous ones that are saving lives which would have been lost under World War I conditions. To compound many of them, fats are essential. . . . Synthetic rubber . . . [is used] for self-sealing plane gas tanks, for life rafts and bomber tires. . . . The synthetic rubber on a battle ship uses up to 4½ tons of used fats. . . . Parachutes, paints, soaps, explosives . . . a hundred other necessities on the battlefield. . . . Keep saving until both Germany and Japan are licked."[117]

With the clothing improved, the army was ready for the brutal European winter. Earlier, officials had loaded twelve rail cars full of ordnance and went north to the coldest part of North America to field test the "anti-aircraft directors and artillery, electrical generating units, clocks and watches, batteries, and sighting and optical equipment."[118] Still, the Germans clearly excelled, as their Panzer tanks were far superior to the Americans' Sherman tank. One story said the Sherman was "clearly out matched."[119] But both tanks, it was said, were inferior to the Russian tank, the "Stalin," with giant guns and heavy plating.

Postwar jobs "for negros" was the subject of one Boston symposium. Another was how to keep racism out of dentistry. A controversy was underway on whether to impose racial quotas in local dental schools. There was no controversy about the effectiveness of the "negro divisions" fighting in Italy, though, as the Associated Press reported, "Due South . . . Negro troops repelled several Nazi counterattacks about a mile north of a little stream Flue la Foce."[120]

Not too long after, American charities gathered together six million pounds of clothing and sent them to Italy for distribution to the poor. Nearly half a million Italians benefited.

In Massachusetts, 61 percent of all jobs were in war or war–related industries.[121] The government slapped an embargo in the Northeast on all civilian shipments by railroad for four days to meet the growing coal shortage. Also, a curb was ordered on natural gas in seven states for domestic consumption due to shortages in war industrial plants in the upper Midwest and stretching eastward.

The German plan to open the dams on the Roer River as a means of halting the Allied advance was a washout. "Today the water level was sinking rapidly . . . when it will no longer be a menace," reported the *Boston Daily Globe*.[122] The rivers flooded but just as quickly receded and the advance continued. The Russian army had advanced thirty-seven miles in one day, according to a news report, and had nearly encircled Breslau while also cutting a road that was being used by the Germans to resupply "Silesia in an effort to prevent a Soviet push into Saxony which would have outflanked Berlin."[123]

To celebrate the thirty-fifth anniversary of the founding of the Boy Scouts, young men in uniform attended churches across the nation in droves, many of them receiving awards. The Boston and Maine Railroad ran newspaper ads politely asking smoking patrons to refrain from smoking in nonsmoking cars: "Half the passengers on some trains, they tell us, are apparently well supplied with 'smokes' and seem to delight in igniting them [while looking] at NO SMOKING signs as they puff."[124]

Two German POWs walked off a logging project in Amelia, Virginia, in mid-February, and a manhunt was organized.

The WAVES (Women Accepted for Voluntary Emergency Service) and the WAC (Women's Army Corps) and the WASP (Women Airforce Service Pilots) got all the attention, but there also existed the women marines. It was the second anniversary of the outfit, which boasted 19,000 members. These women in uniform did real work; it was not about public relations. Women died in this war on the factory floor, on ferrying planes, in combat zones. As of 1945, there were approximately 15,000 WAVES and 5,000 women with the Red Cross overseas, not including the WAVES and women marines just deployed to Hawaii.

Women were everywhere in World War II and not as window dressing for young military personnel. They were in the Mediterranean, in the South Pacific, in the Burma-India-China theater, in Europe, of course, but also in Alaska and Africa.

European refugees streamed hither and yon in the freezing cold to escape the starvation and the Nazis and the coming Russian and American invasions, but they were banned from entering the cities of Munich, Nuremberg, and Augsburg. They weren't just a few stragglers. The refugees totaled, by one report, "several millions."[125]

An apocalyptic statement in a Nazi newspaper exclaimed, "The next eight days will show whether a rope or a collar will encircle our necks. Within the next eight days we will know whether our hundreds of thousands who fell in foreign lands and our own cities will have died in vain. . . . The danger is gigantic."[126]

In Porto Alegre, Brazil, a monkey at a local park was named Hitler, but according to locals, the monkey did not like his name and tried to bite some who called him by the hated appellation. In America, another tale was that the German high command would retreat to the mountains—Bavarian or Austrian—and continue the fight there, a harassing action against the Allies. After kicking out the Nazis, the Belgians again ruled their own country.

Two navy fliers were killed off the Massachusetts coast in training accidents. One burned to death upon crashing on Martha's Vineyard; the other plummeted into Narragansett Bay. The son of St. Louis manager Billy Southworth was killed along with four others when the B-29 Major Billy Southworth Jr. was piloting crashed in Flushing Bay in New York. The highly decorated young Southworth had flown the B-17 *Winning Run* in many missions in Europe without getting a scratch. The handsome young man, who was a professional baseball player before enlisting, had a movie contract waiting for him as soon as the war was over. From Baltimore came the unbelievable story of an airman falling 1,300 feet out of a plane into the Pacific—and surviving: "Wallace C. Montague, 20, of Baltimore, veteran of more than 100 air missions, is recuperating in a hospital following a parachute fall of 1,300 feet into the ocean." He was ribbed by his fellow fliers as "miracle man" and "the man who forgot to die." He told the reporters, "I pulled the rip cord, but my chute failed to open. I made a freefall of 1,300 feet, landing feet first in the water . . . went under 30 or 40 feet . . . struggled to the surface and finally reached the top. I . . . inflated my life vest . . . then passed out."[127] He was picked up shortly after hitting the water, was hospitalized, but had only minor injuries.

Many nautical miles away, on Cape Cod, the family of Ambassador Joseph P. Kennedy was mourning the loss of their eldest son, Lieutenant Joseph P. Kennedy Jr., who had been killed flying a dangerous mission in the European theater. On February 16, 1945, he was posthumously awarded the Navy Cross. The navy's highest decoration was awarded personally by President Roosevelt, "for extreme heroism and courage in aerial flight as a pilot of a United States Navy Liberator bomber on August 12, 1944."[128] The irony was too deep: when the elder Kennedy was FDR's ambassador to Great Britain in the late 1930s, some thought he was too sympathetic to the Nazi cause and, eventually, was recalled. Now his son had been killed by those same Nazis.

Lieutenant Kennedy had volunteered to fly a planeload of explosives aimed at a Nazi U–boat pen, then bail out and let the plane fly into the pen, destroying it. But the plane exploded midflight, and Kennedy was killed instantly. Some thought the hypercompetitive Kennedy family was to blame, as Joe Jr. was jealous that his younger brother Jack had won the Navy Cross the year before for heroic actions in the Pacific. When a Japanese destroyer slammed into Jack's PT boat and destroyed it, the younger Kennedy coolly rallied his men and swam several miles through shark-infested waters to a native island. Jack even towed a very injured crewmate by gripping his life preserver strap in his teeth. Joe Sr. had been grooming his young, dashing, and handsome eldest son for politics and the presidency, but now, with Joe Jr. dead, the ambassador transferred his ambitions to the next in line, John F. Kennedy.

Families were mourning the loss of young sons all over America. In

Texas, the Brock family saw their triplet boys become war casualties, all within five days of one another: one dead, one seriously wounded, and one missing in action. In California, twenty-four navy seamen died when their C-47 crashed in San Francisco Bay. The men were heading home on leave. In Washington, the Reverend Albert McCarthy was tasked with the sad duty of adding another Gold Star to the flag at his church. This Gold Star was for his own son, Lieutenant Albert McCarthy, US Navy, who died of injuries sustained in a bombing mission over Italy.[129] The wounded streamed into America. On one train, a young serviceman said jokingly he could not kick the covers off him in his berth, then revealed he had only one leg. He was one of 988 wounded vets from the European war. "Men with splints and crutches, men with eyepatches and casts, men with head bandages and dangling sleeves, men with blank, staring eyes and empty faces," each had a story, dark and awful, on how they got their injuries. Those that could talk, anyway. One told about how his leg had been ripped open and then had to lie quietly as the Germans shelled the battlefield he was on, hoping against hope for a medic. Another, bandaged from his hips down, told how he'd be all right.[130]

Sacrifice and doing without had been a part of the American landscape since December 1941; throw in a decade of the Great Depression, the American people had been told to do without for a long time. So, when the Gallup polling organization asked Americans about their own sacrifices, an astonishing 64 percent said no, the war years had not caused them too much burden. When asked about sacrifice, a waitress in Dayton, Ohio, said, "All my boy friends have gone overseas; so I can't get married."[131]

THE JAPANESE AIR FORCE was down but not out. Not yet anyway. It was announced they'd sunk an 11,000-ton American carrier *Ommaney Bay* in the Philippines; the Grumman Avengers and the Wildcats flew off her decks. Since October 1944, the Japanese had sunk four aircraft carriers and twenty-two other naval vessels from the American fleet. Sadly, one hundred of the five hundred crew of the *Ommaney Bay* were lost.

Each day brought fresh news of Allied successes and Axis defeats. True, the Germans were still fighting, especially on the high seas, and the Japanese weren't about to quit, but the Allies were irrepressible now, an unspent force.

> The Yanks were on the move in all sectors. They cleaned out enemy pockets at Fort Stotsenburg. They punched closer to the summer capital of Baguio in the north. They seized highway junctions near the foothills of the Sierra Madre Range flanking the Luzon plains in the east, thus severing enemy routes of retreat. American bombers pounded the Cavite naval base in Manila Bay.
>
> Daring P-T boats, operating in cooperation with fighters, swept Batangas Bay south of Manila and . . . to the north, destroying 51 coastal craft. Escorted Liberators bombed the important Japanese air base at . . . Formosa, and 20 planes were destroyed. Patrol bombers hit Japanese shipping in the Sakishima Islands to the east, sinking four freighters and setting two others afire. Further mopping up of bloody Leyte Island yielded 758 more Japanese dead.[132]

The Japanese state media reported that they had planned on the fall of Manila all along. It was a city possessing "no strategic value" whatsoever, they goofily claimed.[133] So why did they take it in the first place, and why did they fight so long to hold on to it? As MacArthur's forces were at one gate, the tank commander yelled to the Japanese, "Open the goddamned thing or I'm coming in anyway."[134] Still, stories of Japanese atrocities flourished. One United Press International story described an "inferno of savagery" as thirteen hundred Filipino civilians and Catholic sisters were slaughtered in Manila.[135] One American woman, the wife of a navy officer, said the Japanese had tried to herd two thousand refugees into a building and then set it ablaze with incendiary grenades. Gruesome tales came out about Japanese soldiers constantly raping women who made the mistake of going to the Manila hospital.

"The most powerful battleship and aircraft carrier force afloat poured upwards of 1,200 Hellcats, Helldivers and Avenger aircraft planes today at Tokyo while warships and Army planes shelled and bombed islands to the south. More flattops than America ever before assembled in a single sea operation are sending raiders in continuous waves against Tokyo's airfields and military defenses, tangling in sky battles with the enemy air force," said a report from the US Pacific Fleet headquarters on Guam.[136] The carriers were protected by thousands of guns mounted on thousands of smaller ships. Speculation was that the wholesale assault was a precursor to a land invasion of the main island of Japan. Smoke, soot, and ash filled the skies over Tokyo and for miles around. And it continued. On around February 20, the War Department communiqué announced that over one hundred Superfortresses dropped thousands of tons of bombs on Tokyo. It was a record force, launched from Saipan and Tinian, and "bombed through clouds using precision instruments."[137]

FLYING WAS GOING ON all over the world. Of course, in Europe, the Pacific, and everywhere there was fighting, but also commercially. America had dozens of commercial airlines in 1945: Piedmont, Eastern, Western, Northeastern, Northwestern, United, Braniff, Pacific Western, Republic, PCA, PBA, Pan Am, Royal Dutch Airlines, and more. Travelers were advised to "Be Careful! Never Travel Without American Express Travelers Cheques!"[138] Eastern Air Lines print ads featured a sexy stewardess with the catchphrase "Call me."[139] PCA Air Lines ads gave their phone number, 737-7070, suggesting patrons call "Republic 7070."[140] And aircraft designers were predicting that, within a few years, jet airplanes would achieve speeds of up to fifteen hundred miles per hour.

So much had gone on in such a short moment that there was hardly time to go back and review or consider what actually had happened. But one intrepid columnist, Ralph McGill, went back to Bastogne, scene of the last German offensive of the war, to survey the destruction. And it was breathtaking.

Bastogne was a peaceful farming village with small shops. Now, let us try to describe it. Those who have seen a city where a tornado, or a cyclone, or a hurricane of great force have struck, will have the best picture of it. But it is worse than that. These houses, for the most part, are of stone. They are two and even three feet thick. They gape. Their floors have fallen in, one on the other. They are a wall and a heap of rubble. They are walls with the insides gone, burned in a raging fire. They are broken, shattered, breeched, slashed, blown flat, twisted into grotesque shapes, pierced with great, ragged, obscene gashes.[141]

"MEAT FROM THE SEA!" shouted one newspaper ad. Fancy shrimp was going for 43 cents a pound, while medium smelts cost 13 cents a pound. Ecco foods were also offering "meat by the dozen."[142] In fact, there was little actual meat being offered in the grocery ads. Again, a rumor swept the nation of a resumption of coffee rationing, and consumers responded in a panic, purchasing great quantities, until the government said there was no planned rationing, but that it might happen if the buying frenzy continued. In fact, government officials said that any rationing of goods was related to supplies and not the coming end of the war, specifically called V-E Day by the International News Service.

But rationing of alcohol did go forward in Virginia, and it was radical too. The monthly allotment for whiskey, gin, or brandy was cut to just one quart a week. But buyers of Series A bonds, especially the aptly named Baby Bonds, would have more than enough in their pockets to buy the booze. The Baby Bond, purchased in 1935, was returning about 33 percent interest, spread over ten years, but if the buyer sold them back to the government and bought Series E bonds for another period of ten years, the return was a skyscraping 77 percent![143] As of 1945, the war had cost America $238 billion.

The *Washington Post* ran a cartoon of an Anglo fist punching a deeply caricatured Japanese soldier and appealed for people to buy war bonds: "Every dollar you put into War Bonds hurts the Japs—hurts 'em badly."[144] The *Washington Post* and other major publications routinely used racist (or unsettling) terms to describe blacks and Japanese and sexist language to describe women. When a black person was suspected of a crime, the paper made reference to "negro," but if a white person was suspected of a crime, they were not referred to as "white" or "Anglo."

FOR FOUR YEARS, DETROIT had been discouraged from making any new cars. All were drafted to build tanks, jeeps, troop transports, and other war matériel. Studebaker was manufacturing the "Weasel" for jungle combat, and according to one ad, "In the forbidding tropical undergrowth of the Pacific Islands, Studebaker's amazing new Weasel personnel and cargo carrier is now in action with our armed forces. . . . The Weasel glides forward in mud and swamp as well as on sand and stone."[145] Studebaker was also making engines for the B-17 bomber.

Looking ahead, the government anticipated a huge consumer demand for new cars once the war was over, as many as twelve to fifteen million cars. "About 4,000 cars daily—nearly 1,500,000 annually—[were] leaving the highways due to such factors as scarcity of tires, replacement parts and mechanical deterioration."[146] But the American driver had firm ideas of what they wanted in their new cars, as they told the Society of Automotive Engineers. They did not want gaudy cars with lots of chrome; they wanted four-door sedans, they wanted large windshields, but they didn't think air-conditioning was worth the price. Interestingly, Californians wanted car seats that turned into beds, and all thought that clocks, radios, heaters, and cigarette lighters should be standard equipment.[147]

Kool, Lucky Strike, Old Gold, Chesterfield, Camel, Marlboro, Chelsea, and Rameses were favorite smokes, coffin nails, ciggies, fags, jacks, butts, stokes, bogies, and joes.

The newest *Superman* comic strip, released February 2, featured the Man of Steel torturing a man by letting him fall off a ledge and then catching him because he was a fair-weather suitor of Lois Lane. Henry Wallace, the forlorn former vice president and beleaguered nominee for secretary of commerce, had a new book coming out: *Democracy Reborn*.

Academy Award winner Orson Welles, in a speech to the National Press Club, said "provincialism" was now the enemy of world peace.

Speaking of the beleaguered, Governor Tom Dewey was to make his first public speech since losing to Roosevelt in November 1944 at a Lincoln Day dinner in Washington. Roosevelt had made the last of his "fireside chats" the year before on June 12, 1944. It was always somewhat of a myth that FDR gave hundreds of such talks. In fact, in all the years he was president, he gave only thirty. In the postmortem of the Battle of the Bulge, it was discovered that nearly a million packages and letters intended to reach American soldiers by Christmas 1944 had been captured by the Germans. However, the army was still able to deliver 90 percent of the sixty-two million packages that were originally sent.

PRIVATE DONALD SMITH WAS a man on a mission. He'd been captured by the Germans on D-Day plus nine and was beaten and tortured by the Gestapo, including being whipped with a cat-o'-nine-tails by a sadistic Nazi. Smith escaped, but he vowed to find the man who had whipped him and get his revenge.[148] On February 4, the *Washington Post* ran a story headlined, "White Race Hardest Hit by Killings." It made the case that white Europeans had suffered more losses in the Second World War than all the other races combined.[149]

The American submarine *Growler*, missing for months, was finally reported as lost. She weighed 1,525 tons and had performed admirably until she was lost with all sixty-five hands. She was later found out to be sunk by Japanese ships in the vicinity of the Philippines. "What adventures they shared, what blows they struck at the enemy, what manner of death came to them, are all among the secrets of the sea. Theirs is a service for which only the resolute and brave are chosen, in which heroism is a routine requirement and glory a remote abstraction," eloquently opined one paper.[150] A week later, the Americans more than evened the score when the navy announced that an unidentified sub sank twelve Japanese ships in one outing, possibly a record for one mission. A week later still, several American submarines sank thirty-one enemy ships, a turkey shoot, for a grand total of 1,020 Japanese ships sunk by American submarines in all of World War II.

Again, the headlines were breathtaking: "Allied Guns and Planes Smash 6 Vicious Nazi Counterblows" and "Yanks Slowly Winning Fight in Manila Bay."[151] Plans were already hatched to move many of the heavy bombers to the Pacific once the European war was concluded.

The Seabees continued to get rave reviews for their work and their courage. All across the Pacific, these men landed; dug in; erected airfields, ammunition dumps, hospitals, and barracks; and brought civilization to places where there had been little before. It was "just north of New Guinea, however, that the astounding construction ability of the Navy [was] more apparent. The islands were hardly more than a war-scarred trading area when the Navy—and the Army—arrived."[152] But Manus was rapidly becoming a great naval base. Many of the men may have been too old to fight, but you couldn't tell them that.

The US Navy as a whole was often doing wondrous things. It had built "a floating Naval Base, somewhere in the Pacific. [It] took its own supply base along . . . for the assault on Iwo Jima. . . . The most gigantic logistics problem in naval history—that of supplying provisions, fuel and ammunition for warships in action far from island bases or docking facilities"—had been solved. It included "floating cranes, hotels, repair units, bakeries. Offices, refrigerated warehouses, wells, dry docks and repair shops." The base had twelve thousand workers, and "enough food was loaded . . . to feed Columbus, Ohio, a city of 306,087, for 30 days and enough candy, shaving cream, tooth paste and miscellaneous items to stock fully 6000 drug stores."[153]

THINGS WERE BECOMING HOPEFUL for the American Indian, at least according to the US Indian Commissioner John Collier, who envisioned a bright economic future that included applying new skills learned in the war to peacetime. According to one news report, "A broad program is in the making to put the Indian on his own economic feet. It is the aim of

John Collier . . . to increase returns from agriculture, the raising of stock and native arts, to develop natural resources on Indian lands."[154]

Women, too, were looking to the future, and it did not include the factory floor. According to the National Association of Manufacturers, women, seeing the end of the war, were "drifting away from their present vital jobs in industry in such numbers as to seriously intensify the current manpower crisis."[155] Anna Rosenberg, director of the War Manpower Commission, "attributed much of the drift to the increasing difficulties of housekeeping. The problems of the woman who tries to maintain a home while working in industry has been constantly multiplied by rationing, difficulties in shopping, crowded transportation and the impossibility of getting anyone to help with her home or children." But the problem remained. "We cannot afford to lose these women. We need them and thousands of additional women in industry. The drift cannot continue without serious consequences," she said. The war industry still needed more women, not fewer, but "it [boiled] down pretty much to their basic interest in the home. Yet women in industry have done magnificently. Certainly, they have won equal pay, equal respect and equal gratitude from industry in this war."[156] Indeed, according to the Gallup poll, an estimated four million women planned on quitting their jobs after the war was over. But as a percentage, 61 percent of women surveyed said they planned to continue working after the war.[157] It was estimated that some fifteen million women were working in war-related work. However, in a subsequent Gallup survey, the majority of Americans opposed military training for women.[158]

In World War II, nearly every American served. War was not just confined to the battlefield, but women were excluded from being drafted in the new labor draft bill. Not too curiously, only a few returning veterans opted to go into the job training program the Veterans Administration was offering as a means of reentry into civilian life. But the first veteran to be hired by the War Relocation Authority was Ken Nishimoto, a "Jap-American" according to the *Topaz Times*. Nishimoto was a veteran of the famed Japanese American outfit in Italy where he was wounded, earning the Purple Heart.[159]

IT WAS SOCIAL HYGIENE Day in America, as proudly proclaimed in some newspapers, but they had a particular target in mind. Opined the *Washington Post*,

> So much has been said about the menace of venereal disease in wartime that the public is often inclined to note only the spread of infection among young girls and men in uniform. Today is an occasion to remember that remarkable progress has been made in the fight against syphilis and the conditions under which that scourge ordinarily flourishes. Not many years had passed since the words "syphilis" and "gonorrhea" were unmentionable in polite society. Commercial prostitution flourished in most cities with the protection or tolerance of local authorities. . . . [But] diseased prostitutes are no longer merely quarantined in "red light" districts. It is true, of course, that promiscuity among young girls—amateur pickups and the so-called "Victory Girls" who, soldiers claimed, lost all sense of moral balance in the presence of a uniform—has created a baffling new problem. And that is accentuated in some measure by the fact that easier cures of venereal disease minimizing the restraint which fear of it heretofore engendered among many people lacking in moral discipline.[160]

The US government produced posters of sultry-looking, disproportionately redheaded women in risqué dresses in bars with such double-entendre captions as "Booby Trap" and "She May Be a Bag of Trouble." This may explain why the director of War Mobilization and Reconversion, James F. Byrnes, had already ordered the adoption of a midnight curfew on all bars and drinking establishments. Specifically covered were "all night clubs, sports arenas, theatres, dance halls, roadhouses, saloons, bars and other enterprises whether public or private."[161]

Ostensibly, the order was to save coal. Even if that were true, the order would be difficult if not impossible to enforce. It did not stop the *Washington Post* from endorsing the idea, however, saying that it was "specious" to worry about GI morale for soldiers on leave, but since it affected relatively few, well, c'est la vie, what were their rights anyway?[162] The government debated harsh penalties for establishments not abiding by the law, including withholding the delivery of food and fuel, a ban on hiring, and so on. Those exempted included USO clubs and other "responsible agencies."[163] The War Manpower Commission had three hundred field offices and intended to use every one of them to enforce the law.

Actually, the general public met the new curfew with a collective yawn. A national survey showed that 95 percent were in bed by midnight anyway.[164] But New York City complied with the directive immediately.

Shirley Temple was a featured speaker on giving advice to teenagers. Her advice was mostly confined to telling teens not to eat chocolate, but she also had time to give out her measurements to the interviewer (34–24–33½), explain how to wash your face, and describe good posture for women, including sucking in your stomach. And, oh yes, she told reporters, "Tell them to remember the gluteus maximus, that's to be held in too!"[165] Hollywood as a whole was looking forward to reopening the European market for their movies now that the war was near the end.

A Daughters of the American Revolution chapter was to hear a talk on the wonders of the future of television as well as lectures about George Washington. On a Sunday in February, whites went to black churches and blacks went to white churches to celebrate "Race Relations Sunday." The Federated Council of Churches issued a statement that said, "Negro servicemen who have fought alongside with their white comrades will not accept in peace that which in war they opposed unto death. The war has made clear how false have been many of our racial attitudes upon a hundred battlefields and in a thousand camps the tests of war have shown that there is no basic difference between men."[166]

The matter of the preferential A-rating treatment given to Elliott Roosevelt's dog, Blaze, an English Mastiff, was a persistent matter. A

Senate investigation was launched and fingers were pointed everywhere, including to the assistant chief of staff for priorities and traffic and to a Mrs. John Boettiger, Elliott Roosevelt's sister.[167]

HITLER HAD PROMOTED THE notion of the perfect Aryan—the blond Germanic "superman"—but American surgeons discovered otherwise. In fact, the German troops were "great physical cowards under pain" and "physically weaker than Americans." Also, the doctors were convinced the Germans were more susceptible to infections than were American troops. And "it is definitely true Nazis often break down and cry . . . when they come to operating tents, but our boys almost never do."[168]

The bombing of Japan and Germany continued night and day. The idea was not just to break their military but also their industrial plants and, finally, the will of the people.

The French underground was not the only partisan group fighting the Germans. So, too, were Norwegians; as a group they boarded and seized twelve German boats of all sizes and shapes. But the French were never completely on board with the Allies. Several French divisions fought alongside the Axis powers against the Allies. France was the only Nazi-conquered country in which a fellow Frenchman ruled instead of a German military general. During the Holocaust, when the Nazis ordered the conquered countries to turn over a certain number of Jews each month for the death camps, France was the only occupied country to exceed its quotas.

TWO GERMAN SPIES WERE quickly tried before a military tribunal of seven officers. They were convicted and sentenced to death by hanging. Erich Gimpel was from Germany; the other was an American from Niantic, Connecticut—William Curtis Colepaugh—whom the prosecution called a "double-crossing traitor." It was a unanimous verdict reached in less than three hours.[169] Colepaugh tried to claim he was a patsy of the Germans. The tribunal didn't buy the argument.

Another traitor, a member of the Dutch underground, had actually been a double agent for three years, feeding sensitive intelligence information to the Nazis. He was so devious that he actually shot certain Germans whose identities were surreptitiously given to him by the Gestapo, as they had planned to execute them anyway.[170] He was captured at a drinking party. This double agent was thrown into the Tower of London, where Sir Walter Raleigh had been sentenced and where some of the wives of Henry VIII had unwillingly visited. Allied justice was swift and decisive. The mayor of a small German town, Bardenberg, was sentenced to ten years in prison for "giving false information to Allied officials."[171]

Mrs. Frank Jay Gould put up $100,000 to "keep the Germans from taking her millionaire husband to Germany."[172] It was blackmail, pure and simple. Her husband was the son of railroad industrialist Jay Gould and had inherited $10 million. He had fallen into Nazi hands during the occupation of France. Germany was also blackmailing Argentina by holding seven diplomats hostage. As a result, Argentina froze Nazi assets, and a "state of tension" existed between the two countries.

Reports stated that on February 15, the Allies began bombing Dresden, starting with four thousand tons dropped by the British and American bombers. They also bombed oil refineries. Berlin radio said Dresden had been "rubbleized" by the bombings.

In Williamsburg, Virginia, the editor of the William and Mary college newspaper *The Flat Hat*, Miss Marilyn Kaemmerle, was fired and the paper suspended by the administration, because she wrote that someday "Negroes should attend the college and 'marry among us.'"[173] An editorial in the *Washington Post* on the whole matter said her piece "could be considered a grievous error in judgment." It called her opinion "highly explosive" and impudently warned that her use of the First Amendment was "a freedom permitted very few journalists."[174] Several days later, a Republican member of the Senate, William Langer of North Dakota, introduced a bill that would have cut off all federal funding from any institution of higher learning that engaged in discrimination—"Race, creed or color"—or anyone who expressed their "views on racial matters." A few days later, the *Washington Post*'s editorial pages noted the beginning of "Brotherhood Week," a campaign that promoted tolerances and brotherhood as virtues. But it did not specify if that included all using the First Amendment or just those so anointed by the knights of the keyboard of the newspaper, although it did mention "discrimination among men."[175] Women were not mentioned, obviously second-class citizens in the eyes of the *Washington Post*, but then the editorial had the audacity to quote FDR, when he said, "It is, therefore, a solemn duty . . . to keep our country free of prejudice and bigotry."[176] Except, of course, in the newsroom of the *Washington Post*.

GERMAN PROPAGANDIST JOSEPH GOEBBELS, the de facto head of the defense of Berlin, went on the radio again to broadcast inanities and absurdities. He hinted that Germany had secret and scientific weapons still to be used against the Allies. Further, he said, "It is, of course, a fact that the enemy has a bigger war potential at his disposal, and particularly so at this time, but only from a material and not from a moral point of view." He then turned really irrational, saying, "If we are to believe the enemy announcements, then every German could choose by which procedure he wants to be liquidated or extinguished in his spiritual, moral and physical life—namely, whether he wants to die from hunger, slave labor or pestilence."[177]

News reports said Nazi officials were now deserting Prague, fearful of retaliation by Czech partisans. In another act of desperation, Hitler declared martial law in Germany with orders to "handle ruthlessly" any Reich citizen who did not help in the war or who "damaged the Reich" by spreading anti-Nazi rumors. It included imposing the death penalty for anyone, "especially through cowardice or of selfishness," who did not assist the Nazis, including offering a shelter for anyone engaged in fighting the Allies.[178] Even as Hitler was committing his country to a suicide pact, rumors surfaced again of backroom peace feelers from the Germans to the Allies. But even if taken seriously, the Allies would have slapped them down. They were committed—all—to unconditional surrender. No exceptions. So were the American people. According to Gallup, 75 percent supported unconditional surrender over a negotiated peace.[179] Germany was to be crushed into nothingness.

The American army arrested 62 more officers and enlisted men embroiled in a black-market scandal in Paris involving stolen supplies for the soldiers fighting. Already, another 157 had been tried and found guilty, with most dishonorably discharged and some sentenced to hard labor, up to fifty years. A similar problem existed in China, where $50,000 worth of equipment, including jeeps and siphoned gasoline, disappeared. There was an enormous black market operating in China.

It came to light that an American sub sank a Japanese prison ship the previous fall and out of eighteen hundred lives, only five American soldiers survived.[180]

A soldier, Earl J. McFarland, a US Marine hero of the South Pacific, was sentenced to die in the electric chair for the brutal rape and murder of an eighteen-year-old girl after his service. In other news, the youngest hero of World War I died at the tender age of forty. Francis Prarie from Mattydale, near Syracuse, New York, enlisted when he was only twelve, after convincing the recruiter he was eighteen. He was a runner of important war messages, was gassed, lost a foot, and along the way, saved the life of Father Francis Kelly, the "fighting chaplain of the Seventy-seventh Division." Prarie was awarded the Medal of Freedom, the Silver Star, and the Distinguished Service Medal.[181] Vilma Suberly was jailed in Portland, Oregon, for marrying "five sailors, one soldier and two civilians."[182]

In Baltimore, city fathers worried about the "wolf girls" preying on defenseless GIs. Young girls, often in their early teens—essentially prostitutes—were roaming the streets, stalking young servicemen with money in their pockets. The headline in the *Washington Post* read "Blow at Street Pickups; Teen-Age 'Wolf' Patrol Girls to Face Arrest in Baltimore."[183]

A more deadly girl in Germany was saved during the daytime by a US military policeman who stopped her from stepping into a minefield.

By the evening, she was writing letters to her "SS sweetheart" that said, "The American is altogether a comical figure. He stands guard with an umbrella. One thing they will never take away from us—we will start our new life under the principles we have been taught. To live means to fight. Wait and see who laughs last." Then into her room walked an American officer and the same MP who'd saved her life and whom she was now mocking. She tried to hide her letters but for naught. She was promptly placed under arrest—"You've been linked with a German agent caught sabotaging"—and subsequently remanded to the military police.[184]

ELEANOR ROOSEVELT WAS BUSIER than ever with her war work, her work on bond drives, her work on American morale, and her duties as First Lady and as Roosevelt's wife. But this did not stop her from helping to raise money for the National Symphony, saying, "Washington has become in truth the center of the United States with people coming from all parts of our country to help in the war effort."[185]

General William "Wild Bill" Donovan, head of the very effective Office of Strategic Services, was now advocating the creation of a permanent "central intelligence service" for the purposes of protecting American interests in a postwar world. In modern warfare, the gathering of political and military intelligence was everything.

The peninsula of Bataan was finally retaken by General MacArthur's forces in only a little over two weeks, using army paratroopers, navy guns, and the infantry. Later, MacArthur visited the hovels and falling down shacks that housed so many Allied POWs who were ultimately killed. He hailed the battle of Corregidor as a decisive fight, one that would delay the Japanese long enough for the Allies to mount a counteroffensive from Australia.

Shortly thereafter, the Americans took the island of Corregidor, first coming in by parachute. Despite all of MacArthur's successes in the last three plus years, it had still not been determined whether he would be given the overall command for the invasion of Japan. The fight for

Corregidor was tough, often hand-to-hand combat, often in the tunnels that honeycombed the island. Many Americans died before the Japanese were cleaned out and the island retaken.

As the Russian invasion moved ahead, giant underground arsenals were discovered, loaded with bombs, land mines, shell casings, and the like. They were built "upon the blood and bones of hundreds of thousands of slaves." After landing at a nearby airfield, one soldier said, "we were conducted to a tunnel entrance camouflaged with artificial trees to a sign posted, 'death to him who enters without a pass.' The slaves were given a number burned upon their breasts. The weak and the sick were killed. The stronger were sent to build other underground arsenals."[186]

The projection of the late winter of 1945 was that there would be little if any cutback in military spending after V-E Day. As he so often did, columnist Drew Pearson had the inside dope. "It has all been kept hush-hush, but top Army officials have made a vitally important decision on war production after Germany's defeat. Original war production schedules called for a 40 percent cutback after Germany caves in, permitting a vast reconversion program and the early production of automobiles, refrigerators, radios and other civilian goods." The decision instead was to keep war production at "full tilt" and to "crate, sort, repair and reship heavy equipment from the Atlantic to the Pacific." Also, "a pile of telegrams 2 feet high cancelling war contracts to be sent out the day Germany is licked has not been culled and . . . may only cancel a few dozen."[187]

A new Gallup survey found it hard for Americans to cut down on meat, sugar, and butter. American GIs fortunately did not have to worry about their diet. Whatever that ate, they immediately worked it off. Up to mid-December 1944, the Army Transportation Corps had sent 485 million hotdogs, 467,000 turkeys, 2.5 million chickens, and 4,906 tons of butter to servicemen in Europe.

Elliot Gurnee, a navy seaman and son of Maryland, came home to tell the astonishing story of his survival at sea. He'd been a boatswain mate aboard the SS *West Lashaway* when it was torpedoed and sunk in five minutes out of West Africa on the way to the Barbados Islands. In the water with other seamen, the U-boat surfaced and machine-gunned many survivors, but Elliot survived in a life raft for twenty-three days. He saw fellow seamen drink seawater and die, another go mad, and their rations destroyed by the salty water. Finally, the current drift took them close to shore and, two miles out, he got into the water and swam for the coast to tell his tale.[188]

In the four years since Pearl Harbor, tales of the brutality of the Japanese at Bataan and a hundred other examples left American nerves rubbed raw. In California, the home of a Japanese American, Bob Morishige, was set to the torch. Another home of a Japanese American was fired at six times; fortunately, no one was injured. Such stories of harassment of Japanese Americans during World War II were, in fact, relatively rare, and while Americans could not walk the streets of Tokyo, Japanese Americans walked the streets of America relatively unmolested.

A mother in Pennsylvania, Mrs. Russell McFarland, already had eight sons on active duty, scattered around the world. She had a ninth son yet to go into action, but if her doctor said her health was in danger as a result, the state draft board could stop him from going. While GIs and women and medical staff of the military were all working overtime, the white-collar bureaucrats in Washington were doing anything but, at least according to Representative Earl Wilson, a Republican from Indiana. He estimated that 40 percent of the average workday was taken up with coffee breaks, long lunches, Coca-Cola breaks, going to work late, coming in drunk, leaving early, and on and on. He called it "deplorable." He'd once proposed a 10:00 p.m. curfew for government employees, including women, so they could "get to work on time and with their makeup." Wilson acknowledged that, as a member of the minority, there was little he could do, but he intended "to make a speech soon."[189]

Secretary of State Edward Stettinius made a speech warning the West that while the forces of Nazism and fascism were being exterminated in Europe, it was possible a new outcropping of the dark ideology could erupt in the Western Hemisphere. "We still face the danger of secret Nazi–Fascist infiltration into the political and economic life of this hemisphere," he said.[190] He made the important policy speech at the Inter-American Conference in Mexico City. As it was, essentially, a restating of the Monroe Doctrine, the representatives there discussed some sort of "blockade" against Nazism and fascism. Curiously, Argentina was suspect, even in the face of its rocky relations with Germany. Unlike other Latin American countries, they had never declared war on Japan.

Absenteeism in the workforce, especially war industries, was up 70 percent among men since 1938. A number of reasons were given, including a lengthened work week, overcrowding, emotional strains, "mental conflicts," and hiring inexperienced workers or "workers excluded from the armed forces."[191] One reason not given was that after the American psyche had been battered for years from the Great Depression and the greater war, maybe Americans were downright tired of the strains of each and just needed a long and relaxing rest from it all.

In an attempt to increase the nation's meat supply, the government increased regulation and subsidies. "The War Food Administration . . . put additional limitations on the amount of non-federally inspected meat eligible for subsidy payments."[192] Meanwhile, the head of the Federal Reserve System was recommending an "excess profits tax" on stocks and real estate speculation.

A young man returned from the dead after three years of working undercover on Luzon, operating a secret radio transmitter and sending vital information to MacArthur. Captain Robert V. Ball emerged, looking for his fiancée. The navy sent word to her to meet him in San Francisco, but she replied she had no earthly idea about the betrothal. She'd already gotten married and wished Ball well. It was but one of many "Dear John" letters sent in this war.

Lend-lease was extended to Belgium, which was now running a deficit of over $35 billion. David Lloyd George, Britain's legendary prime minister during World War I, was reportedly in poor health. He was referred to as the "father of Parliament." Coincidentally, he had both a son and a daughter in that august body.

Strange things sometimes happen in wartime. Two B-24 pilots, flying across the Himalayas from China, swore they saw a mountain in Tibet higher than Mount Everest. No report of seeing Shangri-La, though. Wrigley's chewing gum took out large ads in newspapers announcing it was no longer making Doublemint, Spearmint, or Juicy Fruit gums as they had used up their allotment of ingredients for 1945. But they said they would offer a "plain but honest Wartime chewing gum to help take care of both military and civilians needs" under a different brand name.[193] In mid-February, reports revealed that six executives of the Ringling Brothers and Barnum & Bailey Circus were given extensive prison sentences after 168 patrons had perished in a terrible fire in Hartford, Connecticut, in 1944. In Rochester, New York, "most of the department stores . . . were out of women's panties."[194] Apparently, the War Production Board left women's "unmentionables" off a list of vital, low-cost items, such as diapers and men's underwear. So women flocked to stores to snap them up before the oversight was corrected.

THE FIGHT FOR LUZON had taken about six weeks and cost approximately 92,000 Japanese soldiers, but "only" 12,929 Allies, mostly Americans.[195] Surveying the remains of the decimation left by the Japanese, MacArthur could only shake his head and mutter, "savage barbarism . . . seldom displayed in a more repulsive form."[196]

And the fight for Iwo Jima had just begun.

Already, photographs of American landing craft heading for the shores of Iwo Jima were seen in newspapers. The island, just over eight square miles, was only 750 miles away from Japan, a stone's throw in the vast Pacific. An invading armada of eight hundred ships was heading for the tiny speck of land—modern battleships "as well as resurrected survivors of the sneak attack at Pearl Harbor."[197]

Before the landing craft arrived in force, navy planes, complete with rockets, strafed the beaches and the low foothills on the island. Then other planes, including Avengers, dropped bombs. Then, "a terrific fight was underway as the Japanese recovered from their initial shock. Nippon fire intensified as the marines moved inland. When the more rugged volcanic country back from the beaches was reached, the Leathernecks used flame-throwers to burn out pillboxes."[198] ("Leatherneck" was a nickname for a US marine.)

The marines were firmly established on the island, but it was clear a good number would be killed or wounded before Iwo Jima was taken. "The Japanese fought back with fanatical fury from strong inland positions. They used artillery, mortar, machine gun and rifle fire in their efforts to hold back the determined leathernecks."[199] After six days, there was no end in sight, and marine casualties were heavy. Iwo Jima was described as "eight square miles of unadulterated hell."[200] Fighting was factually going on all over the tiny island. As of February 21, already 3,650 of the 40,000 marines on the island lay dead or wounded. No real gains had yet been made by the Americans, and in fact, Japanese resistance had increased. Suribachi, the summit, was well out of reach.

"On the south, flamethrowers and tanks are being used against well entrenched enemy troops on the Mount Suribachi area," said Fleet Admiral Chester W. Nimitz in a report on February 22. "A counter-attack launched by the enemy east of Mt. Suribachi shortly after noon was thrown back. Numerous land mines have been encountered in this vicinity. Four of our tanks were knocked out of action." Nimitz made no attempt to downplay the losses, saying, "On Mt. Suribachi, an extinct volcano already isolated on the island's southern tip, the Devil-dogs wormed their way 100 yards up perilous slopes. The mountain is 546 feet high. Its rugged slopes and caves contain heavy guns that dominate the battlefield."[201] The next day, Japanese planes made some successful hits on American warships engaged in the battle, but the ships continued pounding the tiny island. The island was so small that it was difficult to maneuver equipment, and the landing beaches were strewn with hardware such as amphibious tractors.

Gains were coming, but it was costly. The Americans were fighting not only the Japanese but also the elements—a rainstorm and the deep volcanic ash beaches. The Americans were now, in late February, driving for the Japanese airfield on Iwo Jima, but it would be a fight to the bitter end. The Americans and the Japanese hated each other. On Saipan, a second lieutenant was wounded in the shoulder by shrapnel, yet he and a friend made their way to a Japanese "nest and wiped out every man there—12 in all."[202] Americans soldiers had to fight the interlocking pillboxes and caves of the Japanese on Iwo Jima. In one outing, American submarines sank twenty-three Japanese ships, including one aircraft carrier. It was a turkey shoot.

Meanwhile, in Europe, just when one thought they'd seen a massive Allied air assault, nine thousand planes with thousands of tons of bombs were launched against Germany's railway system and one hundred communications hubs. It was claimed to be the greatest synchronized air attack in history (in a short time), and something like one hundred tons of explosives fell every minute. The Allies launched bombers from the north and from the south and, for good measure, the Russians sent two thousand planes from the east. Berlin radio went off the air after warning listeners to take cover.

In Berlin, women were now enlisted to build barricades in the streets as a means of slowing the coming Allied forces. "A spirit of innate fatalism" pervaded the city. Electricity was turned off throughout the beleaguered metropolis for hours each day. Women in pearls and fur coats were passing bricks alongside plainly dressed women.

TWO OF THE GREATEST wits of twentieth-century England, Winston Churchill and Lady Nancy Astor, Viscountess Astor, crossed swords over, of all things, whether alcohol should be allowed in England on V-E Day. Astor was controversial in the extreme, suspected of being anti-Semitic and pro-Nazi. American born, she was also an outspoken member of Parliament, to the chagrin of its more stuffy members. Churchill, known to like a drink (any hour of the day or evening), naturally favored letting the booze flow freely. But Lady Astor opposed, arguing for a day of prayer and abstinence. They didn't like each other. It is reported that Lady Astor once said to Churchill, "If you were my husband, I'd poison your tea," to which Churchill responded, "Madam, if you were my wife, I'd drink it."[203]

Events were no better in Washington. "Representative William J. Gallagher, the 69-year-old Minneapolis retired street sweeper who gave up a city pension to come to Congress . . . set House Republicans and Democrats at each other's throats by simply advising them to try to get together."[204]

Meanwhile, the future was looking more and more dicey for Adolf Hitler. For the first time in the war, his palatial and private mountain retreat in Bavaria, Berchtesgaden, was bombed by Allied planes. "Thunderbolts from Italy pumped rockets into Berchtesgaden," and no shots were fired from the town at the attacking planes. "The raid on Hitler's private stronghold yesterday was followed up today with an extensive bombing of the Vienna rail yards which were reported handling a great volume of military traffic destined for the Eastern Front," said reports.[205]

Another assassination plot against the Führer was discovered. This time the Gestapo intercepted a letter between German military officers, who communicated cryptically that "important events were about to occur which might bring an end to the war." The letter was written by Colonel von Kolman, who under questioning "was reported to have revealed existence of a secret organization among German army officers to assassinate Hitler and Heinrich Himmler." At least two dozen German officers were arrested, including Field Marshal Baron Alexander von Falkenhausen and General von Kluge.[206]

It was speculated that four of the principal thugs of Nazi Germany—Hitler, Himmler, Goering, and von Ribbentrop—had hideaway weekend and summer homes on the German-Austrian border, draped with SS guards, and could theoretically hold out there for months. All the properties had been "confiscated" in the worst sense of German law, especially von Ribbentrop's. He was a particularly odious bootlicker who stole his house from Jews in Austria. It was just a few miles outside of Salzburg, which was known for its beautiful music as opposed to the ugly din of

Nazism. Salzburg also had an extensive cave network where someone could disappear for a long time. The location of the retreats for these "four horsemen of the apocalypse" could explain why the Germans continued their fruitless Italian campaign "so bitterly instead of withdrawing behind the Brenner Pass and releasing their troops for the Russian and the British-American invasions."[207] Still, the Germans hung on in Italy, even as the 10th Mountain Division took several key peaks. "The presence of this division on the Italian Front was disclosed officially for the first time, trained in America's Rocky Mountains, its soldiers scaled some of Mount Belvedere's perpendicular surfaces with ropes, seizing a German stronghold. . . . They captured" many villages that were "all over 3,000 feet high."[208] Just a few months earlier, Second Lieutenant Robert J. Dole, a member of the 10th Mountain Division, was savagely cut down by Nazi machine-gun fire while trying to save the life of another soldier. He survived, but the recovery was long and dangerous, and his body was horribly scarred.

THE CHICAGO MOTOR CLUB reported that some twenty-three million drivers planned extensive driving vacations after the war. "Bedeviled by gas and tire rationing and wheezing cars," cooped-up motorists wanted to hit the open road again. Esso gasoline made appeals to drivers to use their product to preserve their old cars, saying, "It may seem hard to realize that the last new cars were built over 3 years ago . . . the average car in use today is over 7 years old!"[209]

Plastic contact lenses were just coming into vogue. Speaking of eyesight, the Americans were fiddling around with a photographic bomb, something that exploded so brightly it blinded the enemy.

The beautiful but very erratic Tallulah Bankhead was touring the nation in her new play, *Foolish Notion*, to rave reviews. She was especially popular in Washington, where her father, William Bankhead, had once been Speaker of the House. Miss Bankhead was a partier's partier and a star of screen and stage. She had a devastating wit, a sexy voice, and a photographic memory. She smoked five to six packs of cigarettes a day. When in Washington, she was known for turning cartwheels at high-society parties without wearing panties. Bankhead once said she was as pure as the driven slush. She drank, she took cocaine, she slept with everybody, male and female. Bankhead was an early member of the famous Algonquin Hotel crowd, matching wits and stomach lining with the best of them. She once remarked that cocaine wasn't habit forming: "I've been taking it for years." And she quipped that "the only two real geniuses were William Shakespeare and Willie Mays . . . but you have to put Shakespeare first." The *Washington Post* described her as a "minx."[210]

THE WALLED CITY OF Manila had fallen to the Americans, but the Philippines had yet to be completely liberated. Fortunately, the Congress wisely passed a series of extensive free-trade agreements for the Philippines and millions for the rebuilding of the infrastructure of the crucial and friendly island, even before the war was over. Before the war, around 70 percent of the island's exports of pearls, coconut oil, sugar, tobacco, rice, and other products went straight to America. American Girl Scouts contributed by collecting used cotton clothes for desperate Filipinos.

American armies crossed the Roer River in force, still heading steadily for Berlin. More towns were overrun. Along a front stretching from north of Belgium to Luxembourg down to western France, a giant line of invasion—Canadians, British, and Americans—were rolling over the Third Reich. "They crossed by small assault boats, bridges and amphibious jeeps and tanks at 3:30 a.m. after one of the greatest barrages ever seen on the Western Front was unleashed by big guns crowded in as close together as 1000 to the mile, with one small area hit by 17,000 shells in 20 minutes."[211] On the other side of the offensive, the Russians killed or captured forty-eight thousand Germans.

In the fall of 1944, General Dwight D. Eisenhower had predicted that the German army would be defeated somewhere between the Siegfried Line and the Rhine. Each day, from Normandy and beyond, Ike was looking to be the perfect supreme commander for the Allies, at this moment, at this time. In public, he appeared down to earth, even folksy and friendly with his wide smile and backslapping behavior. In private, he swore like a longshoreman and smoked like a chimney and had an explosive temper. But he was right about the war. American troops were grinning, marching over "the German swastika black helmets . . . in the fields and along the roadsides."[212] The Germans, it was said, were "bewildered."[213]

On February 25, Americans awoke to see splayed across their front pages the heroic, iconic, gallant, brave, valiant photo of Old Glory being raised by the US Marines atop Mount Suribachi on February 23.

"From the summit of Suribachi, which dominates the tiny volcanic island [Iwo Jima], the American flag waved defiantly amid the clouds of battle smoke. It was planted there Friday by a Marine unit of 14 men led by Lieut. Harold G. Schrier of Richmond, Mo."[214] That Sunday morning, dirty and disheveled soldiers emerged from foxholes to find Protestant and Catholic leaders crawling to them to minister to their spiritual needs. One toughened marine said of the battle, "Guadalcanal doesn't even count, compared to this."[215]

Mount Suribachi may have been taken, but the Battle of Iwo Jima had only just begun.

CHAPTER 3

MARCH 1945

"Thousands of Americans Surge Across Rhine,
Smash Toward Berlin from Firm Bridgehead"
ATLANTA CONSTITUTION

"Last Stand in East Ordered by Hitler"
NEW YORK TIMES

"U.S. Must Learn to View World Problems
Realistically"
STAR TRIBUNE

Comic books and the comic pages were an important and vital part of American culture and society in 1945. Millions of children daily read everything from *Superman* to the new *Captain America* to *Batman* to *Mickey Mouse*. But so did their parents and so did GIs. And it did not end there. Many of the popular radio shows at the time were based on those comics, and children listened to and were thrilled by the exploits of *Little Orphan Annie* and *The Shadow*. The exploits of Annie and Captain America seemed even more relevant as they found themselves fighting the

Nazis and Nazi spies. *The Human Torch*, *Flash Gordon*, *The Phantom*, and *Sub-Mariner* thrilled young boys with their strange and heroic exploits. Comics were funny and comics were serious, like *Classics Illustrated*, which condensed fiction like *Adventures of Tom Sawyer* and *Adventures of Huckleberry Finn* and other American classics. The *Classics Illustrated* comics always featured great art, but then again, most all the monthly comic books, the weekly Sunday funnies, and the daily comic strips were also well drawn.

Mayor Fiorello La Guardia used to read, over the radio, the comics to the kids of New York City. In the strip *Smilin' Jack*, a plane that looked suspiciously like a B-29, whose development had been top secret, was depicted in the first panel. Political cartoons were also important. So much so that newspapers like the *Evening Star* and the *Pittsburgh Post-Gazette* featured them each day on the front pages. Comics also became the basis for the movies and serials during the Saturday matinees, like *Sheena, Queen of the Jungle*, *Superman*, *Batman*, *The Green Hornet*, and many others. They were low budget and often campy, but kids and parents alike enjoyed them. The *Blondie* movies were especially a big hit, starring Arthur Lake and Penny Singleton.

The comics and often the heroic exploits of their characters fired the imagination. The good guys always won, and right always triumphed in the end. The comics were also a metaphor for the events of 1945. The Americans, the British, the Australians, the Canadians, the Russians, the Filipinos, the French, and other Allies were the good guys. The Axis, Hitler, Tojo, Mussolini, Rumania, and others fighting against the Allies were the bad guys. The Second World War was referred to as "The Good War," and while no war is good, a war to save humanity from fascism, national socialism, genocide, and racism was at the very least necessary—and necessary for humanity to win. The Allies were not perfect, but the Axis was the perfection of evil. There was simply nothing redeeming about the Axis except their destruction.

And Dr. Seuss went to war.

From January 1941 to January 1943, the thriving author and

cartoonist, Theodor Seuss Geisel, set aside his children's books and published more than four hundred cartoons in *PM*, a progressive daily in New York City. The cartoons were clever, well made, and utterly merciless. America Firsters, the Empire of Japan, and even the injustices of Jim Crow were all regular subjects of ridicule. Horrific caricatures of the Germans, Japanese, and other races were ubiquitous in his drawings. He joined the war effort as a captain in the US Army, heading up the Animation Department in the First Motion Picture Unit of the United States Army Air Forces. Now he was making propaganda films for GIs, several under the direction of the legendary Frank Capra.[1]

Even though radio stations had been prohibited from using the war to promote the news, the war, popular culture, and advertising mixed easily, such as "And here's the war news, brought to you by Campbell's Soup." Pepsodent tooth powder with "Irium," Listerine Toothpaste, and Parker Pens all advertised their products with a war theme. Parker's featured a young couple embracing, with the man in uniform saying, "Your letters brought me home safe!"[2]

On March 2, upon returning from the Big Three meeting in Yalta, Roosevelt held a press conference in the White House, which was attended by over two hundred reporters. He rubber-stamped a plan by Stalin to take ten million Germans back to the Soviet Union, as essentially slave labor, to help rebuild Russia after all the damage caused by the Nazis in their invasion several years earlier. Stalin wanted the Germans to work for ten years. FDR indicated his approval of the German-conscription-as-slave-labor program, answered questions about war reparations, and speculated on whether America would one day have another treaty with Germany. He then got more serious and said he could not predict the future, so he was content on just winning the war. As far as using Germans as slave labor, the American people had no qualms about it. A full 74 percent, in a new Gallup survey, favored hauling two to three million of the so-called Master Race to answer to their Soviet masters.[3] For Stalin, "only the goal mattered. He was never tormented by conscience or grief."[4]

Two hundred B-29s hit Tokyo for the eleventh time. Just one week before, another two hundred B-29s firebombed the city governing the Land of the Rising Sun, setting over 240 blocks ablaze. No Japanese fighter planes went to meet the B-29s, and they demolished with impunity.

Half a world away, on March 3, British Mosquito bombers pounded Berlin for the twelfth night in a row. That afternoon, American bombers did likewise. "More than 2,000 American bombers and fighters kept the war's most sustained aerial offensive going full blast through its 19th day. The [American] Eighth dispatched 1,100 Flying Fortresses and Liberators."[5]

A sole American P-51 pilot, Roscoe Allen, a lieutenant in the air force, was flying alone over Germany when he spotted fifteen German planes on patrol. He dove on them and single-handedly downed five and may have shot down two more, but he couldn't be sure as the fight was so furious and fast. Another one hundred German planes had been shot down over the cities of Cologne and Dresden. Out over the Pacific was the plane carrying General Millard F. Harmon, who was in charge of all Pacific army air operations. His flight from the Marshall Islands toward Hawaii, filled with top army brass, soared over calm seas with decent weather, but it never reached its destination and was nowhere to be found.

The war still had months to go, but even so, many were already discussing the peacetime applications and future of aviation, including jet engines, rocket flight, radar, and robot application to flight. Some far-fetched talk said jets would soon be in use over Japan.

The shipping routes around the Philippines had been generally cleared. Japanese troops were thought to be scattered and in small numbers around the islands but not enough to mount a serious challenge to the American forces. The same applied to much of the North Atlantic, as the once large German navy ruled the waves no longer. All that remained were roughly three hundred new, faster Nazi U-boats, by estimates, and they were focused in Norwegian waters.

Henry Wallace was finally confirmed as secretary of commerce, despite opposition from Southern Democrats and Republicans. Some saw his new role as a springboard to the Democratic presidential nomination in 1948, when many expected FDR to finally step aside.

The strongman head of the United Mine Workers, John L. Lewis, who had been the author of many strikes and threatened strikes over the years, even though some vague language had been passed back in 1941 prohibiting strikes during the war, was making trouble again in mid-March when he demanded 10 cents of every ton of coal mined as tribute to the mine workers union.[6] Lewis was no fan of Roosevelt, having broken with him in the 1940 election when he supported Wendell Willkie instead. His threats of strikes had prompted FDR to temporarily seize coal mines in 1943. This time Lewis faced a new problem. A bill proposed by Congress would automatically induct any miner who joined a strike into the armed forces. Miners, like other essential workers, were automatically granted a draft deferment. This bill "would go a step further by requiring deferred miners to remain on the job under penalty of loss of deferment status."[7] Thankfully, the bill failed to advance.

THE HEADLINE IN THE *Atlanta Constitution* on March 4 was chilling and infuriating: "Japs Burn Helpless Americans." At the Puerto Princess prison camp, Palawan Island, the Japanese corralled 150 American POWs into a series of underground shelters, "threw gasoline on the helpless Americans, ignited it and machine-gunned or bayonetted any who tried to flee." But apparently several Americans escaped to tell the tale to General Douglas MacArthur's forces, who later reported, "human bones and bits of charred clothing were found in one of the air raid shelters near the barracks . . . testimony of the wholesale slaughter."[8]

According to one of the survivors, "The Japs got word that there was a big convoy at sea. They thought the convoy, which was going to Mindoro Island, was headed their way and became crazy with fear. . . . They herded us into . . . underground shelters. . . . They threw gasoline in . . . and ignited it."[9] Miraculously, three American POWs escaped and all three told the exact same story of the gasoline, the burning alive, and the shooting of the helpless American servicemen.

Three American nurses who had been captives on Luzon for three years—Frances Nash, Mildred Jannette, and Mildred Dalton—finally arrived back at home in Georgia with gruesome tales to tell about the Japanese treatment of civilians: "three years of terror and torture." A typical American, Dalton said upon her arrival, "I feel I am getting too much credit for what I have done. All over the world it is the duty of nurses to serve the sick and wounded. That is all I have done."[10]

Two soldiers who'd been captive for four years in Japanese prison camps in the Philippines finally returned to the Atlanta area. While reporters and people were beginning to learn of the carnage of the Japanese toward American servicemen, these two men were reluctant to talk about their war experiences. It was a harbinger of things to come.

The long-debated bill to draft nurses into the military in response to FDR's request for twenty thousand new nurses for the war effort finally passed the House, and with ease, too, 347 to 42. A woman had to be wed before March 15, 1945, to avoid the draft. There had been the worry of "marriage epidemic," but this provision seemed to solve it. Also exempt were women with dependent children.

Others not worried about credit but well deserved it were the people of the Philippines, especially the guerrillas who had fought in the sweat-soaked jungles and fetid swamps since early 1944. They lived on little and fought with less, but they successfully harassed and harried the Japanese army occupying their homeland. Of the Japanese soldiers, one Filipino guerrilla said, "They have no honor or mercy. They torture the helpless for no reason. Their word is meaningless. They are the most treacherous and most cruel and most insecure people I have ever seen. I did not know there were such people in the world."[11]

Fifty-six days after assaulting the beaches of the main island, MacArthur had been sending daily reports, mostly glowing, about the American offensive. In that month and a half, his forces had killed, wounded, or captured around 262,000 men. A few still remained on the islands, but they were scattered, starving, and demoralized as their supply lines had been cut, a MacArthur specialty. His communiqué said, "The equivalent of six divisions with supporting elements have been destroyed, together with the main supply depots, holding great quantities of ordnance, munitions, trucks, food, clothing and miscellaneous items."[12]

Following the Inter-American Conference in Mexico City, the representatives of twenty republics of the Western Hemisphere signed the Act of Chapultepec. This pledge was an alliance between member nations to act in mutual defense. Considered to be a "new Monroe Doctrine," the Associated Press considered it "the realization of a dream first conceived by Woodrow Wilson thirty-one years ago and later incorporated into Article X of the League of Nations."[13] The war wasn't even over and new alliances were being formed in anticipation of the next one.

Another woman going into battle was war correspondent Barbara Finch of the British Reuters News Agency. She was aboard a hospital plane that arrived at the island of Iwo Jima, "where thousands of American Marines fought and died to gain an essential foothold in Japan's 'front yard.'"[14] The ship carried doctors, medical supplies, corpsmen, and one ton of mail. It also carried equipment for the wounded to be evacuated by air. The hospital plane was fired on by Japanese emplacements on the battle-torn island. "I crawled from the plane, tottering under the weight of a tin hat, trench knife, canteen and typewriter," wrote Finch. Later, she said she got to a hospital tent, was shot at, was thrown down by a marine colonel to protect her, spent the afternoon witnessing and writing about the carnage, and then took off with the plane again, filled with wounded. "We took off smoothly—out over the armada of American ships riding in the blue water: up through the frosty air until Iwo Jima—an island of blood and courage and death—was a memory."[15] Finch, an intrepid reporter, was part of a famous war correspondent duo; her husband, Percy, was also often found in dangerous war zones.

THE MATTER OF FRANK Sinatra and military service arose again. Fed by a Walter Winchell rumor, the story going around was that Sinatra punctured his own eardrum with a sewing needle to avoid service. Another rumor was that he'd spread a lot of cash around to avoid the army. His local board in New Jersey had classified him 2-A-F but in a "necessary job" and "regularly engaged in an activity in support of the national health, safety and interest."[16] Further, "Ira Caldwell, board chairman, said he had ordered the 29-year-old crooner placed in a 2-A-F after receiving notification from Washington . . . that Army physicians and reviewing military officials had disqualified Sinatra for the second time because of a punctured eardrum."[17] Sinatra was first classified as 4-F in December 1943. He issued a statement that said, "I'd like to accept the decision without comment as millions of guys have. I'm sure I experienced the same emotions they did. However, I certainly envied them their privacy."[18] Later, the members of Frank Sinatra's Draft Board #19 in Jersey City voted 4 to 0 to return the singer's draft status to 4-F.

SOME STATES HELPFULLY PRODUCED diagrams, guides, and maps to show what fruits and vegetables would grow best in a given state. Georgia went even further, telling Georgians what vegetables would grow best in the northern, central, and southern parts of the Peach State, with cabbage, beets, potatoes, and radishes doing the best statewide. The War Production Board announced that through the national brownout effort, some three million tons of coal had been saved.

Men's hats had been in style for many years, changing in shape and size. From the early days of America, men wore tricornered hats, beaver hats, stovepipe hats, Homburgs, Stetsons (which included the "Stratoliner," the "Whippet," and the "Diplomat"), bowlers, the Dallas, the "Bentley," boaters, derbies, skimmers, top hats, felts, Panama hats, and fedoras. And ball caps for boys. In 1945, military hats were also in style, from the overseas cap to officer's "slouch" hats to helmets to pilot's hats to sailor caps. No man, military peaked hats or otherwise, went out in public without a hat, and they always removed them when they went inside, and always, always, always tipped their hats to ladies. They also held doors for ladies, held chairs for ladies, and stood up when a lady entered or left a room. No downtown of a big city or small town was complete without a hat store for men.

While Americans sought comfort through familiar luxuries like hats, they were realizing that this war, unlike every other war in the nation's history, touched all, involved all, and called on all to sacrifice, do without, go without. Boys and men who weren't drafted enlisted, and after their tours were up many reenlisted, not for the pay (which was low), not for the food (which was uniformly mediocre), not for the fringe benefits (which were none), but maybe for the camaraderie, definitely for the action, and mainly for the patriotism.

It was reported locally in March that Admiral William "Bull" Halsey had taken off a few precious days in February from commanding his carrier fleets in the Pacific to go to the palatial 4,000-acre Georgia winter estate of John Hay Whitney for some days of hunting and fishing. Whitney, a professional inheritor, descended from the *Mayflower*'s William Bradford and from Lincoln's key aide John Hay. But Whitney was also a genuine war hero. While serving in the Office of Strategic Services, he was taken captive by the Nazis but later escaped when his prison train came under attack by the Allies.

Other local news often included the awarding of medals, posthumously, to saddened parents, as in the case of Private Thestius B. Gunter Jr., who was killed in action after first receiving the Purple Heart and later the Silver Star. In the Battle of Saipan, young Gunter volunteered and then kept delivering ammo to a forward position despite a serious leg injury the previous June. He won the Silver Star on June 17. He was killed in action on June 18. He'd been in the dairy business with his father, to whom the Silver Star was presented.

Serious discussions were underway in Washington to ration cars—"old jalopies"—for essential workers. Few new cars had been made in years, and something like 1.5 million cars a year were being taken off the road. The government estimated that there were barely enough civilian cars on the road to sustain the economy. Even so, the national speed was only thirty-five miles an hour; even an exhumed LaSalle could handle that.

In England, the eighteen-year-old princess Elizabeth, heiress to the British throne, had been granted the honorary rank of subaltern in the Auxiliary Territorial Service, the British equivalent of a WAC. "By the King's order, she [was] to be treated exactly the same as any other student officer with no special privileges because of personal rank." Elizabeth was the first member of the royal family to join the war effort full time.

AFTER TWO WEEKS, THE battle for Iwo Jima was still unsettled. As of March 5, the Americans so far counted 12,864 dead Japanese soldiers and 81 taken prisoner. Yet, Japanese resistance strengthened. Hospital planes took off day and night from Iwo Jima, loaded with wounded. Planes off of carriers continued their assault on the island and also the island of Chichi Jima in the Bonin Island chain, just to the north. Also, islands in the Marshall chain were strafed and shelled. Chichi Jima had previously been bombed by a young Lieutenant Junior Grade named George H. W. Bush, in his TBM Avenger, off USS *San Jacinto*. Bush, a hero, was awarded the Distinguished Flying Cross and three Air Medals as he was shot down but survived, though his two crewmates did not.

Respected *Atlanta Constitution* columnist Gladstone Williams filed a detailed account of Franklin Roosevelt's in-person report to Congress to brief them on his 14,000-mile trip to Yalta, where he met with Churchill and Stalin, and then to Cairo where he again met with Churchill. He was exhausted, bone-weary, but he was hopeful, and his eyes still twinkled. In fact, some members of Congress remarked on how well the president looked and how he might have put on a little much-needed weight. "He has more color in his face, and he seemed to have gained a little weight," remarked Georgia senator Richard Russell.[19] There was no effort to conceal his wheelchair, and unlike in the past when audiences were asked to turn their backs while the president locked his leg braces into place and then labored to stand at a podium, he was wheeled in and helped into a more comfortable chair to read his text. But he frequently departed from it to expand on the importance of Yalta. It was unlike any speech given before to the Congress.

> His tone and manner were conversational throughout, and there was in his speech none of the oratorical flourishes which usually mark the appearance of a chief executive before the congress. It was as though Mr. Roosevelt was sitting in his drawing room with members of congress surrounding him. He talked in much the same conversational style, giving an account of his travels and the problems that were taken up and solved at Yalta. In the first place, Mr. Roosevelt deviated from custom by delivering his speech from a sitting position. This time, he was wheeled in on his little business-like rolling chair—the same type that he gave the King of Arabia, who had envied its leg-saving faculties. Once inside the chamber, the President transferred to a more comfortable red plush-covered chair, from which he delivered his report. He was seated immediately in front of the speaker's dais, whereas ordinarily he stands on the dais itself. Another evidence of the President's informality was found in the number of deviations he made from the written text of his speech.[20]

FDR made a glancing reference to "the world prima donnas with whom he found it necessary to deal, a thrust believed to have been aimed at General Charles de Gaulle, the temperamental head of the French provisional government who refused an invitation to meet with the President on his return from Yalta."[21] Still in a snit, de Gaulle later refused to act as a cosponsor in the San Francisco meeting creating the United Nations. American editorialists and columnists tore into France in general and de Gaulle specifically as rude, ungrateful, and ill mannered. American public opinion about France, our oldest ally, was beginning to shift dramatically. But there was good news. Senator Russell said he "was impressed with the President's condition. He thought he was in as good form as a man of Mr. Roosevelt's 63 years could be expected."[22]

AT WESTERN AUTO STORES across the country, more than automobile parts could be obtained, although tires were going for as low as $14.65 a tire up to $19.95. Inner tubes were "ration free," which was good because tires blew out often, even if they had a ten-month guarantee. Also, rakes could be bought for $1.10, hoes for 89 cents, a Silex glass coffee maker for $3.35, and enamel for repainting a bike to make it look shiny and new was only 23 cents for a young girl or boy. A thermos, handy for picnics, outdoor work, or camping, was fetching $1.15. At drug stores, Vicks VapoRub was 27 cents, Pond's face powder was 43 cents, and Pepto-Bismol was on sale for 89 cents. Heavy mineral oil was 23 cents a pint, "HID" deodorant cream was 25 cents, and Squibb Cod Liver Oil was 98 cents for fourteen ounces. Lifebuoy soap was three bars for 18 cents. "Stubble Trouble?" Berkley Blades was offering eighteen safety razors for only 25 cents.

Eleanor Roosevelt was controversial but also beloved. She was her husband's eyes and ears where he could not be; he always said she was his best political adviser. And though the love had probably been out of their marriage for years (though no one really knew), she was a human dynamo, what with her family; the duties of being First Lady; her work with the United Service Organizations and Civilian Defense; her wide world of travel; her daily column "My Day," which was syndicated to hundreds of newspapers five days a week; her monthly magazine articles; her daily radio show; letters; and much more. Unfortunately, she had a strained relationship with her daughter, Anna. The previous month, it became even more strained when FDR took Anna to Yalta rather than Eleanor, who badly wanted to accompany her husband.

Eleanor Roosevelt was no stranger to controversy, and she put her foot in it again when she proclaimed, "Only the best people should have large families."[23] She probably didn't mean it the way it came out, but it caused a national stir, and letters poured into newspapers condemning the remarks. She later clarified, saying, "The only qualification I put on large families is that they should have enough money to enable the children to grow decently—not to have an easy time or a soft life."[24] But then her "My Day" column on March 9 was full of controversies again, as she took on the Board of Trustees for the University of Texas and defended the recently ousted president, Homer P. Rainey. She also talked about families of POWs and how to address envelopes to purchase war bonds.[25]

A FORTY-ONE-YEAR-OLD GI, MACK Tharpe—who had no business fighting as a navy pilot—died in combat. An editorial praised his heroism but also said, "This is a young man's war."[26] Indeed it was. Boys as young as sixteen, seventeen, eighteen, nineteen were fighting and dying.

People were starting to think about the effects on the twelve million American GIs serving overseas and the effect they would have on the country they would return to. Both had changed radically in four plus years. The boys "who return won't be the same boys who went away," wrote one of the most eloquent columnists in the country, Ralph T. Jones.

> There are some twelve million of them, or more, who are undergoing that strange and wrenching experience of life, for months and years, as units in a vast organization of uniformed men, disciplined and subject to laws and ordinances different from those they knew in civilian life. . . . These young men of ours . . . will come back with a new wisdom deep in their eyes and with a new idealism for the America they helped create. For they will have been looking at us at home and the things we do, from the perspective that gives them, in one sense, a clearer view and a better understanding. For they will come home purged of that handicap of provincialism. . . . No future . . . politician will be able to make stump campaign capital by calling Americans of neighboring countries "furriners."[27]

Another change coming would be that America would never again take a back seat to Great Britain when it came to global affairs. The British Empire was waning and the Pan-America was waxing.

In Atlanta and other cities, plans were underway for their annual

"Woman of the Year" awards. "The idea of recognizing the leading Atlanta woman—instigated here two years ago . . . has circulated throughout the country."[28] The awards went to women who were leaders in culture, style, design, fashion, and business. This national award may have been the inspiration for a movie of the same name, starring Spencer Tracy and Katharine Hepburn.

THE BIG CITY OF Cologne, Germany, was overrun and subdued. It had large factories for the manufacture of war matériel, but they'd been silenced by Allied bombers. The city in which Adolf Hitler had ordered his troops to make a "Stalingrad-like stand" now lay helpless before the Allied juggernaut, abandoned by his disobeying troops. The city residents "cowered in cellars, while the battle swirled about them, [and] they streamed back to the American lines carrying their household possessions."[29] A sure sign of the German army retreat was the blowing up of their own bridges and military installations—anything to slow the Allied advance.

Across Germany, the wholesale slaughter of chickens was ordered to save on grain for human consumption. "All persons living in towns must dispose of their poultry, establishment of new chicken ranches was forbidden, limitations [were] placed on the number of brood hens that may be retained by farmers, and only peasants and poultry farmers [were] allowed to raise chickens at all after April 1."[30]

A writer waxed literary about the taking of Cologne: "Legend tells that the Huns of ancient days slaughtered 11,000 British virgins and their leader, Saint Ursula, at Cologne. Today, American tanks and mobile artillery rumble through the streets of the great city on the Rhine, the fourth largest city in all of Germany, avenging the victims of those modern Huns, the Nazis."[31] The taking of Cologne was a devastating blow to what remained of German morale. It was a factory for war, but it was also one of the most historic cities in Europe, with a cathedral said to be one of the best examples of Gothic architecture on the continent, though now badly damaged by Allied bombing. It was estimated that it would take ten years to repair the ancient structure. Fortunately, most of its treasures had been removed for safekeeping.

According to war dispatches, it was the eighth day of daylight bombing by the British. Nazi soldiers were told they had to go one month without pay so as to help the refugees from Eastern Europe. No one believed it for a moment. Besides, the German mark was nearly worthless.

On Iwo Jima, the Japanese had attempted several times to penetrate American positions but were repelled. Mount Suribachi was an active volcano, and on March 5 it was reported: "the volcano began acting up yesterday. Smoke billowed from the crater and fissures high on its slopes and soon a huge cloud enveloped the volcano and the American flag flying from the topmost crag." It was also noted that the "volcano is pouring sulfur fumes through its caves, flushing out Nipponese soldiers."[32] Meanwhile, American GIs cooked C-rations over the hot lava.

Another veteran died, but this one was a past master of the War Between the States. Aaron Whitfield Dorn, ninety-six, was a "veteran of the Gray," who was born in South Carolina, moved to Georgia, and fought against the Yankees before settling down to become a grocer.

Many of the news reports coming out of the Pacific were "dateline: Guam," as it had become the headquarters for Fleet Admiral Chester W. Nimitz, commander in chief of Pacific naval operations, despite the fact there were still a number of Japanese troops on the island.

The newspapers continued to publish helpful guides for readers. Processed food needed blue stamps, while other stamps, such as X5 and Y5, were identified for certain days. The same with meats and fats, and "your meat dealer will pay you two red points and 4 cents for each pound of used fats." Also, ration stamps were issued for sugar, shoes, fuel oil, and gasoline ("coupons good for four gallons").[33]

Meat continued to be scarce and sometimes even nonexistent. The army was taking some 50 percent of pork and a whopping 80 percent of beef! The situation was not expected to change soon, so the average American would have to make do with only 1.3 pounds of meat a week. A mordant and dismissive editorial writer said, "So if you are getting your

1.3 pounds per week, you are getting your fair share. And the best thing to do when you find the meat market cupboards are bare, is to grin cheerfully, go home, and concoct as satisfying a meal as you can, sans meat."[34]

A new survey was released by the Gallup organization on the national election the previous fall, and FDR, the old master, had once again scrambled the deck. He won the organized, semiskilled, and unskilled labor vote overwhelmingly, as expected, but he also won the white-collar vote and did surprisingly well among the business classes. True, 1944 was a wartime election, but the wartime elections of 1916 and 1864 had sent the country off in a different direction than the path it had been on prior to the national plebiscite. The 1944 election affirmed the Democratic Party as the true governing political party in America, where all the cool people belonged, from academics to Hollywood, including B actor Ronald Reagan. Across most margins, FDR had increased his vote percentage over 1940, in some cases, exponentially. Only among farmers did he go backward, from 54 percent to 48 percent.[35] In cities over five hundred thousand, FDR swept with 61 percent of the vote. In towns under ten thousand, he saw a decline.

The Japanese announced their headquarters in Hanoi—in French Indochina—had been bombed by American forces on March 5, in a daytime attack no less.[36]

The great theatrical trouper, Ginger Rogers, had been spreading her wings from the light, tripping the light fantastic, dancing comedies with Fred Astaire. Now she was the leading lady in the hit movie *I'll Be Seeing You*, costarring Joseph Cotton and Shirley Temple, sans Astaire. The dark but hopeful movie about the war and what it could do to men—and their love lives—was released in 1944, but it was still airing in 1945.

GEORGIA WAS HOME TO some of the smartest—and dumbest—politicians. A group of state legislators happened on the not-so-bright (and unconstitutional) idea that a surcharge should be levied on bachelors in the state, with the funds going to spinsters. They could be excused from the tax if they provided documentation that they proposed marriage to three old bitties—and were turned down by those three spinsters—the previous year.

Meanwhile, everybody in America was scrambling to file their tax returns, due March 15. Taxes, during World War II, reached as high as 90 percent for high-wage earners, but they were high across the board and people were getting sick and tired. A powerful, populist, grassroots lobby was hard at work trying to pass a repeal of the Sixteenth Amendment, which granted income tax authority to Washington, and replace it with an amendment that limited taxes to no more that 25 percent. Over the previous several years, eighteen state legislatures had already approved the measure to call for a constitutional convention, under Article V of the US Constitution, to consider the amendment. Washington was becoming alarmed and aired the same old scare tactics bureaucracies had used in the past. After all, the first rule of bureaucracy is to defend the bureaucracy. Naturally, Congress refused to consider the amendment, so the state-by-state effort was undertaken. The organizer and funder of the Constitutional Government Committee and the American Taxpayer Association was Frank Gannett, owner of the many Gannett newspapers and news services.

The deposits in American commercial banks totaled $21 billion, up by 21.6 percent over 1943.

THE THIRD ARMY ADVANCED thirty-two miles in two days as American troops swarmed over Cologne. General Eisenhower lifted a temporary news blackout (though it was hard to tell) and General George S. Patton was, as always, on the offense. His army captured Lieutenant General Edwin Graf von Rothkirch und Trach, who forlornly declared, "It will be over within four months—five months at the most."[37] The German general was described as "dejected when he was brought to the rear, in a jeep. His grey-green overcoat and black knee-length rubber boots were caked with mud." He muttered, "How can you win a war when you have no gasoline and no horses?"[38] He might have also asked how you win a war without troops as German POWs lined up for miles.

Cologne was a pile of ruins. Full 85 percent of it was estimated to be in shambles as a result of the forty-two thousand tons of bombs dropped from Allied raids. Two thousand acres of the city were devastated. Patton's army was fifty miles inside the Fatherland. About this time, the fantastical rumor swept his troops and the rest of America that he swam the Sûre River in icy cold water as a way to inspire his troops. Stories were increasing about the German civilians throwing themselves at the feet of the American troops. One reporter wrote, "It is beginning. The 'act' by the German people, intended to fool our Army men that the German people they meet, as our invasion progresses, are all quite innocent of any wrong, that they themselves are poor victims of the Nazis and that they welcome us as sympathetic and understanding friends. Pah. The stories already coming out of Cologne about the fawning, sycophantic Germans are sickening, that's all."[39]

Despite offers of beef and cheese and butter and cognac from the German populace, the American troops had longer memories—of the dead and starving children of Holland, of the death camps, of the thousands massacred by the Luftwaffe, of the helpless American soldiers mowed down at Malmedy. A professor shouted, "Heil Eisenhower!" but the Americans were not impressed. When he tried to shake hands with an American GI, the soldier refused and the professor's "dark eyes blazed behind their thick glasses and his smiling face sharpened into hard, angry cruelty."

We must never forget, as the Germans adopt these tactics . . . that the whole nation is responsible for its government and its leadership. We must never forget that these same Germans rejoiced—and laughed—when, in the early stages of the war, they read of the helpless thousands—tens and hundreds of thousands—who were slain. . . . These are the ones who strutted and boasted when their U-boats sent Americans to death in the cold waters of the Atlantic. . . . These are the ones who fantastically proclaimed themselves members of a nation of "supermen." Instead, a nation of under evolved rats, as they are.

Let us pray our men never forget the German record, when they are tempted to become friendly and cordial with some cleverly ingratiating German. Especially when that German is in the guise of an attractive, smiling fraulein.[40]

This explained why the Allies would not negotiate, why they would only accept total war, unconditional war, and unconditional surrender. Winston Churchill and Franklin Roosevelt had not forgotten.

Rumors were flying around that Hitler wasn't finished, that he still had one more trick up his sleeve, one more wicked stunt to delay the inevitable. His propaganda minister, Joseph Goebbels, took to the frequencies again to spout new inanities. He said the war had already "exceeded its climax" and would end "to a furioso in its final phase, then end suddenly and rashly" in a win for the Nazis, as the morale and the purpose of Germany were superior to the Allies. He'd written in an article, "Experience teaches us it is not about the forcible necessities of the war. War comes at the moment it's due with the force of a hurricane and usually ends the same way, quite suddenly after its wildest eruption." The battle, he continued, "is not to be presumed that it will become completely stabilized anywhere at any time."[41] Someone forgot to tell Dr. Goebbels that the Allies were not a force of nature but a force for morality and good, an immovable, irresistible force that would not simply die down until the last Nazi was forced to stand in the dock for crimes against humanity.

Eisenhower went on radio to tell German military officers to quit the German army and think about the rebuilding of their country. "An appeal for Gen. Eisenhower's headquarters, addressed to German army officers via the American broadcasting station in Europe, has urged that they 'reconsider the situation of Germany, the situation of their men and their personal situation' and surrender to the Allies."

Germany has lost the westwall, her most powerful defense in the west. The Allies have reached the Rhine and the Rhur. In the East the

Red Army is standing before Berlin. The industrial areas of Upper Silesia, East Prussia, Posen (Poznan) and parts of Saxony, Brandenburg and Pomerania are in Russian hands. The end is merely a question of time. . . . The responsibility for the outcome of the war no longer rests with the German officer. But the responsibility for his men remains— and this responsibility will indubitably be taken into account by postwar Germany. Germany's future will be hard, but there will be a possibility for reconstruction. The Allies do not intend to destroy Germany—only the politicians know that their number is up. Many German officers whose names must remain unknown have sent parliamentarians to the Allies in a hopeless situation and surrender their troops. Other officers who could not take this course of action ordered their men to cease fire when the attack caught up with them. We cannot expect the German officer to do anything that would be contrary to his honor or to his country's interest. It is in Germany's interest to put an end to this useless bloodshed. The decision is up to the German officer.[42]

The successful surge across the Rhine River was said by some to be second only to the Normandy invasion. According to the Associated Press, "The swift, sensational crossing yesterday was the biggest military triumph since the Normandy landing, and was a battle feat without parallel since Napoleon's conquering legions crossed the Rhine early in the last century."[43] What was left of the German army was caught flat-footed, and only token resistance was offered. The Americans also took the strategically important Ludendorff Bridge at Remagen. The banter among correspondents was that with Patton's Third Army surely crossing the Rhine soon and with the continued advances of the Canadians, British, and Soviet armies, the next battle with the Nazis would be the last of the war. If so, this had to make a lot of GIs nervous. After all, who wanted to die in the last battle of a war? The good news was, for the first time since 1922, the Stars and Stripes were raised before the American troops over the Rhine.

Meanwhile, the Russian army was now just twenty-five miles from the outskirts of Berlin. Much of the crossing had been made using pontoon bridges and assault boats. Heavily censored dispatches reported there were one million combat troops amassed in the center of the front under General Omar Bradley's command, poised on the Rhine to the north.[44] Though the full weight of Allied forces had not yet crossed the Rhine, it was a psychological victory for the Allies—and a psychic defeat for the Germans. It was as if Caesar had crossed the Rubicon. Once the Rhine had been crossed, the destiny of both forces was on a collision course that could be neither altered nor prevented. They were engaged in the final death struggle of the Aryan Nation.

FDR returned to the White House from a long weekend at Springwood in Hyde Park on the Hudson River. Roosevelt loved the family compound despite some difficulty getting around in his wheelchair. During his twelve-year presidency, he made roughly one thousand trips to his home, where he played pinochle, read dime novels, worked in flower gardens, had his "fivesies," and smoked up a storm. He and Eleanor almost always had guests visiting, including his cousins, whom he was fond of, especially Margaret Suckeley and Laura Delano. The fact that he was even reported to be away from Washington was itself a news story as, all during the war, his movements were often hush-hush. The White House said that henceforth it would permit publication of the president's journeys to Hyde Park—after he had returned. When FDR returned to the White House, he was immediately deluged with work. He presented Admiral Halsey with the Gold Star, received and accepted the credentials for new ambassadors for Italy and Belgium, and then met with Vice President Truman and the congressional leadership to discuss pending legislation.

BY THE SECOND WEEK in March, fifteen square miles of Tokyo lay in ruins from a giant B-29 bombing raid by an incredible three hundred planes. In terms of sheer power, if the same attack had happened on the city of Atlanta, half the city would be destroyed. General Curtis LeMay, in charge of air operations against Japan, said the massive assault had been launched from three islands in the Marianas chain. He continued, "The target attacked is now entirely burned. The fire left nothing but twisted, tumble-down rubble in its path. These facts are incontrovertibly established by reconnaissance photographs taken on the afternoon of the strike."[45] The Americans hit Tokyo and bombed other cities in Japan just as hard. Nagoya was hammered by another squadron of B-29s. Military aircraft was made in this city, so it was an important target. Only two B-29s were lost due to antiaircraft flak, but the commander of the Guam fleet of bombers, Brigadier General Thomas S. Power, said, "It looks like the boys did a pretty good job tonight."[46] B-29 crews invented their own cojoined words, or portmanteaus. They merged "Japs" with "apes" and came up with "Japes."

Back home in Chandler, Arizona, the war was in progress, but between irate local citizens and German POWs who'd been interned in a camp there. The prisoners had decided to offend the locals by waving a homemade Nazi banner in front of a sign in town—a roll call of honor that listed local boys who were serving, wounded, missing, or dead. Some citizens, angered by this act, moved to attack the Germans; however, the army guard intervened and led them away. POW camps deep inside the United States did not require the best and the brightest soldiers, and the civilians made charges that the German POWs were not under the best of supervision as the guards got haircuts, drank in bars, and made suggestive comments, "ogling and whistling" at young women. Lax security was often reported by the civilians as the Germans stole oranges out of groves and chickens out of coops.

Like the crumbing Third Reich calling on the people of Berlin to make a last stand against the advancing Allies, the Japanese political leadership was doing the same. The Japanese prime minister, Kuniaki Koiso, in a talk before the Diet, said they must be ready to defend the "sacred motherland" against the coming invasion. He was honest enough to tell them what they already knew: "The present war situation is very serious."[47] In Germany, much of the political leadership was in denial. Koiso, too, avowed, "We'll crush the foe" and an invasion would be "the God-sent opportunity for the decisive battle. . . . If the enemy should invade waters near our mainland we will crush him in the sea."[48] He made similar comments about an invasion moving inland on Japan.

BERLIN HAD BEEN POUNDED ten days in a row now, day and night. This time, the daylight bombing was completed by the British and Canadians flying Mosquitos, Lancasters, and Halifaxes.

Pope Pius XI issued a statement that the common good was more important than labor and capital, but it was the labor and capital of the Allies that was achieving the common good against the common bad of the Axis powers. Good usually triumphed over evil, but only if good was very, very careful and very, very capable. The pope was still laboring under a cloud for his concordat (Reichskonkordat) with Nazi Germany of 1933 as well as for the well-founded belief that the Vatican was less than supportive of the Jews of Europe, as it turned a blind eye toward Germany's treatment of Jews and the coming Holocaust.

So, too, did the Roosevelt administration and most newspapers and politicians in America. While they may not have known about the murderous atrocities of the Holocaust and the specifics, they'd known for years of the harsh treatment of Jews in Germany going back to the "Night of the Broken Glass"—Kristallnacht—in 1938 and even before, with the various anti-Semitic acts brought about by the Nazis. Over the years, Jews could not own pets, bicycles, or typewriters or sit for university exams. All this was done out in the open, and the United States did nothing, not even lodge a protest. Hitler and his minions, over the years, took the silence of the West as tacit approval of their racist acts. Occasionally, a brave writer or political cartoonist would say something about it, but it was rare. In 1945, the cartoonist for the *Atlanta Constitution* depicted Hitler and an animal-like toady as hunched-over, sad-looking misanthropes sitting in a tree with a sign that read "For Aryans Only," while a mocking monkey said, "We can always resort to guerrilla warfare."[49]

More and more of the political intelligentsia were speculating and talking about the fall of Nazi Germany, about how and when it would come. Many were surprised that now, near the end, the German citizenry wasn't falling on their collective sword for Adolf Hitler. They also had expected much of the Nazi hierarchy to withdraw to the Bavarian and Austrian Alps and fight a guerrilla war from there; the Allies had certainly discussed the possibility.

Ralph McGill, a reporter for the *Atlanta Constitution*, wrote, "The population is not only ready, but eager to quit. Both, on the Eastern and Western Fronts, when they see that they are not going to be massacred as they were told by the Nazis. The theory of the solidarity of the German people behind the Nazi regime is due to the total inability . . . to understand the nature of totalitarian regimes." But "they certainly knew there was strong opposition, or they would not have had the Gestapo, SS, concentration camps, the hangings, the universal terror."[50] Now the theory among some clearheaded thinkers was that without the popular support of the civilian population, a guerrilla, rearguard action would be impossible. The civilian population wouldn't support them, arm them, feed them, or hide them. In fact, they would turn on them, turn them in, if only to prove they had never supported the Nazis, which of course they had. The German people knew about the beatings and dislocations and deportations and degradations and deprivations and disgraces and, at least through rumors and whispered late-night conversations, mass exterminations in the death camps. The German people knew.

Upon FDR's return to the United States, Gallup took a survey asking the American people if they approved of the president and of Yalta. Astonishingly, Roosevelt and by extension Yalta were approved by 61 percent of Americans, with only 9 percent disapproving. Among his voters, 71 percent approved and only 6 percent disapproved. Among voters who supported Tom Dewey in the 1944 elections, 55 percent approved and only 12 percent disapproved. It was as much a mandate—and an approval—as any president had ever received.

The Führer returned to the radio waves once more to exhort his people, though they were no longer listening to him. He oddly charged the Allies with being "drunk by their orgy of victory." He urged the German people to fight until the Allies "get tired and will yet be broken."

> Only those who suffer defeat are unworthy of winning victory. . . . We witness both in the east and the west what our people would have to face. Our task is therefore clear: to put up resistance and to wear down our enemies so long that until, in the end, they will get tired and yet be broken. . . . It is my unshakable determination and it must become the unshakable will of all of us to show the world no worse example than our forefathers have given. . . . Even if fate has turned against us now, there can be no doubt that these reverses can be overcome as so often before, with steadfastness and courage, with endurance and fanaticism. To defy all danger with iron determination and to do everything to bring about a turn for the better, and for this purpose to strengthen the power of resistance of our nation and its armed forces. Just as great must be our fanaticism in the destruction of those who are trying to resist our aims.[51]

He also made some bizarre claims that without the German army, "there would be no Germany today."

SATURDAY, MARCH 11, BROUGHT SAD news about six navy men who were killed instantly when their two torpedo bombers collided over the Atlantic just southwest of the Miami Naval Air Station.[52]

All the newspapers avidly and comprehensively covered the war, including from the local level. Some had weekly features not just about the dead, wounded, POWs, or MIA, but also about the assignments, promotions, awards, and men back from overseas, like they would Hollywood celebrities, only these celebrities were paid little and put their lives on the line each day. Interestingly enough, Hollywood did go to war—with the training films; with the actors who enlisted, such as Eddie Albert and Jimmy Stewart, who became legitimate war heroes; and with the inspirational war movies like *Bataan* and *Back to Bataan* starring John Wayne, *Desperate Journey* starring Errol Flynn and Ronald Reagan, *Wake Island* starring Robert Preston and William Bendix, and of course the unforgettable *Mrs. Miniver* and *Casablanca*, two of the most memorable war movies of World War II, or any war.

A favorite stopover in Los Angeles was the Hollywood Canteen, which was founded and operated by Hollywood residents, including starlets like Bette Davis. Anyone in uniform could attend and have a beer and a burger at no cost. These men and women in uniform might find Betty Grable or Rita Hayworth as their waitress or dance partner. The Canteen opened in 1942 and operated through the rest of the war, closing in November 1945.

But life around Hollywood also went on as usual, with the endless cocktail parties and beach parties and marriages and multiple marriages and celebrated divorces and affairs, all of them covered in Louella Parsons's gossip columns.

Radio in rural America was a vital news and entertainment link, and the dial was filled with religious programs such as *Sunrise Gospel*, but also the *Dixie Farm Hour*. For entertainment, *The Kate Smith Hour*, *House Party*, *Our Gal Sunday*, and other programming ran from 9:00 a.m. to the signoff at midnight. *Our Gal Sunday* had been on the air for nine years and starred Vivian Smolen in the title role. Every Tuesday from 8:30 to 9:00 p.m., listeners could hear the famed actor, director, writer, and producer Orson Welles interview other actors on his show *This Is My Best* on CBS radio.

TO MINIMIZE THE DAMAGE done to German workers by Allied bombers, the various aircraft and tank plants had developed the "sleepeasies." Simply put, they were wood on top and concrete below, forming a roof for protection when the bombing began. According to one news report, these small two-man sleeping quarters included "Goebbels tuned radios and a picture of 'Our Beloved Führer.'" They "sleep underground . . . or retire there during daylight raids not caring whether, when the siren sounds the all-clear, the upper structure will exist or have been blown away." If the wood and canvas structure was indeed blown away, "a swastika-marked van will deliver a new superstructure tomorrow, new mass-produced furniture and a kitchen stove."[53]

The American First Army was now well past the Rhine, heading east toward the factory towns where much of the German war arsenal had been assembled. The army was five miles past the big river, which had a bridgehead eleven miles wide, and was now "less than 25 miles from the southern region of the 6000-square mile basin teeming with war factories."[54] The Third Army under Patton's command was also advancing quickly "along the north side of the Moselle River . . . giving Patton's forces control of all the river."[55]

From the east, the Russians were advancing more quickly, though the German high command was in denial that the capture of Berlin was part of the Russian plans. With all the attention focused on the Americans, British, and Canadians advancing from the west and the Soviets from the east, it was forgotten that the Germans were still locked in a fierce battle in Italy. The American Fifth Army was manning the bulk of the attack, and the Germans, under Field Marshal Albert Kesselring, told troops to defend "every inch" of Italy. They were also told, "you do not defend Italy in these battles but Germany itself. Not one inch of ground must be surrendered to our enemies without a battle."[56]

A BITTER LABOR STRIKE enveloped Hollywood and four major studios. RKO, Warner Brothers, Twentieth Century–Fox, and Pathé were all shut down while Paramount, Universal, Columbia, and Metro-Goldwyn-Mayer stayed open. The War Labor Board told the fifteen thousand striking employees to return to work, but to no avail. Betty Grable, Dorothy Lamour, and others reported for work, but just as quickly returned home as their studios were shut down. The strike had been called by the Conference of Studio Unions representing the set decorators. The strike was sometimes bloody and lasted six months, delaying a number of movies, although Hollywood had approximately 130 movies completed in the wings, ready to release. Even so, there was a chance the strike might extend to the movie houses around the country.

The story of the German POWs in Arizona would just not go away. It had gained national attention and national outrage. A Democratic congressman from Arizona, Richard Harless, said the POWs were smoking two packs a day per prisoner and eating "luxury menus, typical of the Waldorf Astoria," and the American guards wouldn't go into prisoners' barracks wearing a necktie "for fear of being strangled."[57] Much of it turned out to be a tempest in a teapot, half-truths and exaggerations, but the German prisoners were being well fed, got three packs of cigarettes a week, and were not forced into slave labor. Fact is, German POWs certainly had it better in an American POW camp than they ever had in the German army, and they definitely had it better than their American counterparts who were forced into labor camps with barely starvation rations.

The editor of the *Richmond Times-Dispatch* was scheduled to give a talk on the "Prospects for Liberalism in the Postwar South" at the Georgia Academy of Social Sciences in Atlanta. There was little fear of an overflow crowd.

THE AMERICANS CONTINUED THEIR pummeling of mainland Japan. Tokyo had been reduced to rubble. Nagoya had been smashed to bits. Now it was Osaka's turn. Three hundred B-29s dropped 2,300 tons of bombs on the city. Japan's three largest cities lay in ruins. In Osaka alone, four square miles of the city were aflame. It was very densely packed, with over 47,000 people squished into each square mile. The flames were visible 125 miles away. "Clustered in the attack area [were] steel, copper and aluminum plants; aircraft parts plants . . . the main truck railroad."[58]

Another Nazi prison camp was liberated in mid-March. In the early reports, no Jews were mentioned in the liberation of this camp near Rheinbach, Germany, although they did mention that the freed and wandering in the local town were "French African troops, Belgians, Poles, Russians and Dutch, with a sprinkling of domestic murderers, prostitutes and thieves. [And that] many of the Europeans were one-time prisoners of war" who had been freed when the Wehrmacht withdrew and the Americans advanced.[59]

Now, it got bizarre. When the 9th Armored Division took the prison camp, they found that while all the prisoners were free, all of their German captors were in the jail cells; the roles were reversed. "Hans Dreschke, the fat Nazi who ran this place, and his 20 guards remained behind. . . . Dreschke and the guards were in the cells, and the keys were in the hands of their one-time prisoners." And a "German guard . . . clicked his heels together and stood at attention in the white light of the American flashlight and said: 'Cell No. 542 . . . Prisoner Koslowsky reporting.'"[60] The cells had no furniture, and the prisoners were made to sleep on the filthy and cold stone floor. The guard, Koslowsky, "who used to beat the prisoners and hold the butts of cigarettes against their cheeks," admitted to his torture but was steadfast in proclaiming he was only following orders.[61]

The shape of the *bon soldat*—the "good soldier" argument—was beginning to take form. The argument by German soldiers that they were only following orders would be used and used again to defend their heinous actions in the field and the camps before and during World War II. The war correspondent W. C. Heinz waxed literary: "No matter how much you read about these Germans and their methods, you never quite believe it, of course, until you finally see the evidence yourself, and then it all seems very familiar and like very old stuff. It seems so familiar because it is exactly like what you have read and heard, and because these Krauts always seem to play their parts just the way Hollywood has been playing them for years."[62]

Newspaper forecasters had nothing better to do, so they once again forecast the end of World War II, now saying the end would come in early summer, when earlier they said it would come in late fall of 1945. They read the tea leaves of such things as the morale of German troops and their supposed willingness to fight and die for Germany. The idea of a sudden German collapse was discounted by all, as was the expectation of the sort of ferocious defense by the Germans of the previous November, December, and January. Nonetheless, there had been a definite change in the mental attitude of German troops, consistently demonstrated by the character of their resistance during the Allies' drive to—and across—the Rhine. "German morale has deteriorated, but seemingly not to the point where Nazi soldiers [were] ready to give up the fight entirely." Right now, the German troops were languidly putting up a struggle, as if they would go through the motions just so long as they didn't get hurt. Still, the Allied commanders in the field believed the Germans, to the end, would stand and fight.

Patton's Third Army captured thirteen towns in the five miles they had advanced while "Allied tactical planes, flying 2,700 sorties, hammered the Germans from the Remagen bridgehead north, destroying or damaging twenty-eight German planes and pounding enemy transports and strong points with a blazing whirlwind of destruction."[63]

Astonishingly, the White Russian anticommunist army was fighting the Nazis alongside the Soviet-Russian communist army as they achieved a breakthrough in their drive toward Berlin. Even more ironic, but very European, both the "Whites" and the "Reds" had been onetime allies of Nazi Germany. Europe was infamous for its shifting alliances. Foes became friends, friends became foes, and no agreement was ever permanent.

A startling rumor swept Europe. Did General Field Marshal Karl von Rundstedt offer to surrender his armies on the Western Front to the Allies? Was the offer rejected? And how did the story get out, since censorship regulations prevented news agencies from carrying any surrender offer until it was made official, for obvious reasons? Besides, the Allied position was unconditional surrender. So was an offer of surrender even entertained? Could Rundstedt offer up the surrender of the German forces also fighting in Italy and against the Russians in the east? Was it even tenable, as the track Germany was on meant "national suicide for the German people"?[64] Then von Rundstedt was removed from his command, fueling even more rumors that he had indeed sought his own armistice with the

Allies. Field Marshal Walther von Model was now the supreme commander of German forces in the west—or what remained of them.

If the Nazi Party leadership was committed to a suicide course, the German civilian population was thinking in a different direction. News reports used words like "docile" and sentences such as "This does not mean the German civilians are welcoming the Allies with open arms. But it does mean that German civilians and ordinary soldiers believe the war is hopelessly lost and once they are overrun, they feel they might well make the best of it instead of struggling on in a hopeless cause. Heavy Allied bombing has also played their part, undoubtedly, in taking the starch out of the German civilians' will to resist."[65]

Once again, American soldiers were being victimized by an invasion, this time by an invading horde of pretty young girls wearing sweaters. The girls in the tight-fitting sweaters were on a mission to separate naive young soldiers from their wallets. It was an old story. The pretty girl approaches a well-scrubbed, corn-fed young GI with some cash in his pocket and innocent lust in his heart. She tells him she needs to sell one more magazine subscription, and if he buys it, she will (a) go out on a date with him, (b) apply for WAC flight school, or (c) be awarded a war bond. These young soldiers, far away from home and girlfriends, fell for the ploy like a ton of bricks. Local law enforcement officials got involved after one GI got stood up on a promised date after buying a newspaper subscription.

The director of the Office of Price Administration, Chester Bowles, urged Congress to grant his bureaucracy the ability to control the prices to all sports and entertainment locales. Bowles had already urged price controls on barbers and beauty salons but now tried to expand his domain to include "entertainment, service, commercial rent and real estate prices and a host of other civilian goods and services. The OPA chief asserted that motion picture admissions had risen 33½ percent from June 1941 to December 1944, although one-third of the increase could be attributable to federal taxes."[66] No one, not in Washington's time or FDR's era, could explain the stupidity, idiocy, or dysfunctionality of the federal government.

Bataan survivor Private First Class Louis C. Zelis, who finally got home to Chicago, revealed a sad tale about one of his fellow prisoners. Captain Arthur Wermuth "was brutally beaten by Japs because he stood up for his men" at Cabanatuan prison camp. According to Zelis, when the men, sick and doubled over with dysentery, were forced to clean a "dung heap" barefoot, "without hesitation, Capt. Wermuth complained to a Jap officer in a manner which could not be misunderstood. The officer pulled a bit of judo on Capt. Wermuth, knocking him to the ground. Then, while [the other prisoners] stood by helplessly, they kicked him. They kicked him in the face. They kicked him in the stomach. They kicked him all over his body with their heavy boots. Unconscious, Capt. Wermuth was taken to a hospital. He was there for some time. We don't know what happened. One morning he was gone. The camp grapevine said he had been taken to Japan."[67] Being taken to Japan for slave labor was akin to a death sentence for an American soldier. (He, in fact, survived the war and died in 1981.)

SOUTHERN BELL TELEPHONE AND Telegraph was running ads featuring a pretty, young telephone operator cautioning customers not to use long distance for too long: "When your Long Distance call is over a line to a war-busy center, she may say—'Please limit your call to five minutes.' That's to help everybody during the rush periods."[68]

The issue of federal taxes and "paying your fair share" (whatever that meant) would not go away. Naturally, newspaper editors liked to moralize in shorthand, often writing trite editorials lecturing the reader to be glad they had so little to pay. One such editorial said, "Compared to the sacrifice which those thousands have made and are making, the highest tax rates pale into insignificance. We are called upon for dollars and cents, they for their very lives."[69]

FOLLOWING ADOLF HITLER'S LATEST radio screed, more and more people were openly speculating that the Führer was a lunatic, a nut case, and that the latest depressing war report had sent him around the bend. It had been talked about for years, but people held back as if the thought of young men fighting and dying against a babbling idiot made it all seem so worthless, so meaningless. Problem was, even though the rest of the world thought Adolf Hitler was insane, the German people thought otherwise. They thought him a genius at one time, a moral crusader. It was one of the greatest examples of mass self-deception and mass hysteria ever seen, and it would be studied for years.

Even now, at the end, he thought Germany would prevail. "Apparently, there is one man in Germany who does not know what is going on. That man is Adolf Hitler," wrote one reporter.[70]

In 1943, psychologist and Harvard professor Henry Murray was commissioned by the US Office of Strategic Services, a precursor to the CIA, "to study Adolf Hitler's personality to try to predict his behavior." Murray provided a 229-page report, "Analysis of the Personality of Adolf Hitler."

Murray described Hitler as a paranoid "utter wreck" who was "incapable of normal human relationships."

"It is forever impossible to hope for any mercy or humane treatment from him," Murray wrote. . . .

Hitler suffered from intolerable feelings of inferiority, largely stemming from his small, frail, and sickly physical appearance during his childhood. . . .

"He never did any manual work, never engaged in athletics, and was turned down as forever unfit for conscription in the Austrian Army," Murray writes.

Hitler managed his insecurities by worshiping "brute strength, physical force, ruthless domination, and military conquest."

Even sexually, Hitler was described as a "full-fledged masochist," who humiliated and abused his partners. . . .

As a child, Hitler experienced the Oedipus complex—love of mother and hate of father—which he developed after accidentally seeing his parents having sex, Murray's report says.

Hitler was subservient and respectful to his father but viewed him as an enemy who ruled the family "with tyrannical severity and injustice." According to the report, Hitler was envious of his father's masculine power and dreamed of humiliating him to re-establish "the lost glory of his mother."

For 16 years, Hitler did not exhibit any form of ambition or competition because his father had died and he had not yet discovered a new enemy. . . .

Another blow to Hitler's masculinity: He was "incapable of consummating in a normal fashion," old sexual partners shared with Murray.

> This infirmity we must recognise as an instigation to exorbitant cravings for superiority. . . .

As mentioned, when Hitler did have sexual relations with a woman, he exhibited masochistic behaviors. . . .

According to Murray, Hitler's cycle from complete despair to reaction followed this pattern:

> An emotional outburst, tantrum of rage, and accusatory indignation ending in tears and self-pity. Succeeded by periods of inertia, exhaustion, melancholy, and indecisiveness. Followed by hours of acute dejection and disquieting nightmares. Leading to hours of recuperation. And finally confident and resolute decision to counterattack with great force and ruthlessness.

The five-step evolution could last anywhere from 24 hours to several weeks, the report says. . . .

Hitler valued "pure, unmixed, and uncorrupted German blood," which he associated with aristocracy and beauty, according to Murray.

[Murray] offered the following explanation of Hitler's contempt for mixed blood:

As a boy of twelve, Hitler was caught engaging in some sexual experiment with a little girl; and later he seems to have developed a syphilophobia, with a diffuse fear of contamination of the blood through contact with a woman. It is almost certain that this irrational dread was partly due to the association in his mind of sexuality and excretion. He thought of sexual relations as something exceedingly filthy.

Hitler denied that his father was born illegitimately and had at least two failed marriages, that his grandfather and godfather were Jews, and that one of his sisters was a mistress of a wealthy Jew. . . .

Murray explains that Jews were the clear demographic for Hitler to project his personal frustrations and failings on because they "do not fight back with fists and weapons."

The Jews were therefore an easy and non-militarised target that he could blame for pretty much anything, including the disastrous effects after the Treaty of Versailles.

Anti-Semitic caricatures also associated Jews with several of Hitler's dislikes, including business, materialism, democracy, capitalism, and communism. He was eager to strip some Jews of their wealth and power. . . .

While the merciless Nazi leader was known to offer a weak handshake with "moist and clammy" palms and was awkward at making small talk, his overall presence was described as "hypnotic" in Murray's analysis.

Hitler received frequent compliments on his grayish-blue eyes, even though they were described as "dead, impersonal, and unseeing" in the report.

Murray notes that the Führer was slightly under average height, had a receding hairline and thin lips, and "strikingly well-shaped hands."

Sources say Hitler appeared to be shy or moody when meeting people and was uncoordinated in his gestures. He was also incredibly picky about his food.[71]

In other words, it was the considered opinion that Hitler was an exceedingly dangerous *non compos mentis* (not of sound mind).

SANELY, THE AMERICAN LEAGUE was scheduled to open April 16, returning to the tradition of holding the first game in Washington, DC, featuring the Senators versus the New York Yankees. President Roosevelt had been invited to throw out the first ball as presidents traditionally did. The schedule had been scaled back and the All-Star game canceled for 1945 to accommodate the directives from the Office of Defense Transportation.

FDR's deceased, confidential assistant, Marguerite "Missy" LeHand, had a navy ship named after her. It was a cargo vessel to be splashed in the Mississippi. LeHand had been FDR's secretary, de facto chief of staff, and suspected mistress for twenty-one years. She had died prematurely, having suffered from fainting spells and strokes before passing in July 1944 at the young age of forty-eight.

Stories of a miraculous rescue of POWs, mostly Americans, were beginning to surface. Back in February, just as some two thousand Americans were about to be lined up and shot at Los Baños prison camp, in floated American paratroopers, soldiers, and Filipino guerrillas to save them. Los Baños was one of the most cruel Japanese prison camps in the Philippines. Those captured included civilian men, women, and children, all of whom had dropped weight precipitously, as over the years they had often survived by eating weeds. Almost every newspaper in March reported stories of local citizens, their family members, or friends who were saved from imminent death.[72]

New bombs were dropped on Germany. Gigantic bombs. Five thousand eleven-ton, twenty-five-foot-long bombs from four thousand planes. For the twenty-third night, the Royal Air Force (RAF) and American planes bombed Germany, but these bombs—the "world shakers"—were so big, the British bombers like the Lancaster had to be rebuilt to accommodate them. These bombs were designed to obliterate underground structures, but one bomb could eradicate up to nine city blocks. The next day, the German army staff headquarters was smashed.

The RAF had bombed Berlin for twenty-four nights in a row, and now the US Air Force, which included 650 Flying Fortresses and Liberators, dropped 3,500 bombs, including incendiary bombs. All told, 2,100 bombers flew this mission. Hitting the target was not difficult as they flew in clear skies, both day and night. Many thought this mission ranked with the best by the 8th Air Force, and the returning crew and officers were jubilant.

The main Philippine island of Luzon was now, almost safely, in the hands of the Allies. But the many, many islands in the Philippine chain still had to be cleaned out of Japanese soldiers. MacArthur announced that two important islands, Romblon and Simara, had been flushed of the enemy. The twenty-second and twenty-third islands, so scrubbed, gave the Allied forces a better hold on the shipping lanes.[73]

More importantly, Iwo Jima had fallen. "Fleet Admiral [Chester W.] Nimitz proclaimed the end of Japanese authority there."[74] An estimated twenty thousand Japanese soldiers had died on the tiny island. The early estimate of American dead was just over two thousand. Tokyo radio informed their listeners that Japanese elementary children were being taught the bayonet thrust and charge. It was reported that the fifth and sixth graders were very enthusiastic.

"The German officer assigned to blow up the Remagen Bridge was drunk when American forces captured it, an American sergeant declared . . . contributing a new chapter to the Rhine crossing. S. Sgt. Joseph de Lisin of Bronx, New York, who captured the German officer, said he was soused. Dynamite was planted at strategic spots on the structure and the last folks in Remagen who wanted to leave were given a chance to cross to the east bank."[75]

A SAILOR ABOARD USS *Enterprise* (CV-6) sent an unusual letter to the Chief of Police of Hapeville, Georgia. The letter contained $20 and a letter of apology to grocer W. K. Rambo, who owned a grocery store. The sailor, whose identity was not revealed, said he and some friends had stolen candy and cigarettes in 1934, and his guilty conscience finally caught up to him. Rambo was dead, so the money and the note were given to his widow. His note ended with a biblical citation.

If Victory gardeners had to drive a distance to their gardens, the government would give them an extra allotment of gasoline.

It wasn't as big and monumental as King Edward VIII abdicating the British throne in December 1936, but the resignation of Edward, the new Duke of Windsor, from the post of commander in chief of the Bahamas caused another stir. The resignation meant that Edward was stepping away from any form of public service to the Crown, in the middle of a war, to live with his twice-divorced, many-loved wife, Wallis Simpson, who'd once been married to a Baltimore auto mechanic and was rumored to have pro-German sympathies as a result of her affairs with at least one high Nazi official, von Ribbentrop. Winston Churchill was so suspicious of her allegiance that he stopped the distribution of sensitive war documents that routinely went to all the royals. In May 1939, NBC paid Edward for a radio broadcast in which he pleaded for peace. The broadcast was seen as appeasement, and the BBC refused to broadcast it. For the rest of their lives, the Duke and Duchess of Windsor remained pariahs and curiosity figures at the same time. It was widely assumed that Edward had been appointed the governor of the Bahamas with a posh estate in Nassau as a means to get him out of the way, where he might use his limited, favorable influence to talk up the Third Reich.

RUMORS AND FABLES WOULD not die out that Hitler, in the end, would not negotiate a sudden surrender but instead would slowly surrender while rebuilding Germany in preparation for the launch of World War III. "Hitler is shaping his defeat in order to confer on coming German generations the illusion that resistance never ceased, and to provide a rallying point for the eventual upsurge of the German spirit and ambition," said one news report.[76]

Rumors and fables on the main island of Japan claimed they sighted an American invasion fleet just off the coast, according to Tokyo radio. Steps were being taken to defend the homeland, including the creation of "civilian special attack corps" to help in this goal. "It was indicated that the special attack corps would be a suicide organization pledged to go to certain death if necessary, to carry out any assigned duty."[77]

FIVE THOUSAND DELIRIOUS MOVIE buffs lined Hollywood Boulevard to ogle their favorite actors and actresses at the annual Oscar awards. During the war years, the ceremony had taken on an austere, even cautious air. Tuxedos were mothballed for business suits. Formal gowns with plunging necklines and ostentatious jewelry were closeted for conservative suits and hats for women. During the war years, the Oscar, which had been sprayed with gold paint, was replaced with plaster of Paris and spray-painted with a bronze lacquer. For best actors of 1944, crooner Bing Crosby won for *Going My Way* while Ingrid Bergman won for *None but the Lonely Heart*. The wonderful Barry Fitzgerald won Best Supporting Actor, also for *Going My Way*. Best movie of 1944 went to *Going My Way* as well, as all the major awards went that way.

The *Atlanta Constitution* published a column advising young American girls not to "wed for pity" to wounded American boys, which sorely underestimated young American girls in love.[78] The column noted one young man, who, after returning from three years of service, wrote his betrothed a letter in which he explained he was at the Walter Reed General Hospital with pneumonia, a broken arm—and both legs gone. "I'm pretty busted up," he said, in the letter. He wanted to spare her feelings by saying they weren't really engaged and just had an "under-standing." Her response was "I still love you, no matter what's happened, or what's left of you."[79] Several days after she arrived at the hospital, they were married.

While the Soviets and the Americans were allies of convenience in this war, they were and had been bitter enemies, down to the United States opposing the rise of Lenin in the Russian Revolution. Now, at war's end, they were becoming rivals again, and eventually would become bitter enemies. Both sides coveted the highly advanced German rocket program, and a race was now on to grab the several hundred German scientists and the V-1 and V-2 rockets. Chief among the top scientists was Dr. Wernher von Braun, the young genius who was, in many ways, the father of the German rocket program. "Research laboratories and documents relating to V-bombs [were] reported to have been removed" from Peenemünde, near the Harz Mountains, famous for its canaries. "It is easy to understand that German high command [was] in haste to prevent V-bomb secrets [from] falling into Russian hands."[80] According to Braun, the German scientists took a vote and decided to cast their lot with the Americans over the Russians.[81] It would become one of the most fateful decisions of the twentieth century.

Again and again, the British bombed Berlin and key cities, such as Hanover, where oil was refined for the German war effort. The Allies scored a direct hit on the German main HQ, destroying "administrative buildings, vital records, barracks, utilities and communications and transport systems. It was the first time the high commands' headquarters in Germany had been attacked by Eighth Air Force Bombers."[82]

WHEN IT CAME TO fashion, hairstyle, and hats, young men and women in their teens had many of their own, such as bobby socks and rolled-up jeans. But when they dressed up to go out—to a restaurant or to church—they dressed like their parents. Young men wore suits, sport jackets, cuffed pants, and adult-looking fedoras. Same with young women, who wore heels and nylons, fashionably cut and chic dresses, and business attire. When they reached a certain age—fifteen to seventeen—young Americans wanted to look like mature Americans.

Clothing sales could be found at high-end department stores like Macy's or at bargain basements like Robert Hall. To save money, many women were styling their hair at home using the "cold wave," yielding "long lasting hair curls and waves in only 2–3 hours at home."[83]

Another American flag was raised over Iwo Jima on March 15, and according to the Associated Press, it was "an improved flagpole." The news agency also reported that approximately twenty thousand Japanese soldiers had lost their lives. It had been twenty-five days since the initial

American invasion of the tiny island. With a bit of black humor, the marines rechristened Mount Suribachi as "Mount Plasma." An honor guard was formed from the 5th Marine Division of the 28th Marine Regiment to surround Old Glory atop Mount Suribachi.

While the Pacific war was envisioned to last many more months, even several years, most in the West thought it would take only one more offensive maneuver for the Allies to win and defeat Germany. At least, that was what Winston Churchill was telling people.

BUTTER WAS ALREADY IN short supply, but the War Food Administration told manufacturers that they would need to set aside 40 percent for April and 55 percent for May 1945.[84] No one begrudged the American fighting man and woman having butter in plentiful supplies, but they did resent it when the butter substitute, oleo, was heavily taxed by the government. To some, it seemed like the old bait and switch. Oleo was a sickly, pasty color when it came home from the grocery store. Little pouches of yellow dye accompanied it to be mixed in and make the condiment a more palatable, appealing butter-like color.

The longtime manager of the Philadelphia Athletics, Connie Mack, claimed his team was first division club and pennant contender in 1945, but who was he kidding? They'd been dead last for years, every year, even behind the perennially awful St. Louis Browns. In 1945, the A's finished with a woeful record of 52–98, dead last in the American League. Their road record was an embarrassing 13–63, and they finished 34 games behind the first-place Detroit Tigers. Spring training was coming, and Major League Baseball announced a sharp curtailment in the travel for teams. Exhibition games would be limited to teams training in the same immediate location or they could be played at military installations as long as the military provided transportation. It was expected to be the most severe curtailment in spring training travel in twenty-five years. But what was making headlines in St. Louis was "Pete Gray Is Starter for Browns; One-Armed Gardener Wins Starting Berth in First Exhibition."[85] Gray had lost his arm in a childhood accident, so he could not serve in the military, but that did not stop him from pursuing his dream of playing in major league baseball. His stats page featured an unusual entry: "Fields Left, Throws Left."

Also getting ready for their spring season was Atlanta's minor league Crackers.

By March 17, the navy was saying that Iwo Jima was "in the bag," though at great cost. So far, marine casualties totaled 19,938, with over 4,000 dead. The island was strategically important, within easy bombing range of Tokyo for planes other than B-29s. But it was taken at a terrible cost. The marines said it was the "bloodiest, toughest and costliest battle in the 168-year history of the United States Marines."[86]

Private First Class Charles Trout wrote a letter to his family about witnessing the American flag going up on Iwo Jima: "On Thursday a.m. I saw the American flag flying so beautifully atop the very center of it. Gosh! It was a wonderful sight to see. An American flag had never, never looked so good as it did atop Mt. Suribachi." But the young Georgian GI also was frank about the enemy: "I saw two Jap prisoners yesterday. The punks were laughing giggling from ear to ear. I felt like dropping a grenade amongst them because I had just seen two dead Marines."[87] He didn't think the marines would take many prisoners as the Japanese preferred to die rather than be someone else's captive. It was all a part of the Shogunate culture. And he was frank about the island too, saying, "This is a hell hole here, no trees, no vegetation, only dust and sand."[88] Trout said he had slept in mud holes and had not bathed in days, and the heat was unbearable.

The Japanese propaganda news agency, Domei, had the last word on Iwo Jima: "An important barrier has been given up to the enemy."[89] Almost immediately, American bombers began landing and taking off for Japan from Iwo Jima's prized airfield. They were not alone. Many American carriers had moved close to Japan and were bombing almost at will.

Nuremberg, the center of Nazism, was heavily bombed by the

British. The precise whereabouts of Adolf Hitler was not known, though some reports said he was living in the party headquarters in Berlin. It was estimated that some 75 percent of all structures in Berlin had been leveled and the refugees streamed out of the German capital by the thousands into Denmark and other surrounding countries. Berlin once housed over four million people; now it had housing for about five hundred thousand. There was water and electricity in a small section of the city that was still standing, but nowhere else. In one area there was a "plague wall" loaded with "corpses [that] have been rotting because it was found impossible to remove them."[90]

In Munich, nothing was working because nothing was standing. Germany once had 250 sizable towns, but most were debris now. According to the Associated Press, Germany as a nation was all but destroyed, except "the Nazi structure still holds together . . . terror of the Gestapo and concentration camps hold . . . elements in check just as stern discipline holds a great part of the German army that otherwise would long ago have been scattered."[91] The notion of foreigners being slaves—or worse—to Germans never seemed to bother the average citizen of the Third Reich. But now, with defeat all around the Fatherland, the thought surely occurred to the average German that they very well could be slaves to the rest of Europe, and it must have terrified them.

Other stories still appeared claiming that Hitler and the rest of the Nazi leadership were closeting themselves in the mountains around Berchtesgaden. "Swiss newspapers reaching London . . . said that Adolf Hitler had completed preparations for a last stand in the fortress of Berchtesgaden from which he hopes—after a twilight period following Allied victory—National Socialist Germany will emerge to dominate Europe. While there have been previous reports of a 'Bavarian fortress' to which leading Nazis will retreat, the new accounts brought about almost grotesque reports of underground jet plane factories, synthetic fuel plants embedded in mountain sides, huge stores of war materials and a vast system of defense."[92] The mountains were almost impregnable;

machine-gun nests were omnipresent where Hitler had made his home and where he had installed his private chancellery.

NOT EVERYTHING WAS TICKETY-BOO in the submarine construction service. In Boston, a worker accidentally opened the torpedo tube of a yet unnamed new sub, and it sank to the bottom of Boston Harbor, forty-five feet deep. The good news was, according to Gallup, a plurality of Americans did not foresee another war for twenty-five years. In Washington, a sixty-one-year-old man on trial for his sanity was declared sane and promptly went home to celebrate with his new bride, who was eighty-two years of age. "I have a reservation tomorrow night at the Willard hotel. We shall celebrate," he said.[93]

The whole matter of food was becoming more and more of an issue. In rival press conferences, FDR said one thing on Friday, March 23, about feeding the hungry of Europe, though Eleanor Roosevelt had said something else the previous day. Mrs. Roosevelt, in her press conference with "feminine reporters," took a hard line, saying that other countries needed to step it up. "I don't see why we should feed Europe. I think that there are a lot of other nations that can and should help," she said.[94] But the president said America "must tighten its belt to feed needy peoples of Europe." He went even further, saying that if Americans could "slash" consumption by 10 percent, it could go to feed the starving of Holland. He then moralized, saying, "[you] can't compromise with decency."[95] Then it was announced by the government that, for the foreseeable future, available meat to the public would be cut by 12 percent, the lowest point in ten years. Beef and pork would go down in availability, but mutton, veal, and lamb would be obtainable. The War Food Administration said it would cut available meat, overall, to 118 pounds per year, per adult. And Great Britain was scheduled to receive 25 million pounds of lend-lease meat from America.

Civic leaders made open appeals to citizens to grow more Victory gardens, ration meat, do without, or use coffee and butter substitutes. They were to forget canned vegetables since they were being shipped overseas. Of course, civil leaders were making constant appeals for blood donations. And, to make matters worse, the chairman of the War Production Board, J. A. Krug, told the International News Agency that America's "inexhaustible horn of plenty" was becoming exhausted. After years of depression and war, a reevaluation was necessary before too much food and resources were shipped out of the country, leaving the cabinet bare. But he seemed to be suggesting that the items Americans were asked to do less with—"meats, fats, oils and shoe leather as well as such basic materials as steel and lead[—were] among the items in which the bottom of the barrel has been reached."[96] However, rumors grew that in the devastated and now liberated countries, left in the wake of the German withdrawal and the Allied advance, all that was left was hunger, devastation, crime, and rape, as no credible government existed. Anarchy ruled many ravaged locales.

It was a testament to the durability and patience of the American people. War was swirling all around them. There was no escaping it. It was in the newspapers and the magazines. It was in the newsreels and the movies. It was in the scrap drives and the rationing and the drafts and the wounded and the dead and constant talk about the war and what people were doing about it. The culture of the peaceful and the culture of the war blended easily, seamlessly, so you read headlines such as "Joseph Gatins Weds Beauty After Nazi Prison Escape."[97] Other marriage announcements often mentioned the rank of the groom, such as Lt., Corp., Capt., or Seaman, as if it were the most natural thing. It wasn't unusual for the newly minted groom to get his orders to report for duty right after the marriage. Many honeymoons were delayed. Many honeymoons were never taken.

A goodly number of Americans expected their income to fall after the war. The conventional wisdom was that the war pulled America out of the Great Depression, but it was actually the passage of the Lend-Lease Act in March 1941, when substantial amounts of war matériel were sent to Great Britain to be consumed, that the country began to gradually rise out of the economic rut.

The "Little Flower," Fiorello La Guardia, mayor of New York City, defied the mandate from the Office of War Mobilization and Reconversion to close his city at midnight. The edict had been in place only a couple of weeks, but Hizzoner wanted it pushed back to 1:00 a.m. for New York. FDR went public with his displeasure and opposition over La Guardia's unilateral decision. So did the rest of the country, who denounced the "Little Flower" with glee. So did New York's nightspots, which moved their closing hours back to midnight. Billy Rose, an owner of a city hotspot, said, "My allegiance to my country goes beyond my allegiance to the Mayor."[98] One paper editorialized, "Even the avaricious operators of the most extortionate clip-joints would be hard-pressed to stomach the sight of civilians roistering after men in uniform, obeying wartime restrictions, had departed the fun spots."[99]

At great risk, four British destroyers, on a mission of mercy, snuck into an Arctic fjord and rescued 525 Norwegian women and children who had been hiding in cave after cave as they were chased by the Germans for three months. They'd survived on fish and reindeer meat. Still, the Germans would not give up. A shower of V-1 and V-2 rockets hit London and killed twelve civilians while injuring dozens. Despite the war and heavy losses, the Germans still managed to manufacture seven hundred V-2 rockets in 1945 alone. In return, British subs, operating in the Pacific, sunk over two hundred Japanese ships of all sizes.

The seeds of the "Red Scare" of the late 1940s and early 1950s may have been found in a March 1945 column by Westbook Pegler, which claimed, "Communists in the Army." Pegler had once won a Pulitzer for uncovering racketeering in labor unions, but he also often saw communists everywhere, and in later years, he was actually expelled from the John Birch Society for being too radical. In a long-winded column, he made a thirdhand accusation of communism in the US Army, writing, "The bold rise of political motivation has been a disturbing development in the Army. Lately, it has been decided that even the precautions against Communists in the commissioned ranks are to be relaxed."[100] Pegler was nothing if not influential and also erratic. He had once been friends with

FDR and Eleanor, but now they were considered enemies. Same with others who fell out of favor with Pegler.

IF POSSIBLE, THE ALLIED advance on Germany was moving even more quickly. It was announced that Russian tanks had traveled twenty-five miles in one day, and Patton's Third Army had moved fifteen miles in one day while capturing another eighty thousand "panic-stricken" German troops.[101] And an army of Norwegians, essentially an underground militia, had laid waste to German railroads, sabotaging them and "pinning down 200,000 German troops in Norway."[102]

The plot to kill Hitler in 1944 still continued to boil, and now, almost a year later, Heinrich Himmler was implicated in the conspiracy. The attempt on July 20 was led by the much-esteemed Colonel Count Claus von Stauffenberg, who was missing a leg and an arm he'd lost in the First World War. The mention in the American press of Himmler so late after the attempt, when his name had never shown up before, may have been a case of disinformation to cause discord in the German high command. The Allies knew the Nazis assiduously monitored the Western newspapers, especially the American papers.

BY LATE MARCH, JAPAN'S four largest cities were smoking holes in the ground, having been hit repeatedly with incendiary bombs. Tokyo, Osaka, Nagoya, and Kobe all had been ruined with thousands of civilians burned to death. One editorial took the measure of the whole ordeal and said,

> It is shocking to think of the thousands who must be burned to death when the incendiary bombs fall. That great areas of these residence sections are burned is unavoidable. The most perfect precision bombing of factories, communications and transportation cannot prevent spread of the flames. It is necessary, however, that the cities of Japan, are, one by one burned to black ash, that we can, and will, do. And with each city thus attacked, we remember the treachery of Pearl Harbor and

find calm satisfaction in the knowledge that the Japanese of one more city have learned there is a bill, which must be paid, for treachery, that retribution for such a deed is implacable.[103]

Three million people began streaming out of Tokyo as a result of the constant American bombing.

Another day, another pounding, this one on March 19. In the Pacific, US Vice Admiral Marc Mitscher led his fleet into waters close to Japan and obliterated much of what was left of the Japanese navy. All told, his armada destroyed 475 planes and more than 15 warships, including 2 light carriers, battleships, and merchant vessels. In 1945 alone, the American fleet had sunk 203 Japanese ships of all sizes and shapes and 603 planes. They had also damaged, by estimates, over 365 ships and 1,247 planes.

It may have been a disinformation ploy, but American newspapers reported that with every delay in the expected surrender of the Third Reich, German citizens would die of starvation each day. According to the *Atlanta Constitution*, "Allied military government officials have estimated, as a result of their study of civilian problems in the Rhineland, that each day from now on, that Hitler prolongs the war he automatically condemns at least 5,000 Germans to death by malnutrition in the immediate postwar period."[104] Everybody knew the end was coming, but when it came, America would first take care of the starving and destitute of Poland, France, Belgium, Holland, and other conquered countries. The German, Rumanian, and Italian people would be last, which meant they would get food and medicine last.

In late March, two major milestones were crossed. March 22 marked the thirtieth night in a row that Berlin had been bombed. Two days later, on March 24, an unbelievable ten thousand Allied planes attacked deep into the Reich. It was a scale of attack not seen since the thirteen thousand planes involved in the Normandy invasion.

Nazi leaders convened to escape Berlin, but not without trouble. The small group gathered at a railway station, waiting for cars heading out of town; also gathered were thousands of enraged local citizens, homeless, and destitute. It was reported that "the smartly uniformed leaders, who were the first to leave . . . Poland . . . as the Red Army approached, carried their luggage and were met by a fleet of motorcars. Their situation contrasted sharply with the misery of . . . refugees," and the civilians "spoke their minds. The crowd grew so threatening the party leaders became nervous and ordered the guards to fire into the air." The people "represented no rabble. Their attitudes represented the true feelings of the German nation and they had to be calmed."[105] As with all illicit governments, socialism was also corrupt, and the German people were finding out at last that there had always been two sets of rules: one for the party elites and another for the rest. There were none for some of the least fortunate—Jews, gypsies, and others not part of the Master Race. The German army was falling apart, and with that the "defeated German armies were swept into a state of disintegration . . . no one [was] safe in his home. Most German soldiers, after six years of army life, [had] no home to which to return."[106] Hitler was astonished that his armies had fared so poorly against the Russian army; he had devoted much to the West to fight the Americans and British, whom he viewed as superior soldiers.

Even now, at the last, Washington was wondering why the Soviets and Japan never engaged each other in the war. Hitler wanted Japan to attack Siberia early in the war, but Tokyo refused, even though they had the troops. And Russia had still not declared war on Japan, as the other Allies had. It was very "Leninist" for Stalin to have cooked up a private deal with the Japanese and very much in keeping with Japan's penchant for secrecy and duplicity (as with Pearl Harbor) to have participated in such a deal.

Foreign correspondents still based in Berlin were urged to evacuate quickly and continue their reporting from southern Germany. Meanwhile, the German editor of *Deutsche Aligemeine Zeitung*, Baron Ernest Ungern-Sternberg, was executed for publishing "peace pamphlets."[107]

Now, toward the war's end, Hitler lamented, "I have fallen victim to the biggest treason in history."[108] Hitler wasn't paranoid; at least not after he learned that 300 Third Army tanks had crossed the Rhine and General Montgomery's British army had taken 100,000 frightened and threadbare German soldiers captive. In the east, the Soviets had taken another 45,000 Germans prisoner.

Berlin was overrun with spies who moved from place to place; they were never in one place more than one night. They had to be careful, though, as the slightest misstep could expose them. Wrote one correspondent, "From the beginning I suspected that women were much more dangerous. Any woman's eye must have reacted strongly to his brandnew English underwear of excellent quality."[109]

IN WASHINGTON, PRESIDENT ROOSEVELT was the guest of the annual male-only White House Correspondents Dinner. Esteemed CBS reporter Bob Trout was the emcee for the evening, and it was laden with entertainment, including "comedian Jimmy Durante, Frank Sinatra," song and dance man Danny Kaye, and songstress and Broadway actress Fanny Brice, along with a couple of straight men: for Durante, Garry Moore, and for Brice, Danny Thomas. Also featured was blues singer Georgia Gibbs.[110] The hard and often boiled gentlemen of the press looked forward to this black-tie, off-the-record drinking fest each year. Dignitaries included Supreme Court justices, members of Congress, and top military and White House brass.

Buick had made few cars for four years now, but they were proud of the M-18 Hellcat tank, which scored impressively in battles. Buick was of course a division of General Motors, the sponsor of the "General Motors Symphony of the Air" each Sunday afternoon. Much of GM's advertising proudly stated: "The Army Navy 'G' flag proudly flies over all Buick plants."[111]

A new shortage was announced—this time, rubber. The FDR administration announced a new tsar for rubber: John L. Collyer, president of the BF Goodrich rubber company. He would try to figure out the mess involving imports, retreading, and synthetics, which had been going on, more or less, since the beginning of the war.

Londoners were at war in more ways than one. Churchill's choice of representatives to go to San Francisco for the organizing meeting of the United Nations was under severe criticism. Anthony Eden, Churchill's foreign minister, would lead the delegation, but this did not sit well with Clement Attlee, deputy prime minister and leader of the opposition; the Labor opposition was not happy with Churchill.

THE FINAL DRIVE FOR Berlin started on March 24. General Patton's Third Army finished crossing the Rhine in force with little opposition. "Patton's Rhine-conquering exploit followed one of the greatest armor and infantry thrusts in military history. . . . These successes [appeared] to be decisive blows against the Germans."[112]

Propaganda Minister Joseph Goebbels narrowly escaped an assassination attempt at his own air-raid shelter because, ironically, Allied bombing had prevented Goebbels from reaching the shelter. A bomb exploded, killing several Goebbels flunkies and destroying the underground structure.

Stories surfaced that the Nazis had depots full of vitamins for the next war. "Since 1943 special emissaries have gone abroad whenever possible and bought vitamin products to assure a proper diet for the children who will fight a future war," reported the Associated Press. They elaborated that the Nazis had also warehoused other strange items like the printing presses, saying, "Throughout the Reich, thousands of 'cells' of Nazis have been organized. Party workers are going, or are ready to go, into prison camps posing as anti-Nazis to undergo fake trials as enemies of the regime to win confidence of Allied circles—then to turn against the Allies."[113] This last sentence may have been a bit too fanciful.

THE BATTLE FOR OKINAWA was just beginning. American war planners could not foresee it, but it would be the last—and one of the bloodiest—of the Pacific war. One American carrier launched 230 planes and destroyed 731 Japanese planes in the air and one on the ground. "The fleet communique said naval fliers shot down 281 Japanese planes, destroyed 275 on the ground or damaged 175 others. . . . Earlier communiques listed 15 to 17 Japanese warships crippled in the Inland Sea." The Americans lost an escort aircraft carrier, but they jumped right back, hitting the main island from "battleships, carriers, B-29s."[114]

Another fourteen thousand Allied planes laid waste to the Third Reich. "This is the opening of the final round," said Air Chief Marshal Sir Arthur Tedder of the RAF.[115] This raid set another record for the number of planes and the number of bombs. "Heavy bombers, medium bombers, fighters, gliders, troop carriers and tactical planes filled the skies over the Reich, shooting down at least 68 German planes and plastering the Ruhr with bombs in support of the big Allied push across the Rhine. American and British planes threw an impenetrable air umbrella over the ground armies, blasted German troop concentrations, strongpoints, armor, gun positions, airfields, railroads and highways. They also bombed two big fuel refineries."[116]

General Eisenhower took to the airwaves to warn the German army, especially the Waffen SS, that treating Allied paratroopers as terrorists would be dealt with in the harshest terms. The story went that a secret Nazi memo "calling for the execution of Allied airborne troops" had fallen into Allied hands. But Eisenhower warned the enemy that "severe punishment would be dealt to any troops carrying out the order."[117] Again, this could have been disinformation, courtesy of the OSS or the MI6, the American and British top secret spy operations, respectively. The Allies were involved in a massive airdrop of troops.

British general Bernard Montgomery, 1st Viscount Montgomery of Alamein, dubbed "Monty" and "the Spartan General," and known for carrying a black umbrella, knew his enemy. He told all Allied troops to exercise extreme caution in dealing with the Germans, including German civilians. He "warned his invading troops against fraternizing with the enemy and said it was too soon to distinguish between good Germans and bad Germans."

In streets, houses, cafes, cinemas, etc., you must keep clear of Germans, man and woman, and child, unless you meet them in the course of duty. You must not walk with them, or shake hands, or visit their homes, or make them gifts, or take gifts from them. You must not play games with them, or share any social event with them. In short, you must not fraternize with them at all.[118]

Montgomery told his troops that Nazism permeated all aspects of German life and culture, right down to "children's schools and churches." He advised that, even as Allied troops were in Germany, Nazis were planning for the next war, and that it was up to the Allies to eradicate all forms of Nazism, "the dangerous elements in German life."[119]

General Bradley was also cautioning Allied troops, but against over-confidence. By this point, the German professional army seemed to have mostly melted away, as had the snows of late March in Northern Europe. "The spirit is something hard to believe. I saw guys returning from the front, cold, shivering and drenched. They were tired and uncomfortable. But they were happy. They are in on the kill now and they are not going to sleep until the race is finished," said one observer. Of the German defenses, the observer noted, "The Germans, hoping to stop this avalanche, are frantically putting in everything possible. They have sent convalescents to the front. They have hurled training companies, raw and unprepared into the battle in a desperate hope of plugging the dykes. But it's no use."[120]

Smoking kills. On Iwo Jima, a Japanese soldier took a break from war to take a drag. One too many as it turned out. Unbeknownst to him, a US marine caught wind or sight of him, raised his gun, and fired. Afterward, marine corporal Bill H. Bryant said, "Maybe I should have let him finish his cigarette."[121]

LUGGAGE STORES ACROSS AMERICA were hawking their own "Army Foot Lockers" by Samson. They were olive drab, large, and cheap, only $9.90, and "a wonderful convenience for all servicemen and women, and just the thing for students."[122] City fathers worried about the potential rise of juvenile delinquency once the war was over. The only boys who made the papers now, for the most part, were handsome Boy Scouts lugging newspapers for a wartime paper drive when the young men were not used by the government to hand out morale posters to bars, churches, and restaurants, including the iconic "Loose Lips Sink Ships."

Six thousand miles away, film heartthrob Clark Gable crashed his car against a tree in sunny and warm Los Angeles, slightly injuring his leg and chest. But he was hospitalized at Cedars of Lebanon medical center, just to be safe.

A NEW DIVISION JOINED the British in Italy to fight the remaining Germans. "The first and only completely Jewish brigade [was] operating with the British Eighth Army in Italy. Lt. General Mark W. Clark, Commander of the Allied ground forces, said that he 'was delighted' to have the Jewish outfit fighting under his command and pleased 'that the Jewish people, who have suffered so terribly at the hands of the Nazis, should now be represented by this frontline fighting force.'"[123] These men had their own terrible stories of families disappearing in the night and of Nazi brutalities, which explained why they wore the Star of David proudly on their uniforms. According to the Associated Press, "The brigade is a self-contained unit consisting of artillery, infantry, engineering, signal, transport, ordnance and medical units. The men were drawn from 35,000 volunteers and although it is estimated 1,000,000 Jewish soldiers are fighting on the Allied side, this outfit is the only group specifically designated as a Jewish unit."[124]

Winston Churchill, his whole life, wanted to be at the scene of a battle, and his long military service showed over and over his courage and physical prowess. But, as the British prime minister and one of the most important men in the world, and age seventy to boot, maybe he should have been more careful when he insisted on going to the front. He was nearly blown up by two German shells, which exploded only fifteen yards away. He crossed the northern Rhine but "showed as little concern over the incident as any youthful combat soldier. . . . He simply broke out with his well-known Churchillian smile and kept puffing away on his equally well-known cigar."[125]

THE FOOD SHORTAGE IN Berlin was getting intolerable. The system of rationing had broken down as party officials put themselves in line ahead of everyone else. "As a result, when the public lined up all the best things were gone."[126] An order was sent out to the populace not to plant any flowers. Only the growth of potatoes and other vegetables was permissible. To live meant to live underground as much as possible. Bridges were mostly out, as saboteurs had blown them up. There were rumors of Baltic-style "troikas"—cells in which three men would work together to one day advance Nazism again. Law enforcement had broken down completely. If a policeman stopped someone to ask for their papers, it was just as likely the officer would get a gun stuck in his face.

The situation in Berlin was dark and grim as of March 26. From the east, the Russians were but thirty-two miles away. In the west, the US Third Army was 235 miles away, the US First Army was 266 miles away, the US Ninth Army was 272 miles away, the British Second Army was 277 miles away, the US Seventh Army was 282 miles away, and the Italian front was 544 miles away. Maps showed giant arrows all pointed toward Berlin.[127]

One hundred and twenty-four German soldiers, all playing cards in the battle for the Rhine, decided to surrender after they were convinced that giving up was better than being wiped out. US tanks entered Frankfurt and Limburg. A radio broadcast called on German leaders to assume command, but apparently no one responded. Other headlines on March 27 cried, "RAF Smashes Nazi Convoys off Norway" and "Red Tanks Chase Nazis in Hungary."[128]

As word spread about the awful treatment of American POWs, some in America wondered if we were being too gentle with German, Italian, and Japanese POWs. The POWs America was holding got three squares and medical treatment, some got decent outdoor work, some got access to books, and none were tortured, according to the Geneva Conventions. The Allies abided by the Geneva Conventions while the Axis powers did not. It was one more example of why people believed we were the good guys and Germany, Japan, Rumania, and Italy were the bad guys. In fact, four captured German nurses did not want to be returned to their country as the rules of war prescribed. "If we go across the line, they will put us in a forward hospital and we will be captured again," they said.[129]

THE US SUBMARINE *ALBACORE* was long overdue and presumed lost at sea with a complement of sixty-five officers and men. It was first reported missing in late 1944 but was officially stricken from the naval register in March 1945. (USS *Albacore* was never found. As of 2020, fifty-two American submarines from World War II are still missing.)

More and more German civilians were speaking out against the Reich now that things were at an end, and they were homeless and hungry. Wrote one reporter, "A fat Nazi with a glistening big tear in his eye has just asked me to present his views to the American army authorities. . . . He thinks . . . this war is now getting way too rough. It is destroying lovely towns, ruining beautiful country estates (like his), smashing great business opportunities (also like his) and causing distressing hardships that are almost more than he can bear to see. Also, he thinks the American public ought to know that our American boys aren't being very polite to Germans."[130] The Allied troops seemed to be following the orders of General Montgomery.

Famed World War I British prime minister Lloyd George passed away quietly from influenza at age eighty-two in his four-hundred-year-old Welsh farmhouse with his second wife, Frances Stevenson, at his side. His first wife, Dame Margaret Lloyd George, had passed away in 1941, and in his dotage, he had married a woman twenty-five years his junior. She had for many years been his secretary.

Stephen Early, who'd been FDR's press secretary for years, was finally hanging up his hat to find work in the private sector. But first, the plan was for him to become Roosevelt's appointments secretary. Early was frank about his many years of public service: "I continued to serve until I went broke serving."[131]

THE INVASION OF BERLIN was being ably aided by the Autobahn, Hitler's specially designed superhighway to move German tanks and other mechanized machinery more efficiently. Now the Allies were using it to race into Berlin. "The great single and double lane highways he built in peace to shuttle his armies out from the heart of Germany to attack neighboring countries [were] proving his undoing."[132]

The Supreme Allied Commander Dwight D. Eisenhower went on radio again to proclaim the Nazis whipped, beaten, defeated, and crushed, although he expected them "to fight on wherever they can . . . and they may try either to hold their seaports or to make a final stand in the southern German Alps." There would be "some darn tough fighting before it's over," he said.

> I would say that the Germans as a military force on the Western Front are a whipped army. That does not mean a front cannot be formed somewhere where our maintenance is stretched to the limit, and their defensive means can better be brought to bear. The elimination of German troops west of the Rhine was one of the greatest victories of this or any other war. One day I shall be able to tell you that the organized resistance in Germany is broken. . . . This is my honest opinion. There will be no negotiated unconditional surrender. There will be an imposed unconditional surrender.[133]

A German soldier captured in Frankfurt told the Allied troops he was fifty-two years old. When asked, "What's a man your age doing in the army?" the reply came, "I'm a member of the Hitler Youth."[134]

The treatment of American wounded by the Germans came to light in late March when US Army members liberated a prison hospital in Heppenheim. What they found was "a living hell of starvation and filth—a factory of slow death for American prisoners of war." Almost three hundred Americans were freed, but after weeks of neglect and slow starvation, these formerly healthy and hearty GIs were little more than stick figures. Those who had not died from starvation or infection were "tearful walking skeletons, their arms and legs shriveled to the size of matchsticks. The ward where Americans were kept reeked of infection and festering wounds. Prisoners pulled back the thin blankets on their beds to show filthy gray and blood-stained sheets. So close were these boys to starvation that one was too weak to unwrap the paper around a candy bar."[135]

The Nazis were "sadistic" haters of Americans. "Downstairs in the storeroom . . . [were] dozens of International Red Cross packages. . . . The Americans said their daily food ration was one-tenth of a loaf of sawdust-filled bread, three marble-sized potatoes, a spot of margarine, a half-pint of meatless gravy and a dish of thin potato peeling soup."[136] As it turned out, the German warlords were monsters to everybody, just as the Japanese warlords were. In fact, the Japanese moved many of their POW camps closer to prime bombing targets, such as docks and factories, in direct contravention of the Geneva Conventions; but so too was starving and torturing and burning POWs alive.

Hitler ordered the destruction of two Graf Zeppelins. Whereas once these giant dirigibles served as propaganda vehicles of Nazi power, they now laid in smoke and ashes, just like everything else in Germany.

German broadcasters went on the air to proclaim that Hitler's grand scheme was over and to plead for mercy from the invading Allies: "The German people can be reproached for many things, but they would be as glad as you if the war were to come to an end soon."[137] In Europe, Allied forces gained thirty-three miles in one day as German soldiers were quitting by the bushel.

The State Department revealed that "the Allies have uncovered a Nazi plot to regain control of postwar Germany and strive anew for world domination through Fifth Column tactics. . . . The plans had been developed by Nazi party members, German industrialists and the German military."[138]

A new rumor swept Europe about a German "superweapon." A member of the Dutch underground told a fantastical story about how German scientists had developed a "new weapon, a tiny gadget which could be placed in a rocket bomb . . . launched with complete effectiveness against the continental United States."[139]

IN SOME WAYS, LIFE in America had not changed all that much. A man went into Saks Fifth Avenue, waved a gun, fired a few shots—hitting no one—and shouted, "Don't you know there's a war on?"

Somewhere in the Pacific, the beloved Ernie Pyle was aboard a mystery aircraft, bound for parts unknown. "There are moments when a voyage to war has much of the calm and repose of a pleasure cruise in peacetime," he wrote.[140] He'd been embedded with soldiers and sailors all over the globe, and millions avidly read his columns daily.

The war was not over, yet the Russians were already stirring up trouble. They had installed a puppet government in Poland and requested that the shadow regime be given a vote at the upcoming United Nations conference to be held in San Francisco, the city by the bay. The Russians expected the Americans and other Allies to be relieved with the request for one vote, since previously, they had asked for three votes on all matters.

Easter Sunday, April 1, was especially important in America in 1945. For the first time in years, America was seeing light at the end of the long tunnel of long depression and long war—but at a terrible cost.

CHAPTER 4

APRIL 1945

"President Roosevelt Is Dead;
Truman to Continue Policies;
9th Crosses Elbe, Nears Berlin"
New York Times

"Hitler Dead"
Stars and Stripes

"'Ike' Calls on Beaten Nazis to Quit"
Washington Post

War Mobilization and Reconversion director, James F. Byrnes, promised a return to a free-market economy as soon as the war was over. Byrnes, whose title was also "assistant president," sent a "cheering report on progress of the war" to President Franklin Roosevelt and the Congress.[1] "It looks as if it will be possible, after V-E Day, to make some increase in basic gasoline ration for private vehicles and in the allocation of gasoline in trucks," he wrote.[2] As it turned out, switching from a wartime economy to a peacetime economy was not like raising a shade. "Munitions production, though reduced, [would] still absorb a large proportion of . . . country's manpower and materials."[3] The question was, would the peacetime economy make the same demands on raw materials that the wartime economy did? The report pointed out that "45 percent of our total productive output in 1944 was for war. To obtain this proportion, essential civilian programs were reduced to a level which demands an even more delicate balancing of military needs against those requirements which must be met if we are not to impair our war effort."[4]

No one wanted the economy to slip back into a depression as a reward for winning the war. But literally everything would change. Contracts for military material would be canceled—everything from P-51s to M-1s, from food rations to GI boots, from tanks to shovels, from tents to transports, from howitzers to hamburgers, from uniforms to underwater gear, from cows to C-47s, from butter to boots. No more blackouts and brownouts, no more rationing, no more gas stamps and different numbered and colored food stamps. The government said by V-E Day, domestic gas supplies would instantly double. No more war posters, no more drafting of men for the army. The war was far from over, but Americans were looking forward to a day when they no longer worried about sons and husbands and fathers and grandsons and nephews dying in the deep blue waters of the Atlantic, in the jungles of some remote island in the Pacific, in a muddy foxhole in Europe, or in the skies over all the world. A multibillion-dollar war industry was about to be brought to a screeching halt, and Americans anticipated waking up to a new and hopefully peaceful world.

Except Hollywood. During the war, movies had been about war, sacrifice and bravery, love, lost love, found love. After the war, movies would be about war, sacrifice and bravery, love, lost love, found love. The message was terribly important as all told of a brighter future and the good guys triumphant over the bad. The era of dark film noir was several years off. For now, you could tell the good guys from the bad guys.

As it was, all the movies followed the exploits of the American fighting man in Europe, the Pacific, and the Philippines. But they were also fighting in Formosa, the China Sea, Borneo, Celebes, Moluccas, Lesser Sunda, New Guinea, Calcutta, and other various and sundry outposts to the world, which most Americans would have never heard of had their country not gone to war.

In four short years, adult Americans and their children became masters of world maps. The war culture had touched their lives in every way imaginable, from civil defense to the draft, from "Rosie the Riveter" to bombing rumors, from scrap drives to high drama and lowly people, from military parades to military funerals, from 4-F to "We regret to inform you . . ." The Second World War touched all facets of people's lives and deaths. It was the alpha and omega. The Second World War was, as Churchill said, "not the end. It is not even the beginning of the end. But it is, perhaps the end of the beginning."[5]

THE WAR TO TAKE "Big Negros Island" in the Philippines was still raging, but the British air schools in Ottawa were closing down, all 256 of them. They'd been a great success, churning out British and Canadian fighters to turn back the vaunted Luftwaffe; for the last three years, they had taken the fight directly to Germany with aerial combat and bombing campaigns. Prior to the war, the Germans had the greatest air force in the world. Now, the Americans and the British ruled the skies.

The battle for Okinawa had been raging for nine days in a row. American battleships and planes from carriers hit the main island of Ryukyu and, on April 1, American troops began landing ashore.

In Europe, General Dwight D. Eisenhower went on the radio once again, this time to tell the Germans "how" to surrender and "cease hostilities."[6] The New York Times wrote, "Nine Allied armies, including the United States Fifteenth Army and the French First Army surged deep into Germany in an irresistible surge of khaki soldiery tonight as Gen. Dwight D. Eisenhower broadcast a message to German units to cease hostilities."[7] He told the Germans they had lost control of vast swatches of the Fatherland, they had lost many soldiers, and their situation was hopeless. He then told the German soldiers to surrender now, under the protection of a white flag, and to no longer take orders from their superior officers.

The political leadership of Nazi Germany was not buying it. They told the German citizenry to help them root out Allied spies spreading disinformation among the remaining troops. "Hinting at guerilla action after the war, the German home radio asserted: 'The formal termination of the war will not be the end of it. We shall reconquer tomorrow what we had to give up today under pressure.' The broadcast declared that 'Eisenhower is trying to initiate us into the rotten civilization of the west and carry away our workers as slaves.'"[8]

Slaves—including Russians—were being freed from forced labor in German factories. There was also an armed uprising in Austria with citizens openly fighting the Gestapo. "Armed clashes between members of the Austrian resistance movement and the Gestapo are occurring in Vienna, Graz and other large cities and the resistance movement is steadily growing," the British radio said. The Austrian resistance was very well organized, with all ideologies and religions active participants. The resistance was "in favor of the punishment of war criminals, the expulsion of all Germans who migrated to Austria since the Anschluss and the re-establishment of the 1933 borders."[9]

Belgium had no sooner been liberated by Allied troops, when people there began to wonder when the Allies would leave. Conversely, they wanted to know when the Allies would get around to rebuilding Belgium. And they also blamed "the Allies for troubles of the country." They argued that "their country is a mess through no fault of their own and it is up to the British and Americans to restore it, since they alone possess the means of doing so."[10]

The Marshall Plan was months away, but Washington was stirring with the idea of "little war mobilization boards" to help rebuild war-torn Europe. According to the *New York Times*, "High civilian officials are considering a plan to establish 'little War Production boards' in each of Europe's devastated countries, designed to make the best of what is left of industrial resources there in order to make the Continent self-sustaining.

Many high United Nation diplomatic and economic officials are said to favor the plan."[11]

The equivalent of six armored divisions of British tanks had now traversed sixty-five miles since crossing the Rhine, while breaking the back of the Third Reich armies. British pilots reported seeing streams of surrendering German troops, many carrying white flags. The retreating Nazis were nothing if not nasty. As General George S. Patton's Third Army sprinted into Germany, "resistance from the thinly spread, badly disorganized German army [continued] to be sporadic, with some . . . units finding it difficult to make contact with the enemy." The "Fourth and Sixth Armored Divisions columns [were] moving so fast that their liaison officers had not returned at a late hour." They knocked out German tank units and scooped up more POWs. They also "overran a prison pen and liberated seventy American fliers. There was no immediate report on the fliers except that they were in good spirits." But that was not the end of the day or war dispatches for the 4th and 6th Armored Divisions. "It was learned that Germans had prepared poisoned food and explosive cigarettes which they [left] behind for [Allied] soldiers to pick up. Among the poisoned items were coffee, sugar and chocolate."[12]

All the bridges across the Rhine were jammed with trucks hauling munitions and other supplies. Before, when the Allied trucks returned, they were empty. Now, they were filled with German POWs. "The prisoner collecting points along the way have large signs outside requesting all empty trucks stop for a load," one reporter said, and "a large number of the trucks' drivers are Negros, who seem to take a great deal of delight in transporting these members of the 'Master Race.'"[13]

There were now more than one million Allied troops amassing east of the Rhine.

Since December, the Allies had captured 1,142,224 German prisoners of war. In many ways, the Soviet Union had borne the brunt of the European war, but American and British troops had captured nearly as many POWs as had the Russians, 552,261 to 589,963. All told, since the beginning of the war, the Allies—except Russia—had captured 1.8 million. And the Russians claimed to have lost 12 million men.[14]

In the month of March alone, the Allies flew 5,700 planes over Germany and dropped an astonishing 165,000 tons of bombs, from Austria to the Baltics. The *New York Times* reported, "Blitzkrieg rolled across Germany last week. The technique the Nazi first visited upon Europe was being returned tenfold on the Reich. Devastation by air, swift and daring penetration by tanks, feints and flanking drives, cutting of communications and spreading of confusion—these had once carried the Wehrmacht at lightning pace across Poland, France and the low countries. Last week, it was Germany that knew the disorganization of a broken front and a superior force raising havoc with communication."[15]

Within a few days, the Red Army was rolling into Austria.

A report from Paderborn read, "a battle of annihilation on the Western Front is under way with German troops. . . . They are fighting with everything they have—dug-in infantry with bazookas, self-propelled guns, tanks, mortars and artillery."[16]

The word everywhere was that Adolf Hitler was a dispirited man, first sullen, then ranting even as some Germans still said they would stand by their Führer.

> They are all agreed that Hitler, though a neurotic, broken man since the attempt to assassinate him last July, still is in the political saddle and is holding the Nazi system together. Two high Wehrmacht officers who [had] . . . received a decoration from Hitler last November: They said he looks "broken," talked of hardships and anguish and that he was suffering and sat through most of the audience. One member of the entourage said that the "Führer" was worried about his life, that he rarely travelled anywhere except from his bunker to the briefing room and that he was suffering from a persecution complex.[17]

Most German citizens thought the generals were keeping the war going, putting German soldiers in harm's way, as a means of protecting their own necks "for a few days or a few weeks longer." And many felt the propaganda minister, Joseph Goebbels, was often in charge of Nazi policy even as he was regarded as an "intellectual without character."[18] Goebbels often broadcast that the alliance between the Americans and the Russians would not hold, would fall apart at the last, and that would be Germany's saving grace. Goebbels's analysis was flawed, though. The Americans and the Russians hated each other, sure, but they hated the Germans even more. Meanwhile, since Germany had almost been bombed out of existence, Reich Marshal Hermann Goering, unbeknownst to the *Washington Post*, which had reported his suicide, was in high dungeon with Hitler and the German people. Goering had a colossal ego, a colossal appetite, and now was a colossal failure. Moving into the void was Goebbels.

Churchill was still in the combat zone, now walking among the ruins of a shattered bridge at Weasel, inside Germany.

What form of government would supplant the Nazi dictatorship after Hitler fell was on the minds of many diplomats and State Department functionaries. But of more interest was the story reported by the *Army and Navy Journal* of the surrender offer by General Field Marshal Karl von Rundstedt. However, according to the publication, he was removed from power before the offer could be seriously considered.

Paris was getting ready for a big patriotic parade celebrating France's role in defeating Nazi Germany.

AMERICAN BOYS HAD SCHOOL, chores, Boy Scouts, scrap drives, and poster distributions to keep them occupied, but they had not entirely left their childhood behind. Abraham & Straus was selling a model kit of a B-29 bomber for boys to build. It was made of balsa, had to be cut with a razor or X-ACTO knife, sanded, and then assembled. These models were difficult and took a long time to build but were a great companion on a rainy Saturday afternoon.

NEW REPORTS FROM OKINAWA were good for Americans. Seawalls had been battered as well as gun emplacements, bridges, and flight operation centers. Carrier-launched planes also demolished forty-six enemy planes and damaged another forty-odd planes.

In the Marshall Islands in the Western Pacific, 452 natives were saved from death at the hands of the Japanese by the Americans. The Associated Press reported, "The rescue started with receipt of a report that the Japanese were threatening to decapitate the entire group, apparently because food was running short and the Japanese knew their by-passed garrison had little chance of getting supplies from home."[19] The Maloelap islanders were rescued by a navy landing craft. The Marshall Islands had been taken by American forces a year earlier, but somehow this Japanese military base had been missed.

Mopping-up operations were still underway in Manila Bay, hard as it was to believe. On Easter Sunday, churches nationwide called for the donation of 150 million pounds of serviceable clothing to send to the poor of the world. The United National Clothing Collection's board included former president Herbert Hoover, First Lady Eleanor Roosevelt, Mrs. Wendell Willkie, and various other civil, religious, and political leaders. As with everything else, Americans opened their hearts and closets and drawers to donate the clothes.

The *New York Times* penned a beautiful editorial on Easter Sunday in a tribute to Christianity.

Down through the centuries to the grieving world of today comes the Easter promise of life victorious over death. The message is for all mankind, all races, all creeds. In simpler words, it affirms the universal law that "death is strong, but life is stronger," that evil is, in the final hour, powerless against good. In the Easter story, heard by millions today, Death has made the Sepulcher sure, as he thought, by sealing the stone and setting a watch. "Let there be no mistake," he said. "Let it be certain and clear to all doubters that I have triumphed." Yet, in the morning, at the rising sun, the stone was rolled away, the Tomb was empty. Life had defeated death. Surely the Risen One who is the symbol of that eternal truth would so speak to troubled mankind today. He said, "Because I live, ye shall live also."[20]

It concluded, "May our belief be true. May this Easter morn indeed be the beginning of a good new day, a day of hope and faith renewed, a day of light and peace and reconstruction of our stricken world."[21]

THE PROFESSIONAL INHERITOR ADOLPH Spreckels divorced his fourth wife, Emily. Spreckels was heir to a vast sugar fortune. They were married in August 1939. Her previous husband, Baron Maximillian von Romberg, had been killed in a plane crash one year earlier. Spreckels was about to be inducted into the army.

A new popular book *Shore Leave*, a hilarious novel about a navy fighter pilot, was out, as was *At His Side*, a nonfiction book about the Red Cross in World War II. Also hitting the stands was a love story *The Small Rain* by the famed novelist Madeleine L'Engle, and the polemic *Can Representative Government Do the Job?* by former government official Thomas K. Finletter.

If anything, toward the end of the war, political cartoons of the daily newspapers had become even harsher. Hitler was depicted as more despicable, more disheveled, viler, and mostly standing among the ruins of Germany, but sometimes he was shown riding the back of a spavin, beaten-down German soldier. The Japanese were drawn shorter, more slant-eyed, more mendacious, and with bigger glasses.

Eisenhower had several immediate goals to accomplish, including isolation of Germany, a connection with the Russian army, the taking of the ports in the Baltics, and reprieve in the Netherlands. The most important was nabbing the Nazi war criminals. There were thousands of such thugs, and in the melee of war it was possible for many to melt away and escape justice.

It is not only the surrender of Germany which the Allies must seek in coming weeks, but some plan must be evolved to catch hold of the chief Nazi criminals after surrender. This will be more difficult than it sounds. Germany will be in a state of confusion which can only be compared with that of Russia 1917, with hundreds of thousands of refugees moving from city to city. Millions of foreign workers, desperately anxious to get home, will be streaming toward the German frontiers. Under these circumstances, the escape from Germany of some Nazi leaders should not be too difficult, especially when it is remembered that the Nazis are the only ones left in the Reich who still have automobiles and gasoline.[22]

There was no need to alter tactics when it came to the Allies and Germany. The heaviest fighting left by the Nazis was probably going to involve the Third Army, but resistance was still being offered in northern Italy, Denmark, and Norway. Still, the tide was ebbing on the thousand-year Reich, 988 years early.

EVEN AS LATE AS early 1945, draft dodgers still posed a problem for the FBI. In the early days of the war, draft dodging was mostly committed by rural boys, who did not routinely get notified by their local draft board, or illiterate boys or boys whose notice got lost in the mail. "Most of these cases of misunderstanding or ignorance of the war were cleared up without difficulty to either the FBI or the evaders. . . . This type of violation still occurred in the backwoods areas." With the rare and real draft dodger, the FBI went into action. Toward the end of the war, with the countryside pretty well cleaned out of country boys who didn't stay down on the farm as essential workers, the FBI could focus on catching them. "As in the last war, the willful violators have resorted to all kinds of schemes, from shooting off a toe or a hand or adopting disguises for acquiring a criminal record." The FBI had handled 464,640 cases since 1940 and "reclaimed enough men for thirteen full divisions." All told, the sentences against all draft dodgers added up to 30,548 years in prison and "fines of $1,019,638."[23]

Epidemics spreading throughout the world were of great concern. Experts were calling for clean water, isolation, and safe food. In America, many grew worried about a downturn in the economy and widespread shortages, especially food. Some predicted a return to Great Depression levels of deprivation after the war.

On Easter morning, Okinawa took center stage. It was a short hop to mainland Japan, only a few hundred miles away, with two airfields, so the Japanese wanted to defend it and the Americans wanted to take it. It was a thin, eight-mile-long island surrounded by a series of tiny islands, all infested with Japanese soldiers. But the Americans met surprisingly light resistance when they waded ashore. "There was little or no resistance from Japanese defenders. . . . At the end of the first day's fighting, any marine regiment casualties could be counted on the fingers of two hands, and so could the total counted Japanese dead in the marine sector of the beachhead."[24] The marines and army were astonished. They expected another Iwo Jima. By the end of the first day, they had seized both airfields. The marines took the Yontan airfield on the north end of the island and the army forces took the Kadena Air Base on the southern portion. Both advanced inland rapidly. Americans had attacked in force; they employed 1,500 planes and 1,400 ships against an estimated force of sixty to eighty thousand Japanese troops. The invading forces over the next several days included the Twenty-Fourth Army Corps and the Third Amphibious Corps of the US Marines. So far, so good.

THE GERMAN ARMY QUIT the Netherlands, although there was no organized retreat. It was helter-skelter, a free for all, a pell-mell rush into chaos. They were in danger of encirclement by British general Montgomery and hence beat a hasty retreat back to Germany. They'd held the Netherlands for five years, but now it was slipping from their iron grip.

Two hundred Japanese civilians on the Kerama island group committed suicide rather than surrender to the Americans. They had bought in to the Japanese propaganda that death is better than the fate that awaits them at the hands of Americans. They had chosen all sorts of strange methods of killing themselves, including self-strangulation.

In New York City, eight hundred thousand Americans turned out to celebrate Easter Sunday and watch the Easter bonnet "burst once again into full glory along Fifth Avenue. Great clusters of flowers rode flamboyantly on feminine hands."[25] There was a joyous, almost carefree attitude to the crowd. They knew the war was coming to an end, and that added to the festive atmosphere. The skies were blue, nary a cloud, and the temperature was warm. "Religious fervor was stronger, too, because of the grim touch of the war during the last year. Last Easter, casualties stood at 162,282. In one year, they had multiplied by five, climbing to 872,862, and there were few who walked in the sun along the avenue yesterday who had not in some way felt" the devastating effects of the war.[26] Earlier that morning, thousands had gathered in front of Radio City Music Hall for a sunrise service. St. John Cathedral of the Divine in New York City was packed to overflowing.

In Rome, the pope led an open-air mass for thousands; some who showed up were in uniform—others in rags. The usual thousands of pigeons, who used to delight the tourists, were gone from St. Peter's piazza as, during the war, starving peasants caught them—and ate them. One year before, no one was in the piazza, as they were hiding from the Nazis.

Admiral Ernest Joseph King gave a long but heartfelt prayer for peace and victory at Arlington National Cemetery. "Grant, O Lord, the reward of Thy blessing to all those who have given their lives that our country dedicated to freedom, may stand," he said.[27] At another outdoor Easter celebration, Vice President Harry Truman led a crowd in prayer at the George Washington Memorial in Alexandria, Virginia.

IN PREPARATION FOR THE invasion of Japan, American soldiers exchanged their dollars for the American-printed Yen. The Allies needed Okinawa, which was approximately 472 miles from Nagasaki, the same as from Nashville to Kansas City. "Tokyo is 972 miles, as far as from Washington to New Orleans. Pearl Harbor, once considered an important 'forward area' is 4,646 miles to the rear, or as far as Berlin is from Juneau."[28] Okinawa was occupied by the Japanese, but residents were vilified by Japanese from the mainland. It took only a matter of hours for the marines to slice through the island to reach the other side.

"THE UNITED NATIONS WAR Crimes Commission announced . . . Adolf Hitler's name headed one of five lists of war criminals that it has compiled and that enemy governmental leaders would not be immune from prosecution for war crimes."[29] Another list was devoted to the Japanese suspects and their various war crimes. Also on the list were Italians, Albanians, Bulgarians, Hungarians, and Rumanians. Hitler's was the only name that appeared—so far; the other names were not made public so as not to warn the other criminals. The debate over how to treat heads of states—as common criminals or another class of criminal—was a subject hotly debated among commission members, as was whether they be tried by the War Crimes Commission or by the courts closest to the scene of their accused atrocities.

Two competing underground movements were operating in Berlin. One was an anti-Nazi, pro-Allied assemblage, while the other was a pro-Nazi, anti-Allied contingent. The Nazis were allowing no break with the directives of the high command. On April 2, "The Nazi party ordered every German . . . to stand his ground and 'do or die' against the Allies armies or be outlawed as a deserter."[30] All were ordered into the last-gasp fight—boys, girls, elderly men, everybody.

As the 6th Armored Division advanced, they liberated a POW camp in Ziegenhain filled with 1,277 American fliers who'd been imprisoned since the Battle of the Bulge. "They had lost from twenty-five to forty pounds a man in three and a half months of a semi-starvation diet. . . . Equally mistreated were other Nationals found in the barbed wire enclosure in an open field near Siegenhaim. . . . They included 2,000 British and Dominion troops, 1,000 Russians, 200 Poles and an assortment of Serbs, Slovaks, Moroccans, Belgians, Senegalese and South

American Negros."[31] The 6th Armored Division also freed about "900 Jewish women between the ages of 16 and 35 who had been imported by the Germans from Hungary as slave laborers for farms and factories."

The American POWs again had been treated like dirt by their German captors, put on meager rations of a half piece of bread each day. They'd been made to march through the mud and snow from Belgium to this filthy and squalid camp. Part of the trip included seven days in railroad cars without food or water. On the march, they sometimes came across German civilians who were particularly cruel, especially against the airmen; and the German women were, in a word, horrible. According to these returning fliers, "German women seemed much more bitter and violent toward captured American airmen. . . . The woman kept calling the American and British murderers." They claimed the fliers strafed women and children. "German fliers, they insisted, never attacked anything but military targets."[32]

Over and over, the columnists and reporters and newsreels warned Americans that, though the Germans were through, the Allies could not give up. And the Japanese still had to be licked. There could be no letdown yet. The *New York Times* reported, "The defeat of the German Armies in the west opens the final campaign to crush organized German resistance, but it also brings clearly into perspective one of the greatest problems this country has ever faced."[33] That problem was the malaise of victory: the fear that the forthcoming euphoria of victory in Europe would sap the will of the Allies to finish the fight in the Pacific.

Several days after sending FDR and the Congress the detailed report on the economy, James F. Byrnes, director of the Office of War Mobilization and Reconversion, tendered his resignation. FDR accepted it but asked that Byrnes stay on until a replacement could be found. The day after, several replacements were suggested, including Fred Vinson, a longtime Truman confidant. To replace Vinson at the Federal Loan Administration, it was suggested that Justice William O. Douglas resign from the Supreme Court. Vinson was later confirmed with a unanimous vote.

The German civilians—when not fighting over the scraps of food left behind by their own soldiers—had mixed attitudes about the Allies. Some were snarlers. "These were mostly members of the National Socialist Party—they are dyed in the wool Nazis whose systems are so choked with party poison that no amount of antidote will cleanse them." Others were ignorers. They treated Americans as "if they did not exist. They [acted] as if the American army was a third-rate road show for a one-night stand." Then there were wavers. They were young, had suffered under Nazism, and welcomed the Americans. But they were a distinct minority. Finally, there were smilers. They were the elderly people who had lost sons, lost houses, but were just glad the shelling appeared to be over.[34]

MANY ACTORS AND FAMOUS athletes served, and many saw actual combat, including former heavyweight champion Jack Dempsey, who was in the US Coast Guard in charge of physical fitness. But he had also made six dangerous landings in the Pacific along the way.

ON APRIL 4, THE LONG-DEBATED manpower bill finally went down in defeat by a 46 to 29 vote in the Senate, despite FDR's personal stamp of approval. FDR even went so far as to say that if the bill were not passed, it would make the "successful conduct even more difficult."[35] Eventually, the matter over "work or fight" was dead and a watered-down "powder puff" bill was considered instead.

Anticipation and friction were growing over the upcoming United Nations conference in San Francisco, scheduled for April 25, although all referred to it as a "parley"—headline writers, the Soviets, Eleanor Roosevelt, everybody. *Parley* was definitely the word of the week.

A POW camp was discovered; this one the worst of all, Stalag 9-B Wegscheide. According to the *New York Times*, "For the last four months, 6,500 Americans have been slowly starved to death there amid scenes of foulest degradation, which are virtually impossible to describe. Into a barbed-wire enclosure 400 square feet these 6,500 men were driven like cattle by German troops to spend four months awaiting slow death or liberation." For one prison barracks, there was but one spigot dribbling cold water. "The toilet was a hole in the floor. These had to serve 160 men who had no soap, no towels, only cold water."[36] The Germans routinely stole Red Cross packages; recreation was some dirty, dog-eared paperbacks and a dozen packs of filthy playing cards.

Yet another concentration camp was liberated by the 2nd Cavalry Regiment, this one with 6,500 Allied POWs. The usual stories of hardship and depravation grew even worse than imagined. Germans "overran an ammunition company manned by Negros and left behind unmistakable evidence of atrocities. Bodies were found side by side with a single shot through their heads, and it was later disclosed that several of the Negros had been forced by their guards to run across fields only to be shot down."[37] Later, the Germans took sixteen Allied nurses hostage and forced them to work in Nazi hospitals.

At a POW camp for captured Russians, if possible, it was even worse. One reporter wrote about the camp, "A war correspondent sees some grim sights. Not often among them, however, is that of men fighting one another frantically for a loaf of bread or scooping up raw flour from the ground and wolfing it down in handfuls." The Russians had been dying of starvation at a rate of twelve to fifteen a day. "They looked like ghosts."[38]

It was estimated there were two million Allied POWs at many camps throughout the Third Reich. "Above them in twelve towers that watched and warded them were two hundred German guards with machine guns."[39]

THE FIGHT ON OKINAWA was going better than expected, with opposition, so far, much lighter than normal. Marine flame throwers were flushing Japanese soldiers from their many caves, and then marine engineers sealed the caves, neutralizing them. The bigger problem seemed to be what to do with the thousands of civilians surrendering to US troops, mostly women and children, as most of the Japanese men had been conscripted

Unknown prisoner talks to ambulance driver Francis Smith of Morely, Iowa, about empty caskets and the horrors he and the other prisoners faced. *(Photo courtesy of Buchenwald and Mittelbau-Dora Memorials Foundation.)*

Germany right after an air raid on February 9, 1945. *(Photo courtesy of Buchenwald and Mittelbau-Dora Memorials Foundation.)*

After the arrival of liberated children and juvenile prisoners from the Buchenwald concentration camp at the Ecoui train station. *(Photo courtesy of Buchenwald and Mittelbau-Dora Memorials Foundation.)*

FDR speaking to the public via radio.

FDR in Warm Springs, Georgia.

FDR's funeral.

General Dwight D. Eisenhower, Allied supreme commander, listens while occupants of a former German concentration camp tell, through an interpreter, of atrocities committed by Germans operating the camp. *(Photo courtesy of Buchenwald and Mittelbau-Dora Memorials Foundation.)*

An inmate smoking a pipe holds a shrunken head that was found in the house of an SS doctor after the liberation. *(Photo courtesy of Buchenwald and Mittelbau-Dora Memorials Foundation.)*

FIRST ARMY SIGNAL SECTION WORLD WAR II
HINDENBERG KASERNEN, WEIMAR, GERMANY MAY 1945

Officers of the First Army Signal Section sit on benches in the grounds of a barracks for a group photo. *(Photo courtesy of Buchenwald and Mittelbau-Dora Memorials Foundation.)*

Tec 5 Levin, Pfc. Miles, and Pfc. Bienz, with the guide, look at a sign of one of the barracks of the political prisoners in the Buchenwald camp. *(Photo courtesy of Buchenwald and Mittelbau-Dora Memorials Foundation.)*

Three American soldiers in front of a pile of corpses in the courtyard of a crematorium. *(Photo courtesy of Buchenwald and Mittelbau-Dora Memorials Foundation.)*

View into three incinerators in the crematorium in which skeletal remains of prisoners who were not completely burned can be seen. *(Photo courtesy of Buchenwald and Mittelbau-Dora Memorials Foundation.)*

View of the camp fence of the Buchenwald satellite camp Magdeburg-POLTE. *(Photo courtesy of Buchenwald and Mittelbau-Dora Memorials Foundation.)*

USS *Missouri* (BB-63) about to be hit by a Japanese A6M Zero kamikaze while operating off Okinawa on April 11, 1945. The plane hit the ship's side below the main deck, causing minor damage and no casualties on board the battleship. A 40mm quad gun mount's crew is in action in the lower foreground. *(Collection of Fleet Admiral Chester W. Nimitz. NH 62696. Photo courtesy of Naval History and Heritage Command.)*

Six USS *Hancock* (CV-19) TBM bombers fly near Okinawa while supporting the invasion forces on April 4, 1945. *(National Archives photograph, 80-G-319244.)*

With the American flag flying over his head, Motor Machinist's Mate Robert Mooty, USN, ferries troops across the Rhine River at Oberwesel, Germany, in March 1945. *(National Archives and Records Administration, Still Pictures Division, College Park, MD, Record Group 119A, SC 204664.)*

African American soldier patrols German POWs.

Men playing cards under an aircraft in New Guinea. *(Photo courtesy of Museums Victoria.)*

Nurses from the Seventh Australian General Hospital marching. *(Photo courtesy of Museums Victoria.)*

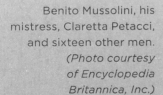

Benito Mussolini, his mistress, Claretta Petacci, and sixteen other men. *(Photo courtesy of Encyclopedia Britannica, Inc.)*

Soldiers embarking on a ship. *(Photo courtesy of Museums Victoria.)*

Generals Eisenhower, Patton, and other leaders during WWII.

Iconic "Kissing the War Goodbye" photo.

Allied military personnel in Paris celebrating the end of WWII.

Cologne Cathedral (German: Kölner Dom) stands unaffected even though Cologne, Germany, is shelled out from an air raid in 1945.

American B-17 over the raid on the Focke-Wulf factory.

American M36 tank destroyers during the Battle of the Bulge.

British troops coming ashore at the Gold Beach on D-Day.

Prime Minister Churchill, Premier Stalin, and President Roosevelt at the Yalta Conference.

German Luftwaffe Heinkel bombers during the Battle of Britain.

German machine gunner marching through the Ardennes in the Battle of the Bulge.

The German Reichstag
after its capture
by the Allies.

US flag over Mount
Suribachi in Iwo Jima.

US marine from the
2nd Battalion on Wana
Ridge in Okinawa.

USS *Bunker Hill* after being hit with kamikaze planes in Okinawa.

US Navy Douglas SBD Dauntless patrolling the skies.

USS *Yorktown* (CV-5) conducts aircraft operations in the Battle of the Coral Sea.

Alan M. Strock, 1943. *(Photo courtesy of Carl Strock.)*

Edward Shirley. *(Photo courtesy of Craig Shirley.)*

Edward Shirley. *(Photo courtesy of Craig Shirley.)*

Edward Shirley. *(Photo courtesy of Craig Shirley.)*

Barney Shirley.
(Photo courtesy of Craig Shirley.)

Ellsworth Abbott "Barney" Shirley, USN killed in action, January 20, 1945. *(Photo courtesy of Craig Shirley.)*

Ronnie Shirley.
(Photo courtesy of Craig Shirley.)

War poster by James Montgomery Flagg.

War poster. *(Photo courtesy of Schiffer Publishing.)*

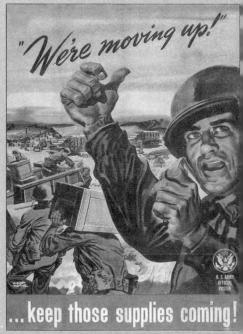

years earlier. Okinawa was an island paradise with lush vegetation but also serpent problems. Vegetables grew well on the island and these were needed for the large population of approximately four hundred thousand.

The popular, handsome, and dynamic Major General Maurice Rose was shot through the head by a German tankman and killed, just as he was surrendering his weapon. His loss was an especially heavy one as Rose was well regarded for his tactical skills and bravery, which was often observed at the scene of a battle.

PLANS WERE UNDERWAY TO create "propaganda" films for the German people detailing the horrors and atrocities of Nazism. Nothing would be held back. Charles Egan at the *New York Times* wrote, "Chief among the subjects for documentary films will be pictures bringing home to Germany the devastation and suffering that her armies caused in conquered areas. . . . Germany's sufferings are mild compared with the starvation and brutal treatment that people under German domination were compelled to undergo. The theme that Germany owes a debt to world society for bringing on a world war and for her behavior in the conflict will be carried throughout the films."[40]

But the Germans had other plans. They leafleted the Rhine with crude handbills promising to be back by May 1, while also vowing that anyone who cooperated with the Allies would be treated as traitors.

Other postwar plans were considered, including where to bury America's dead. Thus, the Congress appropriated an initial $122.9 million for seventy-nine cemeteries overseas. It was figured that about 5,335,500 graves were needed for deceased combat veterans and their spouses. If survivors wanted their dead boys brought home, 70 percent or more of the surviving family had to petition the War Department to do so. It was an odd formulation. New military-based cemeteries were also planned around the country.

The Russians forecast that the war would at least salve the ancient problems of the Slavs. "One of the marked political results of this war will be the liberation of all Slav people and the consolidation of Slav friendship in the struggle against Germany," said the Russian state newspaper *The Red Star*.[41] The paper also noted the gratefulness of the Polish and Czech people for being liberated from the Germans by the Russians.

The Poles and Czech people were saddened, however, when they learned the Nazis had pillaged, carried off, or destroyed virtually all of their libraries; indeed, nearly all the libraries of Europe had been destroyed by the Nazis and priceless works of art and historical manuscripts pilfered. "Hundreds of European libraries including some of the finest institutions of their kind have been devastated by the Nazis." Poland's libraries had been especially hard hit, but all were devastated. "A German commission systematically removed from Polish collections such valuable treasures as illuminated manuscripts, pictures, drawings, engravings and prints. Special files of newspapers and scientific journals were requisitioned and whole collections were carried away to Germany. In Czechoslovakia, the old textbooks have been destroyed and all mention of works by interned or martyred Czech authors have been suppressed."[42] In that country alone, it was estimated that 411 libraries had been sacked. Most of the libraries of Luxembourg, most of the libraries of Belgium, and anything deemed anti-German was destroyed. Kiev libraries were decimated.

The cost of war was measured in death and destruction and the pillaging of libraries, but also in dollars and cents. In March 1945 alone, the cost of war to the United States was $8 billion, though tax revenue brought in only $6 billion through corporation taxation and pay-as-you-go personal taxes or lump payments every March. The national debt grew to $235 billion.

Amphibious assaults by the Allies in Italy netted another two hundred German POWs. But things were moving apace for V-E Day celebrations in the British Isles. One news report said, "The victory atmosphere in Great Britain was strengthened tonight by the Government's announcement of its plans for a V-E celebration. The moment when Allied commanders declare that all organized resistance has ended, that day and the day following will be paid holidays for Government employees."[43]

A NEW AMERICAN INVENTION was for one-stop grocery shopping. The idea was a walk-up, modular dispensary for bread, milk, and breakfast cereals. Customers present tickets to a cashier, who puts them through a machine from dispensing racks in stock rooms through electric control. It was called an "Auto-serve."[44] Because fewer workers were involved, it was forecast that costs would be lower for the consumer.

A new book was about to be published by famed newspaperman and book author Merlo J. Pusey titled *Big Government: Can We Control It?* Another work of nonfiction was *The Nazis Go Underground* by Curt Reiss. The Ringling Brothers and Barnum & Bailey Circus was set to open in Madison Square Garden for an unprecedented forty-seven-day run, with some of the proceeds going toward the seventh war loan drive.

It had been noted that in spite of the war—or possibly because of it—the newspaper ads for 1945 for women's wardrobes, lingerie, sportswear, and furs all depicted slim, chic, stylish, and elegant women. Of course, the entire culture was of well-attired women and men.

American Airlines was offering service to Boston, every hour on the hour, from 7:00 a.m. to 3:45 a.m., almost all flights nonstop. TWA was bragging about its new "Stratoliner," which cost more than $400,000 per plane.

The New York Yankees had ruled major league baseball more or less for years, but one former Yankee, rookie Jack La Rocca, was more interested in second-story jobs than getting safely to second base. La Rocca was arrested for a holdup of a $12,500 payroll, along with several other accomplices.[45] Even so, manager Joe McCarthy was promising a good season for the Bronx Bombers.

Most second-rate movie theaters around America were playing *The Hasty Heart* starring Ronald Reagan and Patricia Neal. It was about a group of wounded American soldiers in a field hospital in Burma at the end of World War II.

The postwar debate had not ebbed. Admiral Ernest King, commander in chief of the fleet, said that America had to maintain its Pacific bases after the war. Already, a new defense and foreign policy was emerging for

America, something vastly different from the one after the last war. The same argument was being made for Europe as well. No one was saying the Russians would be our next enemy, but some were thinking it. As far as the domestic economy, some were forecasting a postwar recession and even a depression, but no one, including Bernard Baruch, an economic adviser to FDR, was peering into the future and predicting a half decade of prosperity. Baruch believed there would be more work than hands after the war. He called for the "deindustrialization" of Germany and Japan, though it seemed Allied bombers and naval ships were doing a fine job at that. Interestingly, he called for a "GI Bill of Rights" in which returning vets could get help reentering society.

THE BATTLE FOR OKINAWA was going well, and already American troops had seized a sizable portion of the island with few casualties. In fact, the initial reports said the fleas and malarial mosquitoes were a greater problem than Japanese troops. So were the three "poisonous varieties of serpents." By one estimate, snakebite deaths numbered more than a thousand a year per the civilian population. Biting fleas were also a problem as they could spread typhus. "All the invading troops underwent inoculations against typhus, cholera and plague before embarking." Despite the lush green foliage and scenic views, Okinawa was not a tropical paradise. "In addition to those diseases (typhus, cholera, plague) the islands inhabitants also suffered from tuberculosis, diphtheria and influenza outbreaks. . . . Mosquitos carried malaria and dengue fever. Hookworm [was] . . . rather frequent because of the natives' habit of going barefoot, while the island's population also included some lepers." And that just scratched the surface. The island also had "mites that [burrowed] into the skin, causing scrub typhus, which takes thousands of lives each year in the Orient. Medical officers were also worried about the prevalence of liver flukes in the salt and fresh waters."[46]

In addition to losing in the air, on the land, and on the sea, the Japanese military faced another problem: hara-kiri. The act, more commonly known as *seppuku*, was committed by thousands of Japanese military because they were losing to the Allies. The Japanese brass implored their troops to stop committing hara-kiri so they could be sent into battle to be killed by the Allies.

Hard as it was to believe, the battle for the Philippines was still being waged. The mopping up that General Douglas MacArthur sometimes referred to was taking longer than expected, but it was understandable. The Philippines comprised 7,641 islands, and the Japanese had established a foothold on many. It wasn't a matter of just one island but many, over 110,000 square miles. On these islands, a soldier could hide for years living off the land.

The *New York Times* was sometimes a good newspaper, but it all too often let its ideological naivete show, as in the case of a page-seven story on April 5, 1945: "Soviets Proclaim Peaceful Intent. Moscow, April 4—The Soviet Union has become the greatest progressive force in the international arena as a stronghold of friendship and the support of all the progressive forces of humanity. The Soviet Union does its best to lay down a stable foundation of peace and friendship with neighbor countries. But the Soviet Union does not hide its deep interest in the point that the neighboring countries must cease to be a corridor for aggressors. The policy of the Soviet Union concerning Poland, Czechoslovakia, Yugoslavia and Bulgaria demonstrates that the Soviet Union rests on a basis of friendship and alliance of and with the Slav States."[47] It was pure propaganda—a reprint of a story from *World Economy and World Policy*— but the *New York Times* printed it in its entirety without challenging one bit of the article; indeed, the paper lauded it and praised the so-called humanitarianism of the Soviets and how the Worker's Party, the "patriotic front," was assisting countries through the "Comintern" to gain their freedom. It was all balderdash.

Nazi high acolyte Arthur Greiser, the "Hangman of Poland," was captured by the Russians. Greiser was particularly hated by the Polish people because he would line up prisoners in chains, force them to dig their own graves, then order them shot in the back. This was repeated continuously.

The 4.5 million people of the Netherlands were starving. The average individual was getting only 350 to 500 calories a day, barely enough to subsist, so they supplemented their diets with tulips and rats. The Nazis had laid waste to everything in the Netherlands and to the Dutch people. Supreme Commander Eisenhower went to the airwaves again to hammer the German people into submission. He told them, "Cease working. Take refuge with your family in the safest place you can find. Factories, mines and rail centers are death traps. Act at once. Delay may mean death. Avoid at all costs being enrolled in the Volkssturm. Untrained and ill-armed, for you the Volksstrum will mean a last-minute death. As the Allied armies approach the areas in which you have taken refuge, follow carefully the instructions in radio and leaflets of the Allied High Command. After the arrival of the Allies, follow carefully the instructions of the Allied Military Government. . . . The end is not far off."[48]

That same day, American troops took the city of Kassel, where the Germans made many airplanes and tanks, without firing a shot. A British flier downed in Germany was on the run. He was hidden by a teenage German girl. They later escaped to Krakow, Poland, where they were married.

For years, the Germans had been working on "wonder weapons," and some in fact were developed, including the V-1 and the V-2, which were considered superior planes for a time; and also self-propelled bazookas, which one reporter said, "The projectile in this case is a pure rocket with its own propulsion charge and thus has considerably longer range. . . . The effects of . . . these projectiles against heavy armor can be considerable."[49] Other, darker rumors had circulated for several years that the Germans were conducting heavy water experiments to create an atomic bomb. Spanish radio broadcast an unshakable faith in the power of the Nazis' secret weapons, even at this date, saying, "Germany possesses secret weapons capable of putting 'a definite and victorious end to the war.'"[50]

BANKS IN AMERICA WERE cathedrals to the American free-enterprise system. Checking was free, printing your name on the checks was free, they often had no minimum balance requirement, and statements on all accounts were mailed every month. Some savings banks offered daily passbook accounts for as much as 7 percent, compounded quarterly.

Clorox had been telling consumers for years that it "Disinfects!" So "Why Take Chances? When it is Clorox-Clean . . . it's hygienically clean."[51]

Mrs. Roosevelt was as busy as ever. She committed a social faux pas when she wore a five-year-old blue, homespun dress to a Fashion Group Luncheon. But she wore that particular dress to make a point: women (and men) could stretch their clothing, and clothing dollar, by hanging on to still-good apparel. As always, Eleanor Roosevelt was a tireless trouper.

Oddly, Rabbi Nathan A. Perilman of Congregation Emanu-El of Chicago called for a postwar pluralistic world, just as there was talk about creating a Jewish state after the war. He attacked those "ministers of the house of Israel" who "preach nationalism for Israel." He accused them of hating isolationism and tribalism while pleading "with the world to guarantee their own tribal rights and their isolationist aims." He did say something profound: "Fascism, wherever it is found . . . leads to deification of the state and deification of the state leads to the desecration of God and the degradation of mankind." Cryptically and perhaps prophetically, he concluded, "The death, devastation, and destruction of millions of lives reveal that when with isolationism—which is repudiationism—we refuse to be our brother's keeper, we become our brother's killer."[52]

Vienna was falling out of Hitler's clutches into the arms of the invading Russians. Beautiful and palatial, Vienna was considered the "queen city" of Europe for its music and happy people, but it was also where Hitler had suffered his first frustration as a failed watercolorist. He had many a bad memory of Vienna, so it seemed natural that this was the first foreign capital he occupied. It was also symbolic for some Germans. Many believed Vienna had once been the capital of the "Holy Roman Empire of German Nationality" and had dominion over a large portion of humanity. Vienna's falling out of German clutches was especially symbolic, since bringing it and all of Austria under German control was the first step in creating the larger Reich. The British Second Army—the "desert rats"—was rolling now toward the German town of Bremen.

MONOGRAMMED SILK HANDKERCHIEFS COULD be purchased, six for $6 from the John Wanamaker Co. by calling STUYVESANT 9-4700. But some men's shoe stores were closed due to "war restrictions on the production of civilian shoes for men."[53]

Life in America was never normal, but some things did go on, like the circus. The Ringling Brothers and Barnum & Bailey Circus had come to the Madison Square Garden in a performance themed "Alice in Wonderland," and thousands of children and their parents thrilled to the flying trapeze, the clowns, the parade of elephants, the magicians, and other acts, including the Flying Wallendas. True to their word, proceeds of the ticket sales did go to the seventh war-bond drive.

A new batch of movies was released for the early spring: *A Tree Grows in Brooklyn, The Princess and the Pirate* starring the American treasure Bob Hope, *The Corn Is Green* starring Bette Davis, *The Life and Death of Colonel Blimp, G.I. Honeymoon*, and *God Is My Co-Pilot* written by ace Flying Tiger Robert Scott. Being held over for the eighth week was the chilling *Gaslight* starring Ingrid Bergman and Charles Boyer. For humor, Abbott and Costello and Laurel and Hardy debuted in new comedies, *Here Come the Co-Eds* and *Music Box*, respectively.

The army was studying a plan to train seventeen-year-olds for future military service in the Army Specialized Training Reserve Program: "Designed to give young men college training in order to enhance their value to the Army, the program provides instruction in mathematics, physics, English, history and geography. Credits received in these subjects may be transferred to any college at the end of the program."[54]

HANDSOME PICTURES OF FIVE-STAR admiral Chester W. Nimitz and five-star general Douglas MacArthur graced the front page of the *New York Times*. The picture showed MacArthur smoking his famous corncob pipe and Nimitz with an unlit cigarette. Nimitz looked happy, and why not? Both had been appointed by FDR and the Joint Chiefs as the absolute land and sea commanders for the invasion of Japan.

> The announcement, regarded here as the most important military command decision since the invasion command for Europe was organized, settles a number of issues of prime strategic importance. It means, in effect, that there will be no "Eisenhower"—or Supreme Commander—of the Pacific, but rather as an Army-Navy team, operating under the direction of the Joint Chiefs of Staff in Washington. General MacArthur, who fought his way back and defeated the Japanese roundly from Australia through the Philippines, will have a gigantic new command, including huge forces to be deployed from the European theatre after V-E Day. His five-star colleague, Admiral Nimitz, who has directed our victories in the Solomons, the Aleutians, the Marianas, Carolines . . . will continue as top Naval Commander.[55]

Eisenhower informed President Roosevelt that there would be no "clear-cut surrender" in Germany, in his opinion. There could be a popular uprising against the regime, he said, but that was unlikely and he was not counting on this eventuality. Eisenhower had written a letter to FDR detailing his best estimates based on intelligence and reports from the front. "In a letter written on March 31 and made public without comment by the White House . . . General Eisenhower said that if the present situation continued a VE-Day would be marked by an Allied proclamation rather than by a definite collapse of German resistance. This would mean, he explained, guerrilla warfare after the formal cessation of hostilities that would require our use of 'very large number of troops.'"[56]

Ike also believed Allied propaganda was continuing and working. German propaganda mills seemed to agree. The Schwarze Korps, directed by Gestapo overlord Heinrich Himmler, said bluntly that Germany is "only days or perhaps weeks from absolute collapse." The publication astonishingly elaborated, "In the remarkable situation of being forced to acknowledge it may be possible to defeat us militarily."[57]

The Soviets condemned their own neutrality accord with the Japanese, saying it no longer made sense. Yes, the Americans had carried the overwhelming majority of the fight against Tokyo, and now, at the brink of victory, the Russians wanted to share in the spoils, just as they were attempting to do so in Eastern Europe. They used the tissue-thin argument that "Japan, an ally of Germany, is helping the latter in her war against the USSR."[58] However, Japan had been an ally of Germany since the Tripartite Pact was signed in September 1940. The Soviets also made the fig-leaf argument that the situation had changed between the Japanese and the Russians in April 1941, when they signed their own deal. But this was four years later. One writer prudently wrote that it would be unwise to believe that more dramatic and decisive events must necessarily go along rapidly.

As always, the United States looked out for its own interests, but maybe naively thought the Russians also wanted a better world. However, Stalin just wanted more power for himself and frankly didn't even care about his own country, as demonstrated by the untold millions of Russians he'd brutally murdered in the last decade. The newspapers were filled with the news of the breakup between the Russians and the Japanese. Some foresaw a quicker end to the Pacific conflagration.

The battle for Okinawa had taken a tougher turn as the marines headed for the center of the island and resistance stiffened. Initial reports said 175 marines and army troops had been killed, with 798 wounded.

Most saw the Japanese defense of Okinawa as futile. Also, it appeared that Japan was running out of experienced pilots. "Incidentally, the possible use of green pilots by the Japanese in haphazard raids on our giant fleet here could account for their relative ineffectiveness," wrote one reporter.[59] Overall, the Japanese defense of Okinawa appeared as if it was scraping the bottom of the barrel, using inexperienced leadership, underperforming equipment, and unproven troops. "Instead of relying on tested military devices, the Japanese [were] acting like a football team with nothing but trick plays and with a line too light to protect the back-field while it is getting plays underway. The best example of this was the mosquito fleet of torpedo boats based in the Kerama Islands, seventeen miles away, for the defense of Okinawa. They could not or did not defend the base from which the torpedo boat attack could have been launched, and their whole plan went awry."[60]

All in all, it was another bad month for Japan. Everybody knew Okinawa was a prime area for the Allies to launch a final invasion of the mainland. "American strategists, for some time had attached great value to the island, but responsible military men who have visited green, neatly terraced Okinawa since the invasion [were] more enthusiastic than ever." It would be, for Admiral Nimitz, one of the greatest prizes of the Pacific, a base for advanced operations for the "concluding stages of the war against Japan."[61]

A contingent of maimed GIs who fought at Iwo Jima were shipped back to the United States, stopping off in San Francisco. For the most part, they were happy, even jubilant, incessantly talking about wives, girlfriends, and beer. One told of getting a letter from his wife. In the letter, she said she had a dream he had injured his right side. Indeed, a Japanese mortar had ripped off his right arm, three days after the letter had been dated and sent. The other patients, amputees, had similar stories involving their mothers.

Another told of getting home to his small town in Texas and sitting in his local favorite gin mill and ordering beer after beer. "There's a nice cool bar back home. I'll get back there and I'll stand in my old place and I'll say 'Start puttin' the beers up here, two at a time,'" he said.[62]

"The wounded from Iwo Island and from other Pacific islands were high-spirited as the huge Navy transport, divided into immaculate wards, bore them swiftly Stateside on smooth waters. They ate with zest, exchanged earthy banter, gorged themselves on ice cream, chocolate and soft drinks from the ship's store and told one and another, over and over again, what they would do to cold American beer when they got home." They were in bunks and some put pictures of girlfriends, wives, and children in the springs of the bed above them and "stared at them for hours, anticipating the moment of reunion." One injured GI said he was not going to let his wife know he was stateside: "I'll just walk in on her."[63]

The Republic Aviation Corporation had developed a newer, faster P-47 Thunderbolt, a feared fighter/bomber, this one with a range of two thousand miles and a top speed of 450 miles per hour. It was hard to imagine that just four years earlier America's air forces consisted of open cockpit biplanes that lumbered along at around one hundred miles per hour.

A Japanese American woman joined the US Army as a nurse, and it made all the newspapers. According to one news report, "Second Lieut. Masako Mary Yamada, 31 years old, just five feet tall told . . . how she applied for military duty two years ago, finally obtaining a release from her job . . . fattened up on rice to meet the weight requirements and was sworn in on Good Friday. She has asked for overseas duty." Miss Yamada's mother was in a "relocation center near Cody, Wyoming, where she was evacuated from Los Angeles in 1942," but she finally got "permission to leave." Her father had passed away but told his daughter to always be proud to be "an American citizen."[64]

Henry Stimson, the much-esteemed secretary of war, reported the newest American casualty figures. As of April 1945, America had suffered 892,900 casualties, with the army suffering the biggest toll: 798,383, including 156,472 killed in action, 486,929 wounded, 88,755 missing, and 66,228 POWs. For the navy, it was 36,649 killed in action, 42,988 wounded, 10,623 missing in action, and 4,266 taken prisoner. Japanese casualties were estimated by Stimson to be more than 300,000, but nobody knew for sure. It was estimated that the ratio of American deaths to Japanese deaths was 23:1.

Nazi Germany had sustained "staggering losses" in the last two weeks. Some numbered it over three hundred thousand in POWs alone, and believed the Germans had been so badly bled that they could not even mount an effective "continuous defense line of any strength." General Omar Bradley was now commanding the First, Third, Ninth, and

Fifteenth, "the largest field command in American history." And "Field Marshal Albert Kesselring threw what was left of the Luftwaffe . . . in a vain effort to delay Allied tank thrusts. The Germans lost heavily in the air and even more heavily on the ground."[65] Shortly thereafter, Bradley received his fourth star.

While the Allies were killing Germans in the battlefield deliberately, a boxcar full of German POWs died inadvertently. "An undisclosed number of German prisoners of war suffocated in the course of a rail journey from the American front to prisoner of war camps. . . . The incident occurred in the American Zone, while the prisoners were in the custody of United States troops."[66] Somehow the ventilation system on the new American-style boxcars was insufficient, but no one knew about it. The number of dead Germans was not reported at the time.

Immediately upon learning of the incident, General Eisenhower ordered an investigation by the Inspector General's Office of the European theater, and he also notified the German high command. It was not yet clear how many Germans had died or who was responsible or what punishment would be meted out. But the last thing Eisenhower wanted was to hand the Germans one last propaganda tool, so he made every effort to notify their leadership (the Ober Kommando of the Wehrmacht), and while he did not apologize, he did want to get to the bottom of the matter and punish those responsible.

The Americans had prided themselves on how well they treated their prisoners, by the lights of the Geneva Conventions, as opposed to the Japanese or Germans and even their allies. According to the deputy chief of the Prisoner of War Division, of the 930,000 prisoners, fewer than 1,500 died in captivity. Meanwhile, "Nineteen special prisoner enclosures [were] jammed . . . as a result of the rapid increase in the number of prisoners taken. About 75,000 Germans have reached these cages in the last three days and 190,000 in the last ten days."[67] As a result, the American Provost Marshal of the American forces now commanded more German troops than did Albert Kesselring in the field. According to the *New York Times*, "Nineteen American enclosures on the Continent now hold 725,000 prisoners. Of this number, 225,000 are in labor battalions, 350,000 in static enclosures, 25,000 in hospitals, and 125,000 in transit. There are 700 women prisoners, most of them nurses. About 100,000 prisoners taken by the American army have been sent to England while another 100,000 have gone to the United States and many thousands are scheduled to go soon, many of them in Liberty ships."[68]

Americans futilely hoped that if they treated their German POWs well, the Germans in turn would treat American POWs well.

The British had captured one thousand German POWs near Lengerich, Germany, and double-timed them, humiliated, through the streets for the civilians to see. German citizens did not like to see the once-honored representatives of the Master Race now treated as human chattel, and some wept. A captured German officer was blunt in his assessment of his own people. He said the German people were lost in romanticism and "there will be no capitulation—you will have to occupy every town in Germany" in order to win the war. He said the fact that all manufacturing plants had been destroyed was of little consequence to the German people. However, their love affair with Hitler, his thugs, and Nazism was over. "Many people feel they made an enormous mistake in following Hitlerism," he said, because under the Third Reich, "life doesn't mean a thing. You are shot right away or hanged. The organization surpassed imagination. I wonder myself that I am living."[69]

Newspapers reported amplifying details of the assassination attempt on Propaganda Minister Joseph Goebbels. He was injured but escaped, and the whole story was garbled among another story that an assassination attempt on Reich Marshal Hermann Goering had transpired.

Patton's Third Army passed Nuremberg's "site of the great Nazi party rallies." It was reported that some new German jets made "isolated attacks," but not enough to stop the Allied surge.[70]

FUNK AND WAGNALL'S WAS offering their annual famous *Standard Dictionary* and promised to improve the dialect of a daily vocabulary peppered in 1945, with "dame" (a good-looking woman), "jive bomber" (a good dancer), "cut a rug" (dancing), "What's buzzin', cousin?" (How are you?), "killer-diller" (something amazing), "chrome dome" (a bald man), "Snap your cap!" (get angry), "armored heifer" (a can of milk), "take a powder" (to leave), "now you're on the trolley" (now you get it), and "hi-de-ho" (hello).

Pravda went out of its way to condemn former president Herbert Hoover, "a leading figure in the Republican Party," as "an enemy of the Soviet Union."[71] Hoover had simply raised some concerns about the upcoming United Nations conference in San Francisco. The pressure was building on the "parley" in San Francisco, and some warned of a dark future for mankind if this organizational meeting of the United Nations failed. Up for discussion, besides the fate of the world, was how many votes the Soviet Union would get, the creation of a Jewish state, the war crimes tribunals, feeding the hungry of the world, the dispersal of postwar shipping problems, the future of aviation, world currency, a children's bureau, and a thousand other things, that's all.

It took massive government programs to defeat the Axis powers, so it stood to reason it would take massive, maybe even global, government to solve the problems of the world. It was suggested that the children's bureau undertake a massive educational effort for the "revamping of the education" of children who had been subjected to totalitarianism "to make it safe for other children to live in the world with them."[72] To try to bring the American position into focus, it was announced that the dean of American anti-communism, John Foster Dulles, would oversee things in San Francisco at the United Nations conference.

George Santayana, eighty-two, was awarded the Nicholas Murray Butler Gold Medal for "distinguished contributions to philosophy or educational theory, practice, or administration." It was awarded only once every five years. He was given the award for the book *The Realm of Being*, which was "a systemic exposition of metaphysics."[73] Santayana was thought to have once coined the phrase "Those who cannot remember the past are doomed to repeat it," but over the years it had become so distorted that no one was ever sure of the original phraseology. The meaning, however, was still well taken. One thing was for sure, though: Santayana must have been a genius, because he gave up teaching philosophy at Harvard.

Lieutenant General George S. Patton Jr. was a busy man. In command of the American Third Army, he was leading thousands of men and hundreds of tanks over many miles on the way to Berlin while contending with the Nazis, the weather, and his running feud with the British general Montgomery. But he still found time to write this letter to the father of one of the troops under his command. It was sent from the "Headquarters, Third United States Army, Office of the Commanding General, A.P.O. 403, 19 March 1945."

My Dear Mr. Schwartz:

Your son, Pfc. Seymour Schwartz, was a member of the Medical Detachment of the 302d Infantry and was killed on Feb. 9, 1945, when he with another soldier went to the assistance of some wounded comrades who were lying in a minefield.

While these two heroic medical detachment men were attempting to evacuate the wounded out of the minefield, they both stepped on mines and were instantly killed. Owing to the fact that it was impossible to recover the body until the minefield was cleared, it was impossible to bury him until Feb. 16. He was then interred with full military honors in the military cemetery in Hamm, Luxembourg, in Grave No. 20, Row 1, Plot F.

In the Bible it says, "Greater love than this no man hath that he lay down his life for his friends." I believe you should take great pride in the fact that your heroic boy did exactly that. For myself, I have more sympathy and sorrow for you who must continue to live than I have for this gallant soldier who did more than his full duty.

With renewed expressions of sympathy, I am

Most sincerely,

G.S. Patton, Jr.[74]

President Roosevelt was also a busy man, but he took the time to write a letter to the spiritual leader of the Congregation Emanu-El, Rabbi Samuel H. Goldenson. FDR said that religion was needed more than ever to bring unity to America.

> The gravity of the times which mark the . . . anniversary of the establishment of congregation Emanu-El, quickens the hearts and souls of thinking men and women an appreciation of their dependence on the strength that can be found only in the everlasting reality of religion.
>
> It seems, therefore, fitting that I should again declare that no greater thing could come to our land today than a revival of the spirit of religion . . . a revival that would stir the hearts of men and women of all faiths to a reassertion of their belief in God. . . . The great majority of Americans find religious unity in a common Biblical heritage— the heritage of the Old Testament. Whether our allegiance is to the tenets of Christian revelation or to the ancient teaching of Israel, we all hold to the inspiration of the Old Testament and accept the Ten Commandments as the fundamental law of God.
>
> It is well, for us, therefore, in the face of global war and world upheaval, to emphasize the many essential things in which we, as a nation, can find unity as we seek solution of the momentous problems before us.
>
> Franklin D. Roosevelt[75]

IN THIS MOST TERRIBLE of times—from the rise of Adolf Hitler and even before with the rise of Joseph Stalin—the more men extinguished other men, women, and children, the more good men turned to God and asked his help in stopping evil. The Second World War was not later called "The Good War" for nothing. We, the Allies—Britain, America, Canada, Australia, and others—were good. They, the Axis—Germany, Japan, and Italy—were bad. There was but one task: good must destroy evil. Hence, only unconditional surrender was acceptable. FDR, Churchill, and the leaders in the field would not negotiate with evil. Everybody saw the war as a struggle between the principled and the unprincipled. There was no moral equivalence, and anybody who was stupid enough to suggest it would have been shunned or worse, and deservedly so. All one had to say was "Remember Pearl Harbor!" and the argument would have been over.

A letter to the New York Police commissioner revealed that two cops in Harlem—who did not know each other as police officers—ended up in the same foxhole in Iwo Jima, both marines, both later wounded. While under Japanese assault, they got to talking and discovered they were both from New York, both cops, both walking adjacent beats.

The annual Jefferson Dinner was approaching for the Democratic Party, and the plan was for the president to address 350 dinners nationwide via "the major networks."[76] The dinners were being held to raise money, but at the main dinner in Washington, FDR would not be in attendance.

The US Navy decided to halt all "all-star athletic teams" in the United States and put the importance on games in the various war zones for morale purposes. Two cigarette dealers were put on trial for selling smokes for "excessive prices."[77] The problem was finding an impartial jury since five were smokers and prejudiced against cigarette dealers, while two jurists were prejudiced against the Office of Price Administration, the government agency that regulated cigarette prices.

THE GERMAN VILLAGES OF Niedermeiser, Herten, Meimbressen, and Weimar all surrendered to American forces by telephone. A First Army colonel spoke of how he called the Bürgermeister for each town and told them the Americans were coming through "and we were ready to accept his surrender." The Bürgermeisters "knew the villages would be destroyed if German troops made a fight, so they gave up to us." The Americans, in this manner, "picked up 300 to 400 prisoners a day" and "fifty to seventy-five former soldiers who had put on civilian clothes" but were now surrendering.[78] In the same vein, three German fliers of Junkers twin-engine planes defected to Madrid and Lisbon. One landed and said to authorities, "We have fled because we are tired of fighting."[79] They casually lit cigarettes of English origin and then ripped off the Luftwaffe insignias and tramped on them.

Four-star general Omar Bradley raised the American flag over a German fortress across the Rhine and was frank in his assessment: "This time we shall leave the German people with no illusions about who won the war—and no legends about who lost the war. They will know that the brutal Nazi creed they adopted has led them ingloriously to total defeat."[80] The flag Bradley raised was the very same American flag raised by US forces at the very same site in World War I. Washington had sent this flag just for this occasion. According to the Associated Press, "The war is not over—but victory is assured. After the defeat of Germany, the struggle with Japan will continue to the same inevitable ending. Until German pride in conquest is mangled beneath our tanks, we shall not find peace."[81]

In two weeks after crossing the Rhine, the Germans lost eighteen thousand square miles of terrain, and the Allies captured over 309,000 German troops. Much of the straggling German army was still at large but on the run, waiting for orders.

The last vestiges of German resistance were scattered and disorganized, often descending into guerrilla action. Berlin radio claimed the Nazi army was going through a "reorganization."[82] And in the east, the Russians were now surprised at the lack of German resistance. It was also reported in the Moscow newspapers that there was gloom in Tokyo since the American landing on Okinawa.

According to the Associated Press, only one marine, Rene A. Gagnon of Manchester, New Hampshire, survived the planting of the American flag on Mount Suribachi on Iwo Jima. "There are six men in the historic photo—five marines and one Navy hospital corpsman."[83] It was later announced that many more marines would have died at Iwo Jima had it not been for the massive shipment of whole blood to the island by the Red Cross: "The Marine Corps death total of 4,189 on Iwo Jima would have been doubled. . . . About one-quarter of the 15,308 wounded were saved from death by the 14,000 pints of blood donated at home."[84] Almost half of the blood used during the battle was right there on the island as the battle ensued. Much of the blood had been donated by civilians just one week before.

As Iwo Jima was now settled, out came the souvenir hunters. Soldiers and sailors picked from among the remains any interesting enemy items to send or take home.

Since the announcement of the Soviets' withdrawal of their peace pact with Japan, the world press had all breathlessly reported on it, except in America, where the Office of Censorship "blocked the transmission from this country of congressional and editorial comment on Russia's denunciation of her neutrality treaty with Japan."[85] But the story got out anyway since it was reported in the overseas press, which eventually made its way to America. The censorship office later said there was "danger" and that responsible parties should "weigh the consequences" of releasing the story. But the government censors never elaborated on what the exact danger was. Even more odd was that neither the British, the Canadian, nor the Moscow governments issued an edict against reporting on this important development in the war. The British office, when asked about censoring the story, dryly said, "I can't see why."[86]

All told, the American forces had destroyed 1,212 Japanese airplanes on the ground and in the air in just nineteen days. "In the same nineteen-day period, 244 Japanese ships—including many small craft—were sunk, forty-three probably sunk and 206 damaged."[87] A day later, on April 8, navy fliers sunk the ship *Yamato*—which weighed 45,000 tons, according to the *New York Times*—the biggest battlewagon the Japanese had ever splashed.[88] The loss of the *Yamato* dealt a severe blow to Japan's morale. For thirty minutes, American fighters tore holes in the deck of the giant battleship before it slowly slipped beneath the waves.

Another six Japanese ships were sunk and hundreds more enemy planes were reportedly shot down, but the Americans did not escape unscathed as they suffered the loss of several ships, including three destroyers and, possibly, a battleship or a carrier. Still, it was estimated by American military experts that the remaining Japanese navy was cut by one-fourth.

Another news report said two B-29 attacks destroyed another 173 Japanese planes. The bombers were escorted by P-51 Mustangs, made by North American Aviation, the toughest and best pursuit plane in the sky now, with a top speed of 440 miles per hour.

The controversy over the auction of surplus military equipment continued, and so did the complaints. The army was putting up used training planes in public sales, and planes that cost $10,000 to $15,000 to build were being sold for as little as $875 to private citizens. The Reconstruction Finance Corporation, a government-sanctioned organization, was selling up to three thousand surplus trainers, including Boeing "Kaydets" and Fairchild "Cornells."[89] The plan for decommissioned bombers and fighters was not yet set, but a decision was made that they would not be auctioned off to the public. Some would be sold or given to friendly countries to help create their own air force, while others would end up in storage, some in the "Boneyard" in Tucson, Arizona, which was becoming a repository for out-of-date aircraft.

THE GROSS ESTATE OF deceased New York baseball great Lou Gehrig was assessed at a mere $171,251, including a $100,000 life insurance policy, with the bulk going to his widow, Eleanor Twitchell Gehrig. But according to the appraiser,

> The trophies that were presented him in happier days seemed to have lost their glamour and value in the schedules of the inventory. The trophy with an eagle on top of a baseball that was presented at his farewell game on July 4, 1939, in the presence of Babe Ruth, his roommate Bill Dickey, Earle Combs, Bob Shawkey, Wally Pipps, Tony Lazzeri, Waite Hoyt, George Pipgras, Herb Pennock, Manager Joe McCarthy and more than 61,000 baseball fans was valued at $5.00. Another trophy awarded for his being the most valuable American League player and which was used after his death to bring in millions of dollars for war

bonds and charitable funds by selling it for a brief space of time to donors of the funds was appraised at $1.[90]

Gehrig set a record by playing in 2,130 consecutive games. The record was considered so unassailable, it was believed no one would ever break it. Gehrig died in 1941.

Six union members were expelled when they engaged in their own work slowdown at a munitions plant. They were also fined and the proceeds turned over to Navy Relief. Store inventories showed a 4 percent decline for 1945, which meant consumption was up, which meant America might now go through a postwar recession after all, especially as sales were up 15 percent.

THE ALLIES MADE AN astonishing discovery in Merkers, Germany. A giant stash of gold—one hundred tons—and cash was found hidden in a German salt mine. "The subterranean vaults contained approximately 100 tons of gold bullion; $2,000,000 in American currency, 1,000,000 francs in French currency, 110,000 [pounds] in British currency, 4,000,000 Norwegian crowns and lesser amounts in other currencies."[91]

As MPs were walking with two German women who had been looking for a midwife for a pregnant friend, they passed a mine entrance. One woman said, "That's where the bullion is hidden." One MP asked her to repeat what she said, and she told them "the gold was brought from Berlin" in early February 1945, "and later the rest of the treasures were brought in."[92]

For a time, the Third Army said there was not yet verification of the vast treasure trove since it had not been officially identified. It took some time to open the vault doors, but finally they were opened, and what they beheld left them speechless. Captain James McNamara, who was one of the first in, said, "Gee, I never saw so much money in my life than when I walked into the room and saw those bags stacked against the wall." But it was more, much more than just gold or money the Nazis had squirreled away, presumably stolen from the best families of Western Europe, many of them Jews. "The storage vaults [were] so deep, that the trip down in an elevator [took] two or three minutes. The statues and paintings were in wooden cases with 'Vienna,' 'Brussels' or 'Paris' stamped on them. Dr. P. O. Rave, curator of German state museums . . . was in charge of the hidden art treasures. He said that originals of Raphael, Rembrandt, van Dyck, Duerer and Renoir were in the mine."[93]

In the giant, multilevel mine were enormous rooms with "1,000 cases of painting and statues, 150 tapestries, 1,000 engravings and 120 cases containing the original Goethe collection." The amount of gold was astounding: approximately 200 tons. The Germans in charge of the vast collection contended that the collection was all Germany's before the war and that it had been hustled out of Berlin with the advance of the Soviets. Experts would have to sort out the problem after the war. At a nearby salt mine, yet another cache was found, but this was of "cognac and champagne."[94]

Shortly thereafter, the Americans blasted a hole in a sealed brick wall to discover "4,000 bags of gold bullion . . . a total of 50 tons. Each bag weighed twenty-five pounds and was worth $14,000."[95] All told, around 200 tons were hidden there, but that was not all. There were also thousands of sacks of coins that were too heavy to lift by one man. A preliminary count also showed 4,050 gold bars. "Another art haul was made . . . by the Fifth Division, which unearthed 200 paintings by Degas and hundreds of manuscripts. The works included some removed from Paris and other European capitals by the Germans. One manuscript dealt with the family history of the Rothschilds."[96]

If nothing else, the story of World War II was also the story of the bizarre. The curator of arts for Hitler and the Third Reich, Count Franz von Wolff-Metternich, and his wife owned four huge estates. They needed labor to tend the field and till the soil, so they called the Berlin labor office and obtained around one thousand slave laborers, mostly Poles and Russians. These laborers worked there for years, fearful of one phone call to the Gestapo. "If any worker became unruly all Count Metternich had to do was to call in the Gestapo and have him removed to a concentration camp. If the worker didn't like their filthy quarters, in the barns or became sullen because the food they ate was not the rich fare enjoyed by the German overseers and workers, then that was too bad." Some slaves labored in these squalid conditions for up to five years. Eventually, they rebelled, and the count and his wife became prisoners in "their own great castle."[97]

To the Germans, George Patton was a figure of fascination but also an enigma. According to the *New York Times*, "Most German commanders would rather fight almost anywhere than in front of Lt. Gen. George S. Patton, Jr. He not only worries them to death with his unorthodox moves but has now added a contemptuousness that must reduce to a minimum any remaining German morale."[98] In short, he had an unconventional way of taking a town or a battlefield; not worrying about German strafing anymore—as the Luftwaffe had nearly been destroyed—he often used smoke screens made by the giant Allied machines, which created this ground fog to help conceal Allied movements.

Okinawa was still not settled and, in fact, the fighting, according to reports, had intensified. On April 7, it was reported that "air battles over the Okinawa invasion had become especially furious. . . . Most attacking aircraft were intercepted by American fighters many miles away and others were picked up [by] patrolling planes on the edge of the screen." The Japanese sent aloft almost 200 planes in the battle and nearly 500 planes over the previous two days, but by one account, US forces "bagged 275 Japanese planes yesterday and today."[99]

A hospital ship neared the harbor in San Francisco, filled with the wounded of Iwo Jima, some of whom had been away from the country for more than three years. Many were amputees or sightless. As best they could, they were up early, had breakfast, cleaned up, and manned the portholes and side of the ship as it came into port. In the ambulances and cars headed for the hospitals, they yelled and whooped at the girls—and the signs for beer. "That's what we were fighting for!" one exclaimed, while another shouted, "Women! Beautiful American women!"[100] Later, some of the wounded were loaded onto a train headed east. They marveled at the snow in the Rockies, and "the days ran swiftly as the train hurried across" the country. "The men played cribbage, poker, hearts and blackjack; checkers, chess and pinochle. They read old books and magazines, smoked endlessly." They looked out the frost-covered windows to catch glimpses of the lights of small towns in the distance. Finally, they arrived at Pennsylvania Station and were transported to military hospitals, again, by ambulances. "This was the last stage but one on the journey home from the Pacific. The wounded were back with their own people."[101]

The drive for the donation of old clothes was in full swing. There were plenty of stories about children, clubs, and churches asking for them. Even ads for department stores asked for old clothing for Italy.

The Germans, despite the pounding to their Luftwaffe, still managed to put a large contingent of planes—one hundred in all—into the skies over western Germany. However, "the battle cost the Germans eighty-seven fighters, including a dozen jet aircraft, according to preliminary estimates of returning American airmen. The enemy pilots fought like fanatics, the American flyers reported, and twenty-two of our bombers and three fighters are missing."[102] The Allies sent aloft around 1,300 B-24 and B-17 bombers, along with some 850 escort fighters. Also, British Lancaster bombers and Spitfire fighters were bombing rail yards and jet bases.

The inventive American propagandists came up with a novel idea. They had German POWs housed in the United States go on the radio and call on the German people to surrender and the German troops to "put down [their] weapons immediately." The American propagandists also went political, as they produced a petition that was signed "'voluntarily by 1,391 of the 3,102 German prisoners of war' held at Ft. Devens, Mass."[103] German people were informed of the petition.

> Listen to us, German brothers, comrades of the armed forces, women and workers. Be not blind facing the danger of a frightful end, about which Hitler is trying to deceive you by telling you tales of secret

weapons . . . only recently Hitler made you promises of victories. Are you still believing anything like that? Only now, the Red Army is carrying the mightiest offensive into the heart of Germany. . . . In view of the catastrophe, which is daily gaining momentum, you will be called upon by the guilty ones for defense to the last. Do you know what that means? That means death. Mobilization of the entire people, insufficiently equipped—everybody a front trooper: children, women, cripples, and old people are given rifles or spades and are instigated, egged on, to their own destruction. That means suicide for Germany. You are not fighting for your native land, but for Hitler, Himmler, Goering, Goebbels, Ley, Koeckner, Krupp and accomplices.[104]

The hard-hitting statement concluded, "There is a future for us, but it must be without Hitler."

Yet, even at the last, US government officials said they had hard evidence of the Nazis' plans to rise up again and mount a third world war. The plan went so far that a radio show was broadcast to discuss the possibility, which included Assistant Secretary of State Archibald MacLeish.

AT THE DEPARTMENT STORE B. Altman & Co., large Oriental rugs, twenty by thirty feet, were going for $1,717. At Gimbels Department Store, an infrared lamp bulb, which relieved "tired muscles," was retailing for $1.60.[105] Appeals were still being made for spare and used clothing for the destitute of the world: "What can you spare that they can wear?" In their zeal, Americans turned in rubber swimsuits and silk lounging pajamas. "The only people who would wear it in the streets are Chinese," said one official.[106] Also donated were corsets of all sizes and shapes, teddy bears, men's underwear, children's underwear. One man came in to a depot and doffed his coat, threw it on the pile, and left, only to return a half hour later to clean out his pockets. "Sorters and checkers in depots [reported] that the cleanliness and excellent state of repair of most of the garments [was] a credit to the American housewife."[107]

America's sixteen commercial airlines—Eastern, Western, TWA, United, Hawaiian, American, Alaska, Piedmont, Braniff, and many others—basically had been commandeered by the US government since December 7, 1941. On that day, all planes in the air were ordered to fly to the nearest airport, deplane their passengers, and await orders. Since that time, they had flown 114,412,093 miles ferrying military personnel. But even so, they still managed to fly 2,264,282,443 miles during the war with civilians—all mannered, well-spoken, clean, neat, and dressed well. These commercial planes and their pilots and crews were underreported and unrecognized heroes of the war. They flew gas and matériel to Normandy, even gasoline trucks cut into three pieces to be reassembled upon arrival. "Dynamite, eggs, war dogs, fresh vegetables, hog bristles, cutting diamonds, Prime Minister Churchill, they all rode the flying box cars both to and from and in between the battlefields."[108]

Everybody was headed to San Francisco. Belgium, which had been pummeled into the ground since the Germans invaded in 1940, was sending a delegation to the originating session of the United Nations. The location of the new "Peace Capital" had not yet been determined, but all knew it would be in the United States, the only superpower in the world, and the British favored Washington, DC. In San Francisco, delegates found transportation difficult since the public transit system was in awful shape, and the cabs were sparse and in even worse shape.

Congress was putting together the initial details of a tax cut to stimulate the economy as soon as the war was over, but some members were fighting for increases in the "excess profits tax," which meant the government would make the moral judgment as to what was a fair profit and what was "excessive." Others, however, were looking at excusing all servicemen from paying deferred taxes during their time in the military. The needs of the fighting man and woman were very much on the minds of many. The "job rights" for many veterans was causing some concern among civilians. Essentially, the government guaranteed to everyone who went into the military a civilian job—or something similar—when they got out, even if it meant firing a civilian who had filled the job.

Early on, the phrase "GI Bill of Rights" was used, but it wasn't about work. What to do with returning veterans who were disabled and could no longer do their old jobs as a result was being debated, with no resolution. Harry Truman gave a speech in which he predicted no postwar recession and, indeed, spoke of how there could be a manpower shortage. Again, he made a reference to the "GI Bill of Rights," and again it was about employment for returning servicemen. Makers of big military vehicles knew they'd be out of work soon. Inflation was not a problem in a wartime economy with so many regulations and requirements; it was running at an anemic 2.2 percent for 1944.

The great Lionel Hampton was bringing the sound of his wonderful jazz to Carnegie Hall, and he was expected to play his signature song, "Flying Home," which brought down houses and nearly brought down a balcony in Connecticut. Nary a word was said about his race.

The headline said it all: "Two Negros Are Tried Out by the Dodgers but They Fail to Impress President Rickey." This story was all about race. Branch Rickey, the general manager of the Brooklyn Dodgers, "Da Bums," was in a headlong rush to integrate his team and be the first team to break the color barrier. Black men had made some strides during the war, but there was still systemic segregation. Black troops did not march with white troops, black fliers did not fly with white fliers, and many were relegated to kitchen duties and steward work aboard a ship or for a senior military officer. The two black ballplayers Rickey was scouting did not impress him, though. Of one, Dave Thomas, he quipped he "could not be interested in him . . . if he was 24 years old instead of 34." Terris McDuffie, the other black player, was 32; again, too old for Rickey's purposes. Rickey wanted a surefire young phenom, a black man who could become an all-star his first year so that the fans and his teammates had to support him. Rickey was a visionary, but also a realist.

The American League champ St. Louis Browns won over the defending World Series champion St. Louis Cardinals, 3 to 2, in an exhibition battle for bragging rights in the Gateway City.

As THE WAR WAS winding down, the territorial goals of the Soviet Union were rising. It was reported, "The USSR has a direct interest in the political attitude and military security of all states within this band which are directly bordering on her own frontiers or relatively contiguous thereto."[109] In Holland, they weren't thinking about secure borders but how to feed millions left behind in the carnage of the war. Famine was widespread; Holland was destitute. Electricity had been off for months, and shops, when they were open, were barren of any food whatsoever. Lice were widespread, and it was estimated that one-fourth of all Dutch citizens were infected, since there was "no soap, no disinfectant, no hot water."[110] The suffering, starvation, deprivation of the Dutch people was impossible to describe.

In Virginia, the Army Corps of Engineers abandoned plans to build a series of fourteen huge dams on the Potomac River, upstream of Washington, DC. While providing electricity to the area, it would have destroyed thousands of acres of good farmland, along with hundreds of homes. Homeowners would be free to continue to dump their sewers into the Potomac, and farmers could continue to allow the runoff of manure to flow freely into the historic and slow-moving, reeking cesspool.

THE PREVIOUS WEEK HAD indicated a lot of movement toward a successful conclusion of the war. The Allies were now on offense throughout the Pacific and Western Europe, and the entire world was changing. The *New York Times* ran a deeply thoughtful piece reflecting on the war: "When a person is living history, it is sometimes difficult to grasp either its extent or its import, to distinguish between the passing shadow and the substance. But who in the country, no matter where he lives, no matter how inadequate his reading, could have escaped the consciousness during the last seven days that he was living one of the greatest weeks of this war, and of our time? The events took place far from our homes and our work, but they affected deeply every one of us. It was a week which saw all but five of the independent nations of the world engaged in the most stupendous battles of history."[111] It made an essential point, comparing and contrasting Woodrow Wilson and World War I and Franklin Roosevelt and World War II: "The difference between then and now is the American people."[112]

Barron's magazine was promoting a cover story on eliminating slums in America once the war was over.[113] Since the Industrial Revolution, impoverished Americans seeking factory work had found refuge in makeshift shacks and dilapidated districts in cities across America. A "slum" was formally defined by the Housing Act of 1937 as

> any area where dwellings predominate which, by reason of dilapidation, overcrowding, faulty arrangements or design, lack of ventilation, light or sanitation facilities, or any combination of these factors, are detrimental to safety, health or morals.[114]

It was expected that widespread spending by private industry, possibly as much as $40 billion, would eradicate these "slums" in favor of new housing. While new low-income housing was the priority, there was no guarantee that the "cleared out" occupants could afford or would be welcome in these newly renovated areas.

Britain's Home Office declared that the era of V-2 bombings had ended. Their building and launch facilities had been overcome by Allied troops. But before that took place, 8,436 English citizens had been killed and another 25,000 injured by the rocket bombs falling from the sky.

Okinawa had grown tougher as the American forces pushed to the finish line. The Japanese resistance had stiffened greatly, and the American gains were small, incremental, yard by yard. The island battle, which at first seemed like a light wind, was quickly becoming a stiffening breeze.

Along with defeating German armies, advancing on Berlin, and finding millions in German loot, the Third Army also had the sad duty of discovering yet another Nazi death camp. "A ghastly extermination center where prisoners said the Germans starved, clubbed and burned to death more than 4,000 European captives in the last eight months has been overrun."[115] This death camp was near Ohrdruf. "Seventy-seven bodies of victims, said by prisoners to have been killed on April 2, the day before the Americans arrived," included American fliers. Also, "ashes and arms and legs of other victims were found around a crude woodland crematory two miles from the concentration camp. The crematory consisted of railway ties over a big pit. . . . Charred remains of ten bodies still lay heaped on top of the grill, and the pit below, where the fire was still burning, was deep in human ashes. The United Press [International] reported that surviving prisoners said some 2,000 of the captives were buried in a huge pit a mile away from the camp." Those innocents murdered by the German SS troops operating the camp "included Poles, Czechs, Russians, Belgians, Frenchman, German Jews and German political prisoners."[116]

A curious tactic was emerging. The American troops liberating the death camps were forcing the local civilian population to tour the camps and witness the carnage at the hands of their kin. Of course, the Germans all denied any knowledge, but the local mayor and his wife both committed suicide by slashing themselves one day after being forced to observe the local holocaust. Some liberated prisoners said as many as 150 more political prisoners had been murdered by the German SS just hours before the arrival of the Americans. One said the bodies were stacked or left where they were, while another said they'd been starved or beaten to death if they could no longer perform any work. Other gruesome reports came from the Gerolstein and Hammelburg POW camps.

Seven German planes carrying a handful of German soldiers flew to Switzerland to surrender. Good thing, too, as reports said four thousand Allied planes, paced by twelve hundred bombers, hit eighteen Nazi targets while blasting eighty-six German planes out of the sky.

On Easter Sunday, the American Ninth Army secured the release of Cardinal August Hlond, the youthful Catholic Primate of Poland. For five years he'd been a captive of the Gestapo. It was thought that the priest and others were held as collateral in the case of a hostage swap. When asked how the Gestapo had treated him, he brushed it all away and said his work was in front of him, not behind him. But he was very appreciative of the Americans, especially for liberating him on such an important Christian holiday.

Following the tradition of Sergeant Alvin York of World War I, Private First Class Wilburn K. Ross of Strunk, Kentucky, in five hours of continuous combat in France the previous October, "turned back nine counter-attacks by a company of German mountain troops, killing or wounding at least fifty-eight of the enemy."[117] Like York, Ross was also awarded the Congressional Medal of Honor.

The segregated troops seemed to fight all that much harder, as if to prove themselves. Americans had already seen it with Jewish and black troops, and now they were seeing it with Japanese American troops. According to one news report, "Somehow it's still incredible to see these dark, slight soldiers, who so uncomfortably suggest our Pacific enemy. Yet, as Tech. Sgt. Andrew Okamura, [a] Hawaiian, put it: 'I can speak more Italian than I can Japanese.'" The Japanese Americans "got on with the job here with typical dispatch and have done remarkably well in a sector where all the efforts thus far have not been brilliant." In Italy, "this regiment of Japanese Americans . . . was tightening its semi-circular grip east and southeast of Massa, below La Spezia. The Nisei (Japanese) troops just back from France mopped Mount Fragolito, pushed to take Mount Belvedere. . . . They used grenades and bazookas to blast the Germans from their last rocky redoubts in the captured heights as fighter-bombers dived beyond the front lines and 155mm. guns punched away at the stubborn enemy. More than anything else the outfit's return here emphasizes the polyglot nature of both the Allied armies in Italy."[118] The news report went on to mention that these Japanese American soldiers were discussing, authoritatively, the sinking of the Japanese battleship *Yamato*, with one "sitting as cross-legged as a Buddha, as he pored over a map and discussed" the sinking "with grave satisfaction."[119]

As Okinawa was coming under more American control, the locals were not as hostile as some thought. "Whereas they had been listed originally as unqualified enemy civilians because of their racial and political connections with the Japanese homeland, American Military Government authorities have discovered that the civilians we have so far encountered seem to reconcile themselves quite happily to the prospect of living under American jurisdiction."[120] Of course, this was only a smattering of opinion based on a very limited sampling of the residents there. The population had been almost completely stripped of Japanese men between sixteen and fifty years old.

IT WASN'T JUST THE government encouraging private citizens to be wise with their food. So was the private industry like Saks Department Store. They were running a promotion aimed at children—but actually aimed at all Americans—called the "Clean Plate Club": "Now as never before saving food is the biggest job you can do. You can pledge your children to clean their plates at every meal!"[121] The enthusiastic ad went on from there, asking readers to "pledge yourself to clean their plate at home and when dining out." The motto was "Food Will Win the War— Don't Waste It!"[122] Saks also hyped their success: 264,000 boys and girls "pledged to clean their plates at every meal. . . . 389 New York schools are enrolled. . . . 720,000 Clean Plate Book Covers remind students to save food for Uncle Sam. . . . Camps from Maine to Florida carry on the summer job."[123]

The magazine aboard the American aircraft carrier USS *Princeton* exploded, and the ship "was sent to the bottom." On the deck of a nearby ship, the USS *Birmingham*, "sand had to be scattered for safe walking to cover the blood."[124] Even with the loss of the *Princeton* and the sidelining of the *Birmingham*, it was evident to all how the war in the Western Pacific was going. According to one news report, "Indeed, it is clear, for all strategic purposes, that Japan's Navy and the Japanese Air Forces already have been defeated; the enemy's army is now our chief obstacle to victory in the Pacific."[125]

THE WAR WAS RAGING in Germany, and the Nazis had been evicted from France only one year before, but it was amazing how quickly Parisians returned to a near normal life in April 1945. Small boys played with sail-boats and mechanical boats on a pond while people tossed bread to the ducks. Harold Callender at the *New York Times* wrote, "The bright purple crocuses and yellow daffodils looked as gay as their pre-war ancestors had looked. The plane and chestnut trees were as richly green as in earlier foliations, quite hiding the Louvre and half hiding the Orangerie and the Jeu de Paume. Nobody talked of Resistance or nationalization or even of greatness. It was as if these Parisians did not read or wanted to forget the Paris press and its politics."[126]

The Girl Scouts launched a national campaign to beef up home safety. Door to door, these girls checked on "yards, porches, stairways and base-ments of more than a million homes." One of the goals of the campaign was to teach these Girl Scouts "the basic requirements of homemaking, namely, to make home a safe and secure place to live."[127] A new book was released, *Robinson Crusoe, USN*, about a navy man marooned for two and half years on Japanese-held Guam. Within a short time, the market would be flooded with books about the exploits of men who had served, and many would be made into fine movies. The unparalleled novelist Booth Tarkington was out with a new book, *Image of Josephine*.

The US Army, not generally known for tenderness or kindhearted-ness, showed just that when it announced it would pay for the passage of twenty thousand British war brides to America. Passports were already being processed, and the army said it would provide "nurses, special diet kitchens and facilities for babies."[128]

The fight for Okinawa was proving to be harder than first expected. "Enemy mortar and artillery fire was extremely heavy. Indications that the Japanese defenders were moving up reinforcements were seen in a marked increase in rifle fire and machine gun action."[129] Casualties among the marines and army were thought to have risen dramatically in just a few days. Gains, which a few days earlier had come in big chunks, now came in mere feet. The Japanese mounted one counterattack after another as the Americans trucked in more and more supplies and ammo.

As an indication of the growing intensity of the battle for Okinawa, air ambulances began flying in and out with the wounded.

The arrows surrounding the Third Reich were closing in on Berlin with the publication of each daily newspaper, and to make matters worse for the Reich, American air forces blew up two airfields used for the Luftwaffe's nascent jet fighter force, including eighty-three aircraft on the ground, many of them jet fighter planes.

The Republicans were demanding an accounting of what the Roosevelt administration was planning to spend after the war as the debate over the extension of the Lend-Lease Act heated up in the Senate.

Private First Class Rene Gagnon returned home to a hero's welcome in Manchester, New Hampshire. Gagnon was one of the six men who raised the second flag—and appeared in the most historic photo—on Iwo Jima. He identified the other men for newspaper reporters, save one unidentified marine who was later killed and whose next of kin had yet to be notified. According to Gagnon, they were: Sergeant Michael Strank, deceased; Pharmacist's Mate 2nd Class John H. Bradley, wounded; Private First Class Ira H. Hayes, deceased; and Sergeant Henry O. Hanson, deceased.[130] As it turned out, Gagnon's memory was not perfect in the heat and danger of battle, though he did carry the flag up to Mount Suribachi.

Marine Sergeant Michael Strank, Marine Corporal Harlon Block, and Marine Private First Class Franklin Sousley—were slaughtered in action during the battle. The other three Marines in the photograph were Corporals (then Privates First Class) Ira Hayes, Harold Schultz, and Harold Keller; Block was identified as Sergeant Hank Hanson (helped raise the first flag and was present at the second flag raising) until January 1947, Schultz (was at both flag raisings) was identified as Sousley who was identified as PhM2c John Bradley (was at both flag raisings) until June 2016, and Keller was identified as Rene Gagnon (carried the second flag up Mount Suribachi) until October 2019. All of the men served in the 5th Marine Division on Iwo Jima.

The battle to defend Germany continued to disintegrate into guerrilla warfare, with the "People's Army," the Gestapo, and the "Elite Guard" suffering heavy losses, often at the hands of escaped slave laborers who had obtained weapons. Civilians captured trains loaded with food and supplies meant for the Nazi high officials and took them for themselves. They also stormed the headquarters of the Wehrmacht and did the same, taking away as much as they could by hand.

WHAT WAS INTERESTING ABOUT men's and women's fashion in 1945 was that the sketches and photographs of the models wearing sporty, elegant, and chic clothing looked exactly like the men and women of Hollywood as well as like the everyday men and women of America. Women wore sporty hats in the ads but also in the movies and in real life. Women wore attractive dresses and shoes, long gloves, and purses in the ads but also in the movies and in real life. Life imitated art, art imitated life, and the people were truly beautiful. "Once again . . . the master of fine tailoring, proves that simplicity of line . . . classic good taste . . . and beautiful fabrics are not only the recurrent themes, but the *sine qua nons* of fashion!" said one ad for Saks Fifth Avenue.[131]

Talk of war crimes and how the new United Nations would manifest itself became more and more prominent. The Czech government wanted "Hitler, members of his government and his 'hangmen' on the first list of war criminals compiled by Allies."[132] Six thousand miles away, Dr. Wang Chung-hui said, "We know whatever organization may be created for the maintenance of peace and security, there must be established the rule of law among nations and there must be cultivated among them the spirit of respect for the law."[133]

Only now, in April, was the evilness of Hitler's Final Solution beginning to come into focus for all the world to see in print. Pictures of the death camps still were not being widely circulated and, curiously, the major newspapers pretty much buried the stories. On page ten of the *New York Times* on April 10 appeared the horrific story of a French Master Sergeant who had been captured by the Germans in 1940. He'd been released as the Americans advanced on Germany, but not before he witnessed "Polish men, women and children slaughtered individually and in thousands by German Elite Guardsmen." He also saw Russian POWs put in cages that were too small to stand up in and too short to lie down in. They were fed only enough to stay alive, but barely. His stories got worse. Much worse. There was no hope for Jews of any nationality at the hands of the Germans.

There one day I saw 100 Jewish men, women and children jammed into a railway car after they had been stripped of all personal possessions and then machine-gunned. Later they ordered all Jews indoors in the Rawa Ruska ghetto, locked the doors, set fire to the houses and shot all those who tried to escape. . . . Jewish women and children who were all barefooted, were forced to do the same work as we, which was principally breaking big stones into little stones. As a general thing, they worked the Jews while they could get work out of them or until the job was finished, then killed them. They marched them from place to place and when any straggled they shot them. I saw one Jewish woman carrying a 2-year-old child fall to the ground. A Gestapo man shot her and then the child. He killed the mother but only wounded the infant. It cried and he went back and finished the job. It was the SS, the Gestapo and the Ukrainian volunteers who did the murdering. They are disgusting beasts. They shot a Jewish girl who tried to escape and left her body lying four days outside the camp. One day when we came past an SS man lifted her garments with his bayonet and asked whether we wanted her. The worst things I saw were at the Lwów. They also closed the Jews in the ghetto, set it afire and shot all who tried to escape. But of course, the whole thing there was on a much larger scale. The ghetto burned for eight days and tens of thousands must have perished there.

I saw corpses hanging out of the windows of ghetto houses. I noticed a naked arm hanging out of a sleigh being driven through the streets. I looked in and saw it was full of Jewish corpses.

Abandon hope all ye who enter here. As it turned out, he was wrong, but what I saw around there almost caused me to lose hope for humanity.[134]

Another news report said the Germans used Russian prisoners for target practice for artillery. They "had turned artillery against the helpless prisoners, killing hundreds." The report continued that, as American troops approached, the Nazis increased the shelling of those "herded inside the barbed wire fence. American aid men tried to save the wounded Russians but many died."[135]

The Russians produced a terrifying report on German atrocities. Two German field marshals, General Walther von Model and General Eugen Schoerner, were charged with "the deaths of 577,000 persons in concentration camps in Latvia and the deportation of 175,000 others as slave laborers in a 6,000-word report . . . by a Russian investigating committee." The report had been researched and written by "prominent Russians." It said, "Germans had methodically destroyed factories, public utilities, libraries, museums, hospitals and homes, had ransacked libraries and art galleries and had slain many Latvian intellectuals. At least 170,000 civilians, including women and children, were slaughtered in mass extermination camps near Riga."[136]

The discovery of yet another death camp was just the beginning. The Nazis had plenty of time and plenty of imagined enemies. And plenty of macabre and evil ways to torture and kill their imagined enemies. Their inhumanity was just starting to be uncovered.

Yet another trove of priceless artifacts was found, hidden by the Nazis. This time it was all Jewish collectibles discovered by the 5th Division at Hungen in the south-central part of Germany. "A huge collection of priceless Jewish manuscripts, painting and other cultural objects stolen by the Germans [from] all over Europe [was discovered]. . . . The collection, which includes objects dating back to the 14th Century, was the second treasure trove uncovered by the Third Army in three days. The Jewish collection had served as the basis for the pseudo-science attacks made by Dr. Alfred Rosenberg, notorious German propagandist, against world Jewry. [He and others] were charged with finding facts that could be twisted to prove that Jews had already been a slave race." The Germans were obsessive. If they were going to enslave people, they wanted proper legal or historical cover. "Most of the manuscripts and books were believed to have been taken from the Oppenheim Museum in Frankfort, the Jewish Historical Museum in Amsterdam and museums in Paris."[137] The army took charge of the purloined possessions, and later the United Nations said it would try to get the thousands of items back to their rightful owners or heirs.

One thousand five hundred American soldiers returned to Boston from the hell of German POW camps. Although "battle scarred and . . . still bearing marks of long confinement, [they were] the largest contingent of liberated prisoners to return from Europe." Many of the Americans had been liberated by the Russian army, and "many told of terrible hardships in Nazi prison camps, of an almost starvation diet, of inadequate clothing in the dead of winter and inadequate shelter."[138] Several died when a German plane bombed the camp. One recalled a boy shot in the back by German troops. Some POWs were captured after the Normandy invasion and forced into cramped boxcars for days on end with only scraps of bread to survive on. Some POWs recalled being beaten by German civilians after parachuting behind enemy lines. But the Poles, they said, were wonderful to the Americans.

After being liberated, they went to wait near the Mediterranean, where a United Service Organizations tour greeted them. They also got food and medical treatment before being sent back to the states. While in captivity, they said, the only thing that kept them alive was Red Cross packages; food was minimal and the "Ersatz" coffee they received was nicknamed "distorted water."[139]

When they were rescued by the Russians, they were surprised to see the Red Army outfitted with almost exclusively American equipment: "Sherman tanks, rifles and even hand grenades."[140] They also saw female troops and a woman tank commander in the Russian army.

THERE WAS TROUBLE BREWING in Winston Churchill's federation government in London. "After a five-year wartime political truce, a battle royal of political name-calling that may result in the early dissolution of Prime Minister Churchill's coalition government has begun among Cabinet Ministers and politicians of the two major parties that will fight for control of the country after the defeat of Germany." The fight involved Churchill, of course; the minister of labor, Ernest Bevin; and the minister of information, Brendan Bracken. "Each side accused the other of starting the fight that is the first round in the campaign that will precede a general election, now expected to be held in the summer or early autumn, the first general election in this country since 1935."[141]

Churchill was charged with saying some "rude things about the Labor party." Bracken, a Churchill ally, was known as one of the more acerbic conservatives in London. "Now that the first blows have been struck by the leaders of two parties, there [was] no compulsion . . . to keep peace and the coalition government may break up in a political brawl." And "with the approach of peace in Europe, both parties have been spoiling for a fight." One participant said he's been experiencing a "sense of frustration" for several years because the temporary unity of the war had delayed what he really wanted, which was a knockdown, drag out brawl, so as to get out of the coalition, and others agreed. "This is where we look like getting into a spot of bother," said one, drolly.[142] Nearly all the tabloids and broadsheets of England forecast the end of Churchill's coalition government as soon as the war ended.

A *New York Times* article on April 10 made a rather unsettling and operatic allusion regarding Nazi Germany's end: "The final act of the drama now drawing near its end in Germany has been often characterized as a 'Twilight of the Gods,' in which the Nazi leaders are attempting to destroy as much of European civilization as possible in a Wagnerian holocaust, before destroying itself."[143]

Perhaps the Nazis, fighting with brutal determination in the face of defeat, were actually executing a long-term plan for victory. Much like the gods in Richard Wagner's legendary opera *The Ring of the Nibelung*, beloved by Hitler, the Nazis would see the world immolated before their own destruction, only to rise from the ashes to conquer once again.

Many in the West were paranoid that the Third Reich was plotting and scheming to make a comeback by hiding caches of arms around Europe. Even as the Allies were stomping over remnants of the German army and the small militias and guerrilla outfits, all still feared the terrors of the Nazis.

HAVING LEARNED NOTHING FROM the monopoly of Standard Oil, Congress was considering the McCarran bill, which would "make one American flag company the sole competitor with foreign lines in post-war overseas air traffic."[144] Seventeen of the nineteen commercial airlines objected and went to Washington to tell their congressmen how they felt. Senator Pat McCarran was an old-style western Democrat, critical of the New Deal but eager to get in on the patronage for his home state of Nevada. He sometimes wore the old-style, upturned shirt collar and striped pants. He was indifferent to ethics and was easily swayed by corporations, such as the insurance industry, which he proposed should be left unregulated by the federal government.

The corrupt Tammany Hall, in charge of all Democratic politics and patronage in New York City for years, for the first time hired a publicity director. Tammany was well-known, feared, and mostly secretive. Curiously, it hired a well-known Republican public relations firm, Russell Potter Associates. The head of Tammany Hall said the hiring was to spotlight their work on promoting democracy.

An eighteen-year-old Manhattan newsboy was sentenced to five days in prison for the black-market sale of cigarettes at 30 cents per pack. At the time, they sold for a few pennies more per pack. President Roosevelt declared that the first day of May 1945 would be "Child Health Day." The nationwide clothing drive for the Italian destitute was so successful, it was estimated some 450 trucks a day were needed to haul all the apparel just in New York City. America's sweetheart, Shirley Temple, age sixteen, announced her engagement to twenty-four-year-old army sergeant John Agar, who later went on to become an actor himself.

As war contracting trailed off, there was a real fear among the thousands of companies that created and manufactured for the arsenal of democracy that the government would be slow in their last payments, as well as the reality of the cancellation of contracts. So banks started to loosen their lending policies while these businesses made the transition to a peacetime economy. As a result, stocks paused in their growth as concerns about a postwar recession or even depression grew.

The policy of lend-lease, which had been a part of US policy since March 1941, was extended by the US Senate for one more year, but it was not overwhelming as Republicans raised objections. It took Vice President Harry Truman to cast the tie-breaking vote. "'The vote,' said the Vice President with a smile, 'is 39 to 39. The chair votes No.'"[145] Senate Majority Leader Alben Barkley of Kentucky scolded his fellow senators for missing so many crucial votes.

THE SOVIET NEWSPAPER THE *Bolshevik* said the cost of the war so far for Mother Russia was 25 billion gold rubles. That cost also included the taking of Vienna, which the Russians were on the verge of doing. And, in so doing, the Russians captured another 2,000 German troops as well as a great swath of field ordnance. All the central parts of Vienna were now in Soviet hands. Eventually, the Russians would take 92,000 Nazi prisoners while killing another 42,000 in their drive through Vienna.

In the Pacific, all eyes were fixed on Okinawa. The invasion by American army and marine forces had gone off without a hitch, at least according to sources. But now, the Japanese were digging in, even though American forces had captured an important Japanese naval base, Unten Harbor. Three more Japanese battleships were sent to Davy Jones's locker by blasts from the American air forces.

In the Philippines, General MacArthur's forces had taken Jolo Island, site of an important enemy airfield. Things were quickly falling apart with the new Japanese government. Premier Kantaro Suzuki had apparently promised "peace," but Tokyo radio had different ideas. It "ridiculed" the suggestion, and instead said it "would devote itself to winning the war."[146] Still, fresh rumors circulated in Washington and diplomatic circles that Japan was about to sue for a negotiated peace. However, the *New York Times* reported, "The official Army-Navy view is that we must prepare for a war in Japan and the Asiatic mainland that may require two years or more after Germany's collapse. Regardless of what optimists think, the Army and Navy certainly are prepared for such a war. Plans are drawn for the immediate redeployment of troops from Europe to the Far East after Germany's collapse, for intensive training of infantry replacements and for continued high quantities of war production."[147]

The War Department was also developing a forceful public relations campaign aimed not at the enemy but at the American people "to acquaint the home front with how vital it is that no efforts be relaxed in delivering the death blow to Japan."[148] The debate in diplomatic circles whirled between the hawks, those who thought the Japanese industrialists would urge Japan to fight to the finish, and the doves, those who theorized Japan's new Suzuki government was more interested in seeking a peaceful end. But as much as the British hated the Germans for civilian bombing of England, the Americans hated the Japanese even more for Pearl Harbor. Three and a half years had elapsed, and nothing banked the hot and justified feelings of all Americans who believed in good sportsmanship and fair play. "Remember Pearl Harbor!" was still heard throughout the country.

Americans all across the country woke up on the morning of April 11 to read this startling story: "The final offensive in the West has begun. Paced by tanks of United States First Army, the elements of five armies, four Americans and one British, have broken out of the center of the Allied Expeditionary Force's line in Germany on a front of 183 miles . . . driving steadily into the heart of . . . Germania for gains of up to twenty-five miles."[149] The ultimate battle to defeat Nazi Germany was on. All knew that Berlin would fall. General Patton knew it. Winston Churchill knew it. Franklin Roosevelt knew it. Joseph Stalin knew it. And Adolf Hitler knew it. The only question was when?

THE CENTER OF THE last German redoubt had been broken by the First and Third Armies. "The Twelfth Army Group [had] taken more than 1,000,000 prisoners . . . since D–Day, a figure greater than the total United States casualties in the war thus far, which [was] at 798,393."[150] Armored forces were slicing through German cities and towns and little could stop the Allied onslaught, as they had been resupplied with ammo and gasoline.

From the heavens, the American air assault continued. The 8th Air Force wiped out 322 German planes, punching through the propeller planes to bomb and destroy what was believed to be eight jet plane air-fields. It was one of the "worst beatings" ever administered to Hermann Goering's vaunted Luftwaffe. Not only had he not defeated England as he'd promised, but he could no longer defend the skies over the Fatherland. Call him Meyer. (Goering had once said "Call me Meyer," a derisive reference to being Jewish, when asked if he could defend Germany by plane.) The British updated their casualty lists. They now totaled over 500,000, with over 200,000 dead and 183,000 either POWs or held in neutral countries.

Another benefit to taking the Pacific islands was that the navy and the Foreign Economic Administration could embark on an aggressive vegetable growing operation. Growing their own in their own backyard, saved time, money, refrigeration, and distance. Instead of gathering and shipping thousands of tons of vegetables (and fruits) on the West Coast, thousands of miles away, now fresh produce could be only hundreds of miles away. In a matter of weeks, something in the order of two million pounds of produce was being harvested on a weekly basis. The program was so successful that the local production of cattle and hogs was being considered.

Steadily, American forces were making their way up the Asian coast from Australia all the way to Okinawa. The goal was to secure advance air bases from which to launch B-29 bombing raids against the Japanese home islands, but many Japanese strongholds still remained dangerously in the Americans' rear. In Luzon, though most was conquered, there were still many Japanese troops squirreled away in the jungles and rocks.

The matter of accommodating troops reassigned from Europe needed to be addressed. Returning wounded veterans to New York were in for a treat. The sports committee of the Red Cross war fund was taking up a collection for tickets to the New York Yankees versus the Brooklyn Dodgers benefit game.

The story of the pilfered European and Jewish art and treasures was not over. The "art treasures captured in a salt mine [represented] the cream of the Prussian State collection including Rembrandts, Holbeins and Titians, but at least 75 percent of the entire collection still [lay] in Berlin vaults."[151] All of it was stolen from museums across Europe, both private and public; all of it priceless masterpieces.

Not surprisingly, as the Allies advanced, they discovered that Germany's public schools had been completely Nazified. At every level, from top to bottom, the public school curriculum was marinated in Hitler worship and Nazi love. Pictures of Hitler adorned every classroom. It had started twelve years earlier under the direction of the Reich Education Ministry. Teachers were fanatical party members and parrots, not educators. Biology was about the genetic superiority of the Master Race, history was about the superiority of the Master Race, as was race studies, "even music . . . taught in the lower schools, [was] used as an emotional drug for German youngsters." One frank teacher said of the Nazi educational system, "Discussion and questions are naturally squelched. Our teaching is a deliberate process of discouraging independent thinking as much as possible." Students were taught the "Hitler salute, prayers for the Fuehrer and political songs."[152]

As the Allied advance continued into Muehlhausen, they came across or picked up sometimes strange things. In this case, they picked up 285 members of Foreign Minister Joachim Ribbentrop's staff without a shot being fired. Among the staff were some diplomats who had spent many years in Washington. "The officials . . . were found cowering in apartments, basements, garages and homes of friends." One of the captured bureaucrats said, "Most of us feel the war is lost, but until now we did not dare to talk about it for fear of what might happen to us."[153] The threat of the Gestapo still hung over the German people, and for twelve plus years they'd been mindful that loose or unacceptable talk was extremely dangerous. Still, they knew there was no miracle weapon to save them. Hitler was alive, they knew this, but it gave them little comfort. They were doubtful that anyone would overthrow the Führer at this late date, but they were also terrified of the coming Russians.

Other strange occurrences happened in wartime. With the First Army, a Red Cross club mobile handing out doughnuts to GIs pulled up one day to a POW paddock and left behind six German POWs; "a pretty girl hopped out, opened the door of the truck, and waved six German prisoners into the enclosure."[154] On another occasion, an elderly German woman approached a POW camp with a young German soldier in tow. She informed the Allied guard that he was her son and she wished to turn him over to the authorities.

Three American reconnaissance planes flew over Berlin and described it as a "dead city."[155] There was no sign of life whatsoever, no pedestrians walking, no street traffic, no train movement. The usual antiaircraft fire was not present, nor did any German planes fly to meet the challenge on this crystal-clear day. But in the port city of Bremen, German troops fought like tigers against the British, who pretty much had the city under their control. But not completely. The Germans were under orders to fight to the death if need be and, to all, it appeared they were determined to achieve that goal. General Eisenhower, for obvious reasons, did not want the ports destroyed, so he made it clear to the Germans not to do so via radio broadcast.

In Seattle, the Boeing Aircraft Company made its 6,981st—and final—B-17 bomber. The B-17 "Flying Fortress" had performed admirably in the European theater and, in a more limited capacity, in the

Pacific war, flying millions of air miles. The crews loved this plane, and all the noses were adorned with often attractive art, declaring their devotion to the plane.

THE MATTER OF FDR versus Montgomery Ward was still not settled. The army, under orders from Roosevelt, had taken over the various department stores and proceeded to act like juvenile delinquents while occupying the stores. Charges were made of frequent drunkenness, "entertaining women friends in the seized stores after hours, improper advances to women employees," and "insulting familiarity on the part of an Army officer toward a customer trying on a dress."[156] Charges were also made of excessive partying, attempting to enter a ladies' lavatory, and violating the store's no smoking regulations. By this point, everybody had forgotten what the original dustup was all about.

As it was spring, Victory gardens were planted all over the country, including rooftop patches in the tenements of the cities, and young children eagerly pitched in.

"On his promise to pay for divorce proceedings for two of his three wives, all professional nurses, James J. Smith, 34 years old, a grocery clerk, got off with a suspended sentence of two to four years."[157]

There was a shortage of bottled beer in the New York City area thought to be caused by a restraint on the use of glass bottles "as well as hoarding by delicatessen and grocery stores."[158] Rabies was also a concern, and city officials picked up animals to test them or kill them.

All the published works of James Thurber were being ballyhooed, as was Tennessee Williams's new play *The Glass Menagerie*, which was hailed by critics as the best drama of the year. But it was a banner year for Broadway as *I Remember Mama* and *Harvey* were also being met with critical praise.

To raise money for the Red Cross, the New York Giants and the Brooklyn Dodgers met in an exhibition game for the first of three fundraising games in a round-robin with the Yankees. Ticket prices were $1.20, $1.80, and $2.40. Meanwhile, due to the manpower shortage, the Brooklyn Tigers and Boston Yanks of the National Football League merged for one year.

STARTLING NEWS REACHED LONDON that Adolf Hitler had died and Heinrich Himmler was now in power. But the same rumor had been floating for two years or more, and also that Nazis, dismayed with the Führer's leadership, had overthrown him. Another rumor was that a fissure was developing in the Nazi leadership. Said one editorial, "All of Germany today is like a landscape in hell, but only the worst spot in the inferno must be the hiding place where the leaders fight like rats in a hole, each blaming the other for the awful punishment that has caught up with them all."[159]

In some ways, it did not matter. True, the Allies wanted to bring Hitler to justice and have him stand in the dock and face his monstrous crimes. But World War II was not just against one man or even one terrible ideology; it was against entire nations, wholly enraptured by evil men. It was also against an entire country of deplorable people.

The tanks of the Allied Ninth Army were now just sixty-three miles from Berlin.

An American submarine sank a Japanese resupply ship, the MV *Awa Maru*. Curiously, the State Department made the announcement and also relayed a message to the Japanese via the Swiss that the ship had been sunk. The ship was under steam without running lights and sank almost immediately.

Germany was down to two, no, make that one pocket battleship as British Lancaster bombs caught the six-hundred-foot *Admiral Scheer* napping in Kiel Harbor, obliterating it.

Okinawa had now heated up into a battle royale. The Japanese, hesitant at first, were now throwing everything into the desperate battle. Japanese airplanes ferociously attacked naval ships of the Fifth Fleet daily despite heavy losses. Japan was now throwing in much more artillery, men, and airplanes, although their favorite weapon was the mortar, which they launched with reckless abandon. These small rockets were fired into the sky and would then land and explode. They also launched over a dozen "suicide" boats at the navy, trying to inflict as much damage as possible. Americans were massacring Japanese at an 11:1 ratio, and they still did not stop.

But things were settling down in the Philippines as Japanese POWs—all wearing POW tags—were put to work rebuilding Manila, the very city they had destroyed.

IT WAS BOUND TO happen. The Anglo-Russian alliance had always been one of convenience. America and Great Britain had a shared history, but the Russians had nothing in common with them, and the naturally paranoid Soviets were made even more paranoid during the war. They were always suspicious and, as a result, were patting themselves on the back over their fight in the east while denigrating the efforts of the Americans and British in the west, going so far as to call the Americans "soft" toward Germany.[160] Meanwhile, the tale of Stalin demanding two hundred thousand Germans in the form of slave labor for twenty years as reparations for war activities would not go away.

LILLY PONS, FAMED OPERA singer, said things were just awful in her native France upon her arrival to the United States. She'd just returned from a four-month, 38,000-mile USO tour in which she gave sixty-three free concerts for the Allies. She also bemoaned the freedom given to Nazi collaborators. She was beautiful, and she was one of the first opera stars to have mass appeal. Just as Miss Pons was lamenting the laxity afforded collaborators, a Nazi collaborator, Lucian Rottee, was sentenced to death by the Paris Court of Justice. He'd worked with the Gestapo to arrest five thousand French opponents to Nazism.

The steel and munitions locale of Ruhr was ablaze. It burned down "over the heads of the trapped troops there."[161] It was estimated thirty thousand to seventy thousand Germans were there.

Soldiers and officers were now taking bets on when and what army would get to Berlin first, as well as when and what army would link up with the Soviets first.

ANOTHER REPORT, ON APRIL 12, appeared in American newspapers about the carnage of Oswiecim (aka Auschwitz). Whereas previous reports had the death toll of Jews, Poles, gypsies, homosexuals, and other innocents at the hands of Nazi Germany in the hundreds or thousands, now reports said five million. "Dr. Bela Fabian, president of the dissolved Hungarian Independent Democratic Party, accused the Germans today of having killed 5,000,000 Jews at the Oswiecim extermination camp in Polish Silesia, from which he himself narrowly escaped." With almost no notice, the Polish Ministry of Information had reported a year earlier that "5 million Jews had been gassed and cremated at this camp, and the International Church Movement's ecumenical committee, in a subsequent report on [Oswiecim's] sister camp of Birkenau, said that 1,715,000 had been killed at the two locations. A spokesman for the American Jewish Committee said that it had been estimated that 4,000,000 to 5,000,000 Jews have been exterminated since the war began in Europe, but the library had no figures to substantiate a report that 5,000,000 had been exterminated in one camp."[162]

Again, serious, substantial, and substantiated charges were made about the mass execution of Jews in Europe, and again, the West failed to comprehend the gravity of what had happed in Nazi-occupied Europe. This later accusation was relegated to page six in the *New York Times*. It may have been the numbers were so staggering that many doubted it. All knew about Hitler's denunciations and laws against Jews, but many European leaders also had inveighed against Jews in the past.

A NATIONAL DAY OF Prayer was announced for Saturday and Sunday, April 21 and 22, for the delegates meeting in San Francisco for the inaugural session of the United Nations.

Doctors and public health professionals were envisioning a country in which there was little to no dental decay. Fluoridation experiments had gone well on children, and the plan was to introduce it into all community water. The impetus behind the drive to improve America's teeth was due to one out of every twelve draftees being barred from service because of bad teeth.

The Census Bureau amended its numbers on women in the workplace as the war wound down. Previously, it was thought a mass exodus of women from the factory floors would take place, but now it was estimated about 18 million women would be working postwar, up from the 17.8 million in 1944.

A London outfitter predicted a day when men would carry purses, just like women, as they had carried musette and haversack bags in the military.

The assistant night managing editor of the *New York Times*, Neil MacNeil, declared at a meeting of teachers that America's newspapers—and especially the *New York Times*—were "the best in all the world" and that they were doing a "splendid and courageous" job in covering the war.[163] He was right when he said that newspapers were a rich source of information for future historians. He also told his audience, "The responsible editors of a responsible newspaper never attempt to make the news more sensational than it is by typographical fireworks." They "do not make the news [but] merely record it."[164]

The Reconstruction Finance Corporation allowed private auctions of surplus military training planes to the public. However, they came with a catch: they could not be flown for the duration of the war, as Washington had slapped strict rationing measures on fuel for pleasure flying.

Old Gold cigarettes had an important announcement to make. They would once again be wrapped in tin foil, now that the limitations on the pliable metal were slackening.

In Okinawa, American forces shot down 118 Nipponese planes; many were trying to fly into US ships on suicide missions. The navy, for the first time, revealed that kamikaze planes were being used against ships. The name *kamikaze* meant "divine wind," referring to an ancient wind that had, legend said, saved Japan from an invading China fleet. The kamikaze pilot was strapped in, and the plane was booby trapped to explode if he tried to get out or land the plane. The pilots all knew they were on a one-way mission. It was loaded with fuel and explosives to cause maximum damage, which they did.

ATOP PINE MOUNTAIN IN Georgia, FDR's last words were, "I have a terrific headache." And then, on the afternoon of April 12, 1945, Franklin Delano Roosevelt, age sixty-three, the thirty-second president of the United States, died. He was only eighty-three days into his fourth term and, like millions of his fellow countrymen, was looking forward to the final victory over the Axis powers. But he was likened unto Moses, who led the Hebrews to the promised land but was forbidden to go there himself.

Roosevelt was the first president to die in office since Warren G. Harding was felled by a heart attack in the lobby of the Palace Hotel in San Francisco in 1923.

Dr. Howard G. Bruenn, the attending naval physician, had examined the president at 9:30 in the morning and found him in "excellent spirits." FDR uttered what would be his final words to Dr. Bruenn at around 1:00 p.m., according to news reports. It was immediately determined that a dangerous headache at the back of his head was the cause of his awful discomfort, and FDR was carried to his bedroom. According to Dr. Bruenn, "Within a very few minutes, he lost consciousness. He was seen by me at 1:30 p.m., fifteen minutes after the episode had started," and the president was unresponsive.[165] Dr. Bruenn called the White House physician, Admiral Ross T. McIntire, and Dr. McIntire, in turn, called Dr. James E. Paullin of Atlanta, an expert in internal medicine and occasional consultant to the navy surgeon general.

Roosevelt was at Warm Springs, Georgia, in the "Little White House" as the press dubbed it, and had planned to be there for several weeks. He'd last been at the Little White House the previous November and December for nineteen days and had intended to be there for several weeks again, arriving on March 30. During the past several months, FDR had lost weight and had a gaunt and tired gray pallor that worried his doctors. It had been rumored that he was not regaining the weight his doctors hoped for. His voice had also become noticeably weaker, his attention span had flagged, and he'd become incontinent.

Several days earlier, Roosevelt met with Sergio Osmena, president of the Philippine Commonwealth, and promised independence and aid quickly for the beleaguered island nation. He also spoke of a great American commitment in the Western Pacific to more quickly defeat the Japanese. The plan was for him to stay at Warm Springs for one more week, then take the train back to Washington and stay there for a few days, before mounting the train again to go to San Francisco to open the first plenary session of the new United Nations.

He'd been going to Warm Springs for years, hoping the warm, natural mineral springs would alleviate his polio, to no avail. One report said he was "unconscious at the end. It came without pain."[166] He was comatose for a little over two hours and "did not regain consciousness. [He] died at 3:35 p.m. (Georgia time)," Dr. Bruenn said in a statement to three wire service reporters.[167]

FDR had been sitting in front of a fireplace, posing for sketches for an oil portrait by Elizabeth Shoumatoff, when he was stricken by a cerebral hemorrhage. He was dressed handsomely, as always, in blue suit and vest, and his tie had been tied in the familiar four-in-hand ("schoolboy") fashion. He had been going through mail and signing letters that morning.

Roosevelt had once been a tall, vital, athletic, and handsome, if also somewhat callow, young man. But he suffered an attack of polio years before at age thirty-nine, and lost the use of his legs as a result for the rest of his life. Confined to a wheelchair for years, he nonetheless was elected governor of New York in 1928, and later, in 1932, the thirty-second president of the United States, with America wallowing in the depths of the Great Depression, a crisis his predecessor, Republican Herbert Hoover, could not solve. Roosevelt was born to the manor, yet he was loved by the working poor of America. He was trained as a lawyer, but his passion was politics and all that it entailed. He'd run for office twelve times and won ten, losing in 1914 in a Democratic primary for the US Senate and, in 1920, when he was the vice-presidential running mate to James M. Cox. It was his narrow win for the New York governorship in 1928, by a little over 28,000 votes in the mostly Republican state, that put him on the national stage and propelled him to the presidency. A split in the GOP ranks helped him win, and then, in the lowest point of the Great Depression, win reelection by 725,000 votes in 1930, making him the frontrunner for the 1932 Democratic sweep of the nation. He carried all of New York overwhelmingly.

Power, gossip, who was up, who was down, who was in, and who was on the outs—Roosevelt played the political game as well as anybody, better than most. He was as comfortable with Hollywood celebrities as he was with world leaders. All had noticed his quickly deteriorating physical condition over the past four months, but no one was prepared for this finality. Indeed, his personal physician, Rear Admiral Ross McIntire, had stayed in Washington rather than make the trip to Warm Springs, and none of the president's family was there.

The White House pharmacist, Commander George Fox; FDR's personal secretary, Grace Tully; and FDR's two favorite cousins, Laura Delano and Margaret Suckley, who were always up on the latest society gossip, were there. Also present but never mentioned in any news reports was FDR's longtime mistress, Lucy Mercer Rutherfurd. He and Lucy had had an affair years earlier when she was Eleanor's personal secretary. Eleanor found a secret stash of love letters between the two and offered her husband a divorce, but FDR's mother, Sara Delano Roosevelt, furiously put her foot down and said her son's burgeoning political career would be ruined if he got a divorce. So he promised Eleanor he'd swear off Lucy, but never really did. Lucy eventually married Winthrop Rutherfurd, a wealthy New York socialite. Still, FDR and Lucy continued to correspond and see each other, often at a surreptitious rendezvous arranged by FDR's niece and Teddy Roosevelt's daughter, Alice Roosevelt Longworth, famous society gossip, pot stirrer, and all-around beautiful and witty troublemaker. Alice once quipped of the affair, "He deserves a good time. He was married to Eleanor."[168] Lucy's husband had died in 1944, and she and FDR picked up where they'd left off years earlier. The Roosevelts' daughter, Anna, arranged for Lucy to visit FDR at Warm Springs, unbeknownst to Eleanor. Everybody it seemed knew about the affair—everybody but poor Eleanor. It was later reported that Eleanor had the Shoumatoff sketches mailed to Lucy. Over the years, FDR had been the subject of other rumored affairs, including with another longtime secretary, Missy LeHand.

By 1945, the marriage of Franklin Delano Roosevelt and Eleanor Roosevelt was as much one of convenience as anything. No one will really know if they'd ever truly been in love, although it seems likely she was once in love with him, more so than he with her. Eleanor had an unhappy childhood and was often treated rudely by her mother-in-law, Sara, who interfered with Eleanor's child rearing, and by her own husband, who often took vacations and trips without her, including to Warm Springs. Still, they did have six children. (The first, young Franklin Jr., died after one year.) After the affair, son James described the state of his parents' marriage as an "armed truce that endured until the day he died."[169]

Eleanor found her fulfillment in a public life. She broke new ground in dozens of ways for future first ladies, and thus, modernized the institution. She held press conferences, wrote a daily newspaper column, wrote a monthly magazine column, hosted a weekly radio show, gave speeches, injected herself into national politics including civil rights, occasionally disagreed with her husband's policies in public, and also sometimes nagged him to distraction about her pet causes.

Although his New Deal never solved the massive unemployment of the nation, FDR's jaunty mood, upbeat nature, eternal optimism, and endless alphabet programs gave the American people hope at a time when they needed it most. And while his leadership during World War II was, in a word, superb, his frequent inspirational speeches helped buoy the morale of the American people and America's fighting men.

Yet part of that leadership was also his uncanny ability to judge men. Aides came and went, but he rarely fired anyone on his political team, save for his old political sidekick Jim Farley, who broke with Roosevelt over Roosevelt breaking the "two terms only" rule for all previous presidents. His economic team was adequate, but his foreign policy and military teams, led by Secretary of State Cordell Hull and Secretary of War Henry Stimson, respectively, were splendid. Roosevelt personally traveled tens of thousands of miles to Tehran, Yalta, Quebec, and the North Atlantic to fashion the Atlantic Charter, with Winston Churchill, and to take part in other important world-altering conferences. Of course, Churchill and FDR met in Washington in December 1941, and again, in June 1942.

"A lover of aviation, who astounded the nation [with] his flight to Chicago to accept the nomination from the Democratic National Convention in 1932, he was grounded by the inflexible orders of the Secret Service until the war gave him valid grounds for breaking the rule that a President must stay on the ground." Roosevelt "flew the Atlantic for the first time in 1943, when he went to Casablanca for his conference with Mr. Churchill. He crossed it again when he went to Cairo for a conference with Mr. Churchill and Generalissimo Chiang Kai-shek at which the decision was made to strip Japan of all her conquests of half a century. And he flew still farther, to Teheran in Asia, for his first meeting with Marshal Stalin at the tripartite conference there."[170]

Roosevelt was the master of subterfuge, never letting anyone know everything he knew. He never wanted to deal all the cards. Only, possibly, his longtime all-around aide Harry Hopkins knew as much as he did.

But it was in the area of military leadership where FDR shined the brightest, as evidenced by the appointments he made: from Secretary of the Army General George Marshall to Secretary of the Navy Frank Knox; from the European supreme commander Dwight D. Eisenhower to General George S. Patton; from General Omar Bradley to Pacific Supreme Commander Douglas MacArthur; from Chief of Naval Operations Admiral Ernest King to Fleet Admiral Chester W. Nimitz; from General Henry H. "Hap" Arnold to FDR's own personal chief of staff Fleet Admiral William D. Leahy, and others. Of course, he relieved Admiral Husband Kimmel and General Walter Short, who were in command of American naval and army installations at Pearl Harbor on December 7, 1941.

He contributed, he asked questions, he gave broad directions, and then he left it to his generals to figure out how to get it done. He was deeply involved in all aspects of the war and was one of the finest wartime presidents ever. He was always curious of new technologies and strategies but never meddled. The top military brass were at the White House often, and military couriers and attachés could be seen coming and going from the executive mansion at all hours, day and night. And, while his love of the navy was common knowledge, he took a keen interest in the army and the army air corps. He gave the green light to Hap Arnold to begin designing a modern air force for a possible war, long before December 1941.

It was simply the finest assembled military leadership in world history, since the days of Caesar, Marcellus, Agrippa, and Mark Antony.

All in the military were thunderstruck at the news of his death. But it was the navy, his personal favorite, that took it the hardest. FDR had been planning a trip to the Pacific in the summer of 1945 for one of his periodic tours of military operations. The American flag at the White House, and then quickly thereafter the ones across the country, were lowered to half-staff. The New York City Fire Department got the word and just as quickly blasted the "four fives signal from the alarm center."[171] Across the country, hotels, restaurants, schools, and even some bars closed for the death of the president. In New York City, "the Hotel Association . . . ordered elimination of all music and all dancing. Some hotels even closed their bars, though others have remained open, but were lined with extraordinarily sobered patrons."[172]

FDR presided over a military that had grown from a bit over three hundred thousand men to a superpower force of twelve million men in uniform. He invented the Joint Chiefs of Staff to better coordinate global military affairs. But his greatest genius may have been to step back and let the military men run the military affairs of the nation. He was an able student of war, was fascinated by Hitler and Nazism, and was able to assemble the most powerful coalition in history.

Frank Knox may have walked the most interesting path to FDR's administration. He'd been a powerful and successful newspaper publisher, who was one of Teddy Roosevelt's "Rough Riders" in Cuba and, in 1936, the vice-presidential nominee along with Alf Landon, whose ticket was shellacked by the Democratic ticket of FDR and John Nance Garner. That the lifetime Republican ended up in Roosevelt's cabinet spoke volumes about both men. FDR was simply one of the shrewdest judges of talent ever to occupy the Oval Office.

The strains of the office and his lifestyle—smoking two packs a day of filterless Camels for years, long days and long nights of managing a domestic government and a military in a far-flung war, holding Churchill's and Stalin's hands, dealing with an often divided Democratic Party and a Republican Party that were looking over his shoulder all the time, not to mention the war reports, often bad, four sons all on active duty, a sometimes contentious wife and political partner, his occasional indiscretions over the years, his secrets, such as his relations with John Franklin Carter, who was his private eyes and ears outside of Washington—took a heavy toll. Roosevelt had been receiving private memos from Carter, a professional correspondent, for years from hither and yon. Carter had sent FDR private memos from the Mexican border, reporting on immigration, to the rough docks of New York City, writing on mob activities and their cooperation with the US government to ferret out Nazi spies.

Time stopped in America, as everyone would remember for the rest of their lives where they were and what they were doing when they heard of the death of Franklin Delano Roosevelt, just as they remembered where they were on December 7, 1941. In a word, Americans were thunderstruck as the news flashed across the nation.

FDR's longtime former press secretary, Stephen Early, told his secretary, "Conference Call," and with that the reporters for the International

News Service, the Associated Press, and United Press International all got on a call. The operator forgot to tell them who was calling, but that did not deter Early. He simply told the reporters, "The President died this afternoon." A disbelieving operator suddenly said, "Do you mean President Roosevelt?" to which Early snapped, "Christ! There's only one president. Of course, I mean President Roosevelt . . . at Warm Springs, Georgia." He spoke quickly and concluded, "death resulted from a cerebral hemorrhage."[173]

There were many tears among the 125 patients at the 2,000-acre Warm Springs Sanatorium, many of whom knew Roosevelt personally as they, too, suffered from polio. He often dined with the patients when he was there and had helped found the facility twenty years earlier. Warm Springs was a tiny southern town of around four hundred people, depending on the year, though the Roosevelts had deep roots there.

The last piece of legislation he signed was a bill to extend the borrowing for the Community Credit Corporation. He also had signed a number of postmaster appointments.

"Newsmen scurried from desks to the night wire editors. At INS [International News Service] Charles Sparenbaugh pressed his bell key four times. In newsrooms all over the United States and in radio stations, this gave him a clear line for news of momentous importance. Then he tapped out the shortest story ever sent:

> FLASH
> WASHN—FDR DEAD.
> INS WASHN 4/12/547 PPH 36

"One minute later the Associated Press bell rang four times and the message read:

> FLASH—WASHINGTON—PRESIDENT ROOSEVELT DIED
> SUDDENLY THIS AFTERNOON AT WARM SPRINGS, GA.

"New York City was indulging its molten flow of people hurrying homeward on sidewalks; rivers of automobiles being dammed by red lights and loosed by green ones. At 485 Madison Avenue, John Charles Daly, young and perspicacious CBS news commentator, sat in the newsroom editing material for the 6:15 p.m. broadcast. His ears heard, without understanding, the soft loudspeaker which introduced a radio serial called *Wilderness Road*."[174]

A few moments later, Daly heard something more distinct, more dominating. The bell on the International News Service teletype rang four times, something reserved for news of major importance. An aide ripped the short story from the machine, read it, and placed it on his desk. Daly read it and then raced into the studio. Then the United Press International machine rang four times, and Daly announced, "We interrupt this program to bring you a special bulletin from CBS World News. A press association has just announced that President Roosevelt is dead. All that has been received is that bare announcement. There are no further details as yet, but CBS World News will return to the air in just a few minutes with more information as it is received in our New York headquarters. We return you to a regular scheduled program."[175]

Stephen Early later issued a full statement that elaborated,

Vice President Truman has been notified. He was called to the White House and informed by Mrs. Roosevelt. The Secretary of State has been advised. A cabinet meeting has been called. The four Roosevelt boys in the service have been sent a message by their mother, which said that the President slept away this afternoon. "He did his job in the end, as he would want to do. Bless you all and all our love," added Mrs. Roosevelt. She signed the message "Mother." Funeral services will be held Saturday afternoon in the East Room of the White House. Interment will be at Hyde Park Sunday afternoon. No detailed arrangements or exact times have been decided upon as yet.[176]

Colonel James Roosevelt was in the Pacific, as were Lieutenant John Roosevelt and Lieutenant Franklin D. Roosevelt Jr., and Brigadier General Elliot Roosevelt was in Europe. It was reported FDR was proud of his four sons in combat, and why not? James had been decorated many times for bravery and fought at Midway and Guadalcanal; Elliot rose to become a brigadier general and had seen action in Tunisia, Sicily, and Italy; Franklin Jr. had been in many battles in the Pacific and the Mediterranean; and the youngest, John, while kept out of combat zones due to poor eyesight, had still served in the Pacific in the Navy Supply Corps.

Word raced around the world and to Washington, where Vice President Harry Truman was presiding over a Senate debate on a water treaty with Mexico. The news had reached him at 5:15 in the afternoon, about one-half hour before the world knew of the death of the president. He grabbed his hat and headed directly for the White House. Even before he was formally sworn in as president, Truman asked the cabinet to stay on.

On April 12, 1945, in the cabinet room of the White House, at 7:09 p.m., Harry S. Truman was sworn in by Supreme Court Justice Harlan F. Stone as the thirty-third president of the United States; he waited until his wife, Bess, and daughter, Margaret, could be in attendance. Truman wore a polka-dot tie and a gray suit. He was grim but firm, and his Midwestern twangy voice was robust.

Truman picked up a Bible from the end of the big table in the cabinet room and repeated the simple thirty-five-word oath that every man, going back to George Washington, had recited, adding the words "so help me God" at the end. President Truman then lifted the Bible to his lips and kissed it. The ceremony did not last more than one minute.

Crowds began to form in Lafayette Park, across from the White House. Nary a sound was heard, but men's hats were doffed, and some women were crying. Some men too. "Some presidents have been held in lukewarm esteem . . . and some have been disliked by the local population, but Mr. Roosevelt held a high place in the rare affections of the capital."[177]

In Hyde Park, all the church bells pealed on and on, telling the citizens of what they already knew. In nearby Poughkeepsie, the fire whistle blasted every ten seconds for two minutes to let locals know something was going on. In Hyde Park, schools were closed and town meetings postponed. At St. James Episcopal Church, where the Roosevelts worshiped, the Sunday service was announced as a memorial service for the president. The portrait of FDR at the church was draped in black as a bugler blew "Taps." Conducting the committal service for Roosevelt on Sunday, April 15, would be the Reverend George W. Anthony from St. James, where FDR had been senior warden. Full military honors for a fallen leader would be rendered at the gravesite at Springwood Estate, the ancestral home of the Roosevelts.

A tenant farmer on the Roosevelt estate, Moses Smith, said he'd been working the land for twenty-five years and FDR's death was the greatest shock of his life. FDR had visited him often on his land, which was also used for meetings during the presidential campaigns.

Many people across the country wept, even Republicans, isolationists, and others who had lost to him. All were now just Americans grieving the loss of an American president. People gathered on street corners, whispering, crying. People gathered around car radios, whispering, crying. For most, he was the first president whose voice they'd actually heard, either over the radio during his "fireside chats" and speeches, such as on December 8, 1941, or in the news reels. Add to that their intimate familiarity with the Roosevelt family and that millions had voted for him four times for president; there was a deep psychic investment. For many, he was family. A personal relationship had grown between the American people and their American friend. Broadcaster Arthur Godfrey said of FDR and Americans, "He was their leader. . . . He was their friend."

"The impact of the news of the President's death on the capital was tremendous. Although rumor and a marked change in Mr. Roosevelt's appearance and manner brought anxiety to many regarding his health, and there had been increased speculation as to the effects his death would have on the nation and world situation, the fact stunned the government and citizens of the capital."[178]

Senator Robert Taft, Republican of Ohio and a "constant adversary on policy," said of FDR, "[He] was the greatest figure of our time" who had died "at the very climax of his career." He was "a hero of the war, for he literally worked himself to death in the service of the American people."[179] Senator Arthur Vandenberg, another Republican, said of FDR, "[He] left an imperishable imprint on the history of America and of the world."[180] *De mortuis nil nisi bonum* (Of the dead, nothing but good is said). But it was more than not violating the ancient Latin edict of not speaking ill of the dead. In life, FDR had his political rivals and more than a few personal opponents. As for the rest of the Congress, most were simply in shock, and thus did not issue statements about the passing of Roosevelt. One exception being the Democratic House leader, John McCormack of Massachusetts, who said, "President Roosevelt was one of the greatest men of all time—a builder of human values. He will go down in history as the savior of democracy. His death is an incomparable loss to the world."[181]

Winston Churchill, who received the news around midnight, did not immediately issue a statement, nor did King George VI. But it was reported both were in a state of shock, as was everybody in London. Britain, too, had a deep affection for Roosevelt. After all, if it had not been for lend-lease and America joining the European war, England may well have gone under. Roosevelt, the patrician, was an honorary Englishman as far as the Brits were concerned. The news was received by many in government in stunned silence. Churchill and the House of Commons planned to adjourn for a day to pay their respects to the fallen American president.

The German news bureau was surprisingly restrained, given that FDR was their mortal enemy: "News of the death of President Roosevelt has, of course, made a deep impression in Berlin. German political circles refrain from drawing any conclusions on the possible effects which the death of the President may have on home and foreign policy of the United States."[182]

At FDR's old prep school, Groton, the flag was lowered to half-staff and the boys there prayed for the president, his family, and the nation. Roosevelt had been born January 30, 1882, at Hyde Park, to James and Sara. He was their only son, a scion of a rich and successful old American family that had made money in shipping, dry goods, real estate, sugar, railroads, importing, and other items. The mansion had been in the family for over one hundred years. The Roosevelts were never as wealthy as the Vanderbilts or the Astors or the Delanos. His mother controlled a great deal of money, but she doled it out to her son and his family only from time to time.

Fiorello La Guardia, the Republican mayor of New York City and sometimes FDR administration official, went on WNYC radio and, for half an hour, spoke extemporaneously and passionately about the loss of FDR, saying it was "our greatest loss. . . . Franklin Delano Roosevelt is not dead. His ideals live."[183] Then Charles de Gaulle weighed in, making it about himself, saying, "It is a terrible loss for our country and me personally."[184]

For the first time in eighty years, the New York Philharmonic Symphony canceled its scheduled performance at Carnegie Hall. The last time they had canceled was for the death of President Abraham Lincoln. For all those years, through strife and panics and wars and the deaths of other presidents and depressions, the New York Philharmonic bravely soldiered on, except for the deaths of these two monumental men.

FDR had known death his whole life; indeed, many key aides had died since he assumed office in March 1933. His longtime political aide, Louis Howe, had died in 1936, and even as late as February 1945, his military aide, Edwin M. Watson, had died. His father, James, had died around the turn of the century; his mother, Sara, had died in September 1941; his close personal secretary for twenty years, Marguerite "Missy" LeHand, had died in July 1944; his navy secretary, Frank Knox, had passed away a year earlier; and his personal bodyguard, August Adolph

"Gus" Gennerich, had died during a good neighbor tour of South America in July 1944. When FDR died, he was still seen often wearing the black mourning armband for his mother.

Just a week before, Pope Pius XII sent a message to Roosevelt in which he said, "I am praying for him and especially for his health."[185] The private missive to FDR was sent via a reporter stationed at the Vatican, who, in turn, gave it to the White House press secretary, who, in turn, gave it to the president, who, in turn, wrote a note back to the Holy Father, thanking him. The pope had told the reporter he was "deeply concerned about the President's well-being."[186]

At the White House, it was Eleanor Roosevelt who formally told Truman of the death of her husband.[187] Truman then asked the former first lady, "Is there anything I can do for you?" But she smiled and said to the new president, "Is there anything we can do for you? For you are the one in trouble now."[188] Jim Bishop wrote in his important book, *FDR's Last Year*, "The second sentence contains an essence of cruelty; a man newly elevated to the Presidency does not appreciate being told he is 'in trouble.' And yet this too was truth. Few, even those in the Senate who admired Truman, felt he had sufficient stature for the Presidency."[189]

Truman, now the most powerful man in the world, left the White House to go to his five-room apartment on Connecticut Avenue, where he lived with his wife, Bess, and their daughter, Margaret. He said he was going home to "go to bed."[190] Before leaving, he sent word to the gathering reporters that he would not have a press conference at that time, and directed the Secretary of State Edward B. Stettinius Jr. that it was his desire that the San Francisco conference go forward as planned. Stettinius, with tears streaming down his handsome face, told the new president "yes."

Truman said he "felt like the moon, the stars, and all the planets had fallen on me." He was replacing a beloved and dynamic Chief Executive who had led America through depression and war, and was now faced with the task of leading America to victory in World War II.

Worse still, Roosevelt had left Truman largely out of the loop during the latter's vice presidency—Truman was not even aware of the
Manhattan Project and other crucial matters. In assuming the presidency, Harry Truman also assumed a daunting burden. Whether he
would measure up to the task of leading the free world remained to
be seen.[191]

TRUMAN WAS IMMEDIATELY SEEN as a poor successor to the giant
Roosevelt. The *New York Times* said of Truman: "He is conscious of
limitations greater than he has . . . but for the time being that is not a bad
thing for the country."[192] That was about the best anybody could muster
about the little man from Missouri.

Truman's bio began to appear in newspapers, from his failed haber-
dashery to his service in Battery D in the First World War to his election
to the US Senate in 1934 to his impressive stewardship of the Senate War
Investigative Committee, which rooted out millions of dollars in fraud.

One of Truman's first actions was to pledge the successful pursuit
of the war to its final and winning end. The statement was issued by
the new White House Press Secretary Jonathan Daniels, who'd been
appointed to the post just one month before, replacing Steve Early: "The
world may be sure that we will prosecute the war on both fronts, East
and West, with all the vigor we possess to a successful conclusion."[193]

Truman was an internationalist, just as FDR had been. Truman had
said earlier, "America can no longer sit smugly behind a mental 'Maginot
Line.' . . . Either America must be constantly ready to repel alone all
and any attacks from the rest of the world or we must be willing to
cooperate with friendly states to check the first sign of aggression."[194]
He was assuming power at a delicate time in world history, with new
alliances and old enemies, with countries teetering on the edge and new
state-sponsored savagery ready to replace the existing state savagery. He'd
said the year before in accepting the vice-presidential nomination, "We
are, in our efforts to make this peace, very definitely in midstream."[195]

Roosevelt was hugely beloved but also hugely hated, even more so than Eleanor. He had changed the very nature of American politics and ushered in a new era of Democratic dominance after the seventy-year reign of the Republicans, from Lincoln to Hoover. True, the onslaught of the Great Depression helped spell doom for the GOP in 1932, but FDR cannily filled the void by remaking the Democratic Party into a blue-collar, "help the little guy," free-trade, internationalist, big-government party of the future. "Happy Days Are Here Again" was the party's unofficial theme song, and they projected a "can-do" air of confidence to the GOP's "green eye shade, eat-your-spinach" dour message. The Democratic Party of 1932 resembled little of the Democratic Party of Grover Cleveland of the late 1880s, save its harshness toward black Americans. As the party of the South, the Democrats had been the party of the Civil War, the party of the KKK, the party of segregation.

THE PLAN WAS TO return FDR's remains the next day, Saturday, April 14, via his beloved train car, the *Ferdinand Magellan*, to his boyhood home at Hyde Park, New York. It was announced he would not lie in state in the Rotunda of the US Capitol, denying tens of thousands a chance to say a last goodbye. Many presidents and generals had lain in state, most using the Lincoln catafalque on which the coffin was laid. Instead, the Episcopal Bishop of Washington, the Right Reverend Angus Dun, would preside over a "simple" ceremony in the East Room of the White House. There would be no eulogy and the seating arrangements would be extremely limited. The list of foreign dignitaries was limited to Anthony Eden, British Foreign Secretary, and a smattering of others like T. V. Soong, the Chinese foreign minister. Also present at the afternoon service were Mrs. Roosevelt, their daughter, Mrs. John Boettiger, and Brigadier General Elliot Roosevelt, who was flying in from Europe.

If there was any place Franklin Roosevelt would have chosen to die, it may have been on a boat at sea, but the wheelchair years before made that prospect problematic; so it may have been either Warm Springs or his beloved family estate, Springwood, high above the Hudson River in Hyde Park. While serving as president those twelve plus years, he traveled to Springwood about one thousand times. He once hosted King George VI and Queen Elizabeth for a famous hot dog roast there, as well as important conferences with Churchill and Prime Minister Mackenzie King of Canada. During his presidency, they were the only two places he could really relax.

The former first lady, Eleanor Roosevelt, said, "I am more sorry for the people of the country and the world than I am for us."[196] Then she left immediately for Warm Springs with her daughter and other family members, but she first asked Truman if it would be all right to use the official plane. The transfer of power was that swift.

Less than ten minutes after Truman was sworn in, Eleanor and Anna got into a limousine under a White House portico—Mrs. Roosevelt dressed in black and her daughter, Anna, in red—and headed to the National Airport, accompanied by Admiral Ross T. McIntire; the wheels were up at 7:40 p.m. Before entering the car, Eleanor "bowed to the little group of ushers, doormen and a few members of her press conference."[197] Earlier in the day, the newspaperwomen had been querying Mrs. Roosevelt about the San Francisco conference. Later she was to speak at a "thrift shop benefit at the Sulgrave Club, when a long-distance message came from Warm Springs, and she was called back to the White House to receive it."[198] Eleanor Roosevelt had a busy week planned, but it was all scrapped now. The Roosevelts had thirteen grandchildren, but the early talk was not to invite them to any funeral for their grandfather.

For maybe the first time in his presidency, a major newspaper, the *New York Times*, talked openly of Franklin Roosevelt's polio and subsequent paralysis, and his lifetime confinement to a wheelchair. For years, the myth had been promulgated that no one knew about his affliction, which was not true. Many people did know about it. It was just considered impolite to talk about it. A young boy recalled going to an outdoor rally at the Boston Common featuring the president in the 1930s. Before the speech started, the crowd was asked to turn their backs to the podium while FDR was wheeling up, and then, after his leg braces were locked in, to turn around to see him, standing there, erect, at the rostrum.

For a man confined to a wheelchair, he was often photographed fishing, swimming, or looking hale and hearty from the back of an open touring car.

FDR almost did not get to serve as president. While making a public appearance in Miami, just before his 1933 inauguration, a deranged man aimed a pistol and fired several rounds into the crowd with the intention of killing Roosevelt. But an unidentified woman in the crowd deflected the assailant's arm at the last second, possibly saving FDR's life. Sadly, the mayor of Chicago, Anton Cermak, who was standing right next to FDR, was killed and several bystanders wounded. The assailant, Giuseppe Zangara of Hackensack, New Jersey, was an anarchist and, according to reports, in deep physical pain. He was later tried, found guilty, and executed. Roosevelt had been returning from a pleasure boating trip aboard the *Nourmahal*, the yacht of wealthy society heir Vincent Astor. FDR had come ashore to board a train to take him home, but before that he was going to address the crowd of well-wishers in Bay Front Park, out in the open.

How bad was the economy FDR inherited? Starting in January 1930 through March 1933, 5,504 banks closed and all deposits vanished, altogether $3.4 billion. The entire savings of a generation was gone, disappeared. It was the greatest economic downturn in history. There were precious few dollars in circulation. When he was sworn in on March 4, 1933, he famously said, "The only thing we have to fear is fear itself." It became one of his signature aphorisms. He used biblical rhetoric to declare war on the rich, "the unscrupulous money changers." He charged that those monied interests "have fled from their high seats in the temple of our administration." He also signaled that his new Democratic Party would be an internationalist one, calling for a "good neighbor policy" toward other countries in the Americas.[199] His speech was, in short, revolutionary. In one fell swoop, he'd redefined two generations of politics.

In 1936, in accepting his party's nomination for the second time, FDR did not back away from bashing his own class, attacking the "princes of privileges" and the "economic royalists." He also unveiled a phrase, given to him by Tommy Corcoran, at the Philadelphia convention: "rendezvous with destiny." He said, "There is a mysterious cycle in human events. To some generations much is given. Of other generations much is expected. This generation of Americans has a rendezvous with destiny."[200]

One of FDR's most fervent supporters was a young Ronald Reagan, twenty-one, who had just graduated from Eureka College in Illinois. He cast his first vote in 1932 for FDR and would go on to cast three more votes for the man. Reagan always had a warm spot for FDR and never forgot that both his father and his brother got jobs at the War Progress Administration in the apogee of despair of the Great Depression.

FDR, using powers a president had not exercised possibly since Lincoln, moved swiftly to alleviate the Great Depression. In his first one hundred days, he began to create an alphabet soup of new agencies, including the Works Progress Administration, the Civilian Conservation Corps, the Public Works Administration, the Tennessee Valley Authority, the National Recovery Act, the Federal Emergency Recovery Act, the Federal Deposit Insurance Corporation, the Civil Works Administration, the Farm Security Administration, the National Labor Relations Board, the National Youth Administration, and more—many, many more. There were even federal programs for perpetually out-of-work writers, who now had no excuse to offer at the bar as to why they had not finished their novel, as well as another federal program for out-of-work artists. The government, for the first time in history, was paying farmers not to produce a crop. There was, it seemed, a federal program for everybody and everything.

He legalized 3.2 percent beer, but before long he would spearhead the repeal of the Eighteenth Amendment, and soon everybody could get a drink. But he also cut veterans' benefits, which would come back to haunt him. He was the last president to be inaugurated in March, a bow to the national crisis and modern travel. He was also the first president to travel the Panama Canal and the first president to visit Hawaii.

If nothing else, FDR was an absolute master at politics. The best.

During the 1932 campaign, the GOP tried to spread the nasty rumor that his health was so bad that seventeen life insurance companies had refused to write him a policy. FDR promptly went out and purchased a $100,000 life insurance policy on himself and named the charitable Warm Springs Foundation as the beneficiary. Game. Set. Match.

At the 1932 convention, he called for "a new deal for the American people."[201] The term "New Deal" stuck, and it became the signature of all of FDR's domestic policies. Even his "Brain Trust" of academics, businessmen, and hard-boiled political operatives became known as "New Dealers" or "New Deal Men." In 1937, he gave his inaugural address in a torrential downpour, but, as always, he was jaunty.

He never had much use for Herbert Hoover and refused to meet with the outgoing president to issue any joint statements on the national emergency. It was a smart move by FDR, but also brutal. He wasn't going to take ownership of any of Hoover's problems.

He and Al Smith had a widely reported rocky relationship that turned bad, as Smith, once the Democratic nominee for president, turned away from his own party and Roosevelt in 1936. FDR was accused by most Republicans (and some Democrats) of being a dictator, but he simply sloughed off the criticism. FDR and the New Deal were so popular, his party actually gained seats in the House and the Senate in the first off-year elections of 1934.

It's not to say there weren't problems with the New Deal. For whatever reason, the FDR administration canceled all the private mail-flying contracts, and instead had army fliers deliver the mail. But there were so many crashes, as the army pilots did not know the routes, the contracts were re-awarded to private fliers.

As of 1936, FDR told Congress in his annual report that no new taxes were needed and that the worst of the Great Depression had passed. But then the economy sank again into the muck.

There were fights over budgets and spending, and FDR's budget director resigned. But while his beloved New Deal came under attack, he remained personally popular. "Mr. Roosevelt was fortunate in other ways that helped his extraordinary career. He possessed unusual personal charm, which held to him many associates who questioned the wisdom of some of his policies. His distinguished bearing, made familiar to millions of people by countless news reel and newspaper pictures, was an asset. So was his richly timbred speaking voice, carried by radio into millions of American homes in countless fireside chats and formal addresses."[202]

He fought with the Supreme Court, which declared parts of his New Deal unconstitutional. He retaliated by trying to add new members, but this "court-packing" scheme failed, rejected by members of his own party.

Of course, the federal bureaucracy had grown exponentially, and he could always count on the support of these public employees. Along the way, he continued to reshape the Democratic Party, making it a coalition of urban sophisticates, academics, youth, the working man, laborers, and farmers, which left the Republican Party nowhere. Indeed, for years, America was ruled essentially by one party, while the GOP was reduced to complaining about the "boondoggle" of the New Deal or the not very appealing "me-tooism" of making the same arguments as the Democrats with negligible difference. His second term featured fights with big labor leadership, but he always enjoyed the support of the working man and woman.

Winston Churchill finally broke his silence to talk of the death of his old friend. He said the loss of FDR was "the loss of the British nation and of the cause of freedom in every land." He also sent a dispatch to Mrs. Roosevelt, which read, "I send my most profound sympathy for your grievous loss. . . . I feel so deeply for you all. As for me, I have lost a dear and cherished friendship which was forged in the fire of war. I trust you may find consolation in the glory of his name and the magnitude of his work. Churchill."[203] Stalin also issued a perfunctory statement, calling FDR "a great organizer."[204] Phone lines across the country became jammed because of the overload, and all four major radio networks—NBC, CBS, Mutual, and the "Blue Network of the American Broadcasting Company"—canceled their regular programming to carry news and tributes to the fallen president.[205]

The phrase "world leader" should have been invented for Franklin Roosevelt. In many ways, as of 1945, he was not only the president of the United States but the president of the world, with the leaders and dictators of the minor countries merely his vassal kings and dukes. Over the course of the past five years, all came on bended knee to touch the hem of his garment. With his jaunty smile and upright cigarette holder and sweeping cape, he was cast as the benevolent power broker. From Churchill to Stalin to de Gaulle to Chiang and everybody in between, they all came to the Leader of the Free World, all asking for something from America. And if he traveled to them, it was not a sign of weakness; no, it was a sign of strength. The president of the United States was willing to come down from Mount Olympus to mingle with the lesser people. They were the "Big Three"—Churchill, Stalin, and FDR—but that was cosmetic, maybe to make the others feel more equal. FDR was first among equals.

The world had changed impossibly since FDR's first inauguration in 1933. Back then he was "Dr. Save the Economy"; now he had become "Dr. Save the World." In his first inaugural address, the status of the world was but one paragraph in his remarks. Since 1939, the world crisis had occupied every sentence of every speech and address and press conference and meeting and casual remark. He entered the office only two months after Hitler had assumed power in Germany, when absolutely no one thought the haranguing nutcase with a funny mustache was a threat to anyone in 1933, except a sleeping Nazi audience member. FDR recognized the rise of the fascist nations and, as early as 1937, called for their "quarantine." According to the *New York Times*, "As the war clouds grew blacker over Europe, Mr. Roosevelt did what he could to dispel them."[206]

In 1938, Roosevelt called for a defense of Canada, should our ally to the north be attacked, but the American public was decidedly unmoved. He later called for the Germans and Czechs to settle the Sudetenland amicably, but that proved fruitless as Hitler simply invaded that part of Czechoslovakia. Later he recalled the American ambassador to Germany,

Hugh Wilson, in protest over Germany's increasingly harsh treatment of Jews.

Early the next year, he appealed to Hitler and Mussolini to pledge to ten years of neutrality, and to sweeten the deal offered American economic aid to the two, but to no avail. Seeing the coming war, Roosevelt asked Congress to amend the Neutrality Act, which covered arms embargos, to a "cash and carry" basis; the United States would help those countries that would help themselves against the Nazi and Japanese onslaught. When the Nazis invaded Denmark and Norway in April 1940, FDR denounced them in no uncertain terms. In May 1940, when Germany invaded the "Low Countries"—Belgium, the Netherlands, Luxembourg—and France, Roosevelt called for an unprecedented buildup of American armaments. He called for an unbelievable fifty thousand airplanes and a two-ocean navy at once, as well as an army draft. His defense buildup would eventually cost the nation over $28.5 billion.

He appointed experienced Republicans, such as Henry Stimson to serve as secretary of war. In the days following Dunkirk, he sought to aid the British without violating the various Neutrality Acts, which were ironically passed by a Democratic, albeit isolationist, Congress and signed by an internationalist Democrat—Franklin Delano Roosevelt.

Dipping into the dusty warehouses left over from the First World War, FDR "loaned" the British more than eighty thousand machine guns and nearly one million rifles. He also "traded" fifty ancient destroyers in exchange for some dubious military bases on English property, including British Guinea and Newfoundland. He arranged for a $100 million loan to China to fight the Japanese and gave assurances to the beleaguered Greek government. All this set the stage for his lend-lease policies, without which England may have succumbed to the Nazi onslaught. In a December press conference, FDR hinted at what he had in mind. He later formalized it in a fireside chat on December 30, 1940, then presented it to the Congress on January 5, 1941. FDR used the memorable phrase, "arsenal of democracy" for the first time in his fireside chat.[207]

Later in January 1941, a bill was introduced in the Congress to give

Roosevelt almost unlimited war powers, but it engendered strong opposition from the isolationist Democrats like Burton K. Wheeler, senator from Montana, who had led the fight against FDR's court-packing scheme of several years earlier. Of the new proposal, he acerbically said, "another New Deal triple A foreign policy—plow under every fourth American boy."[208] Roosevelt was furious and thundered that Wheeler's attacks were "dastardly" and "rotten."[209] Perhaps sensing the coming hostilities as well, the Congress passed the Lend-Lease Act overwhelmingly, which set the country on an inevitable path toward war.

In his third inaugural address, FDR said, "In this day the task of the people is to save that nation and its institutions from disruption. . . . We do not retreat. We are not content to stand still. As Americans, we go forward, in the service of our country, by the will of God."[210] The isolationists were in high dungeon, including America's Lone Eagle, Charles Lindbergh. The president compared him to Vallandigham, "the appropriate leader of a band of 'Copperheads,' who opposed the Civil War."[211] Clement Vallandigham was a prominent Ohio politician and critic of Abraham Lincoln's policies. For criticizing the Civil War publicly—a violation of Military General Order Number 83, an extension of Lincoln's suspension of habeas corpus—Vallandigham was tried, convicted, and, for his punishment, sent into exile in the South. He later became the inspiration for Edward Everett Hale to write *The Man Without a Country*.

In 1941, FDR froze German, Italian, and Japanese assets in America. Then Hitler made a critical mistake by invading Russia. Sentiment in America had been riding high against Joseph Stalin because of communist-induced strikes in essential war industries, but once Hitler invaded the Soviet Union, public opinion swung wildly in favor of Mother Russia. FDR called Germany an "international outlaw" and accused them of "piracy" for sinking American vessels in the North Atlantic. Roosevelt then promised all available aid to Russia, as he had Great Britain, and then, in essence, said America would support anyone fighting Nazism. Later, he ordered the navy in the North Atlantic to shoot on sight Nazi U-boats attacking civilian or military ships at sea. Throughout all this,

Roosevelt remained firmly at the helm of the US government, acting almost always as his own spokesman. After he took his initial steps against Germany, their state-run newspapers singled him out for vitriol and the worst sort of personal invective. Hitler, too, took to childishly referring to FDR as "Frau Roosevelt," though the fact was, in blunt terms, FDR had fathered six children and der Führer none.

But in death, victory had eluded FDR, and the irony was lost on no one. No man—save for the soldier in the field or the sailor on the high seas—had worked harder to defeat Nazi Germany and Fascist Italy and Imperial Japan. He always had time to meet in the Oval Office or at sea or at an army base with those brave men who had been awarded and recognized for their courage in the world conflict; sometimes to pin medals on their chests and sometimes just to give them a kind pat on the arm. And he was at his desk going through memos and telegrams and letters constantly and poring over maps and meeting with the brass, reporters, and other heads of state. For a man confined to a wheelchair most of his adult life, he was poetry in motion. Most men who contracted polio and lost the use of their legs as a result withdrew, became sullen, bitter, even antisocial. Not Roosevelt. He became more empathetic, more outgoing, more resolute, and more energetic. And more able to lead. If anything, his affliction made him a better president, or at least a more tenacious president; certainly, a more cunning president. If there was ever a time in which the talents of a man were so perfectly matched up with the problems of the nation, it was FDR and the Great Depression and FDR and World War II.

Nevertheless, confinement to a wheelchair took a terrible toll on his health. Of course, there was the risk to his overall physical condition, which included trouble with his circulation, blood pressure, heart, and respiration. The list of ailments went on and on. But from 1933 up until 1943, he had aged like most other middle-aged men. He was seen so often in newsreels and the newspapers with a big jovial smile; his upbeat attitude was helpful to his health. It was only in the last year and a half that Roosevelt's health had taken an alarming descent. He looked fifteen years older than he actually was. The White House never let on to the public that he was in poor health, and the reporters covering the White House were in on the conspiracy, just as they'd been in on the conspiracy to not write about or photograph him in a wheelchair.

The White House never officially disclosed the real condition of the president, and for the last several years, his health waxed and waned. He'd had a fifty-foot-long swimming pool installed in the White House and swam at least five days a week, but he'd stopped more or less after the war began. The company of friends, his cousins, and people to blather with also rejuvenated him, as did working on his massive and impressive stamp collection. He had the occasional cold, and once had a small growth removed from the back of his neck, which caused a minor stir. He also contracted the grippe once or twice. But it was clear that, somewhere around 1943, he was beginning to fail. "Official statements regarding" his health "appeared to be in conflict with visible evidence of his physical condition."[212]

FDR had been president for 4,423 days—three terms plus two months and twenty-three days into his fourth term—and almost every one of those days had been filled with drama, conflict, resolution, dismay, humor, trials, and spectacles.

Even his last trip had been hazardous and strenuous. Only two days after his inauguration, he departed Washington for the Yalta Conference. He left by train, then got on a navy cruiser, stopped at Malta, and from there flew to Yalta. All Stalin had to do was wander down the road a bit from Moscow. The accommodations at Yalta, by all accounts, were appalling. Bad food, bad bedding, cold rooms, cold water—Stalin did his worst to roll out the welcome wagon. All in all, the long journey, the arduous meetings, the bad accommodations, and Stalin's harangues took their toll.

THE TRIBUTES ROLLED IN, from world leaders to American politicians, including former president Herbert Hoover, who so eloquently said, "The nation sorrows at the passing of its President. Whatever differences there may have been, they end in the regrets of death. It is fortunate that in this great crisis of war our Armies and Navies are under such magnificent leadership that we shall not hesitate. The new President will have the backing of the country. While we mourn Mr. Roosevelt's death, we shall march forward."[213] Other testimonials came from Cardinal Francis J. Spellman, Senator Alben Barkley, Senator Arthur Vandenberg, General George C. Marshall, Secretary of State Cordell Hull, Soviet ambassador Andrei Gromyko, FDR's former aide James Farley, and his lifetime aide Harry Hopkins. All were grief-stricken. There were occasional references in the press of him being paralyzed or contracting polio, but usually in the most oblique or polite or hushed terms.

In New York City, the Stage Door Canteen, a place for servicemen to eat, drink, dance, relax, and watch live shows, was halted when the manager appeared onstage to tell the audience that FDR had died. They then canceled the rest of the show, although they continued to serve meals. "When the word sank in some of the servicemen began to cry. Some of the girls in the show sobbed audibly. The soldiers, sailors and marines, some limping wounded, filed slowly into the street."[214] Motion picture shows and department stores were also closed across the nation.

EVEN THOUGH THE NATION and the world grieved at the loss of Franklin Roosevelt, the news and events of the war just would not stop. That day, an American Liberty ship in Rome exploded, killing 360 American and British servicemen and wounding 1,730. The ship was loaded with airplane bombs, and only two of the servicemen aboard the ship survived. At the harbor, Bari, three other ships caught fire in the melee. In due time, the next of kin of the servicemen were notified.[215]

The American death toll of servicemen and sailors had risen to 196,999, with the army bearing the great brunt at 159,267 and the navy at 37,402; killed, wounded, missing in action, and POWs totaled 899,390 young men.

HEINRICH HIMMLER ORDERED ALL German towns and villages to be "defended to the last man" and that none could surrender unilaterally to the advancing Allies. It was accompanied by an order that "any who deflect from this duty will be condemned to death." The order was signed by Field Marshal Wilhelm Keitel, Himmler, and Martin Bormann, identified as "head of the party chancellery."[216] Hitler was showing up in fewer and fewer daily news reports, and rumors continued to sweep Germany and the world that he was seriously ill. But the British papers generally dismissed it, while Churchill restated the "unconditional surrender" policy toward Nazi Germany. Labor leader Rhys John Davies begged to differ with the prime minister, citing the history of the Boer Wars, but Churchill responded, saying that Rhys Davies was "not very accurate in his history."[217]

German general Otto Lasch surrendered the city of Königsberg to the Russians without getting Berlin's approval, so the Nazis promised retaliation. "Reprisals will be taken against Lasch's family," promised a high command communiqué. Lasch had once been a hero of the Fatherland, serving well in Operation Barbarossa. Now he was accused of "cowardice."[218]

The Russian army had killed 42,000 Germans and taken 92,000 German POWs. Propaganda Minister Joseph Goebbels wrote in his weekly propaganda broadsheet *Reich*, "We have sunk very low."[219] He elaborated that the war could not possibly go on much longer, not without a greater sacrifice of the German people, who of course had little left to give to the war effort. Like many of the other Nazi leaders, Goebbels was in deep denial about the amount of will the Germans had left to fight in contrast to that of the Allies, which Germany had sorely underestimated since the beginning of the war. Goebbels ranted and called for renewed guerrilla warfare. But he was no expert in warfare, having been excluded from military service in World War I because of a deformed foot, which was noticeable as he walked with a limp.

Meanwhile, the food crisis was skyrocketing in Germany and, indeed, much of Western Europe. The Americans had enough trouble keeping the supply lines for the war machine going, and bringing along tons of food to feed the civilian population was straining resources. The Nazi Party, in addition to many pressing issues, was concerned about the defection of expatriates who were living in other European countries. One of the most respected men on either side, Henry Stimson, the American secretary of war, warned the Germans that resistance was futile. At his press conference, Stimson said something interesting: "But the enormity of Hitler's crime against the world and the responsibility of the German people in its perpetration must be made equally clear to the Germans."[220]

The advancing American army liberated three hundred women who were political prisoners, including a housewife who was sentenced to eighteen months for tearing up a picture of Hitler. The American officer in charge said that some of the women were "crazed" due to extreme starvation, "prison hardships and whippings," and "we found 300 rubber clubs with wrist thongs with which the women were beaten regularly. When we freed them, they were half dead with hunger." The women "were kept under filthy conditions . . . and herded like sheep. In one room about 10 by 20 feet a dozen women were forced to sleep and live," reported the Associated Press.[221] They were of all ages and nationalities, and their only crime had been some sort of opposition to Nazism. When the American GIs opened up tins of sardines, the women cried with joy. They'd been on a meager diet of potatoes for months. As far as the beatings, there had long been a worldwide suspicion that many Germans were committing sexual abuses involving sadism, masochism, bondage, and discipline.

The British announced there would be no more drafting of men over thirty, clearly a sign of how the winds of war were prevailing. They also announced the outfitting of an "Amenity Ship" for her troops in the Western Pacific, complete with a brewery, a movie theater, barber shops, restaurants, snack counters, and more. The party ship could ably entertain up to six hundred men at any given time.

THE NINTH ARMY WAS across the Elbe and closing in on Berlin, but Patton's 6th Armored Division of the Third Army went the farthest, over forty-six miles. "It has smashed . . . east and crossed the Saale River in two places between Naumburg and Jena, scene of one of Napoleon's great victories."[222]

Overhead, American Thunderbolt pilots reported on the increasingly chaotic withdrawal of the Germans in the midst of the advancing tanks and infantry. The Third Army had taken over seventy thousand prisoners since early March. German radio was just as chaotic as they aired that no central front existed anymore. Earlier, the Third Army had taken the city of Weimar and the local German citizens celebrated, not at their conquer but because it meant an end to the war was at hand.

The American civilian and military leadership was especially steamed at the Nazis for their treatment of POWs. The Germans had starved and beaten the American POWs and had now put them on a forced march to the interior of Germany; for what purpose no one knew, but one popular theory was that these prisoners could be used in a hostage exchange or for negotiations. Some 35,000 were on the forced march to join another 34,000 who were already being held there. Some 1,568,580 tons of Red Cross supplies waited in Sweden and Switzerland for transport into Germany for the POWs. "In general, conditions under which American prisoners are held today are deplorable," reported the *New York Times*. "In addition to the suffering caused by the conditions . . . instances are being daily uncovered of deliberate neglect, indifference and cruelty in the treatment of American prisoners, actions which have shocked the entire civilized world. These atrocities are documented by the pitiable condition of liberated American soldiers."[223]

HOUSEWIVES OF QUEENS, NEW York, staged a pro-government, anti-black-market protest over food prices. Standing amid strollers and baby carriages, they chanted poorly composed slogans against an unregulated food market.

Children were not left out of the nation's newspapers. Helpful hints suggested baseball—"383 diamonds are now open throughout the city"—as well as bicycling in Central Park.[224] A headline in the society pages of a New York paper proclaimed, "Miss Vaughan Wed to Fighter Pilot."[225] It was not unusual.

In Okinawa, American guns downed 118 Japanese fighter planes, and the forty-eight Stars and Stripes flew over the Japanese island. The fight had been tough and was not over, but the Allies were now just one step away from a massive invasion of the main Japanese island.

Despite losing her husband, Mrs. Roosevelt had time to tell Americans to consider all the facts of the matter before deciding on the future of Germany.

The US submarine *Scamp* was lost in Pacific action with all sixty-five hands, including her skipper, Commander John C. Hollingsworth. So far, the *Scamp* was the forty-second American submarine lost for reasons unknown while at sea in this war. The new United Nations had grown to forty-seven countries, including Lebanon and Saudi Arabia. General Douglas MacArthur announced that the staff that had served him so well during the southwest Pacific campaign would serve him again during the planned ground invasion of Japan.

"Clean Out Your Closet Week" was announced. Everybody everywhere was asked to check for shoes they no longer wore, as well as sweaters, socks, bedding, blankets, and children's clothing. Collection boxes were set up at schools, churches, and synagogues. The collection was being sponsored by the Civilian Defense Volunteers Office and the American Women's Volunteer Services. Within hours, two tons had been collected in one box in Times Square alone. The used clothing was bound for the destitute of Europe. Across the country, Americans opened their hearts by opening their closets. The eventual goal in Manhattan was fourteen tons of garments and bedding. All this was done under the theme "Uncle Sam Comes to the Rescue."[226]

Everywhere there was discussion of black markets. The government's regulation of the economy at the war's end was breaking down. The investigation of black-market meat was under congressional investigation.

The Jewish Agency for Palestine was assembling plans to resettle some one million European Jews in Palestine after the war. Jews were afraid to stay in Europe and with good reason. So many Jews had disappeared into thin air and, though the Holocaust was still not widely known or believed, "they [were] afraid to stay in Hungary, Rumania and Poland, especially in the small towns. . . . A whole generation have been raised on anti-Semitism. . . . Because of what has happened, Jews [did] not want to stay in the countries where their mothers, brothers and sisters were killed and tortured and where the rest of the population witnessed these acts or even took part in them."[227] Some $8 million had already been raised to purchase rural lands in Palestine, with over $3 million going toward purchasing land for housing. Thousands of laborers would be needed to build a Jewish homeland.

THE TEMPERATURE ON THE East Coast had risen to an unseasonably warm 75 degrees. A new and interesting book out was *Rockets and Jets*, which explored the destructive nature of these two new formidable means of propulsion. The Senate was debating a "war secrets" bill in which harsh penalties were promised to anyone who gave military secrets to any foreign country. Fines of $10,000 and one year in prison were proposed for anyone who disclosed any US secrets to any representative of any other country.

In an exhibition game that raised over $22,000 for the Red Cross, the Dodgers defeated the Yankees, 3 to 1. Present in the stands were several thousand wounded sailors and servicemen, all attending for free. The famed Joe Medwick, his mysterious back problems gone, joined up again with the Giants.

AS OF SATURDAY, APRIL 14, the headlines and front pages were all about FDR's coming last rites in the White House. Everybody was still numbed by the news, and no one could get their arms around the idea that their friend would never again occupy the White House.

Leaving the Little White House, beginning at 9:35 a.m., the

"copper-lined mahogany casket" was accompanied by one thousand troops along the red clay road.[228] Following the hearse was Eleanor Roosevelt dressed in funeral black and covered by a fur cape. Only the president's dog, Fala, was in the car with Mrs. Roosevelt. Hushed drums accompanied the procession. Many of the marching soldiers could be seen crying under the boiling sun while some townspeople watched in silence. FDR had made many friends among the afflicted, the handicapped, and polio victims. They, too, wept and watched as their friend was wheeled slowly to the Warm Springs train station.

The president left Warm Springs in his cherished train car, the *Ferdinand Magellan*. All along the route, crowds filled the scene, most of them crying, standing in subdued silence. For most, it was hard to remember a president who so dominated the world, the country, and their lives. In fact, there was not one since his cousin, Teddy Roosevelt.

Saturday, April 14, 1945, was designated as a national day of mourning. The lead story in the *New York Times* was magically, poetically, tragically, and brilliantly scribed, "Through the black silence of this southern night, the train bearing toward its last resting place the body of Franklin D. Roosevelt is rolling slowly through a sorrowful countryside."[229] Along the way, the slow-moving train encountered knots and clutches of mourning Americans at byways and crossroads. At the stop in Atlanta, the mayor, William B. Hartsfield, presented a large bouquet of flowers.

Mrs. Roosevelt accompanied her husband on the train that arrived at Union Station in Washington, DC, at 10:00 a.m. The coffin, in a procession from Union Station to the White House, was escorted in a motorized car by two noncommissioned officers from each of the services—the marines, the army, the navy, and the coast guard. Army Master Sergeant James Powder commanded the procession. President Truman, the legislative leadership, the cabinet, and the judiciary all met FDR's casket at Union Station. An air corps band played as the flag-covered casket was transferred to a horse-drawn caisson for the trip down Delaware and Constitution Avenues, Fifteenth Street, and Pennsylvania

Avenue to the West Wing gates of the White House. Troops lined the route. Behind them, silent, weeping Americans. The procession was led by the DC Police Force and the Washington Military District, and they were met at the White House by trumpeters as well as the commander of the Military District, Major General Charles F. Thompson; the doctor who had attended him last, Commander Howard Bruenn; FDR's press secretary of long standing, Stephen Early; and some military members who had known and were liked by FDR. CBS radio broadcaster Arthur Godfrey, at one point, was heard to utter, "God give me the strength to do this." He was later heard sobbing by listeners.

The ceremony for the remains of Franklin Delano Roosevelt took place in the East Room of the White House, at 4:00 p.m., with the portraits of George and Martha Washington watching over. Yes, the very same portrait of Washington that Dolly Madison had rolled up just as the British were approaching to burn the White House in 1814.

Roosevelt was a lifetime Episcopalian. The ceremony was billed as a "simple" service. The scene in the East Room was a massive display of lilies behind FDR's casket and catafalque. The American flag was on the left side and the flag of the American president was on the right. Four military personnel—a sailor, a marine, a soldier, and a flier—all stood at post, left arms behind their backs, right arms brandishing a rifle, on the four corners of the small Oriental rug neatly placed under the bier. There were two hundred empty gold straight-back chairs, each with a hymnal on the seat. The big piano had been moved out of the way and the walls had been adorned with gilt-edged mirrors; several large chairs were left for Truman, Mrs. Truman, and their daughter, Margaret, to sit in, silently watching, underneath great dimmed chandeliers.

Afterward, the casket bearing the body of the thirty-second president made its final trip to his beloved Hyde Park. President Truman and other Washington dignitaries accompanied the FDR casket. There were several servicing stops along the way from Washington to the Hudson River, but at each there were "guards of honor."[230] FDR would be buried on the grounds there on Sunday, April 15, at ten o'clock. Roosevelt had always been suspicious of Friday the thirteenths, but it was Thursday, April 12, that was his black day. Truman ordered all federal flags to be lowered to half-staff for one month in remembrance and in honor of Franklin Roosevelt. Naval vessels also lowered their flags to half-mast for one month. Stores across the country posted signs stating they were closed out of respect for the passing of President Roosevelt.

SOME SAW THE ASCENSION of Harry Truman as an indicator that White House policies would turn to the right, after the twelve years of FDR. Many, even in the Democratic Party, had whispered for years that Roosevelt had often behaved like the Congress did not matter. The day before, Friday the 13th, Truman met with congressional leaders for lunch on Capitol Hill. It was significant. Roosevelt would have had the congressional leaders come to him. Truman was a creature of the Congress; FDR was a creature unto himself.

Truman later met with the military leaders and promised no change in European or Pacific policy, saying there would be "no change of purpose or break of continuity in the foreign policy of the United States government."[231]

The papers were filled with stories of those being considered for the new Truman administration: who was up and who was down. The same old Washington parlor game. Harry Truman was not taken seriously by many. He was known to have few hobbies, besides drinking and poker, and he was not thought of as any great or charismatic individual. He was not a great speaker and had a voice that was high-pitched and a bit nasally. Most expected him to serve out the three and a half years of the remaining Roosevelt term of office, but that would be it. Most of all, Truman was seen as a fierce party man who hated most Republicans with a white-hot passion. It was thought in some quarters he would receive the "sympathetic attitude of the press."[232] There was nothing of the majestic to Truman, unlike FDR. Whereas Roosevelt was regal, benevolent, Truman was plebian, even taciturn. Roosevelt had a voice that entered a room before he did. Truman had a voice that made cats yowl.

To commemorate the passing of FDR, workers in war industries worked a full day on Monday at the request of the chairman of the War Production Board, J. A. Krug, who sent a telegram to factories asking that workers continue but that services could be held remembering Roosevelt.

THE WAR CONTINUED UNABATED. Patton's army was storming to a position just thirty-eight miles from Dresden while the Allied air force had downed another 321 German planes. In just one week, at least 1,392 German planes had been destroyed. It was hard to imagine where exactly the Germans were still coming up with planes, but these were definitely older, inferior models being piloted by little more than boys—that is, if they even got in the air; as many were machine-gunned while sitting on the ground. Whether in the air or on the ground, American and British fighters cut through the Germans like a hot knife through butter.

In Japan, the citizenry was ordered to get ready for a massive invasion of the Japanese islands. A message had gone out via Tokyo radio telling civilians to prepare for war and how to fight the invading Allied armies. Analysts said, given the tenacity of the Japanese people, the war could last until 1948.

CURIOUSLY, THE STOCK AND commodities markets closed for the passing of FDR, but the banks were open as it was a day of mourning, not a national holiday. Stocks were advancing when the news of the death of the president reached Wall Street.

New York City was awash in rumors. According to one news report, "Widespread jitters bordering on mass hysteria seemed to sweep New York yesterday . . . as rumors of killings, accidents and deaths involving prominent persons flooded the city."[233] "Newspapers, radio stations, government offices, banks and corner drugstores were deluged with thousands of telephone calls asking, 'is it true?' that such and such a person had been killed." Telephone operators began to wonder if it was an organized campaign to ball up phone lines. Some of the rumors were that Frank Sinatra had died. "Other names mentioned were those of Mayor

La Guardia, Harry Hopkins, Robert Taylor . . . Charles Chaplin . . . Al Jolson, Errol Flynn, Babe Ruth, Jack Benny."[234] The city's phone system could normally handle ten million calls a day, but it shot up that day to many more. The newsroom of the *New York Times* was overwhelmed with over ten thousand calls in one afternoon. Some callers just wanted to play a prank by standing at drug store phone booths and passing along one fable after another. The rumor that actor Van Johnson had died was prominent, as was the rumor that heavyweight champion Jack Dempsey had passed away. This may have been because his restaurant—at Broadway and Forty-Ninth Streets—had posted a sign saying they would be closed because of the death of FDR.

One of the most Republican counties in the nation, Westchester, New York, was in deep mourning for President Roosevelt, with flags lowered, traffic moving slowly, people seen weeping on the streets, and businesses shuttered. Golf courses and beaches were closed, and a vaudeville show was postponed. There was a county-wide memorial service, and church bells tolled at the exact time of FDR's service at Hyde Park. Brooklyn College named a building after Franklin Delano Roosevelt. The president of the college, Dr. Harry D. Gideonse, said, "He is a war casualty, in the same sense as a soldier or sailor under his command. But we must keep our eye on his ultimate goal, the organization of a world community dedicated to law and justice."[235]

All normal radio programming was canceled for the foreseeable future and replaced by . . . static. When stations came back on Monday morning, they consisted of "news broadcasts, appropriate music, memorial services, eulogies and other special tributes to the late President."[236] A collective ad was taken out in the *New York Times*, listing all the businesses that would be closed "out of respect to the memory of the President."[237] They included Bloomingdale's, Gimbels, Hecht's, Lord and Taylor, Saks 34th, and many others. Across the nation, such ads filled the nation's newspapers.

Around the world, people were catching their breath at the death of the American president. Filipinos were shocked. Londoners were shocked. They were shocked in Belgium and Bermuda. France was to observe one day of remembrance. The Brits took it especially hard. They had revered the American presidency for a long time, at least since Abraham Lincoln, so the Court Circular, a sort of daily report on the affairs of the royal family, was also in grief for seven days. A statue of a gloomy Lincoln stood watch outside Westminster Abbey, and now many thought a statue of FDR should someday join him. Churchill was seen leaving Ten Downing Street looking somber and sad. He referred to FDR as "this great departed statesman and war leader."[238] Anthony Eden, the British foreign secretary, would attend the funeral, but all eyes were on Prime Minister Churchill.

The House of Commons received the formal news of FDR's death, and Churchill rose heavily to speak. This was a man who had seen war and peace in many iterations, had suffered personal losses, and now had lost a towering world figure and friend.

> This House will have learned with the deepest sorrow, the grievous news which has come to us from across the Atlantic, which conveys to us the loss of the famous President of the United States whose friendship for the cause of freedom and for the cause of the weak and poor have won immortal fame. It is not fitting that we should continue our work this day. I feel that the House will wish to render its token of respect to the memory of this great departed statesman and war leader by adjourning immediately. I should propose that on Tuesday next, tributes should be paid when we are assembled here by the leaders of the various parties in the House and that we should afterwards proceed with the business already announced.[239]

He did not speak with his usual gusto and bravado, and his voice quavered a few times.

Churchill was dressed somberly, as were all the members of Parliament. Attendance was heavy for the end of the week when the legislative schedule was insignificant. The House of Commons gathered at 11:00 a.m. and recessed at 11:08 a.m. While Churchill called on other parties to eulogize Roosevelt, it later came to pass—and all parties agreed—that he alone should eulogize his friend and fellow warrior. His comments earlier to the House of Commons were drawing frank reactions. "They observed that his enunciation was less clear, that he faltered at two points in his brief speech and that he failed to phrase his sentences in his accustomed style."[240]

Of all the institutions who mourned Roosevelt, it may have been the American military that was most moved. Many of the brass had already held a long friendship with Roosevelt going back to when he was assistant secretary of the navy. But he'd also been friends for many years with General Douglas MacArthur, although he once told friends that MacArthur—along with Governor Huey Long of Louisiana—was one of the most dangerous men in America. From Europe, Eisenhower sent his condolences as did George Marshall. MacArthur, in the Far East, sat alone, listening to the radio reports. A palatable pall went through George Patton's Third Army. Said Private Albert Osborn, "I can remember the President ever since I was a little kid. America will seem a strange, empty place without his voice talking to the people when great events occur. He died fighting for democracy, the same as any soldier."[241]

Latin America was grieving. In Puerto Rico, businesses, schools, and government offices closed. It was the same in Cuba. FDR was called the "greatest modern man" in Panama.[242]

It was the same over nearly the entire world as a grand outpouring of affection and respect was heaped on Franklin Delano Roosevelt, except for the vituperations heaped on him—along with calumny and lies—by the Third Reich.

Still, some of the affairs of America continued. A TWA flight on a Stratoliner was booking passengers on nonstop flights from the East Coast to the West Coast. At the Pennsylvania Railroad, they were touting all the war matériel they could carry, including PT boats, planes, tanks, shells, trucks, and locomotives.

Roosevelt had been working on a speech the night before he died. He was to address three hundred Jefferson Day Dinners across the country via radio. Jefferson was viewed by many as the founder of the Democratic Party, and the Democrats were planning to gather to celebrate the election of 1944. It was not to be; although, as always, FDR's words resonated and touched and moved. His draft spoke of peace: "Americans are gathered together this evening in communities all over the country to pay tribute to the living memory of Thomas Jefferson—one of the greatest of all democrats; and I want to make it clear that I am spelling that word 'democrats' with a small 'd.'"[243] With that, his speech waxed on about peace at home, peace abroad.

> We seek peace—enduring peace. More than an end to war, we want an end to the beginnings of all wars—yes, an end to this brutal, inhuman, and thoroughly impractical method of settling the differences between governments.
>
> The once powerful malignant Nazi state is crumbling. The Japanese war lords are receiving . . . the retribution for which they asked when they attacked Pearl Harbor. . . .
>
> The work, my friends, is peace. More than an end of this war—an end to the beginnings of all wars. Yes, an end, forever, to this impractical, unrealistic settlement of the differences between governments by the mass killing of peoples.[244]

He went on from there, touching third rails, pushing buttons, laying waste to opponents' now-discarded ideas. Even in death, FDR was slaying his opposition and championing his ideas, his friends, his country. His words and the words of other great men and women were timeless.

The crafty old wordsmith had not lost his touch one bit. Indeed, if anything, his flow and composition had probably gotten better. His speech concluded, "The only limit to our realization of tomorrow will be our doubts of today. Let us move forward with strong and active faith."[245]

As THE PLANS FOR the funeral progressed, it was apparent that three of his four sons would not be able to get back in time. All four Roosevelt boys were in uniform, deep in the war. Only Brigadier General Elliot Roosevelt would make it back to Hyde Park to join Eleanor, Anna, and the four wives and family members. Two sons, Franklin and John, were on naval duty, entrenched in the Pacific; it was logistically impossible to get them home in time. Same with James. It was another tragedy as all four Roosevelt boys were serving honorably, serving their commander in chief, serving their father. None of FDR's thirteen grandchildren would attend the White House services.

Tom Dewey, governor of New York and the loser to FDR in the 1944 presidential campaign, was nonetheless invited to attend the funeral services at the White House. He sent Truman a letter pledging his fealty to the new president, saying, "In your every effort on behalf of our country and of the peace of the world you have the fullest support of the Government of the State of New York."[246] For a short time, with the death of Roosevelt, partisanship faded to the background.

FDR was dead. Long live FDR.

TRUMAN SETTLED INTO HIS first day as president, and it had been a hectic one, including a meeting with the editor of the *Kansas City Star*, the same crusading newspaper that had broken up much of the Pendergast political machine from which Truman had once sprung. Truman had been planning to attend the annual Gridiron Dinner (as had FDR) the next night in DC, but he canceled his plans, and then the dinner was canceled.

Truman worked out of the Oval Office. The desk had been cleared of the numerous knickknacks that had accumulated over Roosevelt's many years. But the model ships stayed, as well as the ship and sea paintings. The White House was in a disorganized state. Preparations for the services, accommodations for the Roosevelt family, florists, dozens of people streaming in and out, the White House staff, all in all a controlled muddle. Meanwhile, Truman and his family gave up the small, five-room apartment on Connecticut Avenue to move into Blair House, the official house of the US government reserved for dignitaries. The 120-year-old residence was conveniently located on Pennsylvania Avenue across from the White House. It had been acquired in 1943, and in just two short years, royalty of all sorts had stayed there.

There had never been any protocol or precedent set for a deceased president's family to move out while a new president and his family moved in. Mary Lincoln lingered for five weeks in the White House following the assassination of her husband. This may have been due to her anger at Andrew Johnson for not paying a courtesy call or writing a condolence note. President William Henry Harrison's wife, Anna, was too ill to accompany her husband, "Old Tippecanoe," to Washington. So he asked his daughter-in-law to act as his hostess. But as he took ill and died one month later, there is no account of any of his family residing in the White House. When McKinley was assassinated, Teddy Roosevelt's family moved in less than one week after his death. Harding died in San Francisco in August 1923, while Coolidge was at his family home in Vermont.

The history of the Blair House dates back to Andrew Jackson, when he brought his friend, Francis Preston Blair, to become editor of the *Washington Globe*. Later, Lincoln was friends with the Blair family, who occupied the house. Mrs. Victoria Geany had been the housekeeper there for twenty-seven years.

NAZI GERMANY WAS FALLING fast. But the death of Franklin Roosevelt was seen as some sort of an omen to Hitler, who was maniacally devoted to astrology, fortune-telling, and signs. He was also counting on a weakening of the Allies' resolve with FDR dead, reasoning that the American president was the glue that held together the seemingly fragile alliance. It was a longshot belief. What Hitler never understood was that it was *he* who held together the Allied powers. There was discussion and pronouncements and Hitler's strategists making grand declarations. Oh, there were some food supplies here and ammo dumps there, and a few scattered tanks and planes, but nothing to mount a counteroffensive of any real nature. The idea of FDR's death creating any real opportunity was just a pipe dream for the Nazis. Their day had come and gone. Their idea of withdrawing into two redoubts in the north and south was also always a pipe dream.

In reality, "German resistance [was] crumbling along the fronts of the Twelfth Army Group."[247] And every newspaper map depiction of the assault on Germany proved it. Little American flags from the west and little Russian flags from the east depicted the Third Reich as an ever-shrinking land mass. The 83rd Infantry Division; the 9th Armored; the 3rd Armored; Patton's 4th, 6th, and 11th Armored Divisions; and the 19th Infantry Division—among others—were squeezing in on Germany, wringing the last life out of the evil, terrible monster.

THE END OF THE war may be coming, but that did not stop American companies from advertising their best war products like the "Water Buffalo" made by the Food Machinery Corporation. The print ads touted: "steel clad—the amazing land and water ferry of the Yanks— the 'Water Buffalo'—repeated in daring landings of the Pacific and Normandy when it transported troops and matériel under fire across the never-before-stormed Rhine River."[248] The Food Machinery also made Bean orchard and Crop Sprayers.

TOKYO REPORTED HAVING SUNK twenty-one Allied ships and of fires across the city. The fires were confirmed as they were seen from B-29 nose bubbles; the sinkings were not confirmed.

Admiral Nimitz reported that the kamikaze mission had done considerable damage but had not stopped the American fleet. Everybody now knew about the "divine wind" legend behind the kamikaze pilots who committed suicide by flying their explosive-laden planes into ships. The kamikaze fighter only added to the Americans' imagery of the Japanese as being a savage and insane race.

Fifteen Japanese subs were sunk by the American fleet. That brought the total to 1,098 Japanese ships—transports, escort vessels, cargo vessels, gunboats, tankers, and an array of other vessels, including 124 warships— sunk by the American armada.

Allies captured a V-bomb expert hiding out in a barn in rural Germany with his wife and five assistants. At their ready was a car painted in US Army camouflage and markings.

GOVERNMENT-SPONSORED ADS WERE NOW appearing touting the seventh war loan, which had started on April 9, including the sale of Series E, F, and G savings notes.

Casualty lists continued to fill the newspapers of America. So, too, did favorable editorials about President Harry Truman. As he referred to himself as a "compromise politician," some cheeky papers referred to him as "the second Missouri Compromise." It was openly known that he was a product of "machine politics," but few seemed bothered. Indeed, machine politics often produced well-run cities with good schools, good police and fire protection, and good snow and garbage removal.

Editorials also lamented the plight of American and Filipino refugees in the Philippines who had been killed, wounded, or ground into the sand by the merciless Japanese. Theorists continued to discuss the organization for war crimes trials. One of the central arguing points was, could the victors in war also create fair trials for their sworn enemies and the enemies of humanity?

Two ships collided in the thick fog off Massachusetts, resulting in the loss of nineteen men while thirty-eight ended up in hospitals. One ship was an American freighter and the other was an Allied tanker.

Americans who had served, and prisoners of war, were beginning to return home, richer too. According to the Associated Press, "In sums ranging from $500 up to more than $7,000 each, 2,500 American soldiers, former prisoners of war of the Germans, were paid off today." They were brought to Boston, "outfitted in new uniforms, quizzed by intelligence officers and made ready for forty-five days' leave."[249] The money represented back pay from their time as prisoners.

Churches were invited to oversee the peace proceedings at the San Francisco conclave to create the United Nations. It was announced that "Dr. Reinhold Niebuhr of Union Theological Seminary will join

Rev. Dr. Harry Emerson Fosdick at Riverside Drive . . . the day the conference opens in San Francisco."[250] There would be other religious leaders attending, watching, and hosting religious workshops and services. It was an impressive array of the religious state and the political state. (Years later, many would question it.)

New textbooks were being printed, many with the phrase "a new spirit of international understanding and co-operation."[251] (Years later, many would question it.) A Czech diplomat urged the international supervision of just about everything. "Similarly, the press, radio, movies and other means of influencing public opinion must be supervised," he said.[252]

A Republican congressman, Karl Munt of Michigan, drunk with the world spirit of the time, urged an international education directorate to supervise all textbooks. Globalized education was also urged by the president of Yale as well as NBC. Radio was being urged to spread the words of universality, internationalism, and one world. Church ads and bulletins were devoted to only one topic: the life, times, and death of Franklin Delano Roosevelt.

Even as war and death proceeded at their own pace, so did women's fashion and interior decoration, which probably should not have. A big city newspaper featured a cringing "fashionable" corner of a dwelling that mixed Victorian with modern with art deco with eclectic with colonial. The designer surely would have included shabby chic if it had been invented. Bad interior designers crossed the ages.

The Trimfoot Company of Farmington, Missouri, announced it would keep its "nursery and play school" in place for the benefit of workers after the war. The company made shoes, and women composed 90 percent of its workforce. It's "daily program included a regular health check-chart, mid-morning fruit juice, noon-day meal, and fruit juice or cod liver oil, with the parents' consent."[253] There was also a regular nurse who sent reports home frequently.

Surprise. Surprise. During the recent clothing drive for Europe, someone donated a fur coat. In fact, it was a mink. A young woman walked into a Red Cross donation center, announced she had another coat, and left.

WAR NEWS AND WAR brutalities were never very far away. A French official in charge of prisoners and deportees, Henri Frenay, announced the discovery of 2,040 French citizens brutally shot and killed by the Germans, presumably because they were too weak to march along ahead of the Allied invasion. It was also reported that the Germans shot two hundred American officers they held "while they were being marched from eastern to southern Germany."[254] Other reports included stories of attempts and failures to free American GIs and officers, including General George S. Patton's son-in-law, Lieutenant Colonel John K. Walters. Typhus was sometimes an issue as the Germans and British negotiated a temporary truce while they determined how to handle a German concentration camp.

Preparations were going forth in Hyde Park for Franklin Delano Roosevelt's final resting place. The gravesite would be surrounded by a one-hundred-year-old hedge on the Springwood estate he was so fond of for so many years. The hedge was ten feet high and could be seen from his presidential library in the Springwood home. The site was festooned with over twenty beds of roses, pansies, and daffodils.

British general Sir Bernard L. Montgomery said that as of mid-April, Hitler would never surrender but in fact would destroy everything in the Reichland.

THE SOCIETY PAGES OF the newspapers were crammed with news of new books—the vast majority were about the war or war-related issues, with titles such as *Before Final Victory*, *Air Power for Peace*, *The Military Staff: Its History and Development*, and *The Soldier and His Family*. Charlie Chaplin's paternity suit dragged on, with final arguments being made over the paternity of a little girl whose mother, Joan Berry, claimed Chaplin was the father. The sensationalistic trial had gripped the nation for weeks.

Hollywood was also looking forward to a new season filled with films. It was announced that *Case Timberlane*, a novel by Sinclair Lewis, was going to be made into a movie by MGM for which they would pay $250,000—as soon as Lewis completed the book. Twentieth Century–Fox was planning to star Maureen O'Hara in *The Home Stretch*, a movie about horse racing. Eve Arden and Danny Kaye were set to star in *The Kid from Brooklyn*. And many other movies were due to be released, including *Zoya*, about a young woman hanged by the Nazis, and *This Man's Navy*. The war, as noted, was never far away.

The House was set to hold hearings on the paper shortage in a nation in which trees lined the country from sea to shining sea. A national announcement was made for servicemen and servicewomen that all future dances and social gatherings would be canceled for the funeral of FDR. All baseball exhibition games were canceled for FDR's funeral. "Baseball, joining the rest of the nation in mourning the loss of its No. 1 fan, has suspended all operations for today," reported the *New York Times*.[255] Regular games would start on Monday, including one between the Yankees and the Senators.

In England, ninety thousand soccer fanatics gathered to watch a match between South Cup and Chelsea, which included King George, Queen Elizabeth, and their daughters Elizabeth and Margaret.

The great fastball pitcher, Bob Feller, "Rapid Robert" of the Cleveland Indians, had enlisted in the navy right after Pearl Harbor and thus lost four years of his career. But he gained far more than that in respect, having seen lots of action in the Pacific. No easy duty for Bob. Now the navy was granting him the privilege to pitch for the Great Lakes Navy team. He had been on sea duty from 1942 up until early 1945. In the six seasons he'd pitched, from 1936 to 1941, he had mowed down the competition, winning a phenomenal 107 games and striking out 1,233 batters. In 1940, he had won 27 games and lost only 7. "Rapid Robert" was an otherworldly pitcher and an American hero.

The Pennsylvania Central Airline reported record profits, an increase of $1,025,298. They flew almost sixty thousand passengers in 1944, with eighteen planes in service. The Coca-Cola Company also reported

record profits of $25,021,445 for 1944. In 1945, Coca-Cola was ubiqui-
tous; its image and consumption were everywhere—in the magazines,
on the billboards, on the radio. There were many regional sodas and a
few national competitors, but Coke was considered by many to be the
national soda pop. Others enjoyed by many included Dr Pepper, Hires
Root Beer, Pepsi, Dad's Root Beer, Orange Crush, Kremo, and Nehi,
but Coke dominated the market.

OF COURSE, THE WEEKEND, April 14 and 15, was completely dominated
by coverage of the final respects for President Franklin Delano Roosevelt.
The death of all presidents gripped the nation's attention; only Lincoln's
rivaled that of FDR's. Both held mastery on the nation's devotion and
affection like few other presidents.

Along the way from Union Station to the White House, some five
hundred thousand people lined the streets, quiet; only the sound of various military bands could be heard. Another group of thousands gathered
at Lafayette Park, across the street from the White House. Later, when
black limousines rolled away from the executive mansion, signaling the
end of the services, the large, silent crowd was still there in Lafayette
Park, holding vigil, even as a brief shower hung over them.

At 4:25 p.m., on April 14, the gates to the White House slowly
opened and FDR deliberately left for the last time; this time in a horse-
drawn caisson from the building he had transformed in many ways into
the capital of the world.

Before 1941, the United States had mostly dismantled its military-
industrial complex and almost chloroformed its standing army. America
was not regarded as a world military power, not like Nazi Germany or
Great Britain or even Italy or Russia. At his end, FDR had transformed
America into the greatest force for peace—and the greatest force for
the defense of peace—in the world. He had not really solved the Great
Depression; rather, his policy, the Atlantic Charter, paved the way for
lend-lease aid to Great Britain, which increased production *and* consumption, paved the way out of the Great Depression. As any economics

student would tell you, the key to growth is consumption, not production. And the American economy began to slowly, finally, emerge from the long, dark shadow of the Great Depression.

All over the world, one to three days of mourning had been set aside for the death of Roosevelt.

Bess Furman at the *New York Times* wrote of Eleanor Roosevelt, "For twelve long hours today, from the 10:00 a.m. arrival of the Roosevelt funeral train from Warm Springs, Georgia, until its departure at 10:00 p.m. for Hyde Park, an erect and composed Mrs. Eleanor Roosevelt was the central figure in the majestic ceremonies of farewell accorded by this national and world capital to her beloved husband, Franklin Delano Roosevelt."[256]

The White House put out the word not to send flowers, but devoted Americans sent them anyway, and the mansion was soon overwhelmed. As the service was only for invited family and friends, a hallway was used for the clerks and typists who worked in the White House. They stood and listened to a loudspeaker system while the bells of St. John's Episcopal—often referred to as the church of presidents—pealed their farewell to the president of the United States.

Dignitaries were scarce, there being a war and such. President Truman, British foreign minister Anthony Eden, and a few others were scattered about, as were Supreme Court justices, senators, and those who milled around the Green Room and the Blue Room. The bier was placed in the large, rectangular East Room in front of the French doors, festooned with roses, lilies, and other assorted flowers.

Other dignitaries in attendance included Viscount Halifax and Andrei Gromyko, representing Great Britain and the Soviet Union, respectively, along with Mrs. Woodrow Wilson and longtime FDR aide Harry Hopkins. For much of the service, Eleanor Roosevelt's face was strained while her daughter, Anna, was calm by all accounts. The House passed a resolution mourning Roosevelt, as did the Vatican.

Servicemen paused, wherever they were, and for five minutes bowed their heads in silent prayer.

Bishop Dun moved to the fore, toward the casket, "followed by Rev. Dr. John Magee of St. John's Episcopal Church and the Reverend Howard Wilkinson, rector of St. Thomas Episcopal Church."[257] FDR's favorite hymns were sung, including "Eternal Father, Strong to Save." Then Bishop Dun spoke the invocation. Dr. Magee spoke Psalms 46 and 121. Reverend Wilkinson read from Romans, eighth chapter, fourteenth verse, as well as from St. John.

Bishop Dun prayed for the immortal soul of Franklin Delano Roosevelt: "I am the Resurrection and the Life, saith the Lord." He then ended the service with a final prayer, "In his first inaugural address, the president bore testimony to his own deep faith; so first of all, let me assert my own belief 'that the only thing we have to fear is fear itself.'"[258] With that, the sad procession slowly left the White House, and the casket made its way to FDR's beloved Hyde Park overlooking the Hudson Valley. Hyde Park was draped in purple and black as they awaited the funeral train bearing the remains of Roosevelt.

The next day, at 10:00 a.m., was the funeral. Very few residents were present, though, due to space and security. FDR was buried in a flower-laden plot at the 1,100-acre estate near the New York Central Railroad. The funeral procession proceeded out of the train, through oak and hemlock trees, to the garden where his parents and his firstborn, FDR Jr., were buried. The Reverend George Anthony, seventy-eight, presided over the St. James service and the interment ceremony. The weather was clear, and the aroma of wild apple blossoms and pine perfumed the grounds. Along the way, sometimes surrounded by family, Eleanor Roosevelt was a tower of strength. Somber, mostly silent, erect, she reassured Americans that all would go on.

Before, Ohio and Virginia could claim to be the graveyard of presidents; now New York could make an equal claim on the title with the burial of FDR. Others buried in New York, some of them close by, were Martin Van Buren, Millard Fillmore, Ulysses S. Grant, Chester A. Arthur, and FDR's cousin, Teddy Roosevelt.

THE NAZI PRESS CALLED FDR's death a "miracle," but the rest of the world press was respectful.

There was such finality to Roosevelt's death. So much had been done, yet there was still much to be done, including winning a world war on the European continent and in the Pacific Ocean.

The newspaper coverage began reporting on Truman, from his boyhood exploits to his experiences as a senator or vice president, and now his conduct of the war. A page in history was turning.

While Truman was mourning FDR, he was now the president and moved immediately to succeed him in each field of endeavor, especially the war. The first thing he did was restate the "Good Neighbor Policy." He met with the military brass. He met with the cabinet. He sent telegrams far and wide. He met with Russians. He issued his first presidential order to give priority to returning veterans in hiring policies.

Charles de Gaulle met with some 170 French Resistance women who had been liberated from a German concentration camp. Germany, meanwhile, was burying people. "The German civilians buried . . . 2,700 Allied and political prisoners who had died after months of starvation and torture."[259]

The war continued. The Germans lost over nine hundred planes, most not having taken off yet, and in the Pacific, B-29 planes wiped out half of the Japanese industry over one weekend. The Allies captured over 218,000 German prisoners of war in seventy-two hours. The Allies continued to whittle down Nazi dominion.

THE FDR ESTATE WAS being divvied up and, as expected, Eleanor got the lion's share, with the rest spread among the five children. The will was filed in the late afternoon, and the estimated $1 million bequest from FDR to his wife was very generous.

Truman made an immediate speech before a joint session of Congress, which included the Supreme Court, the cabinet, and much of the diplomatic corps. He outlined his plans for the postwar world.

Truman promised to prosecute the war to a victorious conclusion while asking for world unity. The push was on to end the war quickly and bring the boys home. He promised to carry on the policies of Roosevelt. "I call on all Americans to help me keep our nation united in defense of those ideals which have been so eloquently proclaimed by Franklin Roosevelt," Truman said to the assembled chamber of dignitaries.[260]

Life magazine covered it all. Each week, the magazine went out to millions and was the pride and joy of publisher Henry Luce. It featured starlets and the military brass and FDR and the "slice of life" many readers appreciated. On April 23, President Truman was featured on the cover. Inside were ads for Westinghouse light bulbs and Englander mattresses touting "Better Rest Makes Better Husbands"[261] and BF Goodrich Tires and Cadillac Cars and movies and cartoons and drawings of sexy waitresses serving dinner to diners. A typical issue also featured ads for Buick, not the cars but the M-18 Hellcat, and stories such as "Why the Price Was so Bitterly High" about the cost of war, not just in dollars but in the cost of American lives.

The magazine's top management were all men in 1945, despite the magazine being aimed at women. The April 9, 1945, issue contained a long story about the artists of war, those who drew and photographed the events splayed on the magazine pages. The August 13 issue featured a frightening story on Nazi "super babies." It said, "The Hohenhorst bastards of Himmler's men are blue-eyed, flaxen-haired and pig-fat. They must eat porridge whether they want to or not." And one photo was captioned to say, "This Hohenhorst nurse replaces both Mother and Father in raising this illegitimate SS child."[262] Long after the end of the war, horrors continued to surface. And, of course, more ads; batteries were a staple as were cigarettes and beauty creams.[263] *Look* magazine was a poor country mouse to *Life*.

THE WAR WAS WINDING down, but someone forgot to tell the Germans, despite the call by General Eisenhower for them to surrender. Allied tanks were moving on Berlin as ration stamps were being validated across America. The Russians were deep in Austria, on their way to Berlin, even as German U-boats were still patrolling the North Atlantic. A false rumor was going around that Hermann Goering had committed suicide, and again, the newspapers were filled with war news.

Despite the supposed blessing of FDR's death, Hitler knew the Russians were—as they always had been—the impending threat. Or perhaps he continued to be delusional about a divine victory, as he ordered not only his fanatical followers but the ordinary German to fight to the death. "Reserve units, new formations and the Volkssturm reinforce our front," he reported, to every German on the Eastern Front. "This time the Bolsheviks will experience Asia's old fate. That is, he must and will bleed to death in front of the capital of the German Reich."[264] Anyone who defied this order was to be arrested and executed. So on the morning of April 16, 1945, with the order of unconditional fanaticism hanging over their heads, suburbanites of Berlin were awakened to a barrage of distant artillery, equivalent to small earthquakes, with shaking ground, picture frames falling off the walls, and a constant sense of dread.[265]

As if a prophecy of things to come, a Soviet submarine sunk the German hospital ship *Goya*. It was the worst maritime disaster of the war, with only sixty-five survivors out of the over seven thousand refugees.[266] Americans never knew, though, as no newspaper deemed it worthy of reporting.

While the Russian Bear was bearing down on Berlin, Washington was told a different story. In a communiqué, Soviet general Aleksei Antonov told his Anglo-American allies that they were not yet attacking the Nazi grand prize but instead were simply "undertaking a large-scale reconnaissance on the central sector of the front."[267]

Allied supreme commander Dwight D. Eisenhower cautioned against Nazi Germany surrender anytime soon, and certainly not as a whole, until the nation was occupied. "Nazi units, including divisions, corps, armies, and finally army groups will give up separately," he predicted.[268] Newspapers gleefully ran stories of Germany almost cut in half.[269]

Speculation increased on Hitler's whereabouts and his immediate future. Namely, if the world was to descend on Berlin successfully, what would he do? One possibility was his willingness to kill himself by the hands and guns of his own fanatical SS guards, as a sort of sacrificial lamb. According to those who knew him, though, it was "not probable" that he'd commit suicide. They surmised, "If Germany collapses on one of his active days he most likely will expose himself voluntarily to enemy bullets."[270]

While Soviet thunder was rolling just east of Berlin, President Harry S. Truman addressed a joint session of Congress. A sense of agitation reverberated throughout the country. The soft-spoken Truman, a humble man from Missouri, was now president. What could he do for the war, for the country? Americans were faced with a new man leading their country—for many, they had known only FDR as their president. Who was this new president?

Truman immediately put to bed any doubt of discontinuing Roosevelt's work. He said, "I want in turn to assure my fellow Americans and all of those who love peace and liberty throughout the world that I will support and defend those ideals with all my strength and all my heart. That is my duty and I shall not shirk it. So that there can be no possible misunderstanding, both Germany and Japan can be certain, beyond any shadow of a doubt, that America will continue the fight for freedom until no vestige of resistance remains!"[271] Good to his word, the next day, Truman congratulated Congress on renewing the Lend-Lease Act.

Though no fighting touched the continental United States during the entirety of the war, residents in and around DC were still told to keep a lookout for Nazis. Seven German POWs had escaped over the weekend from military prisons in North Carolina, Virginia, and Maryland. Federal, state, and county police were placed on the lookout. FBI official Harold Nathan, speaking in Richmond, said "this was an all-time record in this area" for escaped German prisoners. One of the seven, twenty-two-year-old Rudolf Strine, was said to "speak broken English"; another, Gerd Roempke, could speak "very good English" as well as Spanish.[272]

Elsewhere in the DC area, the University of Maryland poultry department released a statement that suggested hatching eggs, if carefully transported, could survive by air to war-ravaged Europe. "The results of these [yearlong] tests," announced department head Dr. Morley Jull, "make it quite evident that airplane shipments of eggs can be made to Europe without diminishing hatchability."[273]

THE SECOND HALF OF April brought a lot of the same for the Pacific theater, in a paradoxical and anticlimactic contrast to Europe. Iwo Jima was quiet, disappointingly to some, including Army Captain Nelson Merrill from Hingham, Massachusetts, whose eight-hour flight in his P-51 Mustang encountered no Japanese fighters. "It was a long ride for nothing," he complained.[274]

The bloodbath on Okinawa continued unrelentingly. "Fanatic Japs Lose Air Fight at Okinawa," read one front-page *Los Angeles Times* article.[275] In four days' time, nearly four hundred planes had been destroyed. The B-29 Superfortress bombers continued to reign over Tokyo, with over sixty-five square miles destroyed. Japanese radio admitted that fires burned for over seven hours. Calling American pilots "white albino apes," an intercepted dispatch confessed,

> Those countless numbers who were rendered homeless sought refuge under the protection of the remaining police. A number of sufferers were almost cornered by this huge inferno until they were able to seek temporary shelter in vacant lots fronting the gate of the Shinjuku imperial garden. As the flames began to reach the direction of the lots, the air-raid victims gave up all hope of survival and escape. Then, like a voice from heaven, the huge gate of the imperial garden, by a stroke of fate, opened. A warm, kindly voice calmly said: "Do not hesitate to enter." Then they were let into the garden by police men and imperial guards.[276]

The Philippines, meanwhile, were all but liberated from the Japanese. Very little Japanese resistance existed, but that was expected. The conquest of Japan was believed, though, to be just as important as victory in Europe. Not just for Americans but for every freedom-loving citizen of the world. Australian minister of external affairs, Herbert Evatt, told listeners on the BBC that, despite victory within reach in Europe, "there will be a temptation to feel that the task has been finished, but the steadiness and realism of your outlook will immediately recall the other insolent enemy of human freedom, the other challenger of peace, the other author of barbarities and atrocities beyond telling—Japan." He continued, "There can be no peace while Japan remains strong. . . . Not only victory in Europe but also complete victory over Japan is essential to any sound system of security."[277]

WOMEN WERE VITAL TO the American war effort, both as citizens and wives. Sometimes the husbands they knew would come back different—traumatized, drinking more, scared, maybe even violent. No one, especially the housewives of America, knew how to fix that. In response, the Army Air Forces launched a program to educate "wives of convalescents to their new duties and responsibilities" for "battle-weary veterans." The program encouraged wives to participate "in craft, educational and vocational activities with their husbands. They may study French and Spanish together, or they may work on their postwar homes in the drafting classes."[278] If they so desired, these women could also bond with other wives in the so-called Wives' Headquarters, where they could make food or play bridge.

The economy trusted Truman, a sign of relief for investors and the average American alike. Industrial, rail, and utility stocks rose to 1.5 percent from the day prior. It was the highest peak since 1937.[279]

Over radio, former ambassador to Great Britain and patriarch to the closest thing to Boston royalty, Joseph P. Kennedy, urged the New England states to begin restructuring their infrastructure. They, he believed, "must make a greater effort than they have in the past if they are going" to keep returning veterans in the area. If history repeated itself, any New England vet would emigrate out of the area to find a better job. In particular, Kennedy predicted the growth of the electric industry. "In no field, except aviation itself," he said, "will the demand be greater than in the electrical industries—radar, radio, electronics. New England brains and institutions have been leaders in almost every new effort. . . . But industries always locate with reference to sources of supply, labor, and transportation."[280] He warned that New England governors and statesmen must work harder than they ever had to change the fabric of the area, just so that the vets can live a life they want at home.

THE PATERNITY SUIT AGAINST actor Charlie Chaplin concluded on April 17 with a Los Angeles jury of eleven women and one man deciding that the actor who satirically played Hitler in *The Great Dictator* was indeed the father of eighteen-month-old Carol Ann. Accompanying the news was a photo of Chaplin, head clutched in hand. The caption noted that he seemed "to be suffering from a severe headache."[281] Eventually, Chaplin would be ordered to support the baby girl until she reached twenty-one years of age.

Washington, DC, residents were reminded of the midnight curfew by way of a comic. The "Three Bares" were all in separate beds as two babies looked angrily to a crying and wailing third baby. "Hey, remember the curfew," said the middle baby. "Everything's got to shut up at 12 o'clock!"[282]

"JOIN THE NAVY AND see the world" continued to be a popular turn of phrase, and it was just as true in April 1945 as it was in December 1941. One of Hawaii's own members of the Women's Army Corps (WAC) made some front-page news for being the first Hawaii WAC to step into New York City. "When I saw the skyscrapers did I open my mouth!" exclaimed Private Fujiko "Grace" Kutaka, who had previously been an employee of the *Honolulu Advertiser*. Prior to her deployment to NYC, she had trained in Fort Oglethorpe, Georgia, with fellow WAC members. "We were like sisters, and we shared everything that we had," she wrote to the *Advertiser*, "although at times there were arguments." Detailing a little into her life, Grace said that the women partied "with some Hawaiian girls doing the hula and Mainland girls putting on a skit. It was swell, and one of the C.O.s said she never did see any group of girls who cooperated better."[283]

New York City, where she picked up the task of telegraphing at Mason General Hospital in Long Island, was "better than Georgia" to her. "Spring is here, and the trees are budding and the grass is turning green. . . . The flowers are pretty, too, but not any prettier than the flowers in Hawaii," she said. And despite the cross-country travel by train and seeing sights that she and many others in Hawaii would otherwise probably not see, she admitted, "I wouldn't trade Hawaii for any of these states here."[284]

The owners of Cities Service Refining Corp in Lake Charles, Louisiana, had a rude awakening after President Truman ordered Harold Ickes, secretary of the interior and petroleum administrator of war, to seize their plants and factories. Rent and labor disputes plagued the company, leading to a general lull in production. Truman stepped in. "A production stoppage," explained one administration official, "has existed in this plant for several days. This plant is one of the biggest 100 octane gasoline producing refineries in the country. Its operation is vital to the effective prosecution of the war."[285] Truman's order allowed Ickes to do whatever it took to provide protection for the plant's workers.

With all that was going on, sometimes a sense of normalcy crept into Americans' lives, even if just for small glimpses. This was just as true for the Japanese Americans. Several help-wanted ads popped up in the Japanese American newspaper *Rocky Shimpo* of Denver, Colorado. Prospective waitresses, cashiers, and hostesses were told to call E. Colfax at the New China café. An "attractive salary" was proposed to any girl or woman to help babysit four- to six-year-old girls of Dr. Mengumi Shinoda. Meanwhile, a new beauty shop was advertised to open on Denver's Twentieth Street, owned by Jo Hirota.[286]

The residents of Topaz, the main internment town of Japanese descent in Utah, were greeted with the news that "over 100 certified dealers from Colorado, Idaho, and other parts of the country paid $11,521 for the surplus farm equipment at the sale held here Saturday." The local paper proudly stated that the sale took only two hours, with items sold "on the average of about one a minute."[287]

Still, the reminder of war was always there. Next to the celebratory pride of selling farm equipment on the front page of the *Topaz Times* was a notice "for 7 men to report for active duty to Fort Douglas on May 1."[288]

In England, a secret underground resistance group, which formed "before any other European resistance movement," was officially and publicly disbanded. The "British Maquis" were made up of British civilians "ready at any moment to come to the active defense of their homeland" should the Nazis ever invade the Isles.[289] Now, their purpose was deemed irrelevant. A promising sign.

IN KEY WEST, FLORIDA, the morning of April 17 was a busy court date. Six defendants pleaded guilty to a variety of charges. Louis Phillips was fined $50 for discharging a firearm in the city; Griff Jackson was fined $5 for drunkenness; Ray Fisher, for assault and battery, was fined $10 or sixty days in jail; Elijah Gutman pleaded guilty to not paying child support and was placed under $200 bail to pay for his child $7 a week; Newall Brown was fined $250 or six months in jail for trying to pass a "worthless check"; and Samuel Dawson was sentenced to one year in jail for breaking and entering a car. Dawson, who had served time prior, had arrived in Key West only two weeks earlier to "reform." The presiding judge waved that away, saying, "Key West would be better off without Dawson's presence."[290] Showing the underlying racism and discrimination in a subtle way, the *Key West Citizen* made note of races only when the defendants were black. Presumably, the men whose races were not mentioned were white.

Key West was also the source of some small town controversy. In a letter to the editor, taxi driver, Dwight Russell, corrected a record from the week prior. He was involved, the paper said, in a hit-and-run accident of a little girl, and that she had to be dragged from under the bumper by other children before Russell drove off in a fit of panic. He categorically denied that. "The facts are these. I was going out [of] Division Street when I came to the corner of White. The green light was on and I went very slowly, about 10 miles per hour, as I saw the children around. While I was going, the little girl ran across and the bumper struck her and knocked her down. I stopped the car at once when I saw her coming. If I had been going fast I would have killed her. Before I could get out of my car she jumped up and ran away. . . . I am not as inhuman as [the paper made me out to be]," he argued. He stayed to make sure the girl was okay, and eyewitnesses cleared him of any wrongdoing. However, he admitted, he was fined for not reporting the case. "I did not think it necessary as the child did not get hurt," he said.[291]

Women of Charlotte, North Carolina, saw that they could have miraculous weight-loss with the help of the Tremett tablet, located conveniently at Eckerd's Drug Stores. "They used to call her fatty," said the ad, accompanied by a slim and highly fit woman. "No exercise, no starvation diet, no reducing drugs or cathartics are necessary for those who seek to regain a graceful, youthful figure."[292]

But, if the women, comfortable with their appearance, wanted to spice up their outfits, they could order a slim and "smartly cut" patterned dress for 20 cents in any size from twelve to twenty or thirty to forty. Or, with the summer months approaching, for only 15 cents, they could make their own hat. The *Charlotte News* Pattern and Household Arts Departments, respectively, had these needs covered.[293]

CAPTAIN WILBUR WENDLING'S MOTHER went to visit his grave in Inglewood, California. While she was there, a thief broke into her car and snatched her purse; ration books and $125 were stolen. But also in the purse was her greatest possession: a photo of her deceased son. That, too, was taken. Mrs. Grace Wendling reported it to the police. "He's welcome to everything else," she said, "but I wish he'd send me back that smiling picture of my boy."[294]

BRITISH AND AMERICAN TROOPS in Germany liberated an undisclosed "death factory," with hundreds of gadgets and inventions that would make any engineer blush. Among the "treasures" included corkscrew, bottle opener, bayonet combination, and an unfinished, one-hundred-ton, heavily armored "great what-is-it" with four nine-feet-tall wheels. Also included was the more unimaginative but powerful thirty-foot-long barrel, 120mm anti-tank gun. Estimated cost of all materials and gadgets within the multihundred-acre factory was appraised in the billions.[295]

News arrived of further German and Pacific atrocities. General Douglas MacArthur revealed to the public on April 17 that the Japanese had ordered the murder of hundreds of civilians in Manila months earlier, in February, with "wanton savagery." He called it an "orgy of killing" and a "grisly exhibit of sadism" as churches, convents, schools, and military buildings were burned. Civilians were stabbed, beaten, shot, and burned. A thousand so-called guerrillas were burned in one night on February 9. An estimated 90 percent of religious buildings had been burned, often with priests, religious monks, nuns, and civilians inside.[296]

THE NEW SEASON FOR the great American pastime—baseball—began on April 17. The war had disrupted but not canceled sports as players and managers and staff were drafted, trained, and shipped overseas to fight. Rainy weather ominously threatened and postponed the first game of the season between the Washington Senators and the New York Yankees, which was originally scheduled for the April 16 but moved to April 20. Instead, the Senators' first game was against the Philadelphia Athletics. It proved to be a modest win for the DC-based team, 14 to 8.[297]

"Still Fighting," screamed a full-page ad in *Life*. "Gasoline Is Still Fighting. The Best Gasoline Is Still Fighting." Ethyl Corporation, a world supplier of gasoline, reported that the best gasoline—millions of gallons of it—was being shipped to fighting fronts all over the world. But with that news, it brought the warning that the quality and quantity of gasoline in the United States would be limited: "Only complete, final

Victory will bring car-owners the Ethyl gasoline they look forward to—the Ethyl that will bring out the top performance of any car."[298]

THE THIRD ARMY OF General George S. Patton "slashed across the border of Czechoslovakia" on April 18, "cutting Germany in two geographically." Other Allied troops began capturing Leipzig and Magdeburg, sixty miles south of Berlin. That same day, Patton wrote in his diary that he had his "teeth cleaned at the [HQ's] hospital, where they did an extremely good job."[299] Patton was regarded as the "American Rommel," according to many Germans.[300]

Berliners tried desperately to strengthen the city's defenses for the inevitable onslaught of the Red Army from the east and American and British armies from the west, and they made considerable improvement from the "flimsy" barricades defending the city only weeks earlier. One German newspaper said it would take the enemy "one hour of holding their sides from laughter and two minutes for storming."[301] The Russians were only fourteen miles from the city's borders by April 19, firing up to 325 shells a minute with their new "breakthrough" tanks and artillery.[302] Defenses were needed for Berlin now more than ever. High walls blocked major and minor roads into the city, and streetcars and girders formed barriers. Public schools were closed and universities were converted into hospitals, though it oddly was reported that theaters and concert halls were still open. Anyone under sixty-five was recruited to build, fortify, and defend their city with anything they could. And in a more despicable twist of fate, German women were specifically targeted to dig ditches and trenches, which was crucial to the war effort.[303]

The Pacific armies released a somber report on the situation in Okinawa. In the first eighteen days of the campaign, the United States had suffered nearly 8,000 casualties. The navy in particular was hit badly, with 989 men killed. The Tenth Army alone lost 478 of its troops and 2,500 were wounded. Despite the figures, the gains made in Okinawa continued in America's favor. Gains on the small Ie Island, as well as northern and central Okinawa, proved to be a substantial progress in the war.[304]

PITTSBURGHERS RECEIVED WELCOMED NEWS when they heard that local S. K. Courtney, twenty-one, was among a group of American airmen freed from the Brunswick (German: Braunschweig) prison camp. The camp had been liberated by the Ninth Army only six days earlier; Courtney had been missing since mid-March.[305] An ever-changing landscape.

Cancer kills; it always has. Mrs. Murdock Equen of the American Cancer Society reminded residents of Atlanta, Georgia, of that fact. "Picture a city twice the size of Atlanta—a city of about 600,000—and you will get an idea of the number of Americans who now have cancer," she told them. It was estimated that about 160,000 of those estimated 600,000 Americans will die within the year. So Equen roused fellow Georgians to donate any amount they were willing to help combat such a disease that took extreme prejudice against anyone. "No doubt cancer has killed someone you knew, perhaps someone you loved," she said.[306]

The April edition of *Crisis* continued to shed light on the plight of minorities, even as Americans touted fighting fascism and racism abroad. The magazine, founded in 1910 by W. E. B. DuBois, among others, was the official magazine of the National Association for the Advancement of Colored People. Especially during the Jim Crow era with a segregated military, a black-owned and black-centered paper offered unparalleled solidarity to African Americans throughout the country. "The Negro Soldier Betrayed" read one somber full-page editorial. It declared that it was unwritten army policy in Italy to keep black soldiers as second-class citizens. Namely, the 92nd Division was keeping black soldiers assigned to work units separated from their white comrades at junior ranks. "You cannot separate a man," said the writer, "from his fellows at the induction center, train him in a separate unit, send him, even, to a separate all-Negro isolated training post . . . humiliate him . . . and then expect one day that he will 'join the team' after a little pep talk and give a little superlatives." The editorial homes in on this point: "It must be remembered that these men were beaten up by bus drivers, shot up by military and civilian police, insulted by their white officers, denied transportation to and from the post, restricted to certain post exchanges, and jim-crowed into post theaters." The editorial then pleaded with the War Department that the "race problem" was a substantial problem for the military and could not be ignored. After all, the black solider "can fight as well as any man and is proving it every day."[307]

Readers of *Crisis* noticed the irony in the attached photo of African American Captain Morris S. Young of the 15th Air Force Service Command removing a piece of flak from the cheek of a white bombardier.[308]

Still, discrimination or not, American aspiration and exceptionalism reigned for African Americans. "Wanted: Sea legs and guts . . . to avoid ship delays!" posted one ad for the merchant marines. "Here's a chance for any Negro with Sea Experience to save a lot of American lives. A ship delay—because a man is needed—can cause bloodshed abroad and lengthen the war."[309]

MORALE IN THE GERMAN army started to crack. This was no more evident than to Private Thomas J. Olden of Knoxville, Maryland. Traveling through Remagen in western Germany, he managed to capture a German artillery captain. "I was armed only with my trench knife and scared stiff," he said, "but I guess jerry was plenty frightened himself." The German "eagerly" surrendered to the Maryland native.[310]

The end of the European conflict was in sight with literally each passing hour. The advancement of the Allies on German soil, from both the west and the east, was with speed unseen in history. Truman was slammed with memoranda after memoranda. Samuel Rosenman, White House counsel, informed the new president of specific plans for postwar Europe—namely, what was to be done with war criminals. Conferences with senior officials, both domestically and with other Allies, were ongoing since the New Year, but President Roosevelt hadn't had a chance to review the specifics. It was agreed that, among other things, "the six or more top criminals (Hitler, Mussolini, Goering, Goebbels, Himmler, and [Nazi Minister of Foreign Affairs] von Ribbentrop) should be given a special trial before a mixed military tribunal." They would be charged with "the crimes against humanity." A plethora of crimes were then listed as prime examples of Nazi atrocities. Continued the memo, "The bill of arraignment would be so fully documented that oral evidence would be practically unnecessary."[311]

Of the more unknown war criminals—including the collective organizations of the Gestapo, SS, and Wehrmacht, a number theorized to be in the hundreds of thousands—it was agreed that a military tribunal would charge them "with entering into a common enterprise or conspiracy to persecute and rob minorities . . . to occupy neutral countries by force and in violation of treaties, to commit war crimes and atrocities of all kinds, etc." If these organizations were to be found guilty, then "each member of the organization would be guilty of the conspiracy, and would be punished." It continued, "The punishment would not necessarily be death, but . . . might be hard labor in reconstructing war devastation in Russia, France, etc."[312]

"WOMEN BANKERS PROUD OF SEX," said the *Atlanta Constitution*. Helen Knox and Mrs. Alfred DuPont, "two of America's most prominent bank women," arrived in Atlanta for a regional meeting of the Association of Bank Women (ABW). Though they wouldn't describe themselves as "rabid feminists" (their words), they did have some forward-thinking ideas. Namely, Knox, president of the ABW and manager of the women's department of NYC's Chase Bank, put her foot down: "Women are not going back to the home after the war. Women have shown magnificent patriotic service in the past few years, and they deserve the same recognition as men."[313] It is then with special irony that the paper never revealed Mrs. DuPont's real name, only referring to her as her husband's wife.

FRIDAY, APRIL 20, MARKED HITLER'S fifty-sixth, and final, birthday. In a twist of fate for the Führer, it was this day that the Red Army actually entered the Berlin city limits. The Americans from the west were advancing at a steady pace as well, capturing Leipzig and marching toward Nuremberg and Munich. The British were advancing into Ferrara, northern Italy. Hitler's supposed thousand-year Reich was surrounded on all fronts, from the west, south, and east.

Hitler was quiet. Too quiet. One news report noted, "Hitler's birthday passed with no word from the leader who heretofore has made his natal day a day of festivity throughout Germany."[314]

Though fifty-six years is more obscure and unimportant than other ages, the contrast in mood between 1945 and 1939—his fiftieth birthday—could not have been more obvious. The quinquagenarian day of the German leader, back before the invasion of Poland, before the invasion of France, before the Holocaust was in full swing, was declared a national public holiday. It had been marked with "the largest military review ever witnessed in Berlin," reported the Associated Press at the time, a sure warning of things to come. "New types of long-range air defense artillery" was displayed, along with "a regiment of heaviest artillery"—of 10-inch guns, airplanes, guests from across the globe, paratroopers. Hundreds of thousands of fellow Germans had attended the parade, interrupting the celebrations with shouts of *"wir gratullen!"* ("we congratulate!"). It was called a "mammoth birthday party."[315]

Now, a mere six years later, amid constant rumble of Red Army artillery and impending ruin, Hitler celebrated his birthday comparatively alone. He did leave his bunker, briefly, to greet the new normal of German soldiers: teenage boys, "none of them older than fourteen years old," praising their bravery and loyalty to the Fatherland.[316]

Across the Channel, the date of Hitler's birth took a much more gruesome tone. With more news of German atrocities, more proof was needed. More proof meant more exposure. More exposure meant more witnesses. Residents of Leicester, England, facing these images in cinemas, got up to leave, only to be turned back by Allied soldiers and forced to watch. One soldier said he believed that this was "the only way to break the namby-pamby attitude toward Germans. Many people don't believe such things could be. These films are proof."[317]

AMERICANS WANTED TO DISTRACT themselves with sports, but even that was not without problems. Manager and shortstop Joe Cronin of the Boston Red Sox suffered a fractured right ankle when sliding into second base in the seventh inning against the New York Yankees. The spikes of his cleats caught on infield dirt, and he twisted his ankle in such an unnatural position that, immediately, it was predicted his "long and distinguished playing career" of twenty years had ended.[318]

NEWSPAPERS AND HEADLINES WERE considerably focused on the impending end of the war in Europe, and news of the Pacific theater was relatively light and slow. "American forces [are] mainly concerned with wiping out Japanese air power and wrecking the war industry of the home islands," said one news report.[319]

Admiral William "Bull" Halsey was right about the inevitable defeat of Japan. But he had blood in his eyes. Occupied Japan, he demanded, should be placed under a supreme commander that has "a free hand, with no interference from outside—meaning, of course, well-intentioned but misguided civil governments." The reason? To be free from any punishment done to the Japanese. Halsey demanded that for every American that had been murdered by the Japanese, whether in combat or as a POW, a Japanese must be killed in retaliation. Arguing with evidence of their barbarity—such as cannibalism, rape of nuns, prison torture—he said, "We must make the Japanese race powerless, and then keep it powerless."[320] An eye for an eye.

LESS THAN A WEEK had passed since Hitler's proclamation to fight to the death in a problematic war, when the fatigued and sick leader of the German Reich finally cracked. Calling the Western Front "unfavorable," he ordered all German military to lay "constant attacks on the enemy's rear in conjunction with partisan warfare."[321] The mobilized German military in the west had failed, and the only possible scenario for continued action was guerrilla warfare. The great military of the thousand-year Reich was no more.

THE MEN STATIONED OFF Subic Bay near Manila, the Philippines, were restless, when Lieutenant Bernard Mauer and the men of USS *Blue Ridge* were finally granted leave to go ashore for the first time in months. There were "a lot of tired sailors," but they all wanted off, he wrote to his brother Arnold. Mauer managed to walk miles through "streets of destroyed buildings, torn by bombs and fire . . . ruined wantonly with great loss of life to the native people." He continued, "You'd hardly believe it, so much in ruins yet everyone seems still there, lives there." Mauer noted that somehow, from a distance, Manila looked to be a "city unscratched and full of life." He managed to hitch a ride with a "sombrero wearing guy" who had been imprisoned in a Japanese concentration camp for years and was barely managing to keep himself and his wife and children alive.[322]

Mauer met many more individuals and families whose lives were put at risk for years by Japanese occupation. When invited to supper by the locals, he felt almost guilty that "they might not have enough for themselves," he confessed. There was one unnamed but extremely educated Filipino man, he said, who told story after story of Japanese cruelty. The native man "couldn't speak better English than myself," he joked, adding, after all, "I've got a Bronx accent." The man and his family hosted Mauer with dancing, singing, and showing off their newborn son. All in all, the American sailor was greeted like family.[323]

Back home, the otherwise slow and uneventful war in the Pacific was given a more dramatic flair for the American public: "EXTRA! MacARTHUR LIBERATES MANILA!" Castle Films had exclusive footage compiled into a thrilling "avenging force of fighting Americans." Interviews of former POWs, footage of fighting, destruction, and Japanese defeat were all guaranteed. The film promised to show how General

MacArthur fulfilled his promise to return. Orders could be made in both 8 and 16 mm film, with or without sound.[324]

The men still at home, or perhaps on leave, would be bombarded with ads for the domestic lifestyle. Listerine shaving cream, for only 35 cents, asked, "Why do men like the shaving cream guaranteed not to make shaving a pleasure?" Shaving is a "bore" and a "nuisance." But with Listerine, that chore can, at the very least, be with quality cream. Or, if the reader so chose, he could buy an Alligator raincoat, in which he would look "dashing smart—safe from rain—and money wise as well." If the reader suffered from a dry scalp, then he should look no further than Vaseline Hair Tonic. All it would take is five drops a day to transform the "lifeless-looking hair."[325]

Though the Soviets were clearly dominating the race to Berlin, the American public still had a keen interest in their own army's success. The anxiety was broken up by some entertainment, naturally. Less than a year earlier, smooth and calming-voiced Bing Crosby and the trio Andrews Sisters released the hit song "Hot Time in the Town of Berlin." It immediately hit the number-one spot in the industry, owing much to the zeitgeist of American optimism in winning the war. A year in and the song was still making the airwaves, more appropriate and timely than ever. Papers across the country were asking the record label, Barton Music, to reproduce the lyrics. The *Cincinnati Enquirer* wanted to use the lyrics for the border of a picture of US soldiers in the German capital. According to *Billboard*, "The more heat that goes on in Berlin, the better Barton's pot will boil."[326]

EASY COMPANY OF THE 506th Parachute Infantry in the 101st Airborne Division had their fill of action since their landing behind enemy lines on D-Day. Now, appropriate for their name, they would receive an easy tour through Germany. On April 18, over 325,000 Germans surrendered in the western German region of Ruhr. Easy Company was then assigned the grand prize, short of conquering Berlin itself: the capture of Hitler's Eagle Nest in Berchtesgaden. The Berghof was one of the Führer's many residences, though this home in the very south of Germany, overlooking the Swiss Alps, was his most frequently visited.

So began their long march south to capture the Berghof before it became a new center for Nazi command. On the way, they encountered many Germans, not to fight but to surrender. It was a different situation, surreal for the company. "I couldn't get over the sensation of having the Germans, who only a short time ago had been so difficult to capture, come in from the hills like sheep and surrender," said Private First Class David Webster.[327]

THE WAR ECONOMY CONTINUED unabated across the globe. This of course extended to technology and engineering feats previously unseen. The jet-propelled Messerschmidt Me 163 Komet was said to be the fastest plane in the world, exceeding over six hundred miles an hour by burning a "special fuel" of liquid oxygen, hydrogen peroxide, and calcium permanganate. The Germans' new war toy could fly for up to ten minutes at a time, exceeding a height of ten thousand feet. Within just over forty years of the Wright Brothers' maiden flight in Kitty Hawk, North Carolina, the Nazis had succeeded in creating the first jet. The celebration was short-lived, however, as it descended to a competitive sport. "Ours is faster," simply read an article in *Popular Mechanics*. The American P-80 Shooting Star, developed by Lockheed, was exaggeratedly said to accelerate up to eight hundred miles an hour, faster than the speed of sound. (In reality, the sound barrier was broken two years later by Chuck Yeager, so the boast here was perhaps a bit of patriotic hyperbole.) "Rate and angle of climb are reported 'superlative,'" it bragged.[328] Truly, even then, the world was at a precipice of technology.

With this new technology came dreams of further economic gain for postwar America. Sometimes the love of profit-making exceeded all else. A full-page ad was taken out for a "low-price helicopter for post-war production." It read, "When the war is won . . . we plan to manufacture a jet-propelled, two-passenger helicopter to sell for, approximately, $1,500." It was to be made of the lightweight metals and plastics. The motor "will give you carefree air transportation for as little as one-half cent per passenger mile," a top speed of 200 miles per hour, and a range of one thousand miles, and familiar reliability. "It will be the family car of the air, to fly—'as the crow flies'—over traffic obstacles, to set you gently down on the roof of your office building in the city or at your favorite spot in the country."[329] A slip to fill out was attached to the ad, inquiring about size, method of payment, purpose of purchase, and local aircraft dealers.

Photography was becoming more popular to the American public, evident in the sale and popularity of the appropriately named magazine *Popular Photography*. Founded in 1937, the monthly magazine explored the latest in film and photographs. Its April 1945 edition had a sense of normalcy again after years of exclusively war-related news. "Every day thousands of new photograph fans are born!" read one ad asking for donations of cameras. Burke and Watson Press featured the "Pin Up Girl of 1945," a toddler smooching to the audience. "It's fun for all of us when Daddy takes pictures of me," said the caption. "He wants natural action shots so I give him action poses." Of course, the adorable pose of this little girl, not even a year old, could only have been accomplished with the "flash gun" of B&J's camera. The unnamed Daddy is "no expert," admits the little girl, but he can still capture the cuteness. Of interest to photography lovers was the "photo of the month" by Andre de Dienes, featuring a sunset silhouette of Manhattan in color. The towering silhouette of the Empire State Building against the bright orange sun overwhelmed every other building around, a contrast in colors that anyone would appreciate.[330]

It wasn't all good news. Happy days were not yet here, as discoveries kept creeping in of more and more Nazi atrocities. And it wasn't all about Europeans. One Massachusetts woman, Roberta Laurie, wife of French count and resistance fighter Henri de Maduit, was discovered by Allied troops in a "slave-labor camp." Only forty-five years old, her hair had turned white from trauma and torture. She had not even known her hair had turned white. It was reported, "She hadn't looked in a mirror since

June 1943, when she was taken by the Gestapo from a Brittany chateau." Amid the frenzy of the Americans arriving, she eluded execution by stowing away in a typhoid ward with 265 other women. There, she hid for three days, until she overheard "the most blessed words ever spoken": an American complaining of a "damned lousy bicycle."[331] Without even looking, at that moment, she knew she was saved.

She was but one victim of the many, many horror stories to be recounted in the coming months. It was just the tip of the iceberg.

LIFE REVIEWED PRESIDENT TRUMAN'S first week in office as "firm but humble," an almost impossible task with how busy the Missourian became overnight. Over one hundred appointments with dignitaries, politicians, staff members, foreign ministers, and senators spattered those first seven days.[332] And it was only going to increase. No one envied Truman. All of America recognized he had difficult roads ahead.

HEINRICH HIMMLER, NAZI GERMANY'S number-two man, knew it was over; Hitler, perhaps not. But the scrawny former chicken farmer with the small, round, wire-rimmed glasses knew it. On April 24, Himmler secretly met with the Swedish Red Cross in Luebeck, off the Baltic Coast, and offered Germany's terms of surrender to Americans and British. They, of course, were rejected, on account of the Soviets' lack of say. Either all of the Big Three would be offered the surrender, a true unconditional peace, or nothing. Rumors started to spread of this act of defiance in the press. Was there peace? Was it accepted? What happened? It came from Himmler, not Hitler, so where is Hitler in all of this?

Certainly of no help in the confusion was the United Press International report from an anonymous "high diplomat" that both Hitler and Joseph Goebbels were "shot three days ago."[333] (United Press International unusually did not call the said diplomat "reliable," immediately raising skepticism in other papers.) Yet Himmler himself, in his surrender plea, said that the Führer "may not live another 24 hours."[334] The rumor of Himmler's surrender had the San Francisco

Examiner prematurely scream, in all caps, "NAZIS SURRENDER!"[335] Contradictory reports and announcements flew from world governments. Soviet news *Tass* confirmed there was a bid for peace from the Nazis, though quickly declared it was not accepted. Winston Churchill neither confirmed nor denied such a report. And whereas Truman and Eisenhower declared there was "no foundation for the peace rumors,"[336] that didn't stop a several-thousand-strong spontaneous crowd from gathering in front of the White House singing, "God Bless America."[337] To the disappointment of many Atlantans, theaters, restaurants, and clubs had to close early without their spontaneous nightlong partying. Over $3,000 worth of food, such as pies and hams and cakes, went uneaten, and by the next morning were spoiled.[338]

With the war in Europe all but done, the nations of the world were convening and conversing on what to do. But there was still a legacy of what had come before. Commander and former Republican governor of Minnesota, Harold Stassen, serving as a delegate to the United Nations conference based in California, suggested that Franklin Roosevelt be deemed "President Emeritus of the United Nations of the World." The reason, he argued, was that FDR's presence was still felt, and all work under his presidency would come to fruition. "We may yet say—he is not really gone," Stassen said.[339]

The United Nations conference in San Francisco began on April 25, attended by 850 delegates from 50 nations across the globe. With the state of the world, it was imperative that all nations recognize the importance of establishing global peace. There were two major prerogatives, according to the city's *Examiner*, covering the conference: first, "the good will with which the . . . nations—and particularly the great powers—approach the problem of working together"; second, "the kind of machinery set up to solve disputes as they arise, or if that fails—to put down aggression by force."[340]

Despite that emphasis of peace—a word optimistically thrown around in public the past several days, more so now than at any point during the war—Secretary of State Edward Stettinius stressed that "it is not a peace conference. It is not a deal with boundaries, or reparations or questions concerned with the disarmament and control of Germany and Japan. Its purpose is to prepare a charter of a world organization to preserve the peace in the future."[341]

The religious of the world were also invested in the conference. Pope Pius XII, who had overseen the entire world war as pontiff, had warned the conference a week prior that wars would reoccur if peace was not established. For "the men who will have to decide the destiny of all peoples," the Italian stressed that they "should carefully consider before God that anything surpassing the limits of justice and fairness certainly sooner or later would enormously damage both the victors and the vanquished because this would carry the seed of new wars."[342]

But there was trouble from the outset. The same day the Russians and Americans met on the battlefield, finally linking west and east in a major milestone for the Allied forces, the Soviet Union, represented at the conference by Foreign Minister Vyacheslav Molotov, inexplicably and furiously blocked the election of Stettinius as chairman of the conference. There was "Russian determination to wield decisive, perhaps dominant influence in the creation of world peace machinery," explained the Associated Press.[343] It was feared, perhaps not without merit, that if the Soviet Union blocked this on day one of the conference, what else they would block. What about Poland, now under the thumb of the Russian army? The Soviets demanded that the chairmanship be rotated among the "Big Four"—the United States, the Soviet Union, the United Kingdom, and China.

Meanwhile, in Moscow, Soviet writer A. Sokoloff argued that postwar Europe should not be democratic. Finger-pointing to British colonial rule, he believed it was Western democracies, not soviet-style government, that had led to the current crises. He also said, "It would be a completely hopeless business to demand that democracy in all European countries should be built exactly on the lines of the English or American example. That would constitute an attempt to disturb the internal affairs of other peoples that could not be justified by anything; [except] an attempt to force on them from outside certain political canons."[344]

It was just the beginning of some cold tactics from the Soviets, a sign of things to come.

EVERY DAY, SAN FRANCISCAN papers told their residents to "save all news-papers, magazines, [and] waste basket paper!" because paper could easily pack blood plasma, making any reduction of waste and donations vital to saving lives.[345]

The ban on production, transportation, and selling of alcohol was repealed by the Twenty-First Amendment only twelve years earlier, in December 1933. With its legality back in full force—and the hardship of war—alcoholism became more prevalent. But a local San Francisco chapter of Alcoholics Anonymous, founded four years earlier, promised to tell of the "cures" that saved "thousands of persons with uncontrollable craving for alcohol."[346]

While the nation was eagerly awaiting any news and the excitement of progress in the war was clearly felt throughout the world, tragedy still struck many at home. One Salt Lake City mother's life was upended when her twenty-two-month-old toddler, David John Fowler, fell thirty feet down an elevator shaft and "was crushed to death," a small article buried in the paper's seventh page described.[347] Around the same time, twenty-four-year-old Mack Smith was killed in a fatal car accident in Detroit. The tragedy made front-page news in the *Michigan Chronicle*. He was survived by his wife of two years, Susie Mae Turner-Smith, who was barely able to speak to reporters between sobs of grief.[348]

In Pennsylvania, the headless skeleton of a young girl was found floating in the Allegheny River. Evidence on the body—such as a letter to the girl's parents, dated five months earlier—identified the resident of Worthington, Armstrong County. The head could not be found. Police were unsure but doubted foul play, and theorized that the girl was probably trapped in the water and drowned.[349]

OVER TWO HUNDRED BRITISH bombers obliterated Hitler's Alpine home, the Berghof; a direct hit with a six-ton bomb laid waste the château. "I saw one terrible flash right on Hitler's house," cheered an RAF fighter. "Where's Adolf?" read the subheadline.[350] It wasn't known if Hitler was inside at the time. One could hope.

THE PULLMAN COMPANY WAS enjoying some great advertising during the war. Their eponymous train sleeping cars, already used throughout most of the United States, still had a domestic wartime purpose for the wounded soldiers: "In an almost unbelievably short time after they received their first medical attention at aid stations right in the battlefield, they are in America—on their way to General Hospitals near their homes. . . . No other wounded in the world are brought home so speedily."[351]

For $3.98, women in Mississippi could buy, exclusively offered at the R and K Store in Moss Point, a satin pantie with elastic hip panels and satin elastic gores. "How about a back view of yourself in the mirror?" asked the newspaper ad, with a drawing of a lingerie-wearing woman holding a "Buy War Bonds" flyer. "Hum; we thought so!" The "practical innovation—both fore and aft," it said, and concluded, "[guarantees] freedom of action."[352]

APRIL 28 BROUGHT SOME SHOCKING, though not unwelcome, news to the relatively tame Italian front. Il Duce, Benito Mussolini, the man whose rhetoric, showmanship, and charisma inspired Hitler's own, was quickly tried—though no trial in any legal sense took place—and executed in the small village of Giulino, along with his mistress. Allied troops had been advancing into northern Italy, having already conquered the south last year, and the Duce wanted a way out of the losing war. He had tried to escape three days earlier with his mistress to Spain, but they were captured near the Swiss border. The *New York Times* noted that the "one-time premier begged for life" before the trial found him guilty.[353]

The last words out of Il Duce's mouth were not the words of a dictator or the glory of martyrdom for the cause of fascism but the desperate and sad cries of "No! No!"—of a scared, mortal man.[354] He was then killed by firing squad.

His body was moved to Milan and strung upside down, beaten, urinated and spat on, and displayed for all to see in the public square. One man emptied his pistol into the corpse, and another pushed through guards to beat his body, breaking the lifeless jaw. It was "the unglorious end of a dictator," the *Times* concluded.[355] The same was done to his mistress.

The *London Times* ran a half-page biography of the former dictator, detailing his rise, influence, and failure as an aspiring Roman emperor. "Mussolini liked to parade himself as a man of great physical activity. He went in for the more violent forms of exercise; he was known to have lion cubs as pets. He piloted his own aeroplane, and he had himself photographed at work in the harvest field," it said.[356] His very person was tied to the rise and fall of fascism, bringing a cult of personality unseen in the twentieth century.

"Mussolini's end is deserved but ghastly," wrote an aide of Ike's, warning that "democracies may treat their ex-leaders carelessly and frequently without respect, but the way Mussolini and his mistress were executed . . . should be a warning to all future would-be dictators."[357]

TRAGEDY ALSO STRUCK CAMP Bowie in Brownwood, central Texas, on April 28, when four men were killed and twelve injured in a "premature explosion, which occurred during training in demolition."[358] The story from the *Ft. Worth Star Telegram* noted that all safety precautions were followed.

IN THE PACIFIC THEATER, meanwhile, the same island-hopping that marked the beginning of the year continued. On April 28, the Associated Press reported that Chinese troops killed over a thousand Japanese who were "caught in a pocket 75 miles east of the American airbase at Chihkiang in Hunan Province."[359] In the Philippines, a sixteen-year-old Filipino girl Jeanne Krux found life "too quiet" in Manila. The teenage girl had been a literal fighter during Japanese occupation. "I just remember [killing] 20," she reported. Her first kill was at the age of fourteen. With the

Japanese gone, she had picked up fishing. "Now we catch fish instead of Japs in the nets and traps out there," she said to reporters.[360]

Not far from the relative calm of the Philippines, the Battle of Okinawa was still raging. The capital, Naha, was within sight. Admiral Nimitz reported that 2,800 Japanese planes had been destroyed in one month's time, a vast majority of them near Okinawa. By April 18, a bloody firefight between Japanese and American forces on Ie Island raged on, though two-thirds of the tiny island was in Allied hands. On Okinawa's northwest, Motobu Peninsula, no fewer than 2,500 Japanese tried to capture a strategic hill overlooking the area. Also, US Marines managed to kill over three hundred Japanese.[361]

HAVE INDIGESTION? NEXT TO a full-page article about the details and graphic nature of Mussolini's death sat a small advertisement in DC's *Evening Star*. "Relieved in 5 minutes or double your money back," the ad for Beli-ans Tablets guaranteed. For only 25 cents a bottle, it promised it was "the fastest-acting medicines known for symptomatic relief. No laxative."[362]

THE 42ND INFANTRY DIVISION—THE so-called Rainbow Division—rolled into southern Germany, happening upon the medieval city of Dachau. "Anything with wheels," reported the Associated Press, "rolled down" into the city. There, American soldiers were not greeted with the battered German Wehrmacht but with a series of camps and houses filled with civilians. This was the Dachau concentration camp. Known to have existed before its liberation, Dachau was called in passing the "infamous prison camp" in March, when reports leaked of prisoner revolts.[363]

The sheer scale of the camp, however, surprised even the most hardened American man. Within the past three months, over nine thousand inmates had died of hunger, disease, or murder. Many bodies were not disposed of. As the Americans approached the multilayered and complex camps, SS guards tried to dispose of the evidence of their crimes. Witnesses—four thousand men, women, and children, all slave laborers—were packed into wooden barracks, which were then doused in gasoline and set afire.[364]

Over thirty thousand prisoners were freed the first day. Typhus was rampant in the camp when it was liberated. The Associated Press declared that "the water supply of the city was reported contaminated from 6,000 graves on high ground."[365]

With images of the burned, starving, and tortured men and women of all ages seared into their minds, Allied anger was overwhelming. The revenge was swift. American soldiers, aided by the fury of freed prisoners, rounded up dozens of SS men and Nazi guards and quickly and summarily executed them. One SS guard was slumped over his plate of beans—an ironic and Dante-esque method of execution, with the starving civilians all around—with a bullet to the back of the head.[366] An American GI lent a Jewish prisoner his bayonet with which the starved man proceeded to hack away and behead an SS guard. Another American, a lieutenant, took it on himself to execute three hundred guards alone.[367]

The scene of the bodies was too horrific, beyond literal belief. Said one liberated American POW, "No one will believe us. We got to talk about it, see? We got to talk about it if anyone believes us or not." Marguerite Higgins of the *New York Herald Tribune* reported that "the liberation was a frenzied scene. Inmates of the camp hugged and embraced the American troops, kissed the ground before them and carried them shoulder high around the place."[368]

ARCHBISHOP OF BOSTON, RICHARD J. Cushing, opined to the Massachusetts Chapter of Catholic Alumni that the current age's lack of morality was to be placed solely on women's shoulders. "If our modern world can be characterized as coarse and vulgar—and no one can seriously challenge that characterization of America, at least," he said, "then our womenfolk are mainly responsible." He continued, clearing any ambiguity, "Let it not be charged that men are responsible, for in this manner they take their cue from women." He urged women to counter the "Hollywood culture" made prevalent by "vile movies."[369]

THE UNUSUAL WHEREABOUTS OF a woman named Olga Tschechowa were first discovered when Patton's army captured one of Hitler's retreats a week earlier. Known in the United States for her role as the female lead in Alfred Hitchcock's 1931 *Mary*, Olga had been rumored to be the girlfriend and lover of Hitler for the past two years. In fact, she had apparently married the Führer in Bad Frankenhausen, some thirty miles south from the captured town of Leipzig. A little local boy said, "the Führer is said to be very much in love with her for which nobody can blame him." One German party leader in the area confessed to American troops that recently there had been a huge wedding attended by every high-ranking Nazi official, including Heinrich Himmler. He was not invited, though, as it was too big of a deal even for him.[370] (No newspaper mentioned Hitler's real-life lover, Eva Braun.)

The men who raised the Stars and Stripes on Mount Suribachi on Iwo Jima in the iconic photograph were identified as encompassing the "melting pot that is America and her fighting fortress." The six marines ranged in age from eighteen to twenty-five years old and were from a Pima Indian to the son of Czech immigrants. Private First Class Michael Strank, the Czech, was said to be "one of the nicest, quietest boys in town"; another, Sergeant Henry Hanson, was called (from his mother, no less) "a daredevil who wanted action." Half the men, as reported at the time, had been killed taking the tiny island in later action. "They were my buddies," confessed fellow flag raiser, Private Rene Gagnon.[371]

New York cabbie, Joseph Winston, came across some luck when he discovered a $2,000 diamond clip left in his taxi, which had belonged to a wealthy couple earlier in the day. Like any good man, he turned it over to the police, expecting to never see it again. But fortune and luck were on his side when the police returned the pricey clip to him "for keeps" since the owners could not be located.[372]

"REDS IN BERLIN," SCREAMED the front page of the *Detroit Evening Times*. "Nazis Admit It by Wireless!"[373] It was all the talk, with every paper reporting on the fast-changing landscape. A house of cards brought a new captured city each day. Papers could hardly keep up, with news coming in so fast—a new development every day, if not every hour. The *San Francisco Examiner* reported that over sixteen Soviet armies rampaged in, and the once expansive Reich was "ripped to shreds."[374] One reporter said that the Russians were bringing "fire and death to Berlin," while a Nazi general confessed, "It's hell in there," as child soldiers as young as thirteen tried to repel the advancing Soviets.[375] The Russians were an unstoppable force. Berliners heard the constant rumbling of Marshal Zhukov's tanks, followed by the pops of rifles. White flags of surrender decorated houses as the Soviets marched in. Swiss radio broadcasters reported that "fierce battles are raging but the battle of Berlin is practically over."[376] Three days in, over a fourth of the German capital had been overrun.

WILL AMERICANS CARE? THAT was a question bouncing around many a mind back at home. Day after day brought more news of the Nazis' crimes. But will it even matter to the average American? So opined one anonymous writer in the *Philadelphia Inquirer*. Accompanied by the personification of "history" writing, the first of presumably multiple volumes of "A Permanent Record of German Atrocities," the author of the op-ed "America Must Not Forget—Again!" was scared of such a nonchalant reaction. The "shocking accounts of the horrors of Buchenwald, Dachau, Osweicim and other prison and concentration camps . . . are not propaganda tales concocted for the gullible. They are facts, borne out by photographs, affidavits, and official records," the author wrote.[377]

"Will they be remembered five or ten years from now?" the author asked. "Will we ever learn from history?"[378] After all, the brutality of Germans against Belgium during the First World War—only thirty years earlier—was quickly swept aside as tall-tale legend of propaganda. Will these camps and atrocities similarly be ignored and hand-waved?

To ensure a permanent memory of these atrocities, the editorial suggested that "there should be established in Washington a museum to preserve, so long as such a reminder is necessary, factual, authentic documents, photographs and other displays to keep the American people from forgetting the horrors." For if we are so forgetful, then would not there be a third world war against Germany, just as the second was born from the first? "We must not forget," concluded the editorial, "again!"[379]

The threat of not fully understating the horrors of the death camps was real. General Eisenhower made sure to expose them as much as possible. *St. Louis Post-Dispatch* editor Joseph Pulitzer, grandson of the Pulitzer Prize founder of the same name, was one of many writers to visit the camps at Buchenwald. "I came here in a suspicious frame of mind, feeling that I would find that many of the terrible reports that have been printed in the United States before I left were exaggerations," he confessed.[380]

But it was worse than that. "They have been understatements," Pulitzer said. With an uncharacteristic loss of words, he believed the ghettos and slums of Calcutta, India, to be better and healthier than the German camps. He saw sixteen prisoners sleeping on a 3-by-12-foot shelf, of skin-made lampshades, and read reports of two hundred deaths a day and other horrors. "If the reader is still suspicious," he said, "let him look at the photographs, and when he does so let him remember that they picture only small parts of the mosaic of the Nazi policy of deliberate mass extermination."[381]

Also attending the tour of Buchenwald was writer John Randolph Hearst, son of famed yellow publisher William Randolph Hearst. He wrote of the horrors, "Those who survive will remain for a long time, perhaps for the rest of their lives, in a stunned state of mind. . . . Mentally they will bear forever the crucifying marks." He continued, noting that some German civilians, forced to bury the emaciated corpses of the camps' victims under threat by occupying American troops, committed suicide. "One cannot know," he said, "whether they took their lives because of shame or because of the fear of retribution."[382]

A FULL-PAGE AD RAN in the *Atlanta Constitution* with some rather cruel dissonance: "The Victory which is almost ours, is Living Tribute to the Men of THE THIN GREY LINE." With a large engraving of kneeling

GIs in front of Confederate soldiers, Stars and Bars prominently displayed, the ad claimed that the fight against fascism was the same as in the Civil War. We fight "with the courage and strength inspired of their memory—as we strive to stamp out the tyranny which threatens their Ideals," it said.[383]

THE JAPANESE WERE TAKING a licking from the Americans. Okinawa was still a hot battleground. "Doughboys of the Twenty-third Army Corps have killed 11,738 Japanese and captured 27 in Southern Okinawa alone."[384] Soldiers in Iwo Jima, the center of barbaric attention in the Pacific only a month before, reported a measly sixty Japanese killed. Americans declared victory over Ie Island, finally taking the crucial Hill 178 near an airfield. The battle had been fierce, switching sides several times, before the 7th, 27th, and 96th Divisions advanced for good.[385]

The Yanks also had essentially captured the Philippines; only two Japanese strongholds remained, in Cebu Province and in Mindanao. The latter was nearly guaranteed secured when American 24th Division troops captured Highway No. 1. With that secured, each day, miles of land were occupied by American troops.[386] One report noted that the Americans were advancing over a mile per hour.[387]

In a connection to the past, the 24th Army Corps came across a century-old American cemetery in Naha, Okinawa. In the 1850s, sailors under Commodore Matthew Perry had traveled to the Far East to secure trading rights with both Japanese and the Ryuku Kingdoms. "Murdered in the Market Place," bore two of the headstones.[388]

Out of a warped sense of either fanaticism or desperation, or both, more and more Japanese airmen were trying to ram their planes into US cruisers and battleships. "Every Jap plane is a suicide diver these days," reported Robert Sherrod, war correspondent for *Time* magazine. "They're all 'kamikazes' now. The Japs aren't sending out any planes that are expected to return."[389] But why? There was a shift in tactics to cause as much destruction as possible. Mainly, Japanese high command understood that there was no future for their air force.

PRESIDENT TRUMAN HAD A busy schedule on April 23. He was cast from the frying pan into the fire. It was his first Sunday in Washington since becoming president. The week prior, he had stayed at Hyde Park for Roosevelt's funeral. Among his first duties in DC was to meet the wounded at Walter Reed General Hospital. There, he prayed and worshiped at the chapel with the soldiers. Newspapers noted his enthusiasm in singing the hymns.[390]

That didn't stop others from predicting hard times for him. Of the six vice presidents in US history who assumed the presidency, three had "very stormy political gain." Abraham Lincoln's successor, Andrew Johnson, was impeached but acquitted by the Senate by one vote; Millard Fillmore, who took office after the death of Zachary Taylor in 1850, signed five "compromise bills" on slavery, infuriating northern abolitionists, and perhaps leading to more extremism that took shape in the decade before the Civil War; and John Tyler, vice president of William Henry Harrison, tried to adopt a bipartisan Democrat-Whig platform, leading to disapproval in both parties and the resignation of all but one member of his cabinet. Would Truman, the seventh, have a similarly rocky administration? The odds of history were not on his side.[391]

WOMEN WERE MAKING HEADWAY, not just in jobs, careers, and active participation in American culture but also religion. Two local women were the first to visit the Georgian monastery of Trappist monks, devoted to penance, abstinence, poverty, and seclusion away from the material world. They had to receive approval, but once they were allowed in for a tour, they were struck by the "simple food and life the men of God [lived] within the confines of their small world, in virtual complete silence."[392] The silence was a bit more literal, though, as only the tour guide and the gatekeeper spoke to the women; any and all monks they saw kept silent.

American charity reigned, even during war. In Allegheny and Pittsburgh counties alone, over two million pounds of clothing were donated to the United National Clothing Drive. Fifteen hundred Pennsylvanians assisted the charity group, a monumental task. Though the numbers across the nation were impressive for the first day, the drive was to be an ongoing task for the needy and destitute of Europe.[393] Bostonians, however, were chided by Secretary of State Stettinius. Only eleven days remained in the drive, and Boston had yet to meet its quota. They had to double their efforts.[394]

NORMALCY AFTER THE WAR? Perhaps it was not as far-fetched now as it was four years ago. United Air Lines was looking ahead to a normal postwar America. In late April, they appealed to the Civil Aeronautics Board to introduce a nonstop flight from Washington, DC, to Pittsburgh.[395]

In local sports, fans let off a little built-up frustration in a rather amusing way. After the Chicago Cubs beat the Pittsburgh Pirates twice, disgruntled spectators hurled cushions, oranges, and pop bottles. The oranges, specifically, were outed by *Pittsburgh Post-Gazette* writer Ed Balinger as "rolling to the plate."[396]

The Pacific war may have been brutal, but that didn't stop Hawaii residents from thinking of the what-if scenarios brainstormed years earlier. Immediately after the attack on Pearl Harbor in December 1941, all currency in the islands was replaced with Hawaii-only money. The difference in design was minuscule, though an overprint of "HAWAII" on the back could easily identify these new notes. This was so that in the event of a Japanese invasion of the islands, the US government could easily declare any Hawaii notes invalid, rendering Japanese frustrated with worthless, meaningless wealth that couldn't be used anywhere else in the world.

Soon enough, by late 1944, there was no conceivable threat of a Japanese invasion, so the Department of Treasury reversed their decision, allowing regular greenbacks to circulate in Hawaii while phasing out the special Hawaiian currency. Now natives were asking what to do with all the currency with the overprint. Hundreds of millions of dollars were just sitting in homes and banks and offices. If anything, the plan to be a nuisance to the Japanese backfired; it was now a nuisance to the Hawaii residents themselves.

Stafford Austin, manager of the Honolulu Plantation Company, had one idea. He boiled about $70 million of the currency in his refinery to get the sugar in the bills. "I burned $20,000 in new fives myself with one throw," he said. "It was quite a sensation, I can tell you." He noted, "It's turning out heavy sugar . . . just as sweet."[397] Some army men were reported to have lit their cigarettes made with $1,000 bills.

In Baltimore, sailor Clyde Baker was sentenced to one year in prison for bigamy. He had married two women in five days' time the previous winter "because he was nervous after having ships sunk under him in the South Pacific."[398] The judge denied Baker's request to return to the navy.

THE BATTLE OF BERLIN, or perhaps more accurately, the Battle for Berlin, all came to a head the last week of the month. Soviet tanks—with "On to Berlin" painted on their hulls—and soldiers rushed in, faster than ever before, with such fierceness that the *Washington Post* called it "burning with hatred for everything Nazi and thirsting for revenge." Literally every house along the way was damaged or destroyed. Declared one Russian, "Each stone of the city, each meter of street is against us. We have to take them with our blood." The Soviet paper *Tass* gave a play-by-play: "Fighting in the streets is fierce and stiff. German guns bark. German aircraft fly overhead. However, more and more Soviet regiments pour into the city."[399]

Where was Hitler? The question was still on everyone's minds, more so with the Russians swarming the capital. The question was timely too, as the Free German Press Service (FGPS) predicted that Führer lookalike and double, August Wilhelm Bartholdy, would be filmed "dying on the last Berlin barricades," while the actual leader of the Nazi Reich escaped, alive and well. It was the perfect solution, said FGPS, as Hitler could easily plan from the shadows while creating a heroic figure for postwar Nazi resistance.[400]

Wall Street was not optimistic about Europe's future. With German industry completely destroyed, bankers believed that Nazi resistance would continue to fight fanatically, per their Führer's orders. And that agriculture, too, would be destroyed, forcing "the Reich to rebuild its postwar economic machine from scratch." According to one estimate, it would take Germany thirty years to recover. The bankers' solution was, oddly enough, to maintain "the same type of Nazi control." Otherwise, they reasoned, "an intense shortage of goods will help bid up prices, creating inflation and making the German plight even more chaotic. Rigorous food rationing and price control must be continued. After the war Germans may get some small income from the Army of Occupation, but most dealings will be on a primitive barter basis among citizens of the Reich."[401]

As BERLIN FELL AND millions were liberated from Nazi occupation, and Hitler hid in his bunker, the Battle of Okinawa was still in full swing. Within a little less than two months' time, about half of the Japanese fighting force, about thirty thousand men, had been killed, wounded, or captured.[402] Rigorous fights lay ahead as the Japanese increasingly developed tougher and more brutal means of fighting, slowing the otherwise fast-moving Americans. The Japanese were getting desperate. Kamikaze planes continued to target American navy vessels. The hospital ship *Comfort*, full of wounded patients, was struck by a "suicidal pilot" off the coast of Okinawa. Nearly thirty were reported killed and the ship sustained considerable damage.[403] The ship, however, managed to make it to harbor with the Japanese plane still lodged in her hull.[404]

All is fair in war. In retaliation for the attack on the *Comfort*, over two hundred B-29 Superfortresses unleashed fire and fury on "the suicide-plane bases of Kyushu" for five straight days. Over half of the two hundred Japanese planes attacking American forces were shot down. It was a complete bloodbath of fighter against fighter, though clearly superior American technology persevered.[405]

Eugene Sledge of the 1st Marine Division was less optimistic. On the last day of April, higher-ups gave the go-ahead to move south, into the harsher fighting areas, to replace the 27th Infantry Division. He reported on what he saw: "The stuff has hit the fan down there, boys. The Nips are pouring on the artillery and mortars and everything they've got. Boys, they're firing knee mortars as thick and fast as we fire M1s."[406] For the men in the Pacific, the fighting was far from over.

A GALLUP POLL FROM Princeton revealed that most Americans believed minor Nazis—not just the top administration or leaders—should be punished after the war. Forty-two percent favored imprisonment, 19 percent favored trying and imprisoning if found guilty, 19 percent believed they should be killed outright, 15 percent had no opinion, 3 percent believed reeducation and rehabilitation was the best solution, and 2 percent believed nothing should be done with the captured POWs. The poll also revealed a 98 percent for and 2 percent against punishing Hitler himself. A majority of those polled believed he should be executed.[407]

A NEW MIDWAY-CLASS AIRCRAFT carrier, named USS *Franklin D. Roosevelt* in honor of the newly passed president, was christened by former first lady Eleanor Roosevelt. It was her first public appearance since her husband's passing. The carrier's dedication was somber. Mrs. Roosevelt was quiet, saying, "My husband would have felt keenly and would have appreciated the honor of having a carrier given to him." President Truman sent his regrets that he could not attend, noting that "this vessel is dedicated to winning the war."[408]

"Now fly direct to Boston," announced a large ad in the *Pittsburgh Post-Gazette*. With pride, Trans World Airlines was happy to announce that May 1 would be the start of a new era: "TWA starts a new service which will give Pittsburgh 3 flights daily to Boston plus additional service to New York." The small print gave a caveat, though, bringing the reader back to reality: "Don't travel unless your trip helps win the war."[409]

Victory gardens continued to be popular in the home front, despite how assured victory itself was in Europe. "This gives you exercise," said one ad in the *Boston Daily Globe* in late April, pointing to golf clubs. "But so does this," it continued, pointing to a gardening hoe. "AND you help your Country with a Victory Garden."[410]

Rationing, too, was still in effect, and these stamps were hot commodities. Pennsylvania residents could trade in one pound of used fat for two extra red point rations to buy meat. "Save more used fats until the Japs are licked!" said one ad.[411] Kay Hanson of Boston learned the value of rationing stamps the hard way when his two thousand red ration stamps and "a number of A and B gas stamps" were stolen from his car. Police caught two ten-year-old boys, who claimed that the same stamps in their possession were found in a bag along a cliffside. The police handed the boys over to their parents.[412]

All the war news didn't stop simple day-to-day problems.

"BERLIN IST GEFALLEN," READ the German-immigrant paper in Cleveland, Ohio.[413] Indeed, Berlin had fallen. In the midafternoon of April 30, Adolf Hitler, Führer, chancellor, leader of the Nazi Party, at the age of fifty-six, died by suicide in his Berlin bunker. His now-wife, Eva Braun, joined him in the pact. A simple bullet to the head quickly and efficiently ended their lives. The same man who touted a thousand-year Reich and the superiority of the German people, and who promoted himself as the vanquisher of the Jews, the übermensch, and Messiah to humanity took the coward's way out, refusing to face the oncoming trials awaiting him. To him, it was martyrdom; to others, including those with him in the bunker, it was betrayal.

Only two days earlier, he would have heard of the barbarity and humiliation shown to Mussolini's corpse and may have thought of his own German people—or worse, the Russians—doing the same to him. Would this have driven him to suicide? To prevent such a show and gratification, his body was quickly burned.

Many other fanatics committed suicide rather than be taken alive to face justice from the Allies. A particular fanatical nut was a pint-sized propaganda minister, Joseph Goebbels, who had been with Hitler since the beginning. He had never seen battle and was particularly virulent in his anti-Semitism. Goebbels became the chancellor for a day, after Hitler committed suicide. He and his wife, Magda, who was equally obsessive about Hitler, murdered their six children with cyanide pills in their sleep before killing themselves—he shot her and then took a cyanide capsule. Before taking their own lives, the Goebbels kept muttering about only wanting to live under National Socialism.[414]

All was over. In accordance with the Führer's last will and testament, Grand Admiral Karl Doenitz, supreme commander of the navy, was named to be his successor as the relatively subdued titled, "President of the German Reich."

The news of Hitler's death spread like wildfire. In the following days, much ink was devoted to big, black, bold letters for front-page headlines across the nation:

New York Times (May 2, 1945): "Hitler Dead in Chancellery."
Alaska's Nome Nugget (May 2, 1945): "Hitler Dies in Berlin."
Salt Lake Tribune (May 2, 1945): "Hitler Dead, Says Nazis."
North Carolina's Wilmington Morning Star (May 2, 1945): "Enemy Announces Death of Hitler."
New York Daily News (May 2, 1945): "Nazi Radio Announces: Hitler Dead."
Boston's Daily Record (May 2, 1945): "Hitler Killed."
Washington Post (May 2, 1945): "Hitler Dead, Nazis Say."
Boston Daily Globe (May 2, 1945): "World Hopes It's True: Nazis Say Hitler Dead."
Michigan Chronicle (May 5, 1945): "Hitler's Race Hatred Is Dead."

And so, almost appropriately, April 1945 came to an end.

MAY TO AUGUST 1945

MAY

Americans, alongside the world, learned of Adolf Hitler's death on the first of May, the day after the fateful act. As fast as the headlines were coming in and as fast as newspapers were selling, there were still many who took pause at the news. Was it really so? Would the Führer really have ended it so anticlimactically after decades of touting his martyrdom for the Nazi cause?

It was, after all, a state-run radio that first made the announcement. With solemn music by Richard Wagner and Anton Bruckner's Seventh Symphony, and a dramatic drum roll, the radio announced that Hitler had died fighting "to his last breath against Bolshevism" and exhibited "a hero's death" as he "had recognized the horrible danger of Bolshevism very early and concentrated his entire existence to the fight against it."[1] (The *New York Times* reported that when the German announcer declared "a hero's death," a "ghost voice" was heard on air shouting, "This is a lie!"[2])

Moscow was immediately skeptical, and believed it was a "new Fascist trick" to allow the Nazi leader to escape.[3] Publicly, Truman was more trustful of the announcement, saying, "We have on the best authority possible to obtain at this time that Hitler is dead. But how he died we are not familiar with the details as yet." Indeed, the British Broadcasting Corporation had reported that Hitler died of a stroke.[4] General Eisenhower and his staff were quick to dispel any residual Nazi propaganda aimed at the German citizens that Hitler died a hero. Harry Butcher, naval aide to Ike, wrote in his diary that "the psychological boys were quick on the trigger."[5] Across the pond, Americans throughout New York City were also confused, raising an eyebrow to the news. One Italian man said, "Do not believe what it says. Believe it when you see a picture of Hitler as you saw Mussolini's picture yesterday."[6]

Some Germans were also in disbelief of their Führer's death because they thought he had died the previous summer. They thought the July 20, 1944, plot to assassinate Hitler had succeeded. Per Edward Beattie, United Press International writer and former prisoner of war, many Germans, from "front-line troops to village housewives," thought Hitler had been killed by the suitcase bomb in his Prussian Wolf's Lair. (In reality, he survived by sheer luck; four were killed in the packed room.) Hardly anyone believed he died in a blaze of glory in Berlin. The only ones who did were "Nazi fanatics who also [believed] they can go underground and continue the fight against the Allies for years."[7]

Confusion may have reigned not of the *how* and the *when*, and to many maybe even not of the *if* on Hitler's death, but hearing and imagining the possibility sent a range of emotions throughout the world. Some felt simply numb, as if in a dream. One woman opined, "Too bad he's dead. He should have been tortured." One veteran, Leo Kaplan, who had been injured in the Philippines said, "If it's true, it's the greatest thing I ever heard." Declared Lieutenant Arthur McIntyre, "Good riddance." Sergeant John Eliopoulos was more graphic: "We'd like to spit on his grave, the——."[8] The *New York Times* censored the profanity.

Still, others were more solemn. A policeman confessed, "It would have been good 20 years ago. Late now." Another asked, "So the bum's dead, eh? What difference does it make now?" Joe Sisselman heard the news as bittersweet as a father could; his son, Leonard, had been report-edly killed in Europe ten days earlier. Upon hearing the news, he simply confessed, "Maybe it will save the lives of some of our American kids. For me it comes late."[9]

Despite the news and the effective capture of the Nazi capital, the war in Europe was, at least officially, still ongoing. Wehrmacht and Nazi SS men were still fighting or fleeing. The average American soldier still had to be careful. So learned Staff Sergeant Archie Weathers of the 4th Armored Division, who awoke to another GI in his room after a night's sleep. "Good morning, sir," said the man. Weathers immediately arrested him. The man was secretly a German soldier trying to flee under the Allies' nose. "No GI in his right mind would ever call a sergeant 'sir,'" Weathers reported to United Press International reporters later.[10]

The European war, already battered in April, was now in absolute shatters. Alfred Speer, chief architect and minister of munitions of the Third Reich, admitted defeat himself in a radio broadcast on May 3. Whatever fighting there was, he said, was from a "desire not to allow our German compatriots fleeing from the east to die."[11] Surrender to the Americans or British if you could was the unsaid command.

Speer compared the devastation of Germany the past year to that of the Thirty Years' War, a seventeenth-century religious war that abso-lutely destroyed central Europe with its sheer brutality and death. But it was so much worse now: "Never before was a civilized nation so severely hit. . . . Never yet has any people borne the hardships of war with more perseverance and loyalty than you Germans." He continued, "Now you are all greatly dejected and profoundly shocked. Your faith now turns into despair and your perseverance and toughness into a feeling of tired-ness and indifference."[12]

The terms of surrender to the occupiers are "entirely in their hands," Speer said. Though he stressed that, if allowed, the German people must rebuild "to protect our people against the worst blows." Repairing railways and railroads across the country, building houses and shelters, stockpiling food supplies, and refurnishing factories with coal or wood or any other fuel took precedence and was the basic foundation for any modern society. He concluded the address, "A better providence can alter our future. We, ourselves, can do our share in building this future . . . by meeting the enemy with dignity and self-confidence—at this time becoming more modest and by exercising self-criticism and by firmly believing in the future of our nation, which is eternal. May God protect Germany."[13]

THE MEN OF EASY Company of the 101st Airborne Division reached Hitler's Berchtesgaden residence on May 5, encountering very little resistance as they entered the famed Alpine Eagle's Nest. It had been feared the region would become a redoubt for Nazi resistance, but it turned out to be the opposite. Highly decorated Wehrmacht general Theodor Tolsdorff and his corps willingly and without any resistance surrendered to the Americans. Private Edward Heffron, who caught the convoy of "Tolsdorff the Mad," thought at the time, "A kid from South Philly has a Kraut general surrender to him, that is pretty good."[14]

The goods of the Berghof and its inhabitants were theirs for the taking. Said another private of Easy Company, David Webster, in a letter to his parents a week later, "We obtained pistols, knives, watches, fur-lined coats, camouflaged jump jackets. Most of the Germans take it in pretty good spirit, but once in a while we get an individual who does not want to be relieved of the excess weight of his watch. A pistol flashed in his face, however, can persuade anybody." As for his own booty, "I now have a Luger, two P-38s, a Schmeisser machine pistol, two jump smocks, one camouflaged winter jacket, several Nazi flags about three feet by two, and a watch."[15]

The most important loot was in the cellar. "Lord! I had never seen anything like this before," declared Major Richard "Dick" Winters upon seeing about ten thousand bottles of wine and liquor. It was of course ripe for consumption, and Winters tried (unrealistically, he later said) to put a cap on the drinking. Captain Lewis Nixon, known for his drinking habits, "thought he had died and gone to heaven" upon seeing the cellar, according to Winters. "Take what you want," Winters told Nixon. "Then have each company and battalion HQ bring around a truck and take a truckload. You are in charge."[16]

For the men of Easy Company, who went through D-Day, Operation Market Garden, Bastogne, and the Battle of the Bulge, it was their reward to drink Hitler's alcohol.

FINALLY, IT HAPPENED. VICTORY came on May 8, at 9:00 a.m. Eastern War Time, when President Harry Truman, Prime Minister Winston Churchill, and Premier Joseph Stalin, each simultaneously proclaimed from DC, London, and Moscow, the unconditional surrender of Nazi Germany. The signing had actually taken place twenty-five hours earlier, in a schoolhouse—at the time used as SHAEF (Supreme Headquarters Allied Expeditionary Force)—in Reims, France.

General Dwight D. Eisenhower was not present, but in his place, signing both for the Americans and British, was his chief of staff, Lieutenant General Walter Bedell Smith; for the Russians, General Ivan Susloparov; and for the newly revived French, General François Sevez. Colonel General Gustaf (Alfred) Jodl, the chief of staff for the Nazi Wehrmacht, signed in lieu of Reich president Karl Dönitz.

Jodl signed four documents—perhaps feeling four times the shame—in three languages: German, Russian, and two in English. The first words: "Unconditional Surrender." When signing the end of Germany, Jodl spoke to the crowd of reporters and generals: "With this signature, the German people and armed forces are, for better or worse, delivered into the victor's hands. In this war . . . both have achieved and suffered more than perhaps any other people in the world. In this hour, I can only express the hope that the victor will treat generously with them."[17]

Then there was silence. No celebration, no jubilation, no anger, no weeping. Associated Press correspondent Edward Kennedy appropriately called it "dead silence."[18]

And just like that, the promised thousand-year Reich lasted a measly

into Poland,
nce, and less
rmany came

ration of vic-
ose sixty-first
o be the first
nally moving
if at all. Rats
s molded the
diately got to
ty-one-year-
study proved
e legs off and
d tackle. Dad

n a week ear-
nderstanding
rican people.
bsolute bliss.
Square. "The
rk Times. The
enthusiasm of
ildly jubilant
and filled the
f paper." The
between 8:00
o celebrate or
ns, and at one
gers were, in

ome even five
d through the

radio that New Yorkers get back to work and to save paper, the masses laughed, and confetti and ticker tape fell like rain onto the streets.[22]

Miami Beach, meanwhile, prepared for the news literally like a hurricane as stores boarded up their windows. Elsewhere in the Sunshine State, twelve hundred liquor and beer stores were ordered to close for twenty-four hours to preserve the still-in-place rationing of sugar. The *Miami Herald* nonchalantly said the embargo was "going to upset a lot of Miami's eating and drinking habits."[23]

In contrast to the partying, Hawaii—the epicenter and staging area needed for the United States to enter the war—had a calm, prayer-filled day. "There was no revelry," wrote the *Honolulu Advertiser.* "Business houses and shops remained open. Liquor stores and drinking establishments throughout Oahu were closed by governmental order. . . . Everyone talked about THE day. But there was no revelry. No ticker tape or confetti was thrown. . . . Honolulu has been and continues to be too close to the grim realities of war for that."[24]

Truman established the following Sunday, May 13, as a national day of thanksgiving and prayer, designated "to unite in offering joyful thanks to God for the victory we have won and to pray that He will support us to the end of our present struggle and guide us into the way of peace."[25]

IT WAS TIME TO bring the boys home . . . well, not exactly. Celebrations of V-E Day were dampened by some sobering news. Just because the war against fascism in Europe was over did not mean it was over in Japan. And they needed men in the Pacific more than ever. Even Truman himself, in his announcement of the Nazis' defeat, faced that reality. "We must finish this war," he said. "Our victory is only half won." And Truman promised to rain hellfire on the Japanese. "The longer the war lasts, the greater will be the suffering and hardships which the people of Japan will undergo—all in vain. Our blows will not cease until the Japanese military and naval forces lay down their arms in unconditional surrender."[26] There were those two key words again: *unconditional surrender.* Would the Japanese do so too?

But none of that mattered to the boots on the ground in Europe. Could they go home to their family and loved ones? Could they finally taste real American food again and sit and breathe in real American cities? Don Williams of the *Stars and Stripes*, the war's major military newspaper, broke it down: "No man or woman, no matter how long he or she has been in service, overseas or in combat, will be released from the Army if his or her services are required in the war against Japan." He continued, "In the meantime, don't write home and tell your mother or sweetheart that you'll be home next week or next month. For most of you, it just ain't so."[27] General Patton, a tough guy, took a different tone at the possibility. On May 8, he spoke to the officers of his Third Army that morning, saying that "this was the last regular briefing in Europe." He wrote in his diary that day, "Most of them understood what I meant, and I added that I hope we will have other similar briefings in China."[28]

Of all the formations in Europe, the Third Army was among the toughest. In fact, they were so tough that papers were noting their unique status of being the "only Yanks still fighting" in Europe on May 8, up to the bitter end, right into Prague.[29] The final casualty count in Patton's troop alone was nearly 250,000, including killed, wounded, missing, and non-battle casualties; of those, 21,441 were killed. Also, 308 light tanks and 949 tanks were lost. "2½ years ago today we landed in Africa," Patton wrote. "During all that period until today at midnight we will have been practically in continuous battle. There is going to be a tremendous let down unless we watch ourselves."[30]

Across the world, most US Marines in Okinawa had a simple thought about the European war's end: "So what?" The Nazis weren't exactly the ones firing at them in this Far East island. It was the Japanese, with whom they very much were still at war. "Nazi Germany might as well have been on the moon," recounted Corporal E. B. Sledge. Still, there was some celebration, namely to the tune of a "swishing, roaring, and rumbling" artillery barrage toward Japanese concentrations.[31] Kill two birds with one stone, indeed.

Morale was still essential for the soldiers in Europe. Former president Roosevelt wanted to see to that, and President Truman continued that policy—namely, by supplying sports equipment, such as footballs, baseballs, bats, gloves, and the like. In a war-dominated society, that responsibility dropped onto the War Department. "The Army and Navy," wrote White House Press Secretary Jonathan Daniels to three-time gold medal Olympian John Kelly, "have a very serious responsibility in connection with the morale problems to be solved in this period."[32] Kelly had complained some weeks earlier of the shortage of athletic equipment, which had been discussed by Roosevelt before his passing; however, the White House shut that down, promptly.

On May 14, Soviet Marshal Fyodor Tolbukhin, commander of the 3rd Ukrainian Front, presented General Patton with the Order of Kutuzov, awarded for outstanding military leadership. Patton, ever the rabble-rouser, described Tolbukhin as "a very inferior man [who] sweated profusely at all times." The military he saw, however, was far from it. With Soviet and Western armies increasingly intermingling, partying, and celebrating the European war, there was more clash of cultures. Patton described the award ceremony as a "tremendous show," with a fifteen-mile-long procession of soldiers, standing at present arms, along with "extremely buxom female MP's," Patton noted in his diary. At the château of former Austrian emperor Franz Joseph, they were treated as royalty. Soviet soldiers cleaned and polished their boots, and women retainers "did everything except wipe your face" and even sprayed perfume. Western Allied celebrants were still skeptical of their Slavic friends, however, taking note to drink two ounces of mineral oil before consuming any alcohol. "They did their best to get us drunk," Patton said.[33]

The discipline of the Soviets even impressed the toughened American general. "No Russian could sit down or get up without asking the Marshal's permission. . . . I have never seen in any Army at any time, including the German Imperial Army of 1912, as severe discipline as exists in the Russian army. They give me the impression of something that is to be feared in future world political reorganization," Patton warned ominously.[34]

IMMEDIATELY, THE WORLD LOOKED to the Far East. The Japanese Empire was beaten but not yet down, with still about seven million troops held up in various islands or the mainland itself. Now, with Europe over, an estimated ten million American soldiers, sailors, airmen, and marines were to descend on them. Only a day after V-E Day, Allied transports were shipping troops over. Twelve hundred plus warships bombarded Japanese strongholds, and the Truman administration ordered faster production of B-29 Superfortresses. "Round-the-clock bombing of Japan is in the not too distant future," warned Lieutenant General Barney Giles, head of the Pacific theater's army air force.[35] And, as promised, the attacks and advances sped up.

May 12 saw the 6th Marine Division capture the outskirts of Okinawa's capital, Naha. "They made slow but steady progress with tanks, flame throwers, Tommy guns and bayonets through the toughest defense yet encountered in the Pacific war." The *Honolulu Advertiser* listed a plethora of towns and divisions: the 1st Marine Division seized the village of Dakeshi, northeast of the capital; the 77th Army Division captured decisively important land near Shuri, the second most-populous town in the region; the 96th Division continued to attack the port of Yanabaru. The Naha attacks by the 6th Marines were the most celebratory, though, as they had "the biggest gains . . . with an advance to within 200 yards" of the capital.[36] Forty thousand Japanese had been killed in the Okinawa campaign so far, an average of about one thousand a day.

In mainland Japan, the residents and workers of the third-largest city, Nagoya, saw over five hundred Superfortresses drop 500,760 bombs and incendiary weapons over their city. It was the largest raid on Japanese soil yet, and an "extremely difficult one for fire raids. Nagoya contains more modern construction than Tokyo and also a network of canals, roads, and five square miles of burned-out area from previous raids, which all serve as fire-breaks."[37] Nonetheless, the raid was a success, taking out historical sites such as the city's sixteenth-century castle.

MAY 13 MARKED ONE MONTH since FDR's burial in Hyde Park. For an entire month, flags across the country flew at half-staff. But starting the morning of May 15, flags would again fly at full staff.[38] The period of mourning for Roosevelt was over.

With attention now fully on the Japanese, discrimination and racism was again on the forefront in America. Secretary of the Interior Harold Ickes denounced the "planned terrorism by hoodlums" against Japanese Americans in California. Ickes likened these domestic terrorists to the Nazis themselves. They seem, with the motivation of "false patriotism," he declared, "determined to employ its Nazi storm trooper tactics against loyal Japanese Americans and law-abiding Japanese aliens."[39]

New Yorkers learned just how lucky they were that the war had ended in Europe. "A German submarine tried to V-bomb New York last election day presumably with a jet-propelled or rocket-propelled weapon," read a United Press International story.[40] Luckily, by either a smart-thinking pilot or some fortunate mechanical failure, the launched doodlebug fell short of its target and crashed into the sea.

Heinrich Himmler, SS chief and one of the many brainstormers of the Holocaust, committed suicide in the Lüneburg internment facility two days after his capture. With both Hitler and Goebbels dead, Himmler was the number one most-wanted Nazi official. But somehow, despite a thorough search, he managed to keep a potassium cyanide pill hidden in his teeth. According to London correspondent Terance Duncan, before he took his life, Himmler "was given three choices: to remain stripped, to wear British battle dress, or to wrap himself in blankets." He chose the third option. The examining medical officer searched his mouth, ears, feet, hands, and legs. The doctor had to force his hand inside the Nazi's mouth, on which Himmler animalistically bit down, cracking the vial. And with that one crunch, Himmler fell to the floor and died on the spot. "I am certain," said one at the scene, "that at the time he was first searched the vial already was in his mouth."[41]

As May came to an end, the gaze of the world's politicians and citizens increasingly shifted to the Western Pacific. More Superfortresses raided the Japanese capital; on May 24 alone, over seven hundred thousand bombs were dropped on Tokyo, with fires blazing so high and so intense that they could be seen from two hundred miles away. Brigadier General Thomas Powers, head of the B-29's 314th Air Division, nonchalantly commented, "It looks like a good job."[42] Two days later, the royal palaces—where, in Japanese religion, the god-emperor himself, divine incarnate, resided—were torched. Emperor Hirohito and his wife were unharmed, but ordinary citizens tasked with putting out the fires saw one of the holiest sites turn to ash before their very eyes.[43]

The bloody Battle of Okinawa was still heated and full of death, though Americans continued to gain ground. Naha, the capital, was abandoned as Allies reached eight hundred yards from the city. They then, within days, entered the city itself, finally breaking through fierce resistance. It was an unstoppable force that grew stronger literally by the day as more troops arrived. Most importantly, those who fought survived their wounds. The Americans had the "best medical setup of any Pacific operation," according to army surgeon Frederic Westervelt.[44] It was in no small part due to Americans back on the continent, as a steady supply of donated blood came in. On average, according to Westervelt, two hundred pints of blood were used by medics. One patient used forty pints alone.

The Japanese, just as fanatical as the Nazi leadership by the end, still saw reality and saw the losing battle. Imperial command fired Admiral Soemu Toyoda from three high-ranking positions: commander in chief of the Japanese navy, "commander in chief of overall naval command and commander of the naval escorts command."[45] Such firing was momentous and was a telltale sign of faithless Tokyo; it was akin to sacking General Douglas MacArthur.

It was just one of many ways that, whether many expressed it or not, it was a new world, bringing a renewed feeling of hope (for the Allies) and a new feeling of dread for the future (for the Japanese).

JUNE

The sixth month of the year 1945 was also the first month since the year 1939 that there was no war in Europe.

The war in Europe may have been over, but determining its fate was just as important as ever. So the Allies, with Dwight Eisenhower, Georgy Zhukov, Bernard Montgomery, and Jean de Lattre as signers, announced the "declaration regarding the defeat of Germany and the assumption of supreme authority with respect to Germany by the Governments of the United States of America, the Union of Soviet Socialist Republics, the United Kingdom and the Provisional Government of the French Republic."[46] Consisting of fifteen articles, the declaration, appropriately signed in the former Nazi capital of Berlin, split the German nation into four administrative zones, fulfilling the promise of the Yalta Conference back in February. The Soviet Union was to control East Prussia up to and beyond Berlin; Bavaria, in southern Germany, would be controlled by the United States; the northwest, including the Rhineland, by the British; and the west by the bordering French. In a blow to any Nazi legacy, the German borders were to revert to those of 1937, before the invasions of Czechoslovakia and Poland, before the annexation of Austria, and before the invasion of France.

The German military, all of it, was to be dismantled, and all Germans were to follow their new administrators—depending on the point of view, their new overlords—to the letter. "All German authorities and the German people shall carry out conditionally the requirements of the Allied representatives and shall fully comply with all such proclamations, orders, ordinances and instructions." Such obedience included the complete denazification of Germany, declaring a culture war.

"Germany," the declaration stated, "which bears responsibility for the war, is no longer capable of resisting the will of the victorious powers."[47]

With the swipe of a pen, Nazi Germany and any progress it had made was forever gone. Only the millions of dead civilians remained for its legacy.

AMERICANS COULDN'T LET UP or become too relaxed, despite headline after headline of victories in the Pacific. "The war isn't over," read an ad in the *Cleveland Plain Dealer*. "Not by a LONG SHOT!" The purchase of war bonds was just as important as ever, it declared, and it was a patriotic duty to continue that business: "We've got to lick those Japs . . . but good! . . . and YOU can help!"[48]

Indeed, not all was good news. Just before seizing the airfield in Naha, two American destroyers were crippled and sunk by kamikaze pilots. The destruction of *Morrison* and *Luce* had a combined casualty count of nearly three hundred sailors. Both ships were only two years old, built specifically for the war. The loss of *Morrison* in particular was tragic, as the destroyer was instrumental in saving survivors of the sunk aircraft carrier *Princeton* during the Battle of Leyte Gulf.[49]

WITH MORE NEWS OF B-29 raids, Americans became increasingly curious about these so-called Superfortresses. Both *Life* and *Flying* magazines answered that curiosity with a full-page ad about the aircraft. "A Boeing Superfortress," it opened, "lands on enough nylon to make 4,000 pairs of stockings." With six tires total and weighing up to seventy tons, "any woman can understand why," it continued. "Nylon made stronger stockings than ever before, and it worked the same way with tires." Rubber manufacturer BF Goodrich bragged that these same synthesized rubber tires were also to be found in automobiles.[50]

Boeing was on top of the world. It was less than a year prior that their massive aircraft first attacked Japan. By June 1945, "their valiant crews are regular commuters on the more than 3000-mile round trip from our island bases," they said. The motto "Built by Boeing" was meant to

convey stren
or the Flying
company of
engineering
your use," th

Still, the
Japan? . . . C
the *Beatrice T*
United State
to bring in t
the mainland
the seal on a
again, when
reader were t
or buy "blac
time the rea
more fun [o
really want t

The pre
duction at h
to, in turn,
trying to de
when Amer
general Mits
ted seppuku,
their heads
the narrow
Ocean, not
of staff Lieu
depart witho
51 years."[53]

"Okinaw
on June 21 br

Admiral Nimitz and General MacArthur declared Allied victory in the "bloodiest Pacific battle." Initial reports said that over 90,000 Japanese were killed and only 2,500 taken prisoner, numbers that showed the ferocity and fanaticism that perhaps even the most ardent Wehrmacht soldiers did not have.[54] For an 82-day battle, the average was over 1,000 Japanese lives lost per day. No one knew at the time how many forced civilian conscripts were killed. In contrast, initial estimates said the United States lost 7,000 men, with a staggering 30,000 wounded.[55] Within a week, the Japanese casualty count would rise considerably; by month's end, over 102,000 Japanese were believed killed and 10,000 captured.[56]

The victory over Okinawa was so grand and so important to the Pacific war effort that the *Nome Nugget* in Alaska simply ran a large front-page headline screaming, "Japs Surrender."[57]

THE TRUMAN ADMINISTRATION RECOGNIZED that the United States was at a hinge of history and easily could be on top as the new-found superpower. Secretary of the Navy James Forrestal and Admiral Ernest King, in a closed-door meeting with the House and Senate Naval Affairs, made the case that it was time to build such a military not only to protect Americans themselves but also to protect the world. "The Navy [wanted] a postwar fleet big enough to lick whatever naval forces any other power or combination of powers that 'likely enemies' could bring to bear on the North or South America or Pacific areas."[58]

The United States was also at the forefront of the newly signed Charter of the United Nations. June 26, despite some hiccups and stalls over Soviet and Western values, marked its unanimous approval and signature. China, the first of any nations to be attacked by the Axis, was the first to sign. Many delegates were moved to tears, and thundering applause erupted in the San Francisco War Memorial Opera House.

The Charter, thirty pages in all, opened in a mirror of the Declaration of Independence, and any American would recognize that:

WE THE PEOPLES OF THE UNITED NATIONS
DETERMINED

- to save succeeding generations from the scourge of war, which twice in our lifetime has brought untold sorrow to mankind, and
- to reaffirm faith in fundamental human rights, in the dignity and worth of the human person, in the equal rights of men and women and of nations large and small, and
- to establish conditions under which justice and respect for the obligations arising from treaties and other sources of international law can be maintained, and
- to promote social progress and better standards of life in larger freedom,

AND FOR THESE ENDS

- to practice tolerance and live together in peace with one another as good neighbours, and
- to unite our strength to maintain international peace and security, and
- to ensure, by the acceptance of principles and the institution of methods, that armed force shall not be used, save in the common interest, and
- to employ international machinery for the promotion of the economic and social advancement of all peoples,

HAVE RESOLVED TO COMBINE OUR EFFORTS TO
ACCOMPLISH THESE AIMS

Accordingly, our respective Governments, through representatives assembled in the city of San Francisco, who have exhibited their full powers found to be in good and due form, have agreed to the present Charter of the United Nations and do hereby establish an international organization to be known as the United Nations.[59]

It successfully established a united body of the world's countries, along with a supranational court of justice to oversee any hostilities on the globe. The *Daily Oklahoman* put it succinctly: with this document, "never again shall an Adolf Hitler be allowed to get a head start toward aggression."[60] Small and big countries alike would be able to vote on issues, allowing anyone a voice on the globe.

Truman was confident of its passage from the Senate and House. It was, after all, to be his most crowning achievement yet—and he was barely a month into office. Three decades ago, Woodrow Wilson tried and failed to create a League of Nations. Now, Truman succeeded where Wilson failed. "It will be just as easy," he said to residents of his Missouri home state defending the action, "for nations to get along in a republic of the world as it is for us to get along in a republic of the United States."[61]

July

With the passing of June, the year 1945 had officially passed its halfway mark. Much had happened during the year, and so it was with an odd euphoria that July acted as almost a transitional month. But it was still just as exciting.

On July 5, General Douglas MacArthur made the not-so-surprising announcement that the Philippine Islands had officially been liberated from Japanese forces, ending nearly three years of brutal occupation that started on December 8, 1941, only ten hours after the attack on Pearl Harbor. Japanese killed were estimated over three hundred thousand.

"The entire Philippine Islands are now liberated, and the Philippine Campaign can be regarded as virtually closed," MacArthur opened the communiqué. The Philippines had a combined 115,600 square miles of land with over seventeen million civilians. MacArthur detailed the Japanese forces, consisting of twenty-three divisions, "all of which were practically annihilated," and on sea, "naval battles reduced the Japanese Navy to practical impotence." With the liberation, all six objectives of the campaign—splitting the enemy in two geographically, acquiring "a great land, sea and air base for future operations," establishing a blockade, reintroducing democracy, freeing POWs, and finally, dealing "a crippling blow to the Japanese Army, Navy, and Air Force"—were, in MacArthur's own word, "accomplished."[62]

While fires raged in Japan and the cultural and political shakeup of Germany continued, Americans at home still experienced life as normal. Sometimes, though, unusual small stories appeared in the papers. In Cleveland, Ohio, readers had a chuckle at the guilty verdict of William Johnson, aged forty-four and blind, for robbing Peter Williams, aged seventy-nine and deaf. "Blind Man Robs Deaf Man" read one succinct headline.[63] The news was so unusual, it made the front page in Honolulu.

OKINAWA WAS LIBERATED. THE Philippines were liberated. Berlin was believed to be liberated. The Western Pacific was liberated. Japan was next.

But there was still thorny Germany.

POTSDAM, GERMANY, WAS ABOUT twenty-five miles from devastated Berlin. This eastern German city was the symbolic unification of old Weimar and new Nazi governments, where President Paul von Hindenburg shook newly appointed chancellor Adolf Hitler's hand in 1933. Twelve years later, the fate of Germany hung in the balance of the same nations on which Hitler declared war.

Potsdam itself had been inhabited since the Bronze Age, even making ancient Roman history as a place of fierce Germanic tribes. The Cecilienhof Palace—in which Stalin, Truman, and Churchill met on July 17 to discuss Germany's future—was completed in 1917 by orders of Emperor Wilhelm II for his son, Crown Prince Wilhelm. The prince was impressed by the Tudor mansions in England, which inspired the palace architecture of gardens, landscapes, high ceilings, and almost a natural beauty that contrasted with hard and sharp neo-Gothic architecture throughout Germany. (Joseph Stalin wasn't impressed, though, and couldn't help commenting that it was "nothing much. Modest. The Russian Tsars built themselves something much more solid."[64])

The original plan for a postwar conference was to meet in Berlin itself, but according to Margaret Truman, "too much of the German capital had been destroyed to permit any sizable gathering there." The conference also had to be delayed a day as Stalin was late due to, what else, a heart attack. But it was to Truman's benefit, as that gave him the opportunity to meet Churchill for the first time, cementing Anglo-American relations further. The two immediately hit it off. "Their talk ranged over a wide variety of topics, from the Pacific war to their tastes in music," according to Margaret.[65]

Truman also took the opportunity to visit Berlin proper, or what was left of it. The president met many veterans of the war and even decorated some of them, saying, "I only wish I could have had a more active part in the war itself." He traveled down and visited the crumbled ruins of the Reich chancellery. He paused before the destroyed building and solemnly commented, "It is just a demonstration of what can happen when a man over-reaches himself. I never saw such destruction. I don't know whether they learned anything from it or not."[66] That was to be the central point of the Potsdam Conference.

Elsewhere in the United States, in New Mexico, head of the Los Alamos Laboratory J. Robert Oppenheimer was basking in praise—and fear. On the morning of July 16, a twenty-two kiloton TNT bomb was tested in the desert as part of the top secret Manhattan Project. It was a project three years in the making, using the latest knowledge of nuclear fission.

This new bomb, code-named Trinity, was dropped at 5:29 a.m. Physicist Richard Feynman, also working on the project, described "a big ball of orange, the center that was so bright [it became] a ball of orange that [started] to rise and billow a little bit and get a little black around the edges, and then you see it's a big ball of smoke with flashes on the inside of the fire going out, the heat." Chemist James Conant, expecting simply another conventional bomb, thought "something had gone wrong" and that "the whole world had gone up in flames." Robert Oppenheimer's brother, Frank, feared the ball of fire would engulf everyone twenty miles away.[67]

The next day, Berlin time, Secretary of War Henry Stimson placed a quick note on Truman's desk: "Babies satisfactorily born."[68] And with a literal mighty boom, the world officially entered the Atomic Age.

THE FOLLOWING SEVERAL WEEKS of the Potsdam Conference proved to be difficult for the British prime minister and American president. Despite them all having their own quirky code-names, per Churchill's desire— Stalin was known as "Uncle Joe," Churchill as "Colonel Warden," and Truman as "The Other Admiral"[69]—the thorn in the Anglo-Americans' sides was Stalin, an ominous warning for the future of geopolitics.

What was to be done with Eastern Europe under the thumb of Soviet occupied troops? Rumor had it that the Soviets were gripping tighter on the entire region. Stalin responded angrily, "Fairy tales!"[70] When Stalin asked the other delegates about the Soviet Union controlling the industrial region of the Ruhr in western Germany, an Italian colony in Africa, and for a say in conflicts in the Middle East, War Secretary Stimson raised an eyebrow. He wrote in his diary shortly after that he believed the Soviets were "throwing aside all their previous restraint as to being only a continental power and not interested in any further acquisitions and are now branching out."[71] Even the past crimes of the USSR, such as tens of thousands of Poles in the Katyn Forest murdered in 1940, were shrugged off by Stalin, much to the chagrin of his allies. When questioned, Stalin replied nonchalantly, "They just went away."[72]

The issue of Germany itself was uncontroversial. It had, after all, been decided months earlier in the Yalta Conference. This was simply confirmation.

Potsdam was tiring. Long, brutal days with late hours and late large dinners made it even more tiring for the usually early-riser president. "Stalin gave his state dinner night before last," Truman wrote to his mother on July 23, "and it was a wow." The dinner had "caviar and vodka and wound up with watermelon and champagne, with smoked fish, fresh fish, venison, chicken, duck, and all sorts of vegetables in between. There was a toast every five minutes until at least twenty-five had been drunk. I ate very little and drank less, but it was a colorful and enjoyable occasion."[73]

On July 24, Truman went up to Stalin and plainly said, "The USA tested a new bomb of extraordinary destructive power." Stalin had the perfect poker face—he had his own spies in Los Alamos for years and knew of the Manhattan Project—and replied, "A new bomb! Of extraordinary power! Probably decisive on the Japanese! What a bit of luck!"[74]

A major shift occurred on July 26, when results from the United Kingdom's general election knocked out Churchill as prime minister, replacing him with Labor leader Clement Attlee. It was a rather disastrous election for the Tories, whose wartime victory was thought to guarantee election victory. Instead, the botching of domestic policies from the Conservatives (war notwithstanding) and Labor's promise of social reform in peacetime resulted in the loss of nearly 200 parliament seats for Churchill's party. Labor won an absolute majority, 390 of 640 seats.

Luckily, Attlee was already at Potsdam as part of Churchill's war cabinet, but the shift in tone was noticeable. Admiral William Leahy, chief of staff, noted that the Soviets had a "noticeable coolness in their attitude after Attlee took over." Truman, meanwhile, enjoyed Churchill's company as a leader and certainly as a fellow intellectual, but as a politician, he was wary. Churchill was too bullish at times—thus his nickname, the Bulldog—and the personality did not mesh with Stalin's own iron fist. Truman thought "it may turn out to be all right with the world" with Attlee, and that perhaps it could be different with a more optimistic Labor leader.[75]

JAPAN WAS ON FIRE. The Potsdam Conference in the second half of July did not stop any of the attacks on Japan. Papers ran front-page headline after headline after headline every day of the total destruction of the last Axis power. The *Honolulu Advertiser* was succinct:

July 17: "2,000 Planes over Japan."

July 18: "US–British Forces Again Challenge Jap Fleet."

July 19: "Tokyo Bay Shelled."

July 20: "1,500,000 Japanese Isolated in China."

July 21: "[Fleet Admiral] Halsey Steams Back."

July 22: "Quit! US Warns Japan."

July 23: "416 Jap Ships Sunk or Damaged by US Fleet."

July 24: "Three States Afire! Huge Japan Assault Continues."

July 25: "Jap Fleet Erased!"

July 26: "Jap Cities Brace for New Blow."

July 27: "Japs Defy Ultimatum: War to the Bitter End, Nip Choice."

July 28: "Fierce Malaya Air-Sea Battle."

July 29: "'File-Forget' Jap Fleet."

July 30: "[Premier] Suzuki Says No to Allies: History's Biggest Invasion—US Answer."

July 31: "US Task Force Carries Out Bold Suruga Bay Foray."

AUGUST

August ramped up the pace.

The Potsdam Conference, having now convened for two weeks, was in its final two days. The weather for August 1 was described by White House naval aide William Rigdon as "quite cool . . . as it had been for the past several days. It heralded the fall season and brought out coats and extra blankets."[76] With the coats and cool air also came the agreement that a late-night session would be the final one for the Big Three, as drafts were finalized and reviewed on the agreed-on declarations.

The final meeting began at 10:30 p.m., devoted entirely to the proposed communiqué. It was approved by all an hour and a half later, and at 12:30 a.m., August 2, 1945, the Potsdam Conference was formally disbanded. Truman departed Germany that morning.

There was a bitter taste in Truman's mouth, though. One of the more important issues Truman had pushed for was an opening and internationalization of waterways within Europe. "He envisioned a world," explained his daughter, Margaret, "in which all nations would have the right to free passage of goods and vessels along these waterways to all the seas of the world."[77]

But Stalin wouldn't have it. "We have many more urgent problems before us. This one can be put off," he said. When Truman brought it up again in the late hours of August 1, Stalin objected a second time.

"Marshal Stalin," Truman said, "I have accepted a number of compromises during this conference to conform with your views, and I make a personal request now that you yield on this point."

"Nyet!" the Soviet leader yelled, interrupting his own translator. "Nyet!" He then said in heavily accented English, "No. I say no!"[78] And it was not brought up again.

Writing to his daughter, Margaret, Truman said in early 1947, "I went to Potsdam with the kindliest feelings toward Russia—in a year and a half they cured me of it."[79]

The Potsdam Agreement itself was simple. It was not a peace treaty, and thus did not have to be approved by the US Congress. One of its major accomplishments was the establishment of the Council of Foreign Ministers based in London—comprising ministers of the United Kingdom, Soviet Union, China, United States, and France—to create peace treaties with the lesser Axis powers such as Italy, Rumania, Bulgaria, and Hungary.

For Germany itself, the agreement declared a complete demilitarization and denazification of the region and demonstrated a path forward for democratization. The local governments would be emphasized over centralized federal government, with an explicit order that "no central German government shall be established" except where necessary, such as finance, transportation, and foreign trade. Germany would pay heavy reparations, including a reduction in land and industrial capital.

For Germany's war criminals, the agreement said simply: "The three governments reaffirm their intention to bring those criminals to swift and sure justice. They hope that the negotiations in London will result in speedy agreement being reached for this purpose, and they regard it as a matter of great importance that the trial of those major criminals should begin at the earliest possible date. The first list of defendants will be published before September first."[80] (These would later become the Nuremberg trials, starting later in the year.)

AN INVASION FORCE WAS preparing to conquer Japan, on a scale greater than D-Day, on June 6, 1944. With Japan the sole enemy of the Allied forces, a combined effort from the United States, England, Australia, and Russia would overshadow any invasion seen in history.

And the Japanese were prepared. Japanese radio bragged that their fighters were trained in hand-grenade throwing. They estimated that the invasions could consist of thirty to forty divisions, compared to only ten divisions used on D-Day. "Despite the fact that preparations had been made for two years and 6,000 ships were used 'from the absolutely secure base of Britain,'" Japanese officials thought that the logistical nightmare of managing four times that size from the Philippines would work to their advantage.[81] Little did they know that, weeks earlier, USS *Indianapolis* had delivered a piece of uranium-235 to the 509th Composite Air Group on Tinian Island. The bomb that contained the uranium, dubbed "Little Boy" as a play on a proposed plutonium gun code-named the "Thin Man," was then transported onto a B-29 Superfortress.

This particular Superfortress, named the *Enola Gay*, after the mother of its pilot, Paul W. Tibbets Jr., would change the world and bring about the end of the Pacific theater and the Second World War.

On the morning of August 6, 1945, at 9:15 a.m. Japanese time, a single atomic bomb was dropped onto the industrial city of Hiroshima. It detonated forty-three seconds later, at nearly two thousand feet above the city. About seventy thousand people immediately died from the first wartime use of nuclear weapons. The *Enola Gay*'s mission was complete, and she flew back to base on Tinian.

Harry Truman learned of the drop by message aboard the USS *Augusta*, while traveling back home from his duties at Potsdam:

> Hiroshima bombed visually with only one tenth cover. . . . There was no fighter opposition and no flak. . . . Results clear-cut successful in all respects. Visible effects greater than in any test. Condition normal in airplane following delivery.[82]

"This is the greatest thing in history," Truman said. He ran to the crew of the presidential ship and, with much excitement hidden, declared, "We have just dropped a new bomb on Japan which has more power than 20,000 tons of TNT. It's been an overwhelming success." Lunches were abandoned and food left uneaten in the excitement.[83]

That afternoon, in Los Alamos, J. Robert Oppenheimer received a telephone call from General Leslie Grove, director of the Manhattan Project. "I'm proud of you and all of your people," he said to Oppenheimer.

"It went all right?" Oppenheimer replied.

"Apparently it went with a tremendous bang."

"Everybody is feeling reasonably good about it and I extend my heartiest congratulations. It's been a long road."

"Yes," Groves said, "it has been a long road and I think one of the wisest things I ever did was when I selected the director of Los Alamos."

"Well, I have my doubts, General Groves."

After a day of partying, though, the scientists—Oppenheimer included—became increasingly revolted by their newfound invention. One described Oppenheimer as simply a "nervous wreck."[84]

The *Washington Post* reported the next day that this weapon brought a "new era of power for benefit of man." Because no one could feasibly understand the magnitude of the destruction, the bomb was described as having "a punch equivalent of 2,000 B-29s." If that wasn't clear enough, the paper broke it down into even more manageable figures: four 500-plane raids of Superfortresses.[85] The *Mansfield News-Journal* described the city as having turned into "something that resembled cosmic dust."[86]

The science was so new that the some papers had to run a dictionary definition of an atom. Funk and Wagnall's *Unabridged Dictionary* described the atom as "one of the hypothetical indivisible parts of which all matter is supposed to be formed; in modern scientific usage, the smallest portion into which matter can be divided, even by chemical separation and still preserve its identity; the chemists' unit: now held to be made up of electrically charged particles; some undergo spontaneous disintegration (such as radium)." An editor's note explained further that "there is a constant movement of atoms and scientists have longed believed that if the atoms can be made to collide, or can be smashed by 'bombarding' them with electrons or other particles, the energy released will destroy all matter within the force radius. Apparently, this is the principle on which the atomic bomb operates."[87]

For those who wanted to know more of the science behind the weapon, especially in light of Truman's comments that it "uses the force from which the sun draws it power," the *New York Times* explained: "The sun's power is the sun's heat. For years scientists have known that this heat could not come from ordinary fires like any known on the earth's face. The sun was not big enough to have lasted the billions of years that, there is much evidence, it has been burning at the present rate." Unlike the molecules separated in "ordinary fire" such as wood or coal, the sun "burns not by separation of molecules but by two much more intensely hot methods. One is separation from each other of the atoms, which form molecules. . . . An even greater source of the sun power is the break-up to some extent of the individual atoms."[88]

How was this made into a bomb? For the public, it was only a guess. "For many years scientists have been able to disintegrate atoms in laboratories. There were no explosions because billions of atoms would have to go off at one time even to equal a firecracker. . . . It has been clear to scientists for nearly a half century that if they could get enough atoms in a piece of solid matter, or even gas, the size of a pea, to break up all at once, the explosion would be terrible."[89]

There was no denying the absolute devastation caused by Little Boy. Japan could not hide it. But they tried to spin it, lying that Hiroshima was an "open city," when in reality it was a major industrial and military city. Tokyo officials deemed it an "inhuman" bombing that violated international law. "The destructive power of this new bomb spreads over a large area," Japanese officials reported. "People who were outdoors were burned alive by high temperature while those who were indoors were crushed by falling buildings."[90] The same day of that broadcast, August 8, Russia formally declared war on Japan, ending any hope of Soviet sympathy.

On August 9, Nagasaki, nearly 150 miles southwest of the now-obliterated Hiroshima, was the next target for the second atomic bomb. This one with a more powerful plutonium core, dubbed Fat Man, was dropped by the Superfortress *Bockscar*, and it wiped out the city instantly. "Nagasaki Smashed," said one headline.[91] Japan had not even comprehended the destruction of Hiroshima before the seaport city was bombed.

Oddly enough, that was not the mission. The second bomb's destination was to be Kokura, but, according to one pilot escorting the *Bockscar*, "Bad weather kept us from dropping the bomb on our primary target and cut down our gas supply. We had just enough gas to make one bomb run on Nagasaki." He continued, "We had to run on the target by instruments, and in the last few seconds the bombardier got a sight and let it go right on the town."[92]

The destruction was somehow even worse than Hiroshima. American planes conducting raids 250 miles away could see flames and fires. One described a fireball 8,000 feet high and smoke rising up to 20,000 feet.[93] Major Charles Sweeney, pilot of the observation plane *Great Artiste* (mistakenly described in the *Evening Star* as the bomber of Nagasaki itself), said, "The turbulence from the blast at Nagasaki was greater than at Hiroshima."[94]

The two bombs were the end. Everyone knew it. Even the fanatical

Japanese knew it. On August 10, one day after Nagasaki, Emperor Hirohito informed his cabinet that they intended to surrender unconditionally, if only for the emperor to keep his seat. "Japan accepted [the] surrender term" decided earlier at the Potsdam Conference, "with the understanding that the said declaration does not compromise any demand which prejudices the prerogatives of his majesty as a sovereign ruler." The announcement declared that "His Majesty the Emperor" was "ever anxious to enhance the cause of world peace."[95]

The news of surrender—not yet official—brought celebrations to the street. "Celebrate Ending of Japanese War," said the *Key West Citizen* in Florida. "Boys, millions of American soldiers can go fishing now," read the announcement to the troops.[96] In China, women, subjected to forced prostitution and sex slavery, openly wept. Americans stationed at Okinawa fired artillery in celebration.

On August 14, at 7:00 p.m. eastern time—August 15 in Japan—President Truman announced that the Japanese Empire had officially surrendered to Allied forces, ending the greatest blight of war in American, if not global, history. Truman could not help but smile through the announcement: "Arrangements are now being made for the formal signing of the terms at the earliest possible moment. General Douglas MacArthur has been appointed the Supreme Allied Commander to receive the Japanese surrender."[97] To celebrate the victory—finally, victory, and not just a dream as in the start of the year—Truman requested August 14 and 15 to be federal holidays.

General George Patton took the surrender a little personally and with a tinge of false humility. He wrote in his diary, "Another war has ended, and with it my usefulness to the world. It is for me personally a very sad thought. Now all that is left to do is to sit around and await the arrival of the undertaker and posthumous immortality."[98]

Though the obvious occupation of Japan and its cultural shakeup—much like that of Germany's—would require troops, the United States immediately released the good news: the boys could start coming home, this time for good. During the next eighteen months, about seven million men would be discharged from the armed forces. The army would still "accept" women for their Women's Army Corps, but the women in the navy equivalent, the WAVES (Women Accepted for Volunteer Emergency Service), would be stopped altogether.[99] Overnight, women were seen as unnecessary in the military.

Celebrations erupted across the United States in a mirror to early May after Germany's surrender. At Times Square in New York City, in San Francisco's Market Square, in London's Trafalgar Square, thousands upon thousands gathered in joy. New York itself was intense; one entertainer at a nightclub said it was like "ten New Year's Eves rolled into one." *Life* magazine said it was "as if joy had been rationed and saved up for the three years, eight months and seven days" since the attack on Pearl Harbor.[100] Horns, singing, air-raid sirens, and shouting echoed throughout the country.

In Market Square, San Francisco, sailors on leave drunkenly smashed storefront windows and looted goods. Women were "attacked"—code word for sexually assaulted or raped. The sailors were ordered back to their ships, and authorities had to ward off equally tense civilians. Elsewhere in the Golden Gate City, marines reenacted the famous Iwo Jima flag-raising on top of cars. Women in the WAVES threw pillow fights, and two even stripped nude to go swimming in a lily pond near the Civic Center. "GIs lustily cheered the performances, took some pictures and then politely offered the girls towels as they returned to their taxis," *Life* reassured the readers.[101]

There was plenty of kissing. From coast to coast, men and women embraced. Among the more famous of the photos was in Times Square, where an unnamed sailor jubilantly embraced and kissed a woman. *Life* published the photograph, taken by Alfred Eisenstaedt, with the caption "In New York's Times Square a white-clad girl clutches her purse and skirt as an uninhibited sailor plants his lips squarely on hers."[102] A similar photo, taken by navy photo journalist Victor Jorgensen, published in the *New York Times* and became an instant classic. Both photos passed into the zeitgeist of American celebration.

JAPAN'S SURRENDER WAS OFFICIALLY signed on September 2, 1945, aboard USS *Missouri*. Now on paper, the surrender was the final straw of aggression, signaling final victory.

THE WAR WAS OVER, but the year, more than halfway through, was not. The Nuremberg trials would begin and continue into 1946. Nazi Germany's legacy would die. Japanese imperialism would be reformed into an American-style democracy. The age of the atomic bomb had just begun. And the seeds of the Cold War between the increasingly aggressive Soviet Union and the United States had been planted.

The world, leaving behind one age, would begin another. As the Associated Press wrote in a satirical last will and testament of 1945 on the last day of the year, addressed to the younger year 1946, "OK, son, it's yours. You're young and probably feeling pretty chipper. But before you start feeling sorry for an old codger like me, let me say this: I'll bet you won't get as much done as I did!"[103]

ACKNOWLEDGMENTS

Thank you so much to my precious wife, Zorine, for her timeless efforts in editing and reviewing this book, as well as my daughter, Taylor, and my son, Andrew, for their fantastic editing efforts and my granddaughter, Eleanor, for bringing much joy into my life. Also, thanks to my beloved mother, Barbara Shirley Eckert, my sister Rebecca Sirhal, and our sons Matthew Shirley and Mitchell Shirley for their research and advice as well as Brittany Shirley and Sarah Selip for their friendship, love, and support.

And my infinitely patient editor Jenny Baumgartner for putting up with my many demands. And to Sujin Hong, Stephanie Tresner, Sara Broun, Kristen Golden, Kristina Juodenas, Claire Drake, Sarah Van Cleve, and Jamekra Willis of HarperCollins, and Whitney Bak, Frank Donatelli, Kevin Kabanuk, and Charlie Pratt for their essential assistance. Thank you to my good friend Michael McShane for reviewing this draft. Also Kevin McVicker, Will Hadden, and Carolyn Lisa of Shirley & McVicker for their contributions and support as well as my friend Scott Mauer for all his fantastic editing, drafting, and fact checking. Thank you also to Wes Pippenger for his fabulous research efforts and Caroline Andrews for her shrewd survey of historical books.

NOTES

Prologue

1. Gene Paterson Ames's letter to her mother in April 1945. Courtesy of Craig Shirley. Reprinted with permission.
2. David Brinkley, *Washington Goes to War* (New York: Alfred A. Knopf, 1988).

Chapter 1: January 1945

1. Associated Press, "Germans Will Never Quit, Says Hitler," and "Gen. Kesselring Reported Dead," *Los Angeles Times*, January 1, 1945, 1.
2. Associated Press, "Will Destroy All Shirking War Efforts, He Warns," *Washington Post*, January 1, 1945, 5.
3. "Will Destroy All Shirking War Efforts," 1.
4. "Will Destroy All Shirking War Efforts," 1.
5. United Press International, "Goebbels Hints Desire to End Senseless War," *Washington Post*, January 1, 1945, 1.
6. "Patton Unleashes Full-Scale Offensive," *Washington Post*, January 1, 1945, 1.
7. Associated Press, "Yanks Lunge at Neck of Nazi Bulge in Belgium," *Washington Post*, January 1, 1945, 1.
8. Associated Press, "Blizzards Make Battle of Bulge Weird, Difficult," *Washington Post*, January 13, 1945, 2.
9. "Blizzards Make Battle of Bulge Weird, Difficult."
10. Hamilton W. Faron, "Every New US Pacific Base Adds to Saga of the Seabees," *Washington Post*, January 14, 1945, 5B.
11. Associated Press, "History of Seabees Actually Goes Back to Forming in 1917," *Arizona Republic*, January 7, 1945, 9.
12. International News Service, "117,997 Japs Join Ancestors in Bruising Leyte Campaign," *Honolulu Advertiser*, January 2, 1945, 7.

13. Rembert James, "1945 Fighting to Be Violent, Nimitz Says," *Washington Post*, January 1, 1945, 3.

14. "Job for the Dies Committee," *Los Angeles Times*, January 16, 1944, 4.

15. David Brinkley, *Washington Goes to War* (New York: Alfred A. Knopf, 1988), 17.

16. "War Looks Better," *Los Angeles Times*, January 16, 1945, II-4.

17. Associated Press, "B-29s Open New Year with Bombings in Jap Homeland," *Boston Daily Globe*, January 1, 1945, 2.

18. Associated Press, "New Balloon Investigated," *Los Angeles Times*, January 1, 1945, 1.

19. "Crowds Jam City Streets Greeting 1945," *Los Angeles Times*, January 1, 1945, 1.

20. "Reveling Throngs See New Year In," *Los Angeles Times*, January 1, 1945, 2.

21. "Reveling Throngs See New Year In."

22. Brinkley, *Washington Goes to War*, 269.

23. Brinkley, *Washington Goes to War*, 253.

24. Brinkley, *Washington Goes to War*.

25. Brinkley, *Washington Goes to War*.

26. "Work of Nazis," *Washington Post*, January 4, 1945, 5.

27. United Press International, "Slaying of Yank Prisoners by Nazis Confirmed," *Los Angeles Times*, January 1, 1945, 5.

28. "Nazis Dropped Paratroopers in Plot to Kill US Officers," *Los Angeles Times*, January 30, 1945, 7.

29. "Yanks Find Bodies of Massacre Victims," *Philadelphia Inquirer*, January 14, 1945, 3.

30. "Suitor Slays Forgiven Wife of Soldier, Then Ends Life," *Washington Post*, January 1, 1945, 3.

31. "50 Killed in Utah Train Wreck," *Los Angeles Times*, January 1, 1945, 1.

32. *Los Angeles Times*, January 1, 1945, 5, advertisement.

33. Associated Press, "45 Feared Dead, Scores Hurt in Utah Wreck," *Washington Post*, January 1, 1945, 1.

34. "Greek Regency Is Taken Over by Damaskinos," *Washington Post*, January 1, 1945, 1.

35. "Yank Airmen Down 94 Nazis in Heavy Raids," *Chicago Tribune*, January 1, 1945, 2.

36. "Chiang Offers Early Constitution," *Atlanta Constitution*, January 1, 1945, 1.

37. Daniel M. Kidney, "New FDR Message Slated on Universal Military Training," *Knoxville News-Sentinel*, January 8, 1945, 3.

38. "Appeal Made for New Powers to Speed Victory," *Washington Post*, January 2, 1945, 1.

39. "New Year's Absenteeism Takes Deep Cut in War Production," *Washington Post*, January 2, 1945, 1.

40. "Talk of Tax Cuts," *Washington Post*, January 1, 1945, 2.

41. "Talk of Tax Cuts."

42. "Job-Changing Made Harder Here by WMC," *Washington Post*, January 14, 1945, 3.

43. "This Week in Religion: Moscow Attack," *Pittsburgh Press*, January 7, 1945, 24.

44. "Sermon Themes Stress Unity, Work for '45," *Washington Post*, January 1, 1945, 3.

45. "Brief Respite: Cold to Follow Cloudy, Warm Day in DC," *Washington Post*, January 1, 1945, 3.

46. "GI Gridders Clash Today in Spaghetti Bowl," *Washington Post*, January 1, 1945, 6.

47. United Press International, "Bowl Game Boom Predicted for Postwar Football World," *Washington Post*, January 3, 1945, 9.

48. "Today's Radio Programs," *Washington Post*, January 1, 1945, 9.

49. "Eastern War Time," *Boston Daily Globe*, January 12, 1945, 14.

50. "2 Spies Landed by Submarine Seized by FBI," *Washington Post*, January 2, 1945, 1.

51. "Seize Two Nazi Spies Landed by Submarine," *Kenosha Evening News*, January 2, 1945, 1.

52. "Military Trial Is Expected for Two Alleged Nazi Spies," *Washington Post*, January 3, 1945, 1.

53. "Sabotage Menace Seen," *Honolulu Advertiser*, January 2, 1945, 1.

54. "Big Balloon Found in Tree by FBI Agent," *News-Herald*, January 2, 1945, 1.

55. "Germans Lose 241 Planes in Surprise Raids," *Washington Post*, January 2, 1945, 1.

56. Associated Press, "Reds Push Deeper into Budapest," *Washington Post*, January 2, 1945, 2.

57. Associated Press, "Reds Continue to Blast Ahead in Budapest," *Washington Post*, January 3, 1945, 1.

58. United Press International, "Soviet Troops Begin Systematic Razing of Hungarian Capital," *Honolulu Advertiser*, January 2, 1945, 1.

59. "Eyes Bleeding, Flier Is Guided Home by Buddy," *Washington Post*, January 2, 1945, 3.

60. Associated Press, "Virginia ABC Cuts Rations of Fortified Wine," *Washington Post*, January 2, 1945, 3.

61. *New York Daily News*, January 19, 1945, 179, advertisement.

62. Associated Press, "US to Start Farm Census Next Monday," *Washington Post*, January 2, 1945, 3.

63. Associated Press, "14 Danville Taximen Face Hearing Today," *Washington Post*, January 2, 1945, 3.

64. "The Iowa Poll," *Washington Post*, January 2, 1945, 3.

65. "Water Buffalos," *Washington Post*, January 2, 1945, 3.

66. Leonard Lyons, "Broadway Gazette," *Washington Post*, January 2, 1945, 4.

67. Lyons, "Broadway Gazette."

68. Lyons, "Broadway Gazette."

69. "Montgomery Ward's Answer to the Order of Seizure by the President," *Washington Post*, January 2, 1945, 5.

70. "FDR Seizes Control of Montgomery Ward," History, updated December 21, 2020, https://www.history.com/this-day-in-history/fdr-seizes-control-of-montgomery-ward.

71. "Montgomery Ward's Answer."

72. Associated Press, "Army Fires 11 Officials of Ward Co.," *Washington Post*, January 3, 1945, 2.

73. Barnet Nover, "A Subdued Fuehrer: Hitler's New Year Broadcast," *Washington Post*, January 2, 1945, 6.

74. Nover, "Subdued Fuehrer."

75. Nover, "Subdued Fuehrer."

76. International News Service, "France Hailed as She Joins United Nations," *Washington Post*, January 2, 1945, 7.

77. Dewey L. Fleming, "United Nations Declaration Formally Signed by France," *Baltimore Sun*, January 2, 1945, 11.

78. Walter Lippmann, Today and Tomorrow, *Washington Post*, January 2, 1945, 7.

79. "What Price Conscience?," *Washington Post*, January 2, 1945, 6.

80. United Press International, "Unfaithful Wives Lower Morale in Army, Bishop Says," *Washington Post*, January 4, 1945, 10.

81. United Press International, "Unfaithful Wives Lower Morale in Army."

82. "Babies Bring Up to $2000 in Black Market," *Washington Post*, January 2, 1945, 9.

83. Malrina Lindsay, "The Gentler Sex," *Washington Post*, January 2, 1945, 10.

84. "Roosevelt, Dewey Make Final Major Bids Tonight," *Fort Worth Star-Telegram*, November 4, 1944, 1.

85. "Luce Says FDR Chief Appeaser," *Spokesman-Review*, October 15, 1944, 2.

86. Carolyn Bell, "Town Talk," *Washington Post*, January 2, 1945, 10.

87. Drew Pearson, Washington Merry-Go-Round, *Washington Post*, January 3, 1945, 7.

88. Pearson, Washington Merry-Go-Round.

89. "Congress," *Washington Post*, January 4, 1945, 2.

90. Associated Press, "Enemy Gains Some Ground in Attack on Patton Lines," *Washington Post*, January 3, 1945, 1.

91. United Press International, "Mystery Gun of US Routs Nazi Enemy," *Honolulu Advertiser*, January 6, 1945, 4.

92. "Enemy Gains Some Ground."

93. Ben W. Gilbert, "Roosevelt Indicates Approval of 4-F Edict," *Washington Post*, January 3, 1945, 1.

94. Walter Lippmann, Today and Tomorrow, *Washington Post*, January 4, 1945, 7.

95. Gallup, "American Institute of Public Opinion," *Washington Post*, January 3, 1945, 7.

96. "Public Favors US Projects to Help Postwar Employment," *Washington Post*, January 5, 1945, 3.

97. Associated Press, "Scarce Metal May Reduce Plane Output," *Washington Post*, January 5, 1945, 3.

98. "Allied Rifts Inevitable, President Says," *Washington Post*, January 3, 1945, 1.

99. Joe Brennan, "Shortage of Gasoline Hits 800 Doctors and Nurses Here," *Washington Post*, January 3, 1945, 1.

100. "Party Divisions of the House of Representatives, 1789 to Present," History, Art & Archives, https://history.house.gov/Institution/Party-Divisions /Party-Divisions/.

101. Marquis Childs, "Washington Calling: New Congress," *Washington Post*, January 4, 1945, 6.

102. "4 US Vessels Reported Lost," *Miami Daily News*, January 2, 1945, 23.

103. International News Service, "Casualties Given," *Honolulu Advertiser*, January 6, 1945, 3.

104. "Casualties Given."

105. Associated Press, "Maybe Those Kids Were Softies, but They Sure Held That Line," *Washington Post*, January 7, 1945, 3B.

106. Associated Press, "Patton Tanks, Troops Push into Bourcy," *Washington Post*, January 4, 1945, 1.

107. "Patton Tanks, Troops Push into Bourcy."

108. "2 Nazi Prisoners Flee from Camp in Cumberland," *Richmond Times-Dispatch*, January 2, 1945, 5.

109. United Press International, "Increased Shortage of Meats Seen After Livestock Survey," *Washington Post*, January 3, 1945, 3.

110. "Why Philip Morris *Are* Harder to Get!," *Washington Post*, January 2, 1945, 12, advertisement.

111. "Why Philip Morris *Are* Harder to Get!"

112. "How Cleanliness Ceased to Be Next to Impossible," *Washington Post*, January 3, 1945, 5, advertisement.

113. *Washington Post*, January 12, 1945, 5, advertisement.

114. Associated Press, "Berlin to U.S. Service Opened by Press Wireless," *Chicago Tribune*, January 4, 1945, 6.

115. Craig Shirley, *December 1941: 31 Days That Changed America and Saved the World* (Nashville: Nelson Books, 2011), 16.

116. "On the Line with Considine, NY," *Cincinnati Enquirer*, January 16, 1945, 10.

117. "Nats Reelect Griff President; Vote Dividend," *Washington Post*, January 3, 1945, 8.

118. "Nazis Threaten Visit to GI's Spaghetti Bowl," *Tampa Bay Times*, January 3, 1945, 12.

119. Shirley Povich, "This Morning," *Washington Post*, January 11, 1945, 9.

120. Associated Press, "Orders Dissolution of Charter for Gentile Co-Operative Group," *Freeport Journal-Standard*, January 2, 1945, 9.

121. "25 Jap Ships Set Fire West of Luzon," *Fort Worth Star-Telegram*, January 4, 1945, 1.

122. Associated Press, "Americans Make 2 More Landings on Mindoro," *Washington Post*, January 4, 1945, 1.

123. Associated Press, "Carrier Planes Hit Formosa, Okinawa Jima," *Washington Post*, January 4, 1945, 1.

124. United Press International, "95 Jap Ships Blasted: US Air Fleet Socks 331 Enemy Planes in 48 Hours of Battling," *Honolulu Advertiser*, January 6, 1945, 1.

125. United Press International, "US Carrier Planes First China Attack," *Honolulu Advertiser*, January 6, 1945, 1.

126. "95 Jap Ships Blasted."

127. Associated Press, "Americans Smash South in Luzon: Now 54 Miles from Manila," *Atlanta Constitution*, January 4, 1945, 1.

128. James V. Piersol, "Look Behind for Safety, Bong's Recipe," *Washington Post*, January 4, 1945, 1.

129. Ben W. Gilbert, "Farm Youths Ordered Called for Induction," *Washington Post*, January 4, 1945, 1.

130. Gilbert, "Farm Youths Ordered Called for Induction," 2.

131. Associated Press, "Party-Line Vote in Committee Upholds F.C.C.," *Los Angeles Times*, January 4, 1945, 8.

132. Associated Press, "German Losses in Drive Put at 60,000," *Baltimore Sun*, January 3, 1945, 1.

133. Associated Press, "Eight US Divisions at Bastogne, Nazis Say," *Evening Sun*, January 3, 1945, 1.

134. Anton Chekhov, *The Exclamation Mark* (1886; London: Hesperus Press, 2008), 1.

135. Associated Press, "Torture of Belgians like 'Inquisition,'" *Washington Post*, January 4, 1945, 2.

136. Letter to the editor, "Hitler Was Not Voted into Office," *Washington Post*, March 18, 2016, https://www.washingtonpost.com/opinions/hitler-was-not
-voted-into-office/2016/03/18/04443d06-e615-11e5-a9ce-681055c7a05f
_story.html.

137. Associated Press, "Nazi Winter Push Casualties Estimated at 60,000 by Allies," *Washington Post*, January 4, 1945, 1, 2.

138. "Patton Tanks, Troops Push into Bourcy," 1, 2.

139. "Patton Tanks, Troops Push into Bourcy."

140. "Patton Tanks, Troops Push into Bourcy."

141. Associated Press, "Cigarette Ration Cut to One Pack at Fort Meade," *Washington Post*, January 4, 1945, 3.

142. "Vast Federal-State Health Plan Urged," *Washington Post*, January 4, 1945, 4.

143. "Bowles Calls OPA Pledge a Mistake," *Atlanta Constitution*, January 4, 1945, 1.

144. *Honolulu Advertiser*, January 14, 1945, 9, advertisement.

145. Associated Press, "Morgenthau Sees High Taxes Long After War's Over," *Los Angeles Times*, January 12, 1945, 2.

146. Associated Press, "Chinese Retake Wanting in Offensive Move," *Washington Post*, January 4, 1945, 5.

147. "Localizing Radio," *Washington Post*, January 4, 1945, 6.

148. "Was It Hitler?," *Washington Post*, January 4, 1945, 6.

149. Laurie Johnston, "Sailors Crowd Piers as Ziegfeld-Like Line of WAVES Comes Ashore for Air Station Duty," *Honolulu Advertiser*, January 7, 1945, 1.

150. Leonard Lyons, Times Square Tattle, *Washington Post*, January 4, 1945, 7.

151. Jack Alexander, "The Pugnacious Drew Pearson," *Indianapolis News*, January 3, 1945, 3.

152. Associated Press, "Patton Forces Beating Back Onslaught by 100 Tanks," *Washington Post*, January 5, 1945, 1.

153. "Patton Forces Beating Back Onslaught."

154. Kurt Kelman, "DC Gas Sales Placed Under Special Limits," *Washington Post*, January 5, 1945, 1.

155. Associated Press, "Big Conventions May Be Banned to Ease Rail Strain," *Washington Post*, January 5, 1945, 1.

156. "'Race Service' Hit Lethal Blow; US Asks Ban on Wires, Phones," *Washington Post*, January 5, 1945, 8.

157. Associated Press, "Mustang Pilot Describes Flight of V-2 Rocket," *Washington Post*, January 5, 1945, 1.

158. Associated Press, "No Weather Leak," *Washington Post*, January 5, 1945, 2.

159. Associated Press, "Goebbels Says Allied Error Steeled Nazis," *Washington Post*, January 5, 1945, 2.

160. Ben W. Gilbert, "Labor Draft May Be Asked by Roosevelt," *Washington Post*, January 5, 1945, 2.

161. "Navy Seeks 7½ Billion for Expansion," *Washington Post*, January 5, 1945, 3.

162. George Connery, "Nazi Threat Not Yet Spent, Stimson Says," *Washington Post*, January 5, 1945, 3.

163. Connery, "Nazi Threat Not Yet Spent."

164. Drew Pearson, Washington Merry-Go-Round, *Washington Post*, January 5, 1945, 10.

165. Associated Press, "White-Clad Yanks Stalk Foe in Italy," *Washington Post*, January 9, 1945, 2.

166. "Superman," *Fresno Bee*, January 9, 1945, 8.

167. "50 Packs of Fags Could Have Prevented Strike of Bonny Blue Miners, Says One," *Knoxville News-Sentinel*, January 7, 1945, 9.

168. "Japs Report 3 U.S. Fleets Near Luzon," *Courier Journal*, January 7, 1945, 1.

169. Associated Press, "US Division Is Reported in Lingayen Gulf Area," *Washington Post*, January 9, 1945, 1.

170. "State of the Union Address," History, Art & Archives, accessed April 25, 2021, https://history.house.gov/Institution/SOTU/State-of -the-Union/.

171. Robert C. Albright, "President Asks Full Use of Manpower," *Washington Post*, January 7, 1945, 1.

172. "Radio Address to the Nation re the State of the Union," speech file 1569, January 6, 1945, Franklin D. Roosevelt Presidential Library and Museum.

173. "Opinion Polls Urged for Congress," *Star Tribune*, January 29, 1945, 4.

174. Roosevelt Library, "Radio Address to the Nation."

175. Shirley Povich, "4-F Edict Will Affect All Branches," *Washington Post*, January 7, 1945, 6M.

176. Povich, "4-F Edict Will Affect All Branches."

177. "Diaper March Newest Twist in Protests," *Washington Post*, January 7, 1945, 4M.

178. Associated Press, "Breakthrough Not to Cost Generals Posts," *Washington Post*, January 7, 1945, 1M.

179. "85% of Navy Men on Ships Lost Return to Sea Duty," *Washington Post*, January 7, 1945, 7M.

180. "85% of Navy Men on Ships Lost."

181. "Reserve Board Reports Sales Up 11% in Year," *Washington Post*, January 7, 1945, 8M.

182. Edward T. Folliard, "Ocean Flights Common but Not for a Fellow Riding Conn. Ave. Bus," *Washington Post*, January 7, 1945, 1B.

183. William F. Tyree, "1945 Is 'Most Critical Year' Admiral Nimitz Warns America," *Honolulu Advertiser*, January 12, 1945, 4.

184. "Assault by Naval Forces Moves Close to Mainland," *Scrantonian Tribune*, January 7, 1945, 13.

185. Mary Lyon, "Whole Future to Be Changed by Startling Postwar Products," *Washington Post*, January 7, 1945, 5B.

186. Nat Caldwell, "The Outlook for Southern Cotton Discouraging," *Atlanta Constitution*, January 16, 1945, 7.

187. Associated Press, "38 Companies Will File Plans for Postwar Airlines in South," *Washington Post*, January 15, 1945, 3.

188. *Washington Post*, January 7, 1945, 3S, advertisement.

189. Sterling North, "New Historian Has Written a Brilliant Challenge; Minority Views Steinbeck," *Washington Post*, January 7, 1945, 4S.

190. "MP Killed in Fight as Black Market Gang Is Broken Up," *Washington Post*, January 8, 1945, 1.

191. Associated Press, "GI Looters Get 45 Years," *Atlanta Constitution*, January 12, 1945, 7.

192. *Washington Post*, January 8, 1945, 1.

193. Marquis Childs, "Washington Calling," *Honolulu Advertiser*, January 9, 1945, 6.

194. Associated Press, "Montgomery Asks Fullest Support for Eisenhower," *Washington Post*, January 8, 1945, 1.

195. "Disabled Veterans' Pensions Increase 40 Million a Year," *Washington Post*, January 8, 1945, 3.

196. Drew Pearson, Washington Merry-Go-Round, *Washington Post*, January 8, 1945, 7.

197. Associated Press, "American Air Might Delays Enemy Blows," *Daily Oklahoman*, January 11, 1945, 1.

198. "Here's How Gen. MacArthur Got His Feet Wet at Leyte," *Los Angeles Times*, January 17, 1945, 1.

199. *Honolulu Advertiser*, January 15, 1945, 5, advertisement.

200. Courtenay Moore, "3 Destroyers Swallowed Up by Typhoon," *Honolulu Advertiser*, January 11, 1945, 1.

201. "100,000 Wounded Flown to England," *New York Daily News*, January 11, 1945, 422.

202. Associated Press, "Nazi Officer Aids Yanks to Capture His Entire Outfit," *Washington Post*, January 11, 1945, 5.

203. Drew Pearson, Washington Merry-Go-Round, *Washington Post*, January 11, 1945, 7.

204. Associated Press, "Cigarette Tax Tally Declines," *Los Angeles Times*, January 25, 1945, 4.

205. Associated Press, "French Mob Hangs Woman Convicted of Aiding Gestapo," *Los Angeles Times*, January 11, 1945, 4.

206. Associated Press, "Gestapo Slew 34 Belgians, Survivor Says," *Washington Post*, January 13, 1945, 2.

207. United Press International, "Airliner Crash Costs 24 Lives; Victims Burned," *Dayton Herald*, January 11, 1945, 2.

208. Associated Press, "Thousands Flee Attack by Patton," *Washington Post*, January 12, 1945, 1.

209. Mary Sparge, "Military to Take All Under 30 Who Are Fit," *Washington Post*, January 12, 1945, 1.

210. Sparge, "Military to Take All Under 30 Who Are Fit."

211. Associated Press, "Problems Become More Complex," *Richmond Times-Dispatch*, January 12, 1945, 16.

212. Associated Press, "Nazi Forces Abandon Western End of Corridor," *Washington Post*, January 13, 1945, 1.

213. United Press International, "Only Small Number of Bataan Defenders May Still Be Alive," *Honolulu Advertiser*, January 12, 1945, 5.

214. Jack Fleischer, "Nazi Morals [to] New Low, Letters Show," *Washington Post*, January 13, 1945, 3.

215. Fleischer, "Nazi Morals [to] New Low."

216. Associated Press, "Sailor Eludes Japs, Outwits Them 2 Years," *Washington Post*, January 14, 1945, 2.

217. "Boon to Cities Envisioned in Plan to Reclaim Slums," *Cincinnati Enquirer*, January 22, 1945, 4.

218. International News Service Bulletin, "British Fleet Joins Attack in China Sea," *Washington Post*, January 14, 1945, 1.

219. Associated Press, Paris, "First Army Strikes Ardennes North Flank," *Washington Post*, January 14, 1945, 1.

220. *Los Angeles Times*, January 28, 1945, 1, photograph.

221. "Russ Reported Hurling 2,500,000 Men at Nazis in Smash Across Poland," *Los Angeles Times*, January 14, 1945, 1.

222. Associated Press, "Nazi Saboteur Row Leads to Capture," *Los Angeles Times*, January 14, 1945, 2.

223. Associated Press, "1368 Yanks Back from Europe Look First for Girls and Milk," *Washington Post*, January 14, 1945, 1.

224. "Britain Finances Half of War with Taxes—US, 40 Per Cent," *Washington Post*, January 14, 1945, 2B.

225. *Washington Post*, January 14, 1945, 3S, advertisement.

226. *Los Angeles Times*, January 15, 1945, 10, advertisement.

227. *Los Angeles Times*, January 17, 1945, 5, advertisement.

228. Dougald Werner, "Yanks Smite Luftwaffe in Air Brawl; War's Greatest Victory," *Honolulu Advertiser*, January 15, 1945, 1.

229. *Atlanta Constitution*, January 14, 1945, 4B, advertisement.

230. *Honolulu Advertiser*, January 14, 1945, 11, advertisement.

231. Dorothy Benyas, "Hawaii Veteran Says Nazis Smart but Not Too Tough," *Honolulu Advertiser*, January 14, 1945, 1.

232. Edward Jamieson, "Cradle to Grave Security Planned by Administration," *Honolulu Advertiser*, January 14, 1945, 5.

233. Thomas L. Stokes, "The Role of Lodge?," *Los Angeles Times*, January 10, 1945, 16.

234. "Drastic but Necessary," *Los Angeles Times*, January 19, 1945, II-4.

235. United Press International, "Scientists Consider Plans to Create Japanese Quakes," *Honolulu Advertiser*, January 3, 1945, 3.

236. "Beggar Gets $87 a Day; Told to Find War Job," *Los Angeles Times*, January 16, 1945, 1.

237. "Back to School," *Los Angeles Times*, January 16, 1945, 3.

238. United Press International, "Average GI Mental Age 13, Says Psychiatrist," *Los Angeles Times*, January 12, 1945, 2.

239. Associated Press, "Yank Ace Shot Down by US Machine Guns," *Los Angeles Times*, January 16, 1945, 5.

240. *Los Angeles Times*, January 16, 1945, 11, advertisement.

241. "Job for the Dies Committee: War Looks Better," *Los Angeles Times*, January 16, 1945, 16.

242. Associated Press, "Great Nazi Fortress Falls to Russ Drive," *Los Angeles Times*, January 17, 1945, 5.

243. "Woman Listing Four Husbands Gives Self Up," *Los Angeles Times*, January 16, 1945, II-2.

244. "Hairdresser Arraigned in Draft Case," *Los Angeles Times*, January 14, 1945, 3.

245. Brinkley, *Washington Goes to War*, 234–35.

246. "Job for the Dies Committee: War Looks Better," 4.

247. "Firearms Play Important Part in Bogart Films," *Los Angeles Times*, January 17, 1945, 8.

248. United Press International, "Empire's Casualties Total 1,043,554," *Los Angeles Times*, January 17, 1945, 1.

249. *Los Angeles Times*, January 16, 1945, II-8, advertisement.

250. "Rickenbacker Sees Russia as Key in Conflict," *Los Angeles Times*, January 19, 1945, II-3.

251. Associated Press, "US Sets Schedule of New Draft Call," *Los Angeles Times*, January 17, 1945, 2.

252. Daniel De Luce, "Hungarian Envoy Tells of Visit to 'Mad' Hitler," *Los Angeles Times*, January 17, 1945, 5.

253. William McGaffin, "Indo-China Strikes Show Carriers in Modern Role," *Honolulu Star-Bulletin*, January 17, 1945, 1.

254. Associated Press, "Hirohito Unperturbed by Forts over Tokyo, Jap Radio Says," *Los Angeles Times*, January 17, 1945, 6.

255. George Gallup, "Public's Views Differ in Use of Gas on Japs," *Los Angeles Times*, January 17, 1945, 7.

256. *Los Angeles Times*, January 17, 1945, 9, advertisements.

257. *Los Angeles Times*, January 12, 1945, 8, advertisement.

258. *Los Angeles Times*, January 17, 1945, 10.

259. "Woman Held After Row at Joan Crawford Home," *Los Angeles Times*, January 17, 1945, II-1.

260. "Draft of Garbage Collector Opposed," *Los Angeles Times*, January 17, 1945, II-2.

261. "Casualties in 'The Bulge,'" *Los Angeles Times*, January 17, 1945, II-4.

262. United Press International, "Capital Liberated After Five Years," *Los Angeles Times*, January 18, 1945, 7.

263. United Press International, "Arab Women Toss Off Veil and Ask Limit on Harems," *Los Angeles Times*, January 18, 1945, 1.

264. United Press International, "Grapefruit and Blended Juice Rationed Again," *Los Angeles Times*, January 18, 1945, 1.

265. "'Bumped' Off Plane by Dog, Servicemen Say," *Los Angeles Times*, January 18, 1945, 1, 8.

266. United Press International, "Elliott Roosevelt Named General," *Los Angeles Times*, January 26, 1945, 1.

267. Associated Press, "Missing Navy Ace Comes Back with Jap Saber," *Los Angeles Times*, January 19, 1945, 5.

268. Associated Press, "Yank 'Lost' in 1941 Disclosed Alive," *Los Angeles Times*, January 19, 1945, 5.

269. Associated Press, "Nazis Retreat with Russ 15 Miles from Silesia, Krakow Reported Taken," *Los Angeles Times*, January 18, 1945, 1.

270. "Nazis Admit Crisis in East," *Baltimore Sun*, January 18, 1945, 1.

271. Associated Press, *Decatur Daily*, February 5, 1945, 4.

272. "Himmler Tries Sinister Plan to Raise Cash," *Los Angeles Times*, January 19, 1945, 5.

273. United Press International, "Belgian Battle US Victory, Churchill Says," *Los Angeles Times*, January 19, 1945, 1.

274. "Shore Patrol's Records Show Rise of Menace," *Los Angeles Times*, January 19, 1945, II-1.

275. United Press International, "Shouting Nips Kill 10 Crewmen by Gunfire and Ram Laden Lifeboat," *Los Angeles Times*, January 20, 1945, 1.

276. Associated Press, "British Subs Sink 84 Jap Supply Vessels," *Los Angeles Times*, January 21, 1945, 8.

277. Associated Press, "Nazi Comeback Drive Perils Strasbourg," *Los Angeles Times*, January 20, 1945, 1.

278. Warren B. Francis, "Roosevelt Takes Fourth-Term Oath and Vows Lasting Peace for US; Inauguration Social Aspects Severely Cut," *Los Angeles Times*, January 21, 1945, 1, 3.

279. Francis, "Roosevelt Takes Fourth-Term Oath."

280. Francis, "Roosevelt Takes Fourth-Term Oath."

281. Lorania K. Francis, "Three Historic 'Firsts' Scored in Inauguration," *Los Angeles Times*, January 21, 1945, 3.

282. Associated Press, "Mother Tells Truman to 'Behave Yourself,'" *Kansas City Star*, January 21, 1945, 4.

283. United Press International, "First 12 Years Are Hardest, Says President," *Los Angeles Times*, January 20, 1945, 1, 2.

284. Associated Press, "Wallace Gives Oath to Successor, Truman," *Los Angeles Times*, January 21, 1945, 4.

285. United Press International, "Russ Describe Crimes for Nazi 'Amusement,'" *Los Angeles Times*, January 20, 1945, 2.

286. United Press International, "Dynamite Used by Mob Raiding Returned Japs," *Los Angeles Times*, January 20, 1945, 2.

287. Associated Press, "Warren Deplores Attack on Returned Japs' Home," *Los Angeles Times*, January 21, 1945, 9.

288. "Luftwaffe Officers Are Condemned," *Knoxville News-Sentinel*, January 21, 1945, 4.

289. Associated Press, "Jap Forces Cut in Two by Heavy Luzon Fighting," *Los Angeles Times*, January 21, 1945, 1.

290. Hanson W. Baldwin, "Nazis May Gain Time by Jet and V-Weapons," *Los Angeles Times*, January 21, 1945, 2.

291. *Birmingham News*, January 21, 1945, 18, advertisement.

292. National Postal Museum, "Victory Mail," accessed November 2, 2021, https://postalmuseum.si.edu/exhibition/victory-mail.

293. National Postal Museum, "V-Mail," accessed November 2, 2021, https://postalmuseum.si.edu/exhibition/the-art-of-cards-and-letters-military-mail-call/v-mail.

294. Associated Press, "Reds Smash at Heart of Germany," *Los Angeles Times*, January 22, 1945, 1.

295. Associated Press, "Giant Red Armies Take Insterburg, Prussia Key; Drive on Silesia Capital," *Los Angeles Times*, January 23, 1945, 1, 4.

296. Associated Press, "Hitler Report Taking Command in East," *Los Angeles Times*, January 23, 1945, 1.

297. "Giant Red Armies Take Insterburg."

298. "Life in Germany Told by Ex-'Times' Employee," *Los Angeles Times*, January 23, 1945, 8.

299. United Press International, "Berchtesgaden May Be Capital," *Los Angeles Times*, January 26, 1945, 5.

300. United Press International, "Siegfried Line Fortress Falls to Allied Tanks," *Los Angeles Times*, January 25, 1945, 2.

301. "Siegfried Line Fortress Falls."

302. Associated Press, "Nazis Prepare to Blow Up Berlin," *Los Angeles Times*, January 28, 1945, 1.

303. Associated Press, "Berlin Planes Readied for Nazi Chiefs' Escape," *Los Angeles Times*, January 28, 1945, 1.

304. Associated Press, "US Tells Reich Soldiers Terms for Surrender," *Los Angeles Times*, January 28, 1945, 1.

305. Associated Press, "Allies Caution on Optimism Inspired by Nazi Panic Tales," *Los Angeles Times*, January 28, 1945, 6.

306. Associated Press, "3rd Army Gains on Wide Front," *Los Angeles Times*, January 28, 1945, 1.

307. Associated Press, "Haggard Survivor of Bataan 'March of Death' Joins Yanks after 3 Years' Hiding on Luzon," *Baltimore Sun*, January 22, 1945, 3.

308. Associated Press, "President Issues Plea for Production of Food," *Los Angeles Times*, January 23, 1945, 7.

309. "Dangerous Trophies of War Seized Here," *Los Angeles Times*, January 23, 1945, 7.

310. United Press International, "Louis Only 'Wishes' to Retire; Probably Won't," *Los Angeles Times*, January 23, 1945, 8.

311. "Joe Says Conn Can Run but That He Can't Hide," *Tampa Bay Times*, June 18, 1946, 9.

312. Associated Press, "Ward Stores Seizure Held to Be Illegal," *Los Angeles Times*, January 28, 1945, 1.

313. Russell Brines, "Only Graves Found at Luzon Prison," *Los Angeles Times*, January 24, 1945, 5.

314. Associated Press, "Congress Eyes Pacific Mandates as Bastions," *Los Angeles Times*, January 24, 1945, 5.

315. *Los Angeles Times*, January 25, 1945, II-4, comic.

316. Associated Press, "US Wife, Safe on Luzon, Describes Jap Tortures," *Los Angeles Times*, January 25, 1945, 9.

317. Associated Press, "Eight Yanks Murdered by One Nazi Soldier," *Los Angeles Times*, January 25, 1945, 9.

318. "Woman Told She's One of Conductor's 11 Wives," *Los Angeles Times*, January 25, 1945, 2.

319. "Officer's Wife Questioned on Dual Marriage," *Los Angeles Times*, January 30, 1945, 12.

320. "Soldier's Wife to Face Court," *Los Angeles Times*, January 30, 1945, II-8.

321. Dana Adams Schmidt, "More than 12,000 Yanks Daily Disclosed AWOL," *Los Angeles Times*, January 25, 1945, 7.

322. Associated Press, "Coffee Consumption Soars 28.3 Per Cent," *Los Angeles Times*, January 26, 1945, 9.

323. "Disposal of Surplus War Goods Scheduled on Week-to-Week Basis," *Los Angeles Times*, January 26, 1945, II-1.

324. United Press International, "Food Coupons to Be Canceled After 16 Weeks," *Los Angeles Times*, January 27, 1945, 1.

325. Hedda Hopper, "Gloria Vanderbilt and 'Pat' Di Cicco Separate," *Los Angeles Times*, January 28, 1945, 3.

326. *Los Angeles Times*, January 28, 1945, 18, cartoon.

327. Associated Press, "Official of Breslau Executed as Coward," *Los Angeles Times*, January 29, 1945, 1.

328. Associated Press, "Next Eight Days Will Decide War, Nazi Press Tells German People," *Los Angeles Times*, January 29, 1945, 1.

329. "Berlin," *Los Angeles Times*, January 30, 1945, II-4, cartoon.

330. Associated Press, "Monarchist Editor Sentenced to Life Term by French Court," *Richmond Times-Dispatch*, January 28, 1945, 3.

331. Associated Press, "Gen. MacArthur Under Jap Fire," *Los Angeles Times*, January 29, 1945, 5.

332. Associated Press, "Nazi Leaders Preparing People for Berlin's Loss," *Los Angeles Times*, January 30, 1945, 1.

333. Paul Ghali, "Armed Berliners Battle Police," *Los Angeles Times*, January 31, 1945, 7.

334. Associated Press, "Hitler Calls on Reich for Death Fight: Every German Ordered to Stake Life and Body Against 'Horrid Fate,'" *Los Angeles Times*, January 31, 1945, 1.

335. "Hitler Calls on Reich for Death Fight."

336. United Press International, "Rise Against Hitler or Face Annihilation, Reds Warn Reich," *Los Angeles Times*, January 29, 1945, 2.

337. Patricia McDermott, "Tehachapi's 'Forgotten Women' Also Go to War," *Los Angeles Times*, January 29, 1945, II-1.

338. Alfonso Denoga, "Starvation and Death in Manila Described," *Los Angeles Times*, January 30, 1945, 4.

339. United Press International, "Diet Told Japs Want to Be 'Kind to All Mankind,'" *Los Angeles Times*, January 30, 1945, 5.

340. Associated Press, "Bob Hope Arrives in Florida Unhurt," *Los Angeles Times*, January 30, 1945, 4.

341. Associated Press, "Reduction Ordered in Canned Goods for Civilian Use," *Los Angeles Times*, January 30, 1945, 12.

342. "Father-in-Law Admits Flynn Wed Cigar Girl," *Miami Herald*, January 31, 1945, 16.

343. Associated Press, "Reds Capture Nazi's Gas Death Camp," *Los Angeles Times*, January 29, 1945, 2.

344. Herman Wouk, *War and Remembrance* (Boston: Little, Brown & Company, 1978), 33.

Chapter 2: February 1945

1. "At a Loss for Once," *Los Angeles Times*, January 16, 1945, II-4.

2. Louis M. Lyons, "8,500,000 Surplus Material Available to NE Industries," *Boston Daily Globe*, February 1, 1945, 7.

3. Associated Press, "La Guardia Charges 'Unethical' Auction of War Surpluses," *Evening Star*, February 1, 1945, 1.

4. "La Guardia Charges 'Unethical' Auction of War Surpluses."

5. Ron McKee, "Goldberg May Lose Contract for Surplus," *Washington Post*, February 3, 1945, 1.

6. McKee, "Goldberg May Lose Contract for Surplus."

7. Russell Brines, "Rescued Prisoners, Still Proud in Rags, Can't Believe It's True," *Evening Star*, January 1, 1945, 1.

8. Associated Press, "Japs Move 177 Yank Captives," *New York Daily News*, February 10, 1945, 27.

9. United Press International, "Starved Jap Unit Surrenders Colors Against All Tradition," *Los Angeles Times*, January 28, 1945, 2.

10. Associated Press, "Harry Hopkins Has Talk with Pope," *Los Angeles Times*, January 31, 1945, 2.

11. Associated Press, "Supply Difficulties May Halt Russians Short of Nazi Capital," *Evening Star*, February 2, 1945, 5.

12. Barnet Nover, "Beyond Oratory; More Words by Hitler," *Washington Post*, February 1, 1945, 6.

13. Walter Lippmann, "Not Defeat, but Catastrophe," *Boston Daily Globe*, February 1, 1945, 14.

14. Associated Press, "Captured Rocket Raps Reported Aimed at US," *Washington Post*, February 11, 1945, 1.

15. Associated Press, "WPA Still Exists, but Just to Answer Queries on Records," *Evening Star*, February 5, 1945, 1.

16. Ernest K. Bennett, "Soldier Under Death Sentence Blames His Revolutionary Mind," *Evening Star*, February 7, 1945, 5.

17. Nelson M. Shepherd, "500,000 in US Reassigned as Overseas Replacements," *Evening Star*, February 2, 1945, 1.

18. "Second All-Colored Engine Company Is Established," *Evening Star*, February 2, 1945, B-1.

19. K. S. Bartlett, "If You Want Coal in a Hurry This Winter, 'Come and Get It,'" *Boston Sunday Globe*, February 4, 1945, 3.

20. Associated Press, "Lord Vansittart Says 'Sinister Germans' Escaping from the Reich," *Freeport Journal-Standard*, February 7, 1945, 11.

21. Associated Press, "Vansittart Condemns Neutrals Who Admit Nazi War Criminals," *Evening Star*, February 7, 1945, 7.

22. United Press International, "Nazis Abandon Areas of the Siegfried Line," *Hawaii Tribune-Herald*, February 1, 1945, 1.

23. Associated Press, "Service Plane Bomb Kills Woman," *Los Angeles Times*, January 28, 1945, 1.

24. Associated Press, "Georgia House Votes Poll Tax Repealed by Big Majority," *Evening Star*, February 1, 1945, 14.

25. Associated Press, "Gov. O'Conor Seeks Repeal of Maryland 'Jim Crow' Law," *Washington Post*, February 5, 1945, 4.

26. "Stassen Accepts Invitation to United Nations Conference," *Washington Post*, February 21, 1945, 1.

27. "Working Wives Seen 'Menacing' Family Life," *Evening Star*, February 1, 1945, 1B.

28. "Classified; Help Wanted–Female," *Baltimore Sun*, February 2, 1945, 17.

29. "Jewish Juniors to Meet," *Evening Star*, February 1, 1945, 3B.

30. Genevieve Reynolds, "Junior League Members Take on War Work," *Washington Post*, February 22, 1945, 10.

31. Fred Hampson, "Rescued Yanks Want Health, Visit Home, to Fight Japs," *Bakersfield Californian*, February 2, 1945, 7.

32. Associated Press, "Hysterical with Happiness over Freedom, Flag, Food," *Boston Daily Globe*, February 2, 1945, 7.

33. United Press International, "2 Shots Spelled Freedom for Death Marchers," *Washington Post*, February 3, 1945, 1.

34. "'Don't Wait to Be Drafted,' Nurses Told at Big Rally," *Boston Daily Globe*, February 2, 1945, 7.

35. Harry Hopkins, "You Will Be Mobilized," *American Magazine*, February 1945, 5.

36. Hopkins, "You Will Be Mobilized."

37. "Would Aid Russia in War on Japs," *Baltimore Sun*, February 11, 1945, 3.

38. Carlyle Holt, "Holt Questions Replacement System," *Boston Daily Globe*, February 2, 1945, 11.

39. "An Airman's Prayer," *Democrat and Chronicle*, February 24, 1945, 1.

40. Associated Press, "Fire Drives Out AWOL Soldier Hiding Under Club 15 Months," *Sunday Star*, February 4, 1945, 1, 7.

41. "'No Atheists in Combat Planes,' Former News Writer Declares," *Sunday Star*, February 4, 1945, 10C.

42. "Fighting in Asia Is 'Vacation' to Air Act with 80 Missions," *Sunday Star*, February 4, 1945, 10C.

43. Associated Press, "Schmidt Taken, American Forces Imperil Pruem," *Evening Star*, February 8, 1945, 1.

44. Associated Press, "Yanks Widen Breach: Cross Reich Border at Four New Points," *Boston Daily Globe*, February 1, 1945, 1.

45. Frances Burns, "Carloads of Heroes: Wounded Don't Forget Guys They Left Behind," *Boston Daily Globe*, February 2, 1945, 14.

46. Burns, "Carloads of Heroes."

47. Burns, "Carloads of Heroes."

48. Associated Press, "Soviets Pound Outer Defenses of Berlin Area," *Pensacola News Journal*, February 10, 1945, 1.

49. Associated Press, "Report Goebbels Orders All of Berlin Scorched," *Boston Daily Globe*, February 1, 1945, 3.

50. "Hopkins Charges Colleges Share Blame for War," *Boston Daily Globe*, February 1, 1945, 4.

51. "National Boy Scout Week to Be Observed Feb. 8–14," *Evening Independent*, February 3, 1945, 10.

52. Melville Webb, "Major Leagues Meet Today: Continuance of Game, Election of Commissioner Big Issues," *Boston Daily Globe*, February 3, 1945, 19.

53. *Boston Daily Globe*, February 2, 1945, 23, cartoon.

54. *Boston Sunday Globe*, February 4, 1945, 12, advertisement.

55. Iris Carpenter, "First Army Carves Out 5,000 Yards: Wins Crossroad Center of Siegfried Defense Line," *Boston Daily Globe*, February 3, 1945, 1.

56. Associated Press, "Crack Main Siegfried Belt: Yank Assault Carries 10 Miles Inside Germany," *Boston Daily Globe*, February 3, 1945, 1.

57. Associated Press, "Hour Has Struck, Free Germans Say, Urging Army Revolt," *Boston Daily Globe*, February 3, 1945, 3.

58. Associated Press, "U.S., Reds Call on Nazi Troops to Surrender," *Washington Post*, February 5, 1945, 5.

59. "U.S., Reds Call on Nazi Troops."

60. Associated Press, "Nazis Call Women 16–60 into Army: People Are Vaguely Promised Hitler Will Do Something," *Washington Post*, February 13, 1945, 2.

61. Associated Press, "Germans Freed of Moral Obligations, Nazi Asserts: Big Three Acts Force Grimmer War, He Warns," *Los Angeles Times*, February 14, 1945, 2.

62. "Reich Women Conscripted," *Baltimore Sun*, February 13, 1945, 4.

63. William L. Shirer, "Hitler May Solve Allies' Problem by Dragging Germany Down to Destruction," *Boston Sunday Globe*, February 4, 1945, 1.

64. William L. Shirer, "Shirer Blasts Censor Policy in Washington," *Washington Post*, February 11, 1945, 6B.

65. Mike Levin, "Harvard Professor Finds How Tough Nazis Are," *Boston Daily Globe*, February 5, 1945, 6.

66. Levin, "Harvard Professor Finds How Tough Nazis Are."

67. Henry W. Harris, "Even If Russians Crash Oder, Fortress Berlin Remains," *Boston Daily Globe*, February 4, 1945, 3.

68. M. E. Hennessy, "Round About," *Boston Sunday Globe*, February 4, 1945, 4.

69. "Lauren Bacall Aids Show for Services," *Washington Post*, February 11, 1945, 4.

70. Associated Press, "Nazis Slaughtered on Oder: Reds Close on Kustrin, Frankfurt and Stettin," *Boston Sunday Globe*, February 4, 1945, 1.

71. "Bomber Crash Kills Medford Corporal," *Boston Sunday Globe*, February 4, 1945, 6.

72. Melville Webb, "Major Leagues Going Ahead with Plans to Open Season; Frick and Harridge Appointed to Confer with Government," *Boston Sunday Globe*, February 4, 1945, 20.

73. Associated Press, "Morale Value of Baseball Lauded by J. Edgar Hoover," *Boston Daily Globe*, February 5, 1945, 4.

74. Associated Press, "1st Cavalry Seizes Government Seat," *Boston Daily Globe*, February 5, 1945, 1.

75. Raymond P. Cronin, "After 3 Years: Manila's Fall Lifts Horror of Jap Yoke," *Washington Post*, February 5, 1945, 2.

76. United Press International, "MacArthur Proposed Leader of Nippon Home Island Assault," *Honolulu Advertiser*, February 6, 1945, 1.

77. Associated Press, "Manila Falls to Yanks," *Boston Daily Globe*, February 6, 1945, 1.

78. Associated Press, "Filipino Plays Swing Music on Piano Left by Japs," *Washington Post*, February 5, 1945, 9.

79. Associated Press, "First Cavalry Enters Close Manila Fighting," *Miami Herald*, February 11, 1945, 1.

80. United Press International, "Freed Marines Weep at Sight of Uniforms," *Washington Post*, February 5, 1945, 2.

81. "Freed Marines Weep."

82. Associated Press, "Chinese Draft 500,000; Jap Hold on China Mainland Reported Fast Deteriorating," *Washington Post*, February 16, 1945, 1.

83. Associated Press, "Babe Ruth Dreams of Yesterday on His 51st Birthday," *Boston Daily Globe*, February 8, 1945, 14.

84. *Boston Daily Globe*, February 5, 1945, 5, advertisement.

85. Dorothy Dix, "Wife Tires of Serfdom," *Boston Daily Globe*, February 5, 1945, 3.

86. George Connery, "US Western Front Clothing: A Factual Report," *Washington Post*, February 18, 1945, 1B.

87. United Press International, "London Ignores Nazi Uniform until Yanks Grab Its Wearer," *Washington Post*, February 18, 1945, 5B.

88. "French and American Troops in Alsace Cut Colmar Pocket in Half," *Baltimore Sun*, February 6, 1945, 1.

89. Joseph F. Dinneen, "Boston Is Focus of USO Nation-Wide Celebration," *Boston Daily Globe*, February 6, 1945, 1.

90. "The German War Criminals," *Democrat and Chronicle*, February 5, 1945, 6.

91. Associated Press, "Reich Warned of 'Trickery' by Big Three," *Washington Post*, February 3, 1945, 1.

92. "Reich Warned of 'Trickery.'"

93. Associated Press, "Big Three Believed Fixing Reich Fate," *Washington Post*, February 3, 1945, 2.

94. Edward T. Folliard, "Only Defeat Is Certain: How Long Will Nazis Fight? Nobody Knows," *Washington Post*, February 11, 1945, 1.

95. "6 Yanks Die of Poison Liquor, 3 Blinded, Cafe Is Closed," *St. Louis Post-Dispatch*, February 11, 1945, 2.

96. "France in Puritanic Mood, Campaigns Against Alcohol," *Baltimore Sun*, February 14, 1945, 3.

97. Roman Carmen, "Russians Fill Berlin Path with Corpses," *Salt Lake Tribune*, February 11, 1945, 3.

98. Carmen, "Russians Fill Berlin Path with Corpses."

99. Associated Press, "German Guards Skip Out; 2 DC Men Among 27 Rescued from Prison Camp in Poland," *Washington Post*, February 20, 1945, 1.

100. "Dewey Pledges Support of His Party for FD at Big Three Parley," *Boston Daily Globe*, February 9, 1945, 4.

101. Ben W. Gilbert, "US Punitive Plans Include Inner Reich," *Washington Post*, February 2, 1945, 5.

102. Gilbert, "US Punitive Plans Include Inner Reich."

103. "United Nations Meet in US April 25, Solution of Polish Problem Adopted," *Boston Daily Globe*, February 13, 1945, 1.

104. "5-Point Program to Oust New Deal Outlined by GOP," *Boston Daily Globe*, February 13, 1945, 1.

105. Ben W. Gilbert, "White House Officially Discloses De Gaulle's Rebuff to President; Roosevelt Reported 'Much Disappointed'; Jap War Discussed," *Washington Post*, February 21, 1945, 1.

106. Gilbert, "White House."

107. Ernie Pyle, "What Am I Going to Do About Seasickness?," *Boston Daily Globe*, February 7, 1945, 10.

108. Letter to the editor, "The Mae West Skit," *Philadelphia Inquirer*, December 19, 1937, 28.

109. *Boston Daily Globe*, February 7, 1945, 18, advertisement.

110. Leland Stowe, "The Betrayal of Europe's Suffering Millions," *Charlotte Observer*, February 13, 1945, 4.

111. Stowe, "The Betrayal of Europe's Suffering Millions."

112. Leland Stowe, "Leland Stowe Says: Little People Aren't Getting Break in Liberated Countries," *Boston Daily Globe*, February 9, 1945, 7.

113. "'Don't Want to Sing,' Says Sinatra as He Waits Army Decision," *Boston Daily Globe*, February 9, 1945, 10.

114. International News Service, "Navy to Add 24,000 Ships, 28,000 Planes; Fleet to Have Total of 75,000 Landing Craft for Far East," *Washington Post*, February 1, 1945, 1.

115. Associated Press, "Navy's Fire Power in 1500 Hours Put at 36 Million Tons," *Washington Post*, February 2, 1945, 5.

116. *Boston Daily Globe*, February 9, 1945, 11, advertisement.

117. *Boston Daily Globe*, February 12, 1945, 11, advertisement.

118. Associated Press, "Army's Ordnance Faced Arctic Test Before Europe Use," *Washington Post*, February 3, 1945, 2.

119. George Connery, "Today's Tank Story: Speed and Mobility vs. Giant Power," *Washington Post*, February 4, 1945, 1B.

120. Associated Press, "Negro Divisions Fight German Attacks on Soggy Italian Front," *Boston Daily Globe*, February 13, 1945, 2.

121. Associated Press, "61% of Bay State Labor in War Jobs, NAM Finds," *Boston Daily Globe*, February 11, 1945, 10.

122. Iris Carpenter, "Nazis 'Washed Out' with Failure of Dam Strategy," *Boston Daily Globe*, February 12, 1945, 1.

123. Associated Press, "Russians Drive for Dresden; 37-Mile Gain Cuts Berlin-Breslau Road," *Boston Daily Globe*, February 12, 1945, 1.

124. *Boston Daily Globe*, February 12, 1945, 5, advertisement.

125. Associated Press, "Nazi War Refugees Perish by Hundreds Fleeing Red Armies," *Boston Daily Globe*, February 16, 1945, 1.

126. Associated Press, "Berlin Builds City Defenses; Goebbels Lays Plans to Scorch Capital If Beaten," *Baltimore Sun*, February 1, 1945, 2.

127. Associated Press, "Sans Parachute; Md. Airman Alive After 1300-Ft. Fall," *Washington Post*, February 2, 1945, 7.

128. "Lt. J. P. Kennedy Jr. Gets Navy Cross Posthumously," *Boston Daily Globe*, February 16, 1945, 1, 3.

129. Anne Hagner, "Bombed City He Loved; Pastor to Conduct Gold Star Ceremony for Bombardier Son," *Washington Post*, February 18, 1945, 6B.

130. Associated Press, "Faces, Sleeves Empty, GIs Come Home," *Washington Post*, February 20, 1945, 9.

131. George Gallup, "The Gallup Poll; Made Real War Sacrifices, Only 36% Feel They Have," *Washington Post*, February 14, 1945, 9.

132. Associated Press, "Yanks Seize Naval Base in Subic Bay," *Washington Post*, February 1, 1945, 1, 2.

133. "Yanks Tighten Manila Circle, Gain on Bataan," *St. Louis Post-Dispatch*, February 15, 1945, 11.

134. "Tank Smashes in Gate of Santo Tomas, Soldiers Subdue Guards," *St. Louis Post-Dispatch*, February 5, 1945, 1.

135. United Press International, "Japs Slaughtering Manila Civilians, Refugees Report," *Washington Post*, February 14, 1945, 1.

136. Associated Press, "Hundreds of Planes Are Sent into Battle by Mitscher Force," *Richmond Times-Dispatch*, February 16, 1945, 1.

137. Frank Tremaine, "B-29s Again Hit Tokyo with Record Force," *Washington Post*, February 20, 1945, 1.

138. *New York Daily News*, February 18, 1945, 114, advertisement.

139. *Washington Post*, February 21, 1945, 8, advertisement.

140. *Washington Post*, February 23, 1945, 3, advertisement.

141. Ralph McGill, "People of Bastogne Live in Scarred, Ruined Homes," *Boston Daily Globe*, February 16, 1945, 16.

142. *Boston Daily Globe*, February 16, 1945, 19, advertisement.

143. Associated Press, "'Baby' Bonds Grow Up," *Kansas City Star*, February 12, 1945, 8.

144. *Washington Post*, February 25, 1945, 3B, cartoon.

145. *Boston Sunday Globe*, February 18, 1945, 7, advertisement.

146. *Washington Post*, "Auto Demand to Take 3 Years of Record Production to Fill," February 3, 1945, 1.

147. Richard Tompkins, "Public Asks Postwar Car Be Practical," *Washington Post*, February 11, 1945, 5S.

148. John B. McDermott, "Yank Stalks SS Officer to Avenge Cruel Beating," *Washington Post*, February 3, 1945, 3.

149. John J. O'Neill, "White Race Hardest Hit by Killings," *Washington Post*, February 4, 1945, 3B.

150. "Growler," *Washington Post*, February 4, 1945, 4B.

151. Associated Press, "Goch Outflanked: Allied Guns and Planes Smash 6 Vicious Nazi Counterblows," *Washington Post*, February 15, 1945, 1; and Associated Press, "Yanks Slowly Winning Fight in Manila Bay," *Washington Post*, February 15, 1945, 1.

152. Hamilton W. Faron, "Every New US Pacific Base Adds to Saga of the Seabees," *Washington Post*, January 14, 1945, 5B.

153. United Press International, "America's Secret Weapon: Floating Repair Shops, Hotel, Dry Docks Aiding Iwo Battle," *Washington Post*, February 20, 1945, 1.

154. A. V. Gullette, "Both Land, Jobs Needed for Economic Progress," *Washington Post*, February 4, 1945, 6B.

155. Robb Inez, "Women Deserting Jobs in Vital War Plants," *Washington Post*, February 4, 1945, 3S.

156. Inez, "Women Deserting Jobs."

157. George Gallup, "The Gallup Poll; 4 Million Women May Quit Jobs After War, Poll Indicates," *Washington Post*, February 10, 1945, 5.

158. George Gallup, "The Gallup Poll; Peacetime Military Training for Young Women Opposed," *Washington Post*, February 28, 1945, 3.

159. "Nisei Veteran Appointed Washington Relo. Officer," *Topaz Times*, March 15, 1945, 3.

160. "Social Hygiene Day," *Washington Post*, February 5, 1945, 6.

161. Ben W. Gilbert, "Midnight Closing Edict Effective February 26," *Washington Post*, February 20, 1945, 1, 4.

162. Gilbert, "Midnight Closing Edict."

163. Gilbert, "Midnight Closing Edict."

164. "The Gallup Poll: Curfew Effect Seen Slight; 95% Are in Bed by Midnight," *Washington Post*, February 24, 1945, 3.

165. Ida Jean Kain, "Shirley Temple Gives Advice to Teen Agers," *Washington Post*, February 5, 1945, 10.

166. "Better Race Relation Aims Stressed in District Pulpits," *Washington Post*, February 12, 1945, 7.

167. Robert C. Albright, "'Blaze' Definitely Grounded: Dog Fight Sparks Inquiry into All Travel Priorities," *Washington Post*, February 11, 1945, 1.

168. "Nazi Supermen Are Cry-Babies," *Spokesman-Review*, October 31, 1944, 10.

169. Associated Press, "Army Court Finds Pair Guilty on Three Counts," *Washington Post*, February 15, 1945, 1.

170. Associated Press, "Held by British: Dutch Traitor Is Blamed for Arnhem Loss," *Washington Post*, February 18, 1945, 1.

171. Associated Press, "War Sidelights: AMG Court Gives Nazi 10-Year Term," *Washington Post*, February 16, 1945, 4M.

172. Associated Press, "$100,000 Paid Nazis to Protect Gould, Wife Says," *Boston Sunday Globe*, February 18, 1945, 19.

173. Associated Press, "Editor Fired, W. & M. Paper Will Suspend," *Washington Post*, February 15, 1945, 3.

174. "What Price Freedom?," *Washington Post*, February 15, 1945, 6.

175. "Brotherhood," *Washington Post*, February 20, 1945, 6.

176. "Brotherhood Week, Extension of Remarks of Hon. Brooks Hays of Arkansas in the House of Representatives," Congressional Record, vol. 91, part 10, January 4, 1945, A30.

177. United Press International, "Goebbels Vows 'Boldest' Defense," *Washington Post*, February 16, 1945, 2.

178. Associated Press, "Martial Law Ordered Throughout Reich," *Washington Post*, February 17, 1945, 2.

179. George Gallup, "Crimea Agreement Reiterates Previous Gallup Survey Replies," *Washington Post*, February 18, 1945, 5B.

180. Associated Press, "Nearly 1,800 Yanks Die When Sub Sinks Rat-Trap Jap Prison Ship; Wisconsin Survivor Tells Story," *Kenosha Evening News*, February 16, 1945, 2.

181. Associated Press, "Youngest War I Vet Dies; Fibbed to Enlist at 12," *Atlanta Constitution*, February 20, 1945, 5.

182. "Chameleon Bride Used 28 Names, Wed 8, FBI Charges," *New York Daily News*, February 25, 1945, 3.

183. Associated Press, "Blow at Street Pickups; Teen-Age 'Wolf' Patrol Girls to Face Arrest in Baltimore," *Washington Post*, February 17, 1945, 1.

184. United Press International, "Not So 'Comical'; Girl GI Saved Arrested as Saboteur Aide," *Washington Post*, February 17, 1945, 5.

185. "National Symphon Fund Indorsed by Mrs. Roosevelt," *Washington Post*, February 16, 1945, 4.

186. Associated Press, "Underground Arsenals Built by Nazi Slaves," *Washington Post*, February 19, 1945, 2.

187. Drew Pearson, "VE Day Cutback Will Be Slight," Washington Merry-Go-Round, *Washington Post*, February 18, 1945, 5H.

188. "Heroes Come Home," *Tampa Bay Times*, December 26, 1942, 10.

189. United Press International, "Rep. Wilson Charges Laxity in US Offices," *Washington Post*, February 19, 1945, 12.

190. Associated Press, "'Peace for All Men' Is Goal of US, Stettinius Says," *Richmond Times-Dispatch*, February 23, 1945, 5.

191. Frank Carey, "Sickness Rate Up 70% Among War Workers," *Washington Post*, February 20, 1945, 4.

192. Christine Sadler, "US Seeks Boost of Supply of Meat," *Washington Post*, February 21, 1945, 4.

193. *Washington Post*, February 21, 1945, 10, advertisement.

194. "Women! Panties Are Reported Nil," *Burlington Daily News*, February 23, 1945, 5.

195. "Third of Tiny Island Won Despite Fierce Resistance by Jap Forces," *Chicago Tribune*, February 21, 1945, 1.

196. Associated Press, "Only Dead Jap Soldiers Left on Bataan," *Washington Post*, February 22, 1945, 1.

197. Associated Press, "Landing Follows 72-Day Bombing," *Atlanta Constitution*, February 20, 1945, 1, 5.

198. "Landing Follows 72-Day Bombing."

199. "Landing Follows 72-Day Bombing."

200. "Just 8 Square Miles of Hell—That's Iwo," *Washington Post*, February 21, 1945, 2.

201. Associated Press, "Rising Jap Resistance Slows Yanks," *Washington Post*, February 22, 1945, 1.

202. United Press International, "Wound Angers Buddies, So They Wipe Out Jap Nest," *Washington Post*, February 25, 1945, 5M.

203. Larry Stewart, "Morning Briefing; Looks Like Shoe's Not on Other Foot Yet," *Los Angeles Times*, September 26, 2004, 1.

204. Robert C. Albright, "'Freshman' Lectures House; Rep. Gallagher Starts a Battle in Congress by Urging Unity," *Washington Post*, February 22, 1945, 1.

205. Associated Press, "Berchtesgaden Hit Its First Air Blow," *Washington Post*, February 22, 1945, 2.

206. United Press International, "German Officers Reported Held in Plot Against Hitler," *Washington Post*, February 23, 1945, 2.

207. Louis Lockner, "Nazis' Hideouts Ready in Mounts; Wild Terrain, Loyal Guards Could Delay War Criminals' Doom," *Washington Post*, February 25, 1945, 3B.

208. Associated Press, "10th Mountain Division Takes Italian Peaks," *Washington Post*, February 26, 1945, 2.

209. *Washington Post*, February 26, 1945, 7, advertisement.

210. Nelson B. Bell, "Miss Bankhead Enjoys Five Years of Triumph," *Washington Post*, February 25, 1945, 6S.

211. Associated Press, "2 US Armies Pour Across Roer in Drive for Rhine," *Washington Post*, February 24, 1945, 1.

212. United Press International, "Nazis Quit in Droves as Yanks Exploit 'Real Breakthrough,'" *Washington Post*, February 28, 1945, 1.

213. Associated Press, "Yanks Routing Bewildered Nazi Forces; US Column Races Within 18 Miles of Duesseldorf," *Washington Post*, February 28, 1945, 1.

214. Associated Press, "Marines Making Slight Gains in Drive Against Bitter Resistance," *Washington Post*, February 25, 1945, 1.

215. Lisle Shoemaker, "Capture Appears Near; Foot-by-Foot Advance on Iwo's Central Airfield Continues," *Washington Post*, February 26, 1945, 1, 2.

Chapter 3: March 1945

1. Richard H. Minear, *Dr. Seuss Goes to War: The World War II Editorial Cartoons of Theodor Seuss Geisel* (New York: New Press, 2001).

2. *Birmingham News*, March 4, 1945, 55, advertisement.

3. "Reparation in the Sweat of Their Brow," *Berkshire Eagle*, March 27, 1945, 8.

4. Dimitri A. Volkoganov, *Stalin: Triumph and Tragedy* (London: George Weidenfeld and Nicolson, 1991), 478.

5. Associated Press, "Berlin Handed 12th in Row," *Atlanta Constitution*, Sunday, March 4, 1945, 4A.

6. "Coal Operators Spike Lewis Pact Demands," *Atlanta Constitution*, March 16, 1945, 1.

7. "Miners Who Strike May Face Induction," *Atlanta Constitution*, March 4, 1945, 16.

8. Associated Press, "Japs Burn Helpless Americans," *Atlanta Constitution*, March 4, 1945, 1.

9. "Japs Burn Helpless Americans."

10. Cecile Davis, "Jefferson Flags Flutter, Stores Close Early as Folks Hail 'Miss Mildred,' Heroic Nurse," *Atlanta Constitution*, March 6, 1945, 1.

11. Robert Quillen, "No Quick Cure for Japanese," *Atlanta Constitution*, March 6, 1945, 6.

12. United Press International, "US Destroys 6 Divisions in 56 Luzon Days," *Atlanta Constitution*, March 6, 1945, 1.

13. "Contents Reveal Document as New Monroe Doctrine," *Atlanta Constitution*, March 11, 1945, 6.

14. Barbara Finch, "'Down on Your Face'; Woman's Brief Visit to Iwo Jima Exciting," *Atlanta Constitution*, March 4, 1945, 2.

15. Finch, "'Down on Your Face'; Woman's Brief Visit to Iwo Jima Exciting."

16. Associated Press, "Somewhere a Voice; Probe Looms as Board Terms Sinatra Essential," *Atlanta Constitution*, March 4, 1945, 4.

17. "Somewhere a Voice."

18. "Somewhere a Voice."

19. Gladstone Williams, "President's Report Was Well Received," *Atlanta Constitution*, March 5, 1945, 6.

20. Williams, "President's Report Was Well Received."

21. Williams, "President's Report Was Well Received."

22. Williams, "President's Report Was Well Received."

23. Ollie Reeves, "Just a Rhyme a Day," *Atlanta Constitution*, March 5, 1945, 7.

24. "Mrs. Roosevelt Denies Urging Birth Control," *Pittsburgh Sun-Telegraph*, February 26, 1945, 4.

25. Eleanor Roosevelt, "My Day," *Pittsburgh Press*, March 9, 1945, 36.

26. "At 41, Mack Tharpe Dies in Action," *Atlanta Constitution*, March 6, 1945, 6.

27. Ralph T. Jones, "They'll Be Different After They Return," *Atlanta Constitution*, March 6, 1945, 6.

28. "Woman of Year Group Begins Plans for 1945," *Atlanta Constitution*, March 6, 1945, 4.

29. Associated Press, "Cologne Nazis Flee Before US Tanks; 3 Divisions Smash into

4th Reich City; Only 1,000 Troops Defend Rhine Prize," *Atlanta Constitution*, March 6, 1945, 1.

30. Associated Press, "Stop Brooding: City Chicks Doomed in Reich," *Atlanta Constitution*, March 6, 1945, 3.

31. "Cologne, Where the Virgins Died," *Atlanta Constitution*, March 6, 1945, 6.

32. "Volcano Awakens to Discomfit Japs," *Knoxville News-Sentinel*, March 5, 1945, 8.

33. "Ration Dates," *Atlanta Constitution*, March 6, 1945, 5.

34. "Where the Meat Has Gone," *Atlanta Constitution*, March 13, 1945, 6.

35. George Gallup, "Gallop Poll; Diverse Following of FDR," *Atlanta Constitution*, March 6, 1945, 7.

36. United Press International, "Thrust Perils Main Jap Guardians of Mandalay," *Los Angeles Times*, March 6, 1945, 5.

37. Edward D. Ball, "V-E in Four Months; Germans Near Defeat, Captured General Admits," *Atlanta Constitution*, March 7, 1945, 1.

38. Ball, "V-E in Four Months."

39. Ralph T. Jones, "We Mustn't Be Fooled by Fawning Germans," *Atlanta Constitution*, March 9, 1945, 8.

40. Jones, "We Mustn't Be Fooled."

41. Associated Press, "Goebbels' Latest State of War Spiel: Climax Past, Furioso Coming, Victory," *Atlanta Constitution*, March 9, 1945, 2.

42. Associated Press, "Quit and Leave Door Open for Reich to Rebuild, Ike Tells Nazi Officers," *Atlanta Constitution*, March 6, 1945, 2.

43. Associated Press, "Nazis Reel Before Bold Blow," *Atlanta Constitution*, March 9, 1945, 1.

44. United Press International, "Troops Pour into Reich," *Tucson Daily Citizen*, March 9, 1945, 1.

45. United Press International, "15 Square Miles of Tokyo Reduced to Ashes, Rubble," *Atlanta Constitution*, March 11, 1945, 1.

46. Associated Press, "Japan's Third City Ablaze After Raid by 300 B-29s," *Atlanta Constitution*, March 12, 1945, 1.

47. Associated Press, "Invasion at Any Minute; 'Sacred' Japan to Become Battleground, Koiso Warns," *Atlanta Constitution*, March 12, 1945, 1.

48. "Invasion at Any Minute."

49. *Atlanta Constitution*, March 12, 1945, 6, cartoon.

50. Ralph McGill, "A Sudden End to Nazi Resistance?," *Atlanta Constitution*, March 12, 1945, 4.

51. Associated Press, "Hitler Sees German Doom in Allied 'Orgy,'" *Atlanta Constitution*, March 12, 1945, 9.

52. "Georgian, 5 Others Die as Two Bombers Collide," *Atlanta Constitution*, March 12, 1945, 9.

53. Gault McGowan, "Underground Living: Nazi 'Sleep-Easies' Resist Allied Bombs," *Atlanta Constitution*, March 13, 1945, 1.

54. Associated Press, "Pontoon Bridges Span Rhine as Americans Advance Mile," *Atlanta Constitution*, March 12, 1945, 1.

55. "Pontoon Bridges Span Rhine."

56. Associated Press, "Defend 'Every Inch' of Italy, Kesselring Orders Troops," *Atlanta Constitution*, March 13, 1945, 5.

57. Julian Hartt, "POW Charges Exploded; Two-Packs-a-Day, Rich Menus Untrue," *Atlanta Constitution*, March 13, 1945, 8.

58. United Press International, "Great Fires Rage in Osaka as B-29s Dump 2,300 Tons; Four Square Miles of Jap Port Ablaze," *Atlanta Constitution*, March 14, 1945, 1.

59. "Krauts in Hollywood Just Like Hollywood," *Charlotte Observer*, March 13, 1945, 3.

60. W. C. Heinz, "Hollywood Has Goods on Krauts; US Rolls into Nazi Prison Camp, Traps Fiendish Rubber-Hose Boys," *Atlanta Constitution*, March 14, 1945, 1.

61. Heinz, "Hollywood Has Goods on Krauts."

62. Heinz, "Hollywood Has Goods on Krauts."

63. United Press International, "US Assault Boats Storm Rhine to Outflank Nazis," *Atlanta Constitution*, March 14, 1945, 1.

64. Kingsbury Smith, "Move to End War in West Hinted; Did Von Rundstedt Offer to Quit for One-Sided Peace at Rhine?," *Atlanta Constitution*, March 14, 1945, 1.

65. Wes Gallagher, "'VE' Day Seen Early in Summer," *Atlanta Constitution*, March 14, 1945, 1, 2.

66. International News Service, "OPA Urges Ceilings on Movies, Sports Events," *Atlanta Constitution*, March 14, 1945, 1.

67. Associated Press, "Jap Justice; Bataan Hero Is Brutally Beaten," *Atlanta Constitution*, March 14, 1945, 5.

68. *Atlanta Constitution*, March 14, 1945, 5, advertisement.

69. "Comparatively, We Pay but Little," *Atlanta Constitution*, March 14, 1945, 6.

70. Ralph McGill, "The Psychopathology of Adolf Hitler," *Atlanta Constitution*, March 14, 1945, 6.

71. Amanda Macias, "'A Fully-Fledged Masochist': Inside the CIA's Psychological Profile of Adolf Hitler," *Journal* (Dublin), February 28, 2016, https://www.thejournal.ie/hitler-psychological-profile-2620137-Feb2016/.

72. "Daring Yank Raid Frees 2146 More Near Manila," *Boston Daily Globe*, February 24, 1945, 1.

73. Associated Press, "Two More Islands Seized in Philippines," *Atlanta Constitution*, March 15, 1945, 2.

74. "Two More Islands Seized in Philippines."

75. Associated Press, "Dynamiter Tipsy; Big Show at Remagen Bridge Flops," *Atlanta Constitution*, March 15, 1945, 1.

76. L. S. B. Shapiro, "Hitler Acts to Avert Full Surrender and Leave Door Ajar for Next War," *Atlanta Constitution*, March 16, 1945, 1.

77. United Press International, "Invasion Fleet 'Sighted,' Japs Fear Doorstep Blow," *Atlanta Constitution*, March 16, 1945, 1.

78. United Press International, "'Don't Wed for Pity,' Girls Told," *Atlanta Constitution*, March 16, 1945, 3.

79. "'Don't Wed for Pity,' Girls Told."

80. "Germans Rush V-1, V-2 Secrets Out of Russian Army's Pathway," *Atlanta Constitution*, March 16, 1945, 3.

81. Encyclopedia Britannica Online, s.v. "Wernher von Braun," accessed September 9, 2021, https://www.britannica.com/biography/Wernher-von-Braun.

82. Associated Press, "US Bombers Smash German Army's Staff Headquarters," *Chicago Tribune*, March 16, 1945, 6.

83. *Atlanta Constitution*, March 22, 1945, 13, advertisement.

84. "Butter Quota for Civilians to Be Reduced," *Indianapolis News*, March 19, 1945, 1.

85. Associated Press, "Pete Gray Is Starter for Browns; One-Armed Gardener Wins Starting Berth in First Exhibition," *Atlanta Constitution*, March 18, 1945, 10.

86. Associated Press, "Iwo Isle in the Bag, Navy Says," *Atlanta Constitution*, March 17, 1945, 1.

87. "Atlantan Sees Flag Go Up on Iwo Jima," *Atlanta Constitution*, March 25, 1945, 5.

88. "Atlantan Sees Flag Go Up."

89. United Press International, "Japs Speed Plans to Meet Invaders," *Atlanta Constitution*, March 22, 1945, 1, 5.

90. Associated Press, "Gnawing Fear over Reich; Deportation Threat Steels Germans Against Surrender," *Atlanta Constitution*, March 21, 1945, 1.

91. "Gnawing Fear over Reich."

92. Associated Press, "Grotesque Twilight; Berchtesgaden Fixed for Revolt and Chaos," *Atlanta Constitution*, March 22, 1945, 1.

93. International News Service, "Declared Sane, He'll Celebrate," *Atlanta Constitution*, March 17, 1945, 1.

94. International News Service, "Eat Less or Let Others Help? Europe's Pantry Woes Place FDRs at Odds," *Atlanta Constitution*, March 18, 1945, 1.

95. "Eat Less or Let Others Help?"

96. International News Service, "US Horn of Plenty Drained, Krug Warns," *Atlanta Constitution*, March 18, 1945, 1.

97. "Sally Forth Says: Joseph Gatins Weds Beauty After Nazi Prison Escape," *Atlanta Constitution*, March 18, 1945, 6C.

98. "New York Nightspots Come into the Union," *Atlanta Constitution*, March 23, 1945, 8.

99. "New York Nightspots."

100. Westbrook Pegler, "Communists in the Army," *Atlanta Constitution*, March 19, 1945, 7.

101. United Press International, "Four More Bridges over Rhine Blown," *Atlanta Constitution*, March 20, 1945, 1.

102. Associated Press, "Norwegians Cage 200,000 Nazis," *Atlanta Constitution*, March 20, 1945, 1.

103. "Tokyo—Osaka—Nagoya—Kobe—?," *Atlanta Constitution*, March 20, 1945, 8.

104. L. S. B. Shapiro, "5,000 in Reich Are Doomed Each Day Hitler Delays Peace," *Atlanta Constitution*, March 21, 1945, 1.

105. Christer Jaederlund, "Hitler Woos Masses; Nazi Leaders Anger Berliners, Pay for Error with Their Lives," *Atlanta Constitution*, March 22, 1945, 1.

106. Jaederlund, "Hitler Woos Masses."

107. Associated Press, "Nazi Editor Prints Peace Plea, Dies," *Atlanta Constitution*, March 23, 1945, 2.

108. Gladstone Williams, "Did Japanese Double-Cross Adolf?," *Atlanta Constitution*, March 22, 1945, 8.

109. Christer Jaederlund, "But Always Candidates for Death; Spies in Germany Will o' Wisps Who Gain Information Readily," *Atlanta Constitution*, March 23, 1945, 2.

110. United Press International, "Newsmen Host to FDR, Other High Officials," *Atlanta Constitution*, March 23, 1945, 3.

111. *Atlanta Constitution*, March 22, 1945, 11, advertisement.

112. Edward D. Ball, "3d Army Storms Across River Without a Shot," *Atlanta Constitution*, March 24, 1945, 1.

113. Associated Press, "Nazis Store Pills to Win World War III," *Atlanta Constitution*, March 24, 1945, 1.

114. Associated Press, "Battleships, Carriers, B-29s Hurled Against Japan," *Atlanta Constitution*, March 25, 1945, 1.

115. United Press International, "14,000 Warplanes Rock Reich in Record Raid," *Atlanta Constitution*, March 25, 1945, 1.

116. "14,000 Warplanes Rock Reich in Record Raid."

117. Associated Press, "Ike Broadcasts Grim Warning," *Atlanta Constitution*, March 25, 1945, 1.

118. Associated Press, "No Fraternity; Monty Bans Friendship with Nazis," *Atlanta Constitution*, March 25, 1945, 2.

119. "No Fraternity."

120. United Press International, "Madcap Race for Berlin; Elation Sweeps GI Ranks; Cold, Wet, but in on Kill," *Atlanta Constitution*, March 25, 1945, 2.

121. "Jap Smoking on Iwo Blows Up When Shot by Tate Marine," *Atlanta Constitution*, March 25, 1945, 5B.

122. *Atlanta Constitution*, March 25, 1945, 2A, advertisement.

123. Associated Press, "Jews Join Allies on Italy Front," *Atlanta Constitution*, March 26, 1945, 1.

124. "Jews Join Allies on Italy Front."

125. International News Service, "Churchill, over Rhine, Cheats Death," *Atlanta Constitution*, March 26, 1945, 1.

126. Christer Jaederlund, "Must Whittle Goering's Pants; Berliners Weigh Food Against Duration," *Atlanta Constitution*, March 26, 1945, 1.

127. Associated Press, "Road to Berlin," *Cincinnati Enquirer*, March 26, 1945, 3.

128. United Press International, "Homeward Bound: RAF Smashes Nazi Convoys off Norway" and "Red Tanks Chase Nazis in Hungary," *Atlanta Constitution*, March 27, 1945, 1.

129. W. C. Heinz, "Captured German Army Nurses Don't Want to Be Sent Back," *Atlanta Constitution*, March 27, 1945, 1.

130. Morley Cassidy, "Fat and Wealthy Nazi Sobs for More Gentlemanly War; Cries 'GIs Too Rough, Impolite,'" *Atlanta Constitution*, March 27, 1945, 1.

131. Associated Press, "Early Goes Broke Working for FDR, Hunts Paying Spot to Hang Hat," *Atlanta Constitution*, March 27, 1945, 3.

132. Hal Boyle, "Joyride in Germany: Hitler Paved Way to Defeat with Super-Roads in Reich," *Atlanta Constitution*, March 28, 1945, 1.

133. United Press International, "Nazis Whipped on West Front, Eisenhower Says," *Atlanta Constitution*, March 28, 1945, 1.

134. Associated Press, "'Hitler Youth' Feels His Age," *Atlanta Constitution*, March 28, 1945, 9.

135. Malcolm Muir Jr., "'Don't Come Too Close!' US Prisoners Freed from 'Living Hell,'" *Atlanta Constitution*, March 29, 1945, 1.

136. Muir, "'Don't Come Too Close!'"

137. Associated Press, "Mighty Herrenvolk Change Tune; We're Lost, Cry Nazis, Begging Sympathy of Allied Conquerors," *Atlanta Constitution*, March 29, 1945, 1.

138. United Press International, "'Tomorrow the World' Still Germany's Goal," *Miami Herald*, March 31,1945, 1,

139. Associated Press, "'Almost Inconceivable,' Fears Nazi Weapon Will Wipe Out World," *Atlanta Constitution*, March 30, 1945, 1.

140. Ernie Pyle, "In the Western Pacific," *Bakersfield Californian*, March 28, 1945, 16.

Chapter 4: April 1945

1. John H. Crider, "Byrnes Promises to Speed Return to Free Economy," *New York Times*, April 1, 1945, 1.

2. "Text of the Official Summary of the Report of James F. Byrnes to the President," *New York Times*, April 1, 1945, 28.

3. Crider, "Byrnes Promises."

4. "Report of James F. Byrnes to the President."

5. Winston Churchill, "The End of the Beginning," speech, Lord Mayor's Luncheon, November 10, 1942, London, http://www.churchill-society-london.org.uk/EndoBegn.html.

6. Drew Middleton, "15th Army Attacks," *New York Times*, April 1, 1945, 1.

7. Middleton, "15th Army Attacks."

8. Associated Press, "Germans Ordered to Root Out Spies," *New York Times*, April 1, 1945, 7.

9. "Austrian Patriots Clash with Gestapo," *New York Times*, April 1, 1945, 10.

10. David Anderson, "Brussels Worries over Allies' Plans," *New York Times*, April 1, 1945, 11.

11. United Press International, "'Little WPB' Plan Urged for Europe," *New York Times*, April 1, 1945, 27.

12. Gene Currivan, "Poison Food Left by Fleeing Enemy," *New York Times*, April 1, 1945, 3.

13. Currivan, "Poison Food Left by Fleeing Enemy."

14. Associated Press, "1,142,224 Germans Taken Since Dec. 16," *New York Times*, April 1, 1945, 1.

15. "Blitz on the Reich; As the Wehrmacht Cracks," *New York Times*, April 1, 1945, 1B.

16. Hal Boyle, "Last Big Battle of West Rages at Paderborn, Vital Road Hub," *Richmond Times-Dispatch*, April 1, 1945, 1.

17. Hal Boyle, "Battle of Annihilation in West on as Enemy Tries to Hold Paderborn," *New York Times*, April 1, 1945, 1.

18. Raymond Daniell, "Germany Depicted as Land of Gloom; Travelers Reaching Bonn Say They Will Not Quit Hitler Despite Their Despair," *New York Times*, April 1, 1945, 4.

19. Associated Press, "452 Pacific Natives Saved from Death," *New York Times*, April 1, 1945, 19.

20. "Easter 1945," *New York Times*, April 1, 1945, 8E.

21. "Easter 1945."

22. Drew Middleton, "Eisenhower Drives Toward Four Big Objectives," *New York Times*, April 1, 1945, 3E.

23. Samuel A. Tower, "FBI Keeps Plugging at Job of Catching Draft Dodgers," *New York Times*, April 1, 1945, 7E.

24. George E. Jones, "Okinawa Invasion Amazing Walk-In," *New York Times*, April 2, 1945, 1.

25. "Record Throng of 800,000 Fills 5th Ave. in Gayest Easter of War," *New York Times*, April 2, 1945, 1.

26. "Record Throng of 800,000 Fills 5th Ave."

27. Ernest Joseph King, Ernest Joseph King papers, 1908–1966 (bulk 1936–1952), manuscript/mixed material, https://lccn.loc.gov/mm70038687.

28. "Mileage Data Show Value of Okinawa Base for Bombing of Japan and Occupied Cities," *New York Times*, April 2, 1945, 3.

29. Clifton Daniel, "Heads of States Will Not Escape War Crime Penalties, Allies Decide; United Nations Commission Puts Hitler at Top of First of Five Lists Now Ready—Plea of 'Superior Orders' to Be Insufficient," *New York Times*, April 2, 1945, 6.

30. "Nazi Underground in Action, Foe Says; German Radio Asserts It Is Fighting in Occupied Areas—Issues 'Do or Die' Order," *New York Times*, April 2, 1945, 7.

31. Associated Press, "1,277 US Captives Liberated in Reich; Soldiers Captured in Belgium Lost from 25 to 40 Pounds on Starvation Diet," *New York Times*, April 2, 1945, 7.

32. "1,277 US Captives Liberated in Reich."

33. Hanson D. Baldwin, "The 'Let-Down' Problem; Nation Must Combat VE-Day Easing Off and Push Fight to Finish Against Japan," *New York Times*, April 2, 1945, 8.

34. Gene Currivan, "Herrenvolk Catalogued in 4 Classes," *Courier Journal*, April 3, 1945, 2.

35. C. P. Trussell, "Draft Bill Is Lost in Senate, 46 to 29; Next Step in Doubt," *New York Times*, April 4, 1945, 1.

36. Richard J. H. Johnston, "Yanks Bare Prison Horror; 'Ghosts' Fight over Food," *New York Times*, April 4, 1945, 1, 6.

37. Johnston, "Yanks Bare Prison Horror."

38. Johnston, "Yanks Bare Prison Horror."

39. Johnston, "Yanks Bare Prison Horror."

40. Charles E. Egan, "Movie Propaganda for Reich Planned," *New York Times*, April 4, 1945, 10.

41. C. L. Sultsberger, "Russians Foresee End of Slav Feuds; Red Army Organ Believes War Has Cohesive Effect, Uniting Peoples of East Europe," *New York Times*, April 4, 1945, 11.

42. "Library Pillaging by Nazis Surveyed; Some of Finest Collections in World Have Been Destroyed or Stolen, Report Shows," *New York Times*, April 4, 1945, 12.

43. "2 VE-Day Holidays Promised Britons," *New York Times*, April 4, 1945, 13.

44. Jane Holt, "News of Food; Post-War Store to Serve Its Customers by Conveyor Belt Loaded in Stockroom," *New York Times*, April 4, 1945, 18.

45. "La Rocca, Ex-Yankee, Is Guilty in Hold-Up," *New York Times*, April 4, 1945, 23.

46. "Mosquitos, Fleas Plague Okinawa; Marines Keep Guard Against Malaria and Scrub-Typhus—No Snakes Encountered," *New York Times*, April 5, 1945, 3.

47. "Soviet Proclaims Peaceful Intent; Russian Publication Declares Country Is Most Progressive Force in World Arena," *New York Times*, April 5, 1945, 7.

48. Associated Press, "'The End Is Not Far Off,' Eisenhower Tells Reich," *New York Times*, April 5, 1945, 10.

49. Hanson W. Baldwin, "Two German 'Secret Weapons'; As New Crisis Approaches the Enemy, His Vaunted Anti-Tank Projectiles Fail to Halt Onrushing Allies," *New York Times*, April 5, 1945, 13.

50. "Spain Backs Nazi Secrets; Radio Professes Its Belief in Weapons to Win Victory," *New York Times*, April 5, 1945, 15.

51. *New York Times*, April 5, 1945, 20, advertisement.

52. "Perilman Urges Unity Among Jews; Assails Those Who Denounce Nationalism Among Others but Seek It Themselves," *New York Times*, April 5, 1945, 21.

53. *New York Times*, April 5, 1945, 24, advertisement.

54. "Army Study Plan Reopened to Boys; High School Graduates from 17 to 17¾ Years Old May Take Tests April 12," *New York Times*, April 5, 1945, 27.

55. "MacArthur and Nimitz Get Team Job to Deal Knockout," *New York Times*, April 6, 1945, 1.

56. "Clear-Cut Reich Surrender Is Doubted by Eisenhower," *New York Times*, April 6, 1945, 1.

57. "Himmler Paper Admits End Near," *Baltimore Sun*, April 6, 1945, 1.

58. Susan Butler, *My Dear Mr. Stalin: The Complete Correspondence of Franklin D. Roosevelt and Joseph V. Stalin* (New Haven, CT: Yale University Press, 2005), 313.

59. Warren Moscow, "Japanese Defense Futile on Okinawa," *New York Times*, April 6, 1945, 5.

60. Moscow, "Japanese Defense Futile on Okinawa."

61. George E. Jones, "Okinawa Glitters as Military Prize," *New York Times*, April 6, 1945, 5.

62. Meyer Berger, "Curfew and Blackout in the States Irk Wounded Returning from Iwo; 'We're Fighting to Keep the Lights Burning at Home,' They Declare—A Groping for the Sanity of Peacetime Is Evident," *New York Times*, April 6, 1945, 6.

63. Berger, "Curfew and Blackout."

64. "Japanese-American Joins as Army Nurse," *New York Times*, April 6, 1945, 6.

65. Drew Middleton, "Big Gains in Reich; British Leap 25 Miles—US 9th Spans Weser to Close on Hanover," *New York Times*, April 6, 1945, 1, 9.

66. "A Number of German Prisoners Suffocate in US Boxcars; Eisenhower Investigates," *New York Times*, April 6, 1945, 10.

67. "German Prisoners Suffocate."

68. "German Prisoners Suffocate."

69. "Foe Said to Admit Collapse Is Near; SS Paper Reported Warning End Is 'Days or Weeks' Off, but Sees No Yielding," *New York Times*, April 6, 1945, 1, 11.

70. Sydney Gruson, "5,000 Planes Rip Shrinking Reich," *New York Times*, April 6, 1945, 11.

71. Associated Press, "Pravda Hits at Hoover," *Wilkes-Barre Times Leader, The Evening News*, April 5, 1945, 1.

72. "Children's Bureau Is Urged on Parley," *New York Times*, April 6, 1945, 18.

73. "Author at 82 Will Get the Butler Gold Medal," *New York Times*, April 6, 1945, 13.

74. "Brooklyn Hero, 20, Praised by Patton; General in Letter Cites Bible's 'Greater Love' in Telling How Youth Died," *New York Times*, April 6, 1945, 17.

75. "Roosevelt Asks Spiritual Rebirth in Congratulations to Emanu-El; Tells Congregation All Problems Would 'Melt' Before Faith in God—Spellman also Praises Institution on Its Centenary," *New York Times*, April 6, 1945, 17.

76. Associated Press, "Jefferson Dinners to Hear Roosevelt," *New York Times*, April 6, 1945, 18.

77. "Smokers Deny Prejudice in Trial of Cigarette Case," *New York Times*, April 7, 1945, 17.

78. Associated Press, "Americans Now Capture German Towns by 'Phone,'" *New York Times*, April 7, 1945, 3.

79. Associated Press, "Planes Fleeing Germany Land in Portugal, Spain," *New York Times*, April 7, 1945, 3.

80. Associated Press, "Bradley Depicts Crushing Victory; Says Germans Will Know This Time Who Won as Flag Is Raised at Ehrenbreitstein," *New York Times*, April 7, 1945, 3.

81. "Bradley Depicts Crushing Victory."

82. Associated Press, "Reich Army Seen in Loose Grouping," *New York Times*, April 7, 1945, 3.

83. Associated Press, "Marine Survivor of Iwo Flag-Raising Due Home," *Baltimore Sun*, April 7, 1945, 5.

84. "Whole Blood Cuts Deaths, Hailed at Iwo," *Democrat and Chronicle*, April 9, 1945, 18.

85. Associated Press, "Only US Affected by Censorship Ban," *New York Times*, April 7, 1945, 6.

86. "Only US Affected by Censorship Ban."

87. "1,212 Japanese Planes Blasted in 19 Days," *New York Times*, April 7, 1945, 6.

88. Bruce Rae, "U.S. Fliers Sink Japan's Biggest Warship," *New York Times*, April 8, 1945, 1.

89. "Army Planes That Cost $10,000 to $15,000 Auctioned to Public at $875 to $1,990," *New York Times*, April 7, 1945, 16.

90. "Lou Gehrig Estate Is Listed at $159,475," *New York Times*, April 7, 1945, 10.

91. United Press International, "100 Tons of Gold and Cash Found in German Salt Mine," *New York Times*, April 8, 1945, 1, 16.

92. "100 Tons of Gold and Cash Found."

93. "100 Tons of Gold and Cash Found."

94. "100 Tons of Gold and Cash Found."

95. Associated Press, "Blast Opens Way to Golden Hoard; Third Army Engineers Break Wall in German Salt Mine Used as Hiding Place," *New York Times*, April 9, 1945, 6.

96. "Blast Opens Way to Golden Hoard."

97. Associated Press, "Metternich Acres Seized by Slaves," *New York Times*, April 8, 1945, 13.

98. Gene Currivan, "Patton's Contempt of German Army Deals Hard Blow to Enemy Morale," *New York Times*, April 18, 1945, 1.

99. George E. Jones, "Enemy Fliers Hit Troops on Okinawa; Attack, Later Smashed, Had an Intensity Seldom Seen in Warfare in Pacific," *New York Times*, April 8, 1945, 4.

100. Meyer Berger, "Two Wounded Hail First US Woman," *New York Times*, April 8, 1945, 10.

101. Meyer Berger, "First Home Scenes Hearten Wounded," *New York Times*, April 9, 1945, 12.

102. "Air Fleet Battles Nazis in Big Blow," *New York Times*, April 8, 1945, 15.

103. Associated Press, "Prisoners in US Bid Reich Yield," *New York Times*, April 8, 1945, 16.

104. "Prisoners in US Bid Reich Yield."

105. *New York Times*, April 8, 1945, 22, advertisement.

106. "Clothing Streams into City's Depots; Wearables Donated for War Relief Include Such Freaks as Rubber Bathing Suit," *New York Times*, April 8, 1945, 34.

107. "Clothing Streams into City's Depots."

108. "Giant War Tasks of Airlines Told; Over 2½ Billion Miles Flown Overseas for Army, Navy Since Pearl Harbor," *New York Times*, April 8, 1945, 26.

109. C. L. Sulzberger, "Soviet Union Has Mapped Extensive Foreign Policy," *New York Times*, April 8, 1945, 5E.

110. David Anderson, "Starving Holland Soon to Get Help," *New York Times*, April 8, 1945, 5.

111. "1917 to 1945," *New York Times*, April 8, 1945, 8E.

112. "1917 to 1945."

113. "Slum: Is a Nationwide Slum-Clearance Boom in the Making?," *Indianapolis Star*, April 8, 1945, 41.

114. Modibo Coulibaly, Rodney D. Green, and David M. James, *Segregation in Federally Subsidized Low-Income Housing in the United States* (Westport, CT: Greenwood Publishing Group, 1998), 47.

115. Associated Press, "3d Army Overruns Reich 'Death Camp,'" *New York Times*, April 9, 1945, 5.

116. "3d Army Overruns Reich 'Death Camp.'"

117. "Wins Honor Medal for One-Man Drive," *New York Times*, April 9, 1945, 7.

118. Milton Bracker, "Nisei Troops Take Mountain in Italy; Japanese-American Infantry Returns from France—Foe Stiffens in East," *New York Times*, April 9, 1945, 8.

119. Bracker, "Nisei Troops Take Mountain in Italy."

120. George E. Jones, "Okinawans Seem to Like Our Rule," *New York Times*, April 9, 1945, 11.

121. *New York Times*, April 9, 1945, 11, advertisement.

122. *New York Times*, April 9, 1945, 11, advertisement.

123. *New York Times*, April 9, 1945, 11, advertisement.

124. Associated Press, "Carrier Blast Hit 649 on Rescue Ship," *New York Times*, April 9, 1945, 12.

125. Hanson W. Baldwin, "Okinawa's Fate Sealed; Sinking of Battleship Yamato Shows Japan's Fatal Air and Sea Weakness," *New York Times*, April 9, 1945, 12.

126. Harold Callender, "Parisians Throng to Sun-Bathed Gardens of Tuileries as Nation Emerges to New Life," *New York Times*, April 9, 1945, 13.

127. "Girl Scouts to Open Home Safety Check," *New York Times*, April 9, 1945, 16.

128. "Army Will Pay Way for 20,000 Brides," *New York Times*, April 10, 1945, 1.

129. Bruce Rae, "Fierce Battle Blazes in South on Okinawa; Marines Gain," *New York Times*, April 10, 1945, 1.

130. Associated Press, "A Marine Returns to Identify His Buddies on Iwo," *New York Times*, April 10, 1945, 5, photo caption.

131. *New York Times*, April 10, 1945, 8, advertisement.

132. "War Crimes Policy of Allies Rebuked," *New York Times*, April 10, 1945, 9.

133. Lansing Warren, "Delegates, Jurists Begin Parley Task," *New York Times*, April 10, 1945, 1, 9.

134. "Frenchman Tells of Prison Killings; Saw Poles and Jews Butchered by Germans Individually and in Thousands," *New York Times*, April 10, 1945, 10.

135. Associated Press, "Artillery Used on Prisoners," *New York Times*, April 10, 1945, 10.

136. Associated Press, "Two Field Marshals Accused," *New York Times*, April 10, 1945, 10.

137. "Jewish Art Cache Found in Germany," *New York Times*, April 10, 1945, 12.

138. William M. Blair, "1,500 Ex-Captives Home from Europe; Largest Unit of Liberated Men, Land at Boston—Tell Horrors of Nazi Camps," *New York Times*, April 10, 1945, 13.

139. Blair, "1,500 Ex-Captives Home from Europe."

140. Blair, "1,500 Ex-Captives Home from Europe."

141. Clifton Daniel, "Bevin Signals End of Truce in Britain; Greenwood Backs Labor's Aim to Break Tie on V-E Day—Bracken Hits Dissidents," *New York Times*, April 10, 1945, 13.

142. Daniel, "Bevin Signals End of Truce in Britain."

143. "Hitler's Last Failure," *New York Times*, April 10, 1945, 18.

144. "Competition in Air Urged by 17 Lines," *New York Times*, April 10, 1945, 20.

145. C. P. Trussell, "Senators Extend Lend-Lease Act; Reject Taft Curb," *New York Times*, April 11, 1945, 1.

146. United Press International, "Tokyo Denies Bid for Peace Is Near; Broadcasts Say Suzuki Will Follow Predecessors' Plans for Winning the War," *New York Times*, April 11, 1945, 3.

147. "Unofficial Observers Look for Jap Peace Bid," *Los Angeles Times*, April 11, 1945, 6.

148. Sidney Shalett, "Talk of Tokyo Bid Rife in Washington," *New York Times*, April 11, 1945, 4.

149. Drew Middleton, "Whole Line Moves; Americans By-Passing Brunswick—3d Army Is Enfolding Erfurt," *New York Times*, April 11, 1945, 1.

150. Middleton, "Whole Line Moves."

151. "Best of Reich Art Found in 2 Mines," *New York Times*, April 11, 1945, 8.

152. Raymond Daniel, "German Schools Wholly Nazified," *New York Times*, April 11, 1945, 10.

153. Associated Press, "GIs Seize 285 Ribbentrop Aides Cowering in Refuge Near Weimar," *New York Times*, April 11, 1945, 12.

154. United Press International, "Red Cross Girls Deliver 6 Nazi Captives at Camp," *New York Times*, April 11, 1945, 12.

155. United Press International, "Fliers Scout Berlin, Find Nothing Moving," *New York Times*, April 11, 1945, 13.

156. "Army 'Misconduct' Charged by Ward," *New York Times*, April 11, 1945, 17.

157. "To Divorce 2 Wives So He Can Keep 3d," *New York Times*, April 11, 1945, 25.

158. "Bottled Beer Shortage Is Developing Here; Retail Price Is Increased by 1 Cent a Pint," *New York Times*, April 14, 1945, 11.

159. "Hitler to Himmler!," *New York Times*, April 12, 1945, 22.

160. "Russians Belittle Western Success; Americans Accused of 'Soft' Attitude to Germans and Injustice to Deportees," *New York Times*, April 12, 1945, 3.

161. Virgil Pinkley, "Ruhr Area Aglow from Explosives; Every Brick in Cities Is Broken Twice—German Civilians Look Fat and Well-Fed," *New York Times*, April 12, 1945, 5.

162. Associated Press, "5,000,000 Reported Slain at Oswiecim; Hungarian Liberated by US Troops Says Jews Were Killed over 10 Months," *New York Times*, April 12, 1945, 6.

163. "Press of America Held World's Best," *New York Times*, April 12, 1945, 21.

164. "Press of America Held World's Best."

165. Associated Press, "Last Words: 'I Have a Terrific Headache,'" *New York Times*, April 13, 1945, 1.

166. "Last Words."

167. "Last Words."

168. Anthony Bergen, *Dead Presidents* (blog), Tumblr, January 7, 2014, https://deadpresidents.tumblr.com/post/72563792397/he-deserved-a-good-time-he-was-married-to.

169. Roger K. Miller, "All the President's Women," *Pittsburgh Post-Gazette*, May 18, 2008, 5E.

170. "Roosevelt Fond of His Home on Hudson, Haven of Rest, Family Life, Conferences," *New York Times*, April 13, 1945, 5.

171. Meyer Berger, "City Is Stunned by News of Death," *New York Times*, April 13, 1945, 10.

172. Berger, "City Is Stunned by News of Death."

173. Jim Bishop, *FDR's Last Year, April 1944–April 1945* (New York: William Morrow & Company, 1974), 598.

174. Bishop, *FDR's Last Year*, 599.

175. Albert J. Baime, *The Accidental President: Harry S. Truman and the Four Months That Changed the World* (Boston: Houghton Mifflin Harcourt, 2017), 29.

176. Associated Press, "White House Statement," *New York Times*, April 13, 1945, 3.

177. "Roosevelt Is Dead; Truman President," *New York Times*, April 13, 1945, 3.

178. "Roosevelt Is Dead; Truman President," 1, 8.

179. Arthur Krock, "End Comes Suddenly at Warm Springs," *New York Times*, April 13, 1945, 1, 3.

180. Krock, "End Comes Suddenly at Warm Springs."

181. Frederick R. Barkley, "Shock, Disbelief Echo in Congress," *New York Times*, April 13, 1945, 4.

182. "Churchill Will Honor Roosevelt Today; Commons Expected to Adjourn in Tribute," *New York Times*, April 13, 1945, 7.

183. "'Our Greatest Loss,' La Guardia Declares," *New York Times*, April 13, 1945, 3.

184. "De Gaulle Voices Sorrow," *New York Times*, April 13, 1945, 3.

185. "Pope Pius Recently Gave His Special Blessing to FD," *Boston Daily Globe*, April 13, 1945, 4.

186. "Pope Blessed President in Message of Week Ago," *New York Times*, April 13, 1945, 2.

187. "Mrs. Roosevelt Flies to Georgia; Was at Benefit When News Came," *New York Times*, April 13, 1945, 4.

188. Bishop, *FDR's Last Year*, 598.

189. Bishop, *FDR's Last Year*, 598.

190. Krock, "End Comes Suddenly at Warm Springs."

191. Will Hickox, "Marching to Victory: 'The President Is Dead,'" April 12, 1945, Truman Library Institute, https://www.trumanlibraryinstitute.org/wwii-75-marching-victory-7/.

192. Krock, "End Comes Suddenly at Warm Springs."

193. "Statement by the President After Taking the Oath of Office," April 12, 1945, Harry S. Truman Library and Museum, https://www.trumanlibrary.gov/library/public-papers/1/statement-president-after-taking-oath-office.

194. James B. Reston, "Security Parley Won't Be Delayed," *New York Times*, April 13, 1945, 1, 2.

195. Reston, "Security Parley Won't Be Delayed."

196. "Mrs. Roosevelt Flies to Georgia."

197. "Mrs. Roosevelt Flies to Georgia."

198. "Mrs. Roosevelt Flies to Georgia."

199. "Roosevelt Highlights," *Pittsburgh Press*, July 20, 1945, 9.

200. Jean Edward Smith, *FDR* (New York: Random House, 2008), 368.

201. "Acceptance Speech to the 1932 Democratic Convention," July 2, 1932, Franklin D. Roosevelt Presidential Library and Museum, https://www.fdrlibrary.org/dnc-curriculum-hub.

202. "Roosevelt Regime, from '33, Longest in Nation's History," *New York Times*, April 13, 1945, 7.

203. "Churchill Will Honor Roosevelt Today."

204. "Stalin Says F.D. 'Great Organizer' Against Enemy," *Boston Daily Globe,* April 13, 1945, 5.

205. "Radio Networks Cancel Commercial Programs," *New York Times,* April 13, 1945, 10.

206. "Policies Expanded by World Crises," *New York Times,* April 13, 1945, 8.

207. Mark Seidl, "The Lend-Lease Program, 1941–1945," Franklin D. Roosevelt Presidential Library and Museum, https://www.fdrlibrary.org/lend-lease.

208. "Talk of the Week," *Cincinnati Enquirer,* January 15, 1941, 8.

209. "Roosevelt Hits Lend-Lease Foes with Vigor," *Boston Daily Globe,* January 15, 1941, 1.

210. "Inaugural Address," January 20, 1941, Franklin D. Roosevelt Presidential Library and Museum, https://www.fdrlibrary.org/documents/356632 /390886/1941inauguraladdress.pdf/1ea00842-0ea7-4237-ab52-a96af4d6862f.

211. "An Almost Forgotten American Whose Record Has Been Revived," *Arizona Republic,* April 30, 1941, 36.

212. "Roosevelt Health Long Under Doubt," *New York Times,* April 13, 1945, 9.

213. Associated Press, "Nation Mourns Death," *News and Observer,* April 13, 1945, 1, 8.

214. Berger, "City Is Stunned by News of Death."

215. United Press International, "360 Die, 1,730 Injured in Bari Ship Blast," *New York Times,* April 13, 1945, 11.

216. Associated Press, "Himmler Bars Towns' Surrender; End Not Far Off, Goebbels Says," *New York Times,* April 13, 1945, 12.

217. Associated Press, "Surrender Policy Stands; Churchill Says 'Unconditional' May Be Applied 'Piecemeal,'" *New York Times,* April 13, 1945, 12.

218. "Himmler Bars Towns' Surrender."

219. Walter Kiernan, "One Man's Opinion," *Arizona Republic,* April 17, 1945, 12.

220. "Stimson Warns Reich Resistance Is Folly," *New York Times,* April 13, 1945, 12.

221. Associated Press, "300 Women Prisoners Rescued in Germany," *New York Times,* April 13, 1945, 12.

222. Drew Middleton, "US and Red Armies Drive to Meet; Americans Across the Elbe in Strength Race Toward Russians Who Have Opened Offensive from Oder," *New York Times,* April 13, 1945, 1, 12.

223. "Reich's Cruelty to US Captives Denounced by Stimson, Stettinius," *New York Times,* April 13, 1945, 13.

224. "Things for Children to Do," *New York Times,* April 13, 1945, 14.

225. "Miss Vaughan Wed to Fighter Pilot," *New York Times,* April 13, 1945, 14.

226. "Clean Out Attic Also," *New York Times,* April 13, 1945, 19.

227. "Shift of 1,000,000 to Palestine Set," *New York Times*, April 13, 1945, 19.

228. Frank Kluckhorn, "Crowds in Tears Watch Funeral Train Roll North," *New York Times*, April 14, 1945, 1, 4.

229. Kluckhorn, "Crowds in Tears."

230. Kluckhorn, "Crowds in Tears."

231. Associated Press, "Truman Does Not Plan to Attend Parleys; Will Follow Roosevelt's Foreign Policies," *New York Times*, April 14, 1945, 1.

232. Lewis Wood, "Turn to the Right Seen," *New York Times*, April 14, 1945, 1.

233. "Flood of Rumors Gives City Jitters," *New York Times*, April 14, 1945, 4.

234. "Flood of Rumors Gives City Jitters."

235. "Building Named for Him," *New York Times*, April 14, 1945, 4.

236. "Radio Today," *New York Times*, April 14, 1945, 4.

237. *New York Times*, April 14, 1945, 4, announcement.

238. Associated Press, "Mourn in Britain; A Solemn House of Commons Adjourns After Churchill Speaks Empire's Grief," *Kansas City Star*, April 13, 1945, 13.

239. "Mourn in Britain."

240. "Churchill Tribute Heard by Commons; Adjourns After Prime Minister in Faltering Voice Lauds Roosevelt's Career," *New York Times*, April 14, 1945, 5.

241. Gene Currivan, "Generals and GIs Mourn Late Chief; Men on Fronts, Where Death Is Commonplace, Shocked by Unexpected Passing," *New York Times*, April 14, 1945, 6.

242. "Latin-Americans Mourn Roosevelt; Crowds Pour into American Embassy in Rio de Janeiro to Express Condolences," *New York Times*, April 14, 1945, 6.

243. Franklin Delano Roosevelt, "Franklin D. Roosevelt's Last Message to the American People," April 12, 1945, Library of Congress, https://www.loc.gov/item/rbpe.24204300/.

244. Roosevelt, "Last Message."

245. Roosevelt, "Last Message."

246. United Press International, "Dewey Pledges Full Support to New Chief," *Press and Sun-Bulletin*, April 13, 1945, 28.

247. Drew Middleton, "Patton Lashes Out; Fourth Armored Division Reaches Point Only 89 Miles from Red Army," *New York Times*, April 14, 1945, 1, 9.

248. *New York Times*, April 14, 1945, 10, advertisement.

249. Associated Press, "War Prisoners Returning; 2,500 US Soldiers Are Paid—Easterners Home Sunday," *New York Times*, April 14, 1945, 17.

250. "Churches to Watch Peace Conference; Addresses on Problems Up in San Francisco Parley to Be Given at Riverside," *New York Times*, April 14, 1945, 18.

251. "Textbook Revision Urged to Aid Unity," *New York Times*, April 14, 1945, 18.

252. "Textbook Revision Urged."

253. "Factory to Continue Nursery After War," *New York Times*, April 14, 1945, 19.

254. Dana Adams Schmidt, "3,040 French Dead Found in Nazi Camp; Minister Says Deportees Were Shot—US Rescue Column Is Lost in Ambush," *New York Times*, April 14, 1945, 28.

255. John Drebinger, "Baseball Cancels Activities Today," *New York Times*, April 14, 1945, 20.

256. Bess Furman, "Mrs. Roosevelt Retains Her Calm," *New York Times*, April 15, 1945, 3.

257. "Rites at Capital; War Leader's Fearless Faith Called by Bishop Dun a Bequest to All," *New York Times*, April 15, 1945, 1, 3.

258. "Rites at Capital."

259. "Germans Forced to Bury Victims," *New York Times*, April 15, 1945, 9.

260. Associated Press, "Truman Calls for Unity to End War," *Los Angeles Times*, April 17, 1945, 1, 9.

261. *Life*, April 23, 1945, 96, advertisements.

262. "Illegitimate Nazi 'Super Babies' Live in German Chateau," *Life*, August 13, 1945, 37.

263. *Life*, April 9, 1945, 47, advertisement.

264. Daniel T. Brigham, "Last Stand in East Ordered by Hitler," *New York Times*, April 17, 1945, 6.

265. Anthony Beevor, *The Fall of Berlin, 1945* (New York: Viking Publishing, 2002), 224.

266. Beevor, *Fall of Berlin*, 188.

267. Beevor, *Fall of Berlin*, 233.

268. Associated Press, "Formal Surrender by Nazis Unlikely, Eisenhower Says," *Washington Post*, April 17, 1945, 1.

269. "Yanks Spearhead Reaches Berlin, Nazis Say," *Los Angeles Times*, April 16, 1945, 2.

270. George Axelsson, "Hitler's Death at Hands of His Own Aides Seen," *Los Angeles Times*, April 15, 1945, 7.

271. Harry S. Truman, "Address Before a Joint Session of the Congress," April 16, 1945, Harry S. Truman Library and Museum, https://www.trumanlibrary.gov/library/public-papers/2/address-joint-session-congress.

272. "Tri-State Area Hunts Seven Nazi Fugitives," *Washington Post*, April 17, 1945, 3.

273. "Hatching Eggs May Be Sent Abroad by Air," *Washington Post*, April 16, 1945, 3.

274. "Hingham Pilot Finds No Planes in Fight over Japan," *Boston Daily Globe*, April 17, 1945, 17.

275. "Fanatic Japs Lose Air Fight at Okinawa," *Los Angeles Times*, April 17, 1945, 1.

276. "Fire Raid Routs 'Countless' Japs," *Los Angeles Times*, April 17, 1945, 4.

277. "Victory over Japan Essential," *London Times*, April 17, 1945, 2.

278. "Army Teaches Wives How to Assist Mates," *Miami Herald*, April 15, 1945, 7A.

279. John Rogers, "Stock Upswing Reflects Faith in New Leader," *New York Daily News*, April 17, 1945, 19C.

280. "NE Must Provide Jobs for Vets, Kennedy Says," *Boston Daily Globe*, April 18, 1945, 1.

281. Flora Bel Muir, "Chaplin's the Papa, Jury Finds," *New York Daily News*, April 18, 1945, 4C.

282. "The Three Bares," *Washington Post*, April 17, 1945, 7, cartoon.

283. Laurie Johnson, "A Boy . . . and a Guitar . . . Her Hawaii Calls!," *Honolulu Advertiser*, April 18, 1945, 1.

284. Johnson, "A Boy . . . and a Guitar."

285. "Truman Orders Louisiana Refinery Seized in Dispute," *Honolulu Advertiser*, April 18, 1945, 1.

286. *Rocky Shimpo*, April 16, 1945, 2, advertisement.

287. "100 Dealers Buy Up Surplus Farm Equipment Here," *Topaz Times*, April 17, 1945, 1.

288. "Seven Get Active Duty Calls May 1," *Topaz Times*, April 17, 1945, 1.

289. Eveline Dienes, "Secret Underground Setup in England Is Now Dissolved," *Boston Daily Globe*, April 16, 1945, 6.

290. "Six Defendants Pleaded Guilty in Court Today," *Key West Citizen*, April 17, 1945, 1.

291. Letter to the editor, *Key West Citizen*, April 16, 1945, 2.

292. *Charlotte News*, April 17, 1945, 7A, advertisement.

293. *Charlotte News*, April 17, 1945, 2B, advertisement.

294. "Thief Takes Soldier's Photo While Mother Visits Grave," *Los Angeles Times*, April 17, 1945, II-1.

295. Wes Gallagher, "German Death Factory Yields Amazing Gadgets," *Los Angeles Times*, April 18, 1945, 5.

296. "'Orgy of Killing' in Manila Related," *Los Angeles Times*, April 18, 1945, 7.

297. "Both Major Leagues Begin Games Today," *Key West Citizen*, April 17, 1945, 1.

298. *Life*, April 16, 1945, 2, advertisement.

299. "Patton Crashes Deeper Inside Czechoslovakia," *Los Angeles Times*, April 19, 1945, 1; *George S. Patton Papers: Diaries, 1910 to 1945*, April 18, 1945, Library of Congress, https://www.loc.gov/collections/george-s-patton-diaries/about-this-collection/.

300. Gault MacGowan, "Germans Regard Gen Patton as American Rommel," *Boston Daily Globe*, April 20, 1945, II-5.

301. "Berlin Strengthens Barricades," *Salt Lake Tribune*, April 19, 1945, 2.

302. "Reds Throw Secret Weapons at Berlin," *Los Angeles Times*, April 19, 1945, 2.

303. Ludwig Popper, "Berlin Walled In with Ring of New Defenses," *Honolulu Advertiser*, April 19, 1945, 1.

304. Associated Press, "Okinawa Casualties 7895; Marines Reach North Coast," *Boston Daily Globe*, April 19, 1945, 1.

305. "Pittsburgh Flier Freed in Germany," *Pittsburgh Post-Gazette*, April 19, 1945, 1.

306. "600,000 in US Now Suffering Cancer Inroads," *Atlanta Constitution*, April 19, 1945, 9.

307. "The Negro Soldier Betrayed," *Crisis*, April 1945, 97.

308. "New York Bars Economic Jim Crow," *Crisis*, April 1945, 101.

309. "Wanted: Sea Legs and Guts to Avoid Ship Delays," *Crisis*, April 1945, 114, advertisement.

310. Associated Press, "Maryland Soldier Says Nazi Officer 'Eagerly' Gave Up," *Washington Post*, April 19, 1945, 3.

311. "Memorandum," April 19, 1945, Harry S. Truman Library and Museum, https://www.trumanlibrary.gov.

312. "Memorandum," Harry S. Truman Library and Museum.

313. Cecile Davis, "Women Bankers Proud of Sex," *Atlanta Constitution*, April 21, 1945, 3.

314. Howard P. Bailey, "War Review," *Evening Star*, April 22, 1945, 1C.

315. "50th Birthday of Hitler Marked by Review," *Evening Star*, April 20, 1939, 1.

316. Richard J. Evans, *The Third Reich at War* (New York: Penguin, 2008), 722.

317. "Moviegoers Made to View Horror Films," *Pittsburgh Post-Gazette*, April 21, 1945, 1.

318. Harold Kaese, "Cronin Suffers Broken Ankle," *Boston Daily Globe*, April 20, 1945, 1.

319. Howard P. Bailey, "War Review," *Evening Star*, April 22, 1945, 1C.

320. "Kill a Jap Officer for Each Yank Murdered, Says Halsey," *New York Daily News*, April 20, 1945, 21B.

321. "Hitler Admits Defeat of His Armies in West," *Los Angeles Times*, April 22, 1945, 1.

322. "Letter from Bernard Mauer to Arnold Mauer," Mauer Archives (Private), April 20, 1945.

323. "Letter from Bernard Mauer to Marie and Frederick Mauer," Mauer Archives (Private), April 23, 1945.

324. *Popular Photography*, April 1945, 12, advertisement.

325. *Life*, April 30, 1945, 4, 7, advertisements.

326. "War Beats Pitch for Barton," *Billboard*, April 21, 1945, 19.

327. Stephen E. Ambrose, *Band of Brothers: E Company, 506th Regiment, 101st Airborne from Normandy to Hitler's Eagle Nest* (New York: Simon & Schuster, 2001), 259–62.

328. "Nazi Rocket Plane 'Burns' Sky at 600 MPH," *Popular Mechanics*, April 1945, 6.

329. *Flying*, April 1945, 132, advertisement.

330. *Popular Photography*, April 1945, 15, 17, 55, advertisements.

331. Thomas E. Henry, "American Woman Hid in Typhus Hospital to Dodge 'Death March,'" *Evening Star*, April 22, 1945, 4A.

332. "President Truman's First Week," *Life*, April 30, 1945, 19.

333. "Hitler, Goebbels Killed Swiss Report Declares; Himmler May Surrender," *Honolulu Advertiser*, Extra, April 28, 1945, 1.

334. "Himmler Slays Hitler—Report," *Atlanta Constitution*, April 29, 1945, 12A.

335. "NAZIS SURRENDER," *San Francisco Examiner*, April 29, 1945, 1.

336. United Press International, "Stettinius Denies Link to Rumors," *Philadelphia Inquirer*, April 29, 1945, 2.

337. "Rumor Is Spiked as Crowds Sing at White House," *Miami Herald*, April 29, 1945, 1.

338. Paul Jones, "Night Spots, Restaurants Close on False Peace Story," *Atlanta Constitution*, April 29, 1945, 12A.

339. Associated Press, "Title Proposed for Roosevelt," *Arizona Daily Star*, April 17, 1945, 7.

340. Sigrid Arne, "Here Are Complete Details of World Security Organization," *San Francisco Examiner*, April 22, 1945, 7.

341. Arne, "Complete Details of World Security Organization."

342. "Pope Urges Fair and Just World Peace Organization," *Boston Evening Globe*, April 18, 1945, 3.

343. John M. Hightower, "Russian Determination to Wield Decisive, Perhaps Dominant Influence in Creation of Peace Machinery Threatens Conference," *Crowley Post-Signal*, April 27, 1945, 1.

344. C. L. Sulzberger, "Democracy for Europe Criticised by Russian," *Los Angeles Times*, April 22, 1945, 2.

345. *San Francisco Examiner*, April 22, 1945, 16, advertisement.

346. "'Alcoholics' to Tell Cures," *San Francisco Examiner*, April 22, 1945, 16.

347. "Baby Killed Between Elevator and Shaft," *Des Moines Tribune*, April 28, 1945, 7.

348. F. M. Leonard, "Youthful War Worker Dies in Auto Accident," *Michigan Chronicle*, April 28, 1945, 1.

349. "Girl's Skeleton Is Found Along Bank of River," *Pittsburgh Post-Gazette*, April 23, 1945, 1.

350. "Hitler Chalet Is Erased by 6-Ton Bomb," *Washington Post*, April 26, 1945, 1.

351. *Life*, April 30, 1945, 33, advertisement.

352. *Independent Record*, April 8, 1945, 12, advertisement.

353. Milton Bracker, "Mussolini Killed; Slain by Partisans," *New York Times*, April 30, 1945, 1.

354. James E. Roper, "Cries of No! No! As Partisan Shoot Him, Girl Friend," *Washington Post*, April 30, 1945, 1.

355. Bracker, "Mussolini Killed."

356. "Mussolini: Autocrat of Italy, Rise and Collapse of Fascism," *London Times*, April 30, 1945, 3.

357. Harry C. Butcher, *My Three Years with Eisenhower: The Personal Diary of Captain Harry C. Butcher, USNR, Naval Aide to General Eisenhower, 1942–1945* (Kingsport, TN: Kingsport Press, 1946), 819.

358. "Camp Blast Kills Four," *Ft. Worth Star Telegram*, April 29, 1945, 1.

359. "Chinese Troop Kills 1,200 Japs," *Tucson Daily Citizen*, April 28, 1945, 5.

360. W. H. Shippen Jr., "Filipino Girl, 16, Who Killed at Least 20 Japs, Now Finds Life Too Quiet in Manila Area," *Evening Star*, April 28, 1945, 1.

361. Frank Tremaine, "2,813 Jap Planes 30-Day Bag," *New York Daily News*, April 19, 1945, 12B.

362. "Heartburn," *Evening Star*, April 10, 1945, 293.

363. "Dachau Prison Camp Taken, 32,000 Set Free by Yanks," *Baltimore Sun*, April 30, 1945, 2.

364. Stephen E. Ambrose, *Citizen Soldiers: The U.S. Army from the Normandy Beaches to the Bulge to the Surrender of Germany, June 7, 1944–May 7, 1945* (New York: Simon & Schuster, 1997), 464.

365. "Dachau Prison Camp Taken."

366. Howard Cowan, "Notorious Nazi Prison Camp Is Liberated, 32,000 Are Freed," *Evening Times*, April 30, 1945, 1.

367. Ian Buruma, *Year Zero: A History of 1945* (London: Penguin, 2013), 76.

368. Ambrose, *Citizen Soldiers*, 463.

369. United Press International, "Today's Vulgarity Blamed on Women," *Citizen News*, April 30, 1945, 1.

370. Iris Carpenter, "Hitler Reported Married: Big Wedding to Mysterious Beauty 'Olga,' Three Weeks Ago," *Boston Daily Globe*, April 21, 1945, 1.

371. Trudi McCullough, "Heroic Iwo Jima Flag Crew Typifies US Melting Pot," *San Francisco Examiner*, April 22, 1945, 1.

372. "Police Give $2,000 Find to Driver," *San Francisco Examiner*, April 22, 1945, 4.

373. International News Service, "Reds in Berlin," *Detroit Evening Times*, April 22, 1945, 1.

374. "Reich Ripped to Shreds," *San Francisco Examiner*, April 22, 1945, 1.

375. C. L. Sulzberger, "Russians Bring Fire and Death to Berlin in Wild Battle That Shatters Nazi Dream," *Honolulu Advertiser*, April 23, 1945, 1, 6.

376. "Flags of Truce Reported Flying in Blazing City," *Pittsburgh Post-Gazette*, April 23, 1945, 1.

377. "America Must Not Forget—Again!," *Philadelphia Inquirer*, April 24, 1945, 14.

378. "America Must Not Forget—Again!"

379. "America Must Not Forget—Again!"

380. Joseph Pulitzer, "Descriptions of Atrocities Found to Understate Facts," *St. Louis Post-Dispatch*, April 29, 1945, 1A.

381. Pulitzer, "Descriptions of Atrocities Found to Understate Facts."

382. John R. Hearst, "Concentration Camp Visit Horrifies US Senators," *San Francisco Examiner*, April 29, 1945, 1.

383. "Rich's Atlanta," *Atlanta Constitution*, April 23, 1945, 11.

384. "11,738 Japs Killed in One Okinawa Area," *Pittsburgh Post-Gazette*, April 23, 1945, 2.

385. Frank Tremaine, "Raise Flag on Ie Peak," *Honolulu Advertiser*, April 22, 1945, 1.

386. "Yanks Close in on Last Two Jap Philippine Strongholds," *San Francisco Examiner*, April 22, 1945, 3.

387. "Yanks Advance Mile an Hour Toward Davao," *Honolulu Advertiser*, April 20, 1945, 1.

388. "Okinawa Had Old Yankee Cemetery," *San Francisco Examiner*, April 22, 1945, 1.

389. Laurie Johnston, "All Jap Planes Suicide Craft, Says Sherrod Why?," *Honolulu Advertiser*, April 20, 1945, 1.

390. "Truman Attends Service with War Wounded," *Pittsburgh Post-Gazette*, April 23, 1945, 8.

391. Alexander George, "Three Ascending Vice Presidents Have Had Stormy Political Going," *Atlanta Constitution*, April 22, 1945, 8A.

392. "First Women Visit Home of Trappists," *Atlanta Constitution*, April 22, 1945, 9A.

393. "Clothes Aid Response Is Pleasing," *Pittsburgh Post-Gazette*, April 23, 1945, 11.

394. "Boston Spurred to More Effort in Clothing Drive," *Boston Daily Globe*, April 20, 1945, 7.

395. "United Air Seeks to Extend Service," *Pittsburgh Post-Gazette*, April 23, 1945, 5.

396. Ed Balinger, "Disgusted Fans Hurl Cushions," *Pittsburgh Post-Gazette*, April 23, 1945, 14.

397. Frederick C. Othman, "'Hot' Money (70 Million of It) Burned in Hawaii After Blitz," *Honolulu Advertiser*, April 24, 1945, 1.

398. "Sailor Gets Year for Bigamy," *Washington Post*, April 26, 1945, 3.

399. Eddy Gilmore, "Thirst for Revenge Spurs Berlin Attack," *Washington Post*, April 27, 1945, 2.

400. "Fake Hitler in Berlin?," *Atlanta Constitution*, April 27, 1945, 1.

401. Hudson Phillips, "Reich Held Knocked Out for at Least 30 Years," *San Francisco Examiner*, April 29, 1945, 9.

402. "Half of Jap Garrison in Okinawa Is Knocked Out," *Henderson Daily Dispatch*, May 2, 1945, 1.

403. W. H. Lawrence, "Enemy Suicide Pilot Dives Plane on US Hospital Ship off Okinawa," *New York Times*, April 30, 1945, 1.

404. "Hospital Ship Hit by Plane; 63 Casualties," *Honolulu Advertiser*, April 30, 1945, 1.

405. Associated Press, "B-29s Blast Jap Suicide Bases After Hospital Ship Attack," *Evening Times*, April 30, 1945.

406. Eugene B. Sledge, *With the Old Breed at Peleliu and Okinawa* (Oxford: Oxford University Press, 1990), 202.

407. George Gallup, "US Public Favors Punishing Minor Nazis for War Crimes," *Washington Post*, April 27, 1945, 7.

408. "New Carrier Bears Name of Roosevelt," *Honolulu Advertiser*, April 30, 1945, 1.

409. *Pittsburgh Post-Gazette*, April 30, 1945, 9, advertisement.

410. *Boston Daily Globe*, April 30, 1945, 2, advertisement.

411. *Pittsburgh Post-Gazette*, April 23, 1945, 12, advertisement.

412. "Ration Stamps Stolen; Boys Claim Alibi," *Boston Daily Globe*, April 30, 1945, 11.

413. *Volksblatt*, May 3, 1945, 1.

414. Beevor, *Fall of Berlin*, 381.

Epilogue

1. "Hitler Dies in Berlin," *Nome Nugget*, May 2, 1945, 1.

2. Associated Press, "Hitler Is Dead, Say Nazis," *New York Times*, May 1, 1945, 1.

3. "Russia Skeptical of Hitler Report," *Baltimore Sun*, May 2, 1945, 1.

4. "Brain Stroke Killed Hitler, Eisenhower's Evidence Indicates," *Pittsburgh Press*, May 2, 1945, 1.

5. Harry C. Butcher, *My Three Years with Eisenhower: The Personal Diary of Captain Harry C. Butcher, USNR, Naval Aide to General Eisenhower, 1942–1945* (Kingsport, TN: Kingsport Press, 1946), 819.

6. Meyer Berger, "City Takes Report of Death in Stride," *New York Times*, May 2, 1945, 9.

7. Edward W. Beattie, "Germans Believe Hitler Died in 1944 Bomb Plot," *Miami Herald*, May 6, 1945, 4.

8. Berger, "City Takes Report of Death in Stride."

9. Berger, "City Takes Report of Death in Stride."

10. United Press International, "GI Captures German Who Called Him 'Sir,'" *Falls City Journal*, March 20, 1945, 2.

11. "Reich's Future Up to Allies, Speer Says," *Washington Post*, May 4, 1945.

12. "Reich's Future Up to Allies."

13. "Reich's Future Up to Allies."

14. Stephen E. Ambrose, *Band of Brothers: E Company, 506th Regiment, 101st Airborne from Normandy to Hitler's Eagle Nest* (New York: Simon & Schuster, 2001), 266–70.

15. Ambrose, *Band of Brothers*.

16. Ambrose, *Band of Brothers*.

17. Associated Press, "Reich's Chief of Staff Begs Mercy for Nation, Stresses Its Suffering," *Miami Daily News*, May 8, 1945, 1.

18. "Reich's Chief of Staff Begs Mercy for Nation."

19. Margaret Truman, *Harry S. Truman* (New York: William Morrow and Company, 1973), 241.

20. "Truman Asks No V-E Celebration but Re-Dedication to Task Ahead," *New York Times*, May 2, 1945, 9.

21. "Wild Crowds Greet News in City While Others Pray," *New York Times*, May 8, 1945, 1.

22. "GIs on Battlefront Solemn, Masses Wild over V-E News," *Dallas Morning News*, May 8, 1945, 1.

23. "V-E Day Will Upset Miami's Drink Habits," *Miami Herald*, May 6, 1945, 1.

24. "Honolulu Observes V-E with Prayer, Hard Work, Programs," *Honolulu Advertiser*, May 9, 1945, 1.

25. "Sunday Set as Day of Thankful Prayer," *Washington Post*, May 9, 1945, 1.

26. James E. Chinn, "Terrible Days Face Japan, Truman Says," *Washington Post*, May 9, 1945, 1.

27. Stephen E. Ambrose, *Citizen Soldiers: The U.S. Army from the Normandy Beaches to the Bulge to the Surrender of Germany, June 7, 1944–May 7, 1945* (New York: Simon & Schuster, 1997), 464.

28. Martin Blumenson, *The Patton Papers: 1940–1945* (Boston: Houghton, Mifflin Company, 1974), 699.

29. "Americans Drive on Last Pocket in Czechoslovakia," *Miami Herald*, May 6, 1945, 5.

30. *George S. Patton Papers: Diaries, 1910 to 1945*, May 8, 1945, Library of Congress, https://www.loc.gov/collections/george-s-patton-diaries/about-this-collection/.

31. Eugene B. Sledge, *With the Old Breed at Peleliu and Okinawa* (Oxford: Oxford University Press, 1990), 223.

32. Letter from Jonathan Daniels to John S. Kelly, May 10, 1945, Franklin D. Roosevelt Presidential Library and Museum.

33. *George S. Patton Papers: Diaries, 1910 to 1945*, May 14, 1945, 712.

34. *George S. Patton Papers: Diaries, 1910 to 1945*, May 14, 1945.

35. "1,200 Warships Will Ring Nip Home Islands," *Honolulu Advertiser*, May 9, 1945, 1.

36. "6th Division Marines Fighting in Suburbs of Okinawa's Capital," *Honolulu Advertiser*, May 12, 1945, 1.

37. United Press International, "Big Blow Aimed at Factories," *Arizona Republic*, May 14, 1945, 1.

38. "FDR Mourning Period to End," *Courier*, May 14, 1945, 1.

39. United Press International, "Ickes Ired by Attacks on Returned Japs," *Hanford Morning Journal*, May 15, 1945, 1.

40. United Press International, "Sub's V-Bomb Missed New York," *Miami Herald*, May 15, 1945, 1.

41. Associated Press, "Gestapo Chief Takes Poison," *Miami Daily News*, May 24, 1945, 4, 5.

42. "550 B-29s Drop 700,000 Fiery Missiles on City," *Honolulu Advertiser*, May 24, 1945, 1.

43. "Tokyo Laid Waste!," *Honolulu Advertiser*, May 26, 1945, 1.

44. "Mortality Rate of Wounded on Okinawa Low," *Honolulu Advertiser*, May 27, 1945, 1, 2.

45. "Jap Navy Shakeup Aimed at All-Out Suicide Strategy—Tokyo," *Honolulu Advertiser*, May 29, 1945, 3.

46. "Statements by Big 4 Powers on Control of Germany," *Philadelphia Inquirer*, June 6, 1945, 1.

47. "4-Power Military Rulers Take Over Reich, Plan to Sever Conquests, Fix Control Zones," *Washington Post*, June 6, 1945, 1.

48. *Cleveland Plain Dealer*, June 4, 1945, advertisement.

49. Associated Press, "2 Ships Sunk by Kamikazes," *Baltimore Sun*, June 9, 1945, 2.

50. *Flying*, June 1945, 3, advertisement.

51. *Life*, June 11, 1945, 103, advertisement.

52. *Beatrice Times*, June 14, 1945, 6, advertisement.

53. Associated Press, "Jap Describes Hara-Kiri Rites of Commanders," *St. Louis Post-Dispatch*, June 27, 1945, 1.

54. William F. Tyree, "Japanese Death Toll Heavy on Okinawan Island," *Honolulu Advertiser*, June 21, 1945, 1.

55. "Japs' Losses in Defending Island Exceed 90,000," *Evening Star*, June 21, 1945, 1.

56. "US Victory on Okinawa Cost 46,319 Casualties," *Washington Post*, June 28, 1945, 1.

57. "Japs Surrender," *Nome Nugget*, June 22, 1945, 1.

58. "Navy Desires US Fleet to Top the World," *Honolulu Advertiser*, June 21, 1945.

59. *Charter of the United Nations and Statute of the International Court of Justice* (San Francisco, 1945), Preamble, https://www.un.org/en/about-us/un-charter/preamble. Copyright United Nations. Used with permission.

60. Associated Press, "Peace Charter Voted, Truman to Talk Today," *Daily Oklahoman*, June 26, 1945, 1.

61. "Truman Proposes Republic of World as War Antidote," *Honolulu Advertiser*, June 29, 1945, 1.

62. "MacArthur's July 5, 1945, Communique 'The entire Philippine Islands are now liberated . . . ,'" July 4, 2000, National WWII Museum, https://www

.nationalww2museum.org/war/articles/macarthur-philippine-islands-liberated-1945.

63. "Blind Man Robs Deaf Man," *Honolulu Advertiser,* July 1, 1945, 1.

64. Simon Sebag Montefiore, *Stalin: The Court of the Red Tsar* (New York: Alfred A. Knopf, 2003), 498.

65. Truman, *Harry S. Truman,* 267.

66. William M. Rigdon, *Log of President Harry S. Truman's Trip to the Berlin Conference,* 18–19, Harry S. Truman Library and Museum, www.TrumanLibrary.gov.

67. Kai Bird and Martin J. Sherwin, *American Prometheus: The Triumph and Tragedy of J. Robert Oppenheimer* (New York: Random House, 2005), 307–8.

68. Truman, *Harry S. Truman,* 497.

69. Truman, *Harry S. Truman,* 264.

70. Montefiore, *Stalin,* 498.

71. Truman, *Harry S. Truman,* 271.

72. Truman, *Harry S. Truman,* 280.

73. Truman, *Harry S. Truman,* 279–80.

74. Montefiore, *Stalin,* 490.

75. Truman, *Harry S. Truman,* 277–78.

76. Rigdon, *Truman's Trip to the Berlin Conference,* 38.

77. Truman, *Harry S. Truman,* 278.

78. Truman, *Harry S. Truman,* 278–79.

79. Truman, *Harry S. Truman,* 279–79.

80. "Text on Big 3 Report on Berlin Parlay," *Washington Post,* August 3, 1945, 2.

81. "US Invasion Fleet Is Massing, Japs Say," *Washington Post,* August 4, 1945, 1.

82. Truman, *Harry S. Truman,* 282.

83. Truman, *Harry S. Truman,* 282.

84. Bird and Sherwin, *American Prometheus,* 315–17.

85. "Atomic Bomb Packs Punch of 2000 B-29s," *Washington Post,* August 7, 1945, 1.

86. International News Service, "150,000 Japs Die as Atom Bomb Turns City to Dust," *Mansfield News-Journal,* August 8, 1945, 1, 3.

87. "What's an Atom? Here's the Description from Dictionary," *Washington Post,* August 7, 1945, 1.

88. Howard W. Blakeslee, "Power of Atom Likened to Sun's," *New York Times,* August 7, 1945, 5.

89. Blakeslee, "Power of Atom Likened to Sun's."

90. "Enemy Calls Use of Atomic Bomb Violation of International Law," *Evening Star,* August 8, 1945, 1.

91. "Nagasaki Smashed," *Detroit Evening Times*, August 9, 1945, 1.

92. Associated Press, "First Atomic Bomb Declared Outmoded by Deadlier New One," *Evening Star*, August 12, 1945, 5.

93. Associated Press, "Nagasaki Atom Bombing Seen by Fliers 250 Miles Away," *Daily Times*, August 10, 1945, 1.

94. "Atomic Bomb Declared Outmoded."

95. Associated Press, "Text of Japan's Message Concerning Surrender," *Wilkes-Barre Times Leader, The Evening News*, August 10, 1945, 1.

96. "Celebrate Ending of Japanese War," *Key West Citizen*, August 10, 1945, 1.

97. Edward T. Folliard, "Japs Quit Unconditionally," *Washington Post*, August 15, 1945, 1.

98. *George S. Patton Papers: Diaries, 1910 to 1945*, August 10, 1945.

99. George Connery, "Act to Speed Discharges During Next 18 Months," *Washington Post*, August 16, 1945, 1.

100. "Victory Celebrations," *Life*, August 27, 1945, 21–27.

101. "Victory Celebrations."

102. "Victory Celebrations."

103. Associated Press, "Last Will and Testament," *Globe-Gazette*, December 31, 1945, 12.

BIBLIOGRAPHY

BOOKS

Acheson, Dean. *Present at the Creation: My Years in the State Department*. New York: W. W. Norton & Company, 1969.

Adleman, Robert H., and George Walton. *The Devil's Brigade*. Philadelphia: Chilton Company, 1966.

Ambrose, Stephen E. *Band of Brothers: E Company, 506th Regiment, 101st Airborne from Normandy to Hitler's Eagle Nest*. New York: Simon & Schuster, 2001.

———. *Citizen Soldiers: The U.S. Army from the Normandy Beaches to the Bulge to the Surrender of Germany, June 7, 1944–May 7, 1945*. New York: Simon & Schuster, 1997.

Ambrose, Stephen E., and Günter Bischof, eds. *Eisenhower: A Centenary Assessment*. Baton Rouge: Louisiana State University Press, 1995.

Andrew, Christopher, and Vasili Mitrokhin. *The Sword and the Shield: The Mitrokhin Archive and the Secret History of the KGB*. New York: Basic Books, 1999.

Applebaum, Anne. *Iron Curtain: The Crushing of Eastern Europe, 1944–1956*. New York: Doubleday, 2012.

Arthur, Max. *Churchill: The Life; An Authorized Pictorial Biography*. Ontario: Firefly Books, 2015.

Atkinson, Rick. *The Day of Battle: The War in Sicily and Italy, 1943–1944*. New York: Henry Holt and Company, 2007.

———. *The Guns at Last Light: The War in Western Europe, 1944–1945*. New York: Henry Holt and Company, 2013.

Ayer, Frederick, Jr. *Before the Colors Fade: A Portrait of a Solider; George S. Patton, Jr.* Boston: Houghton Mifflin Company, 1964.

Baime, Albert J. *The Accidental President: Harry S. Truman and the Four Months That Changed the World.* Boston: Houghton Mifflin Harcourt, 2017.

Beevor, Anthony. *The Second World War.* New York: Little, Brown and Company, 2012.

———. *The Fall of Berlin, 1945.* New York: Viking Publishing, 2002.

Berry, Henry. *Semper Fi, Mac: Living Memories of the US Marines in World War II.* New York: Arbor House, 1982.

Bird, Kai, and Martin J. Sherwin. *American Prometheus: The Triumph and Tragedy of J. Robert Oppenheimer.* New York: Random House, 2005.

Bishop, Jim. *FDR's Last Year, April 1944–April 1945.* New York: William Morrow & Company, 1974.

Black, Conrad. *Franklin Delano Roosevelt: Champion of Freedom.* New York: Public Affairs, 2003.

Blumenson, Martin. *Patton: The Man Behind the Legend, 1885–1945.* New York: William Morrow and Company, 1985.

———, *The Patton Papers: 1940–1945.* Boston: Houghton Mifflin Company, 1974.

Bourke-White, Margaret. *They Called It Purple Heart Valley.* New York: Simon & Schuster, 1944.

Brinkley, David. *Washington Goes to War.* New York: Alfred A. Knopf, 1988.

Brough, James, and Elliott Roosevelt. *Roosevelts of the White House: A Rendezvous with Destiny.* New York: G. P. Putnam's Sons, 1988.

Bruun, Erik, and Jay Crosby, eds. *Our Nation's Archive: The History of the United States in Documents.* New York: Tess Press, 2009.

Burgin, R. V. *Islands of the Damned: A Marine at War in the Pacific.* New York: New American Library, 2010.

Burkett, Christopher. *50 Core American Documents: Required Reading for Students, Teachers, and Citizens.* Ashland, OH: Ashbrook Press, 2015.

Buruma, Ian. *Year Zero: A History of 1945.* London: Penguin, 2013.

Butcher, Harry C. *My Three Years with Eisenhower: The Personal Diary of Captain Harry C. Butcher, USNR, Naval Aide to General Eisenhower, 1942 to 1945.* Kingsport, TN: Kingsport Press, 1946.

Butler, Susan. *My Dear Mr. Stalin: The Complete Correspondence of Franklin D. Roosevelt and Joseph V. Stalin.* New Haven, CT: Yale University Press, 2005.

Cant, Gilbert. *The Great Pacific Victory from the Solomons to Tokyo*. New York: John Day Company, 1946.

Carmichael, Thomas N. *The Ninety Days*. Chicago: Bernard Geis Associates, 1971.

Chekhov, Anton. *The Exclamation Mark*. 1886; London: Hesperus Press, 2008.

Churchill, Winston. *Blood, Sweat, and Tears*. New York: G. P. Putnam's Sons, 1941.

———. *The Second World War*. Vol. I, *The Gathering Storm*. Boston: Houghton Mifflin Company, 1948.

———. *The Second World War*. Vol. II, *Their Finest Hour*. Boston: Houghton Mifflin Company, 1949.

———. *The Second World War*. Vol. V, *Closing the Ring*. Boston: Houghton Mifflin Company, 1951.

———. *The Second World War: The Grand Alliance*. Vol. III. Boston: Houghton Mifflin Company, 1950.

———. *The Second World War: The Hinge of Fate*. Vol. IV. Boston: Houghton Mifflin Company, 1950.

———. *The Second World War: Triumph and Tragedy*. Vol. VI. Boston: Houghton Mifflin Company, 1953.

Clark, Alan. *Barbarossa: The Russian-German Conflict, 1941–45*. New York: William Morrow and Company, 1965.

Costello, John. *The Pacific War: 1941–1945*. New York: Harper Perennial, 2009.

Coulibaly, Modibo, Rodney D. Green, and David M. James. *Segregation in Federally Subsidized Low-Income Housing in the United States*. Westport, CT: Greenwood Publishing Group, 1998.

Craig, Gordon A. *Europe Since 1914*. Hinsdale, IL: Dryden Press, 1961.

Crisp, Robert. *Brazen Chariots: Fighting Against Rommel's Crack Afrika Korps—the Allied Side of the Desert War*. New York: Ballantine Books, 1961.

Cronkite, Walter, and Maurice Isserman. *Cronkite's War: His World War II Letters Home*. Washington, DC: National Geographic, 2014.

Cunningham, W. Scott, and Lydel Sims. *Wake Island Command*. New York: Little, Brown and Company, 1961.

Deighton, Len. *Blitzkrieg: From the Rise of Hitler to the Fall of Dunkirk*. New York: Ballantine Books, 1982.

———. *Blood, Tears and Folly: An Objective Look at World War II*. New York: Castle Books, 1993.

Dobbs, Michael. *Six Months in 1945: From World War to Cold War*. New York: Alfred A. Knopf, 2012.

Drea, Edward J. *Japan's Imperial Army: Its Rise and Fall: 1853–1945*. Lawrence: University Press of Kansas, 2016.

Eisenhower, Dwight David. *Crusade in Europe*. Garden City, NY: Doubleday and Company, 1940.

Eisenhower, Susan. *Mrs. Ike: Memories and Reflections on the Life of Mamie Eisenhower*. Moosic, PA: HarperCollins, 1996.

Evans, M. Stanton, and Herbert Romerstein. *Stalin's Secret Agent: The Subversion of Roosevelt's Government*. New York: Threshold Editions, 2012.

Evans, Richard J. *The Third Reich at War*. New York: Penguin, 2008.

Fleming, Thomas. *The Forgotten Victory: The Battle for New Jersey—1780*. New York: Reader's Digest Press, 1973.

Gallagher, Hugh G. *FDR's Splendid Deception*. Arlington, VA: Vandamere Press, 1994.

Goodwin, Doris Kearns. *No Ordinary Time: Franklin and Eleanor Roosevelt; The Home Front in World War II*. New York: Touchstone, 1996.

Graebner, William. *The Age of Doubt: American Thought and Culture in the 1940s*. Boston: Twayne Publishers, 1991.

Guderian, Heinz. *Panzer Leader*. New York: De Capo Press, 1996.

Haskew, Michael E. *Western Allied Forces of World War II: Order of Battle*. London: Amber Books, 2009.

Hastings, Max. *Inferno: The World at War, 1939–1945*. New York: Alfred A. Knopf, 2011.

———. *Overlord: D-Day and the Battle for Normandy*. New York: Touchstone–Simon & Schuster, 1984.

Hastings, Max, and George Stevens. *Victory in Europe: D-Day to VE Day in Full Color*. New York: Little, Brown and Company, 1985.

Heinrichs, Waldo H. *Threshold of War: Franklin D. Roosevelt and American Entry into World War II*. Oxford: Oxford University Press, 1988.

Hilsman, Roger. *American Guerrilla: My War Behind Japanese Lines (Memories of War)*. McLean, VA: Brasseys (US), 1990.

Hitchcock, William I. *The Bitter Road to Freedom: The New History of the Liberation of Europe*. New York: Free Press, 2008.

Hull, Cordell. *The Memoirs of Cordell Hull*. New York: Macmillan Company, 1948.

Ickes, Harold L. *The Secret Diary of Harold L. Ickes*. Vol. III, *The Lowering Clouds, 1939–1941*. New York: Simon and Schuster, 1955.

Jordan, Jonathan W. *American Warlords: How Roosevelt's High Command Led America to Victory in World War II*. New York: NAL Caliber, 2015.

Kass, Amy A., Leon R. Kass, and Diana Schaub, eds. *What So Proudly We Hail: The American Soul in Story, Speech, and Song*. Wilmington, DE: ISI Books, 2011.

Kaufmann, J. E., and H. W. Kaufmann. *Hitler's Blitzkrieg Campaigns: The Invasion and Defense of Western Europe, 1939–1940*. Mechanicsburg, PA: Combined Books, 1993.

Keegan, John. *The Second World War*. New York: Viking Publishing, 1989.

Kenez, Peter. *Hungary: From the Nazis to the Soviets; The Establishment of the Communist Regime in Hungary, 1944–1948*. New York: Cambridge University Press, 2006.

Kennet, Lee. *G.I.: The American Soldier in World War II*. New York: Charles Scribner's Sons, 1987.

Kerr, E. Bartlett. *Surrender and Survival: The Experience of American POWs in the Pacific, 1941–1945*. New York: William Morrow and Company, 1985.

Ketchum, Richard M. *The Borrowed Years, 1938–1941: American on the Way to War*. New York: Random House, 1989.

Kotani, Ken. *Japanese Intelligence in World War II*. Oxford: Osprey Publishing, 2009.

Larrabee, Eric. *Commander in Chief: Franklin Delano Roosevelt, His Lieutenants, and Their War*. New York: Harper & Row Publishers, 1987.

Lash, Joseph P. *Eleanor and Franklin: The Story of Their Relationship, Based on Eleanor Roosevelt's Private Papers*. New York: W. W. Norton & Company, 1971.

Lawson, Ted W. *Thirty Seconds over Tokyo*. Garden City, NY: Blue Ribbon Books, 1944.

Leckie, Robert. *Helmet for My Pillow: From Parris Island to the Pacific*. New York: Bantam Books, 2010.

———. *Okinawa: The Last Battle of World War II*. New York: Penguin, 1995.

———. *Strong Men Armed: The United States Marines Against Japan*. New York: Bonanza Books, 1962.

Levi, Primo. *Survival in Auschwitz*. New York: Collier Books, 1958.

Liddell Hart, Basil Henry. *The German Generals Talk*. New York: William Morrow and Company, 1948.

Low, David. *Low on the War: A Cartoon Commentary of the Years 1939–41*. New York: Simon and Schuster, 1941.

Lukacs, John D. *Escape from Davao: The Forgotten History of the Most Daring Prison Break of the Pacific War*. New York: Simon & Schuster, 2010.

MacArthur, Douglas. *Reminiscences*. New York: McGraw-Hill, 1964.

MacDonald, Charles Brown. *The Mighty Endeavor: The American War in Europe*. New York: William Morrow and Company, 1986.

Manstein, Erich von. *Lost Victories*. Chicago: Henry Regnery, 1958.

Marshall, Samuel Lyman Atwood. *The Soldier's Load and the Mobility of a Nation*. Quantico, VA: The Marine Corps Association, 1950.

Mauldin, Bill. *Up Front*. New York: Henry Holt and Company, 1945.

McCullough, David. *Truman*. New York: Simon & Schuster, 1992.

McElvaine, Robert S. *The Great Depression: America, 1929–1941*. New York: Three Rivers Press, 1984.

Meacham, Jon. *Franklin and Winston: An Intimate Portrait of an Epic Friendship*. New York: Random House, 2004.

Minear, Richard H. *Dr. Seuss Goes to War: The World War II Editorial Cartoons of Theodor Seuss Geisel*. New York: New Press, 2001.

Morton, Louis. *United States Army in World War II: The War in the Pacific; The Fall of the Philippines*. Washington, DC: Office of the Chief of Military History, Department of the Army, 1953.

O'Neill, William L. *A Democracy at War: America's Fight at Home and Abroad in World War II*. New York: Free Press, 1993.

Overy, Richard J. *Why the Allies Won*. New York: W. W. Norton & Company, 1995.

Patton, George S. *War as I Knew It*. Boston: Houghton Mifflin Company, 1947.

Perret, Geoffrey. *There's a War to Be Won: The United States Army in World War II*. New York: Random House, 1991.

Phillips, Sid. *You'll Be Sor-ree!* Denver: Valour Studios, 2010.

Polenberg, Richard. *The Era of Franklin D. Roosevelt, 1933–1945: A Brief History with Documents*. New York: Bedford/St. Martins, 2000.

Prior, Robin. *When Britain Saved the West: The Story of 1940*. New Haven, CT: Yale University Press, 2015.

Pyle, Ernie. *Brave Men*. New York: Henry Holt and Company, 1944.

Redmond, Juanita. *I Served on Bataan*. New York: J. B. Lippincott, 1943.

Richler, Mordecai, ed. *Writers on World War II: An Anthology*. New York: Alfred A. Knopf, 1991.

Roberts, Geoffrey. *Stalin's Wars: From World War to Cold War, 1939–1953*. New Haven, CT: Yale University Press, 2006.

Roosevelt, Eleanor. *This I Remember*. Garden City, NY: Doubleday and Company, 1961.

Roosevelt, Franklin D. *F.D.R.: His Personal Letters: 1928–1945*. New York: Duell, Sloan and Pearce, 1970.

———. *The War Messages of Franklin D. Roosevelt December 8, 1941, to April 13, 1945: The President's War Addresses to the People & to the Congress of the United States of America*. USA: United States of America, 1945.

Rowley, Hazel. *Franklin and Eleanor: An Extraordinary Marriage*. New York: Farrar, Straus and Giroux, 2010.

Ryan, Cornelius. *A Bridge Too Far*. New York: Simon and Schuster, 1974.

———. *The Last Battle*. New York: Simon and Schuster, 1966.

Schultz, Duane. *Wake Island: The Heroic Gallant Fight*. New York: St. Martin's Press, 1978.

Schweikart, Larry, and Dave Dougherty. *A Patriot's History of the Modern World*. Vol. II, *From the Cold War to the Age of Entitlement: 1945–2012*. New York: Penguin, 2013.

Sebag Montefiore, Simon. *Stalin: The Court of the Red Tsar*. New York: Alfred A. Knopf, 2003.

Service, Robert. *Stalin: A Biography*. London: Pan Books, 2004.

Shaw, Antony. *World War II: Day by Day*. New York: Chartwell Books, 2010.

Shirer, William L. *20th Century Journey: A Memoir of a Life and the Times: The Start: 1904–1930*. New York: Simon and Schuster, 1976.

Shirley, Craig. *December 1941: 31 Days That Changed America and Saved the World*. New York: Nelson Books, 2011.

Shogan, Robert. *Hard Bargain: How FDR Twisted Churchill's Arm, Evaded the Law, and Changed the Role of the American Presidency*. Boulder, CO: Westview Press, 1995.

Sledge, Eugene B. *With the Old Breed at Peleliu and Okinawa*. Oxford: Oxford University Press, 1990.

Smart, Charles Allen. *The Long Watch*. Cleveland: World Publishing Company, 1968.

Smith, Jean Edward. *FDR*. Manhattan: Random House, 2008.

Spector, Ronald H. *The Eagle Against the Sun: The American War with Japan*. New York: Free Press, 1985.

Tatum, Charles W. *Red Blood, Black Sand: Fighting Alongside John Basilone from Boot Camp to Iwo Jima*. New York: Berkley Publishing Group, 2012.

Taylor, Robert L. *Winston Churchill: An Informal Study of Greatness*. Garden City, NY: Doubleday and Company, 1952.

Thomson, Robert Smith. *A Time for War: Franklin D. Roosevelt and the Path to Pearl Harbor*. New York: Prentice Hall Press, 1991.

Toland, John. *Adolf Hitler*. New York: Ballantine Books, 1976.

———. *But Not in Shame: The Six Months After Pearl Harbor*. New York: Random House, 1961.

———. *The Last 100 Days: The Tumultuous and Controversial Story of the Final Days of World War II in Europe*. New York: Random House, 2003.

Townsend, Peter. *Duel of Eagles*. New York: Simon and Schuster, 1969.

Truman, Harry S. *Memoirs by Harry S. Truman*. Vol. I, *Year of Decisions*. Garden City, NY: Doubleday and Company, 1955.

———. *Memoirs by Harry S. Truman*. Vol. II, *Years of Trial and Hope*. Garden City, NY: Doubleday and Company, 1956.

Truman, Margaret. *Harry S. Truman*. New York: William Morrow and Company, 1973.

Tuttle, William M., Jr. *Daddy's Gone to War: The Second World War in the Lives of America's Children*. New York: Oxford University Press, 1993.

Ungváry, Krisztián. *Battle for Budapest: 100 Days in World War II*. London: Bloomsbury Academic, 2019.

Volkogonov, Dmitri A. *Stalin: Triumph and Tragedy*. London: George Weidenfeld and Nicolson, 1991.

Weinberg, Gerhard L. *A World at Arms: A Global History of World War II*. Cambridge: Cambridge University Press, 1994.

Weintraub, Stanley. *Final Victory: FDR's Extraordinary World War II Presidential Campaign*. Boston: Da Capo Press, 2012.

Weisbrode, Kenneth. *The Year of Indecision, 1946: A Tour Through the Crucible of Harry Truman's America*. New York: Viking Books, 2016.

Wheeler, Richard. *A Special Valor: The US Marines and the Pacific War*. New York: Harper & Row, 1983.

Wheeler-Bennett, John, and Anthony Nicholls. *The Semblance of Peace: The Political Settlement After the Second World War*. New York: W. W. Norton & Company, 1974.

Willmott, H. P. *June 1944*. New York: Blandford Press, 1984.

Winters, Richard D., and Colonel Cole C. Kingseed. *Beyond Band of Brothers: The War Memoirs of Major Dick Winters*. New York: Penguin, 2006.

Woolner, David B. *The Last 100 Days: FDR at War and at Peace*. New York: Basic Books, 2017.

Wouk, Herman. *War and Remembrance*. Boston: Little, Brown & Company, 1978.

ARTICLES

"Ace Killed by US Fire." *Washington Post*. January 16, 1945.

"Agony in Japanese Hellship Portrayed by Yank Survivor." *Boston Daily Globe*. February 17, 1945.

"Aviation Gas Tax?" *Boston Daily Globe*. February 14, 1945.

Albright, Robert. "New Blast by Wheeler Sparks Acrid Policy Fight." *Washington Post*. January 16, 1945.

"B Cadets Who 'Wash Out' Given New Aviation Assignments by Navy." *Boston Daily Globe*. February 17, 1945.

"Beachhead Is Quickly Won at Mariveles, Japs Trapped: Four Divisions Last of Foe in Manila." *Boston Daily Globe*. February 17, 1945.

"Bombardment Silences Jap Island Batteries." *Boston Daily Globe*. February 17, 1945.

"Captured 'Superman' Line Up." *Boston Daily Globe*. February 17, 1945.

Connery, George. "Stimson Reports 18,000 Missing Indicates 22,000 Dead, Wounded." *Washington Post*. January 16, 1945.

"Ernie Pyle at Honolulu: Entirely Different War in Pacific—Nothing Behind for 1000 Miles—Unhuman Enemy." *Boston Daily Globe*. February 17, 1945.

Gilbert, Ben. "Outdoor Lighting 'Brownout' Ordered for US February 1." *Washington Post*. January 16, 1945.

"Halsey's Planes Hit Day After Sinking 41 Ships Off Indo-China." *Washington Post*. January 16, 1945.

Hamlin, I. R., Lieutenant. "Suddenly in Strode Gen MacArthur" [Editorial]. *Boston Sunday Globe*. February 18, 1945.

Higgins, Marguerite. "WTU Backs Use of German Labor, but No 'Slavery.'" *Boston Daily Globe*. February 17, 1945.

Levin, M. "Nazi War Captives Dull as to Future of Reich: Common Soldier Has Only Vaguest Notions About Government if Free to Choose." *Boston Daily Globe*. February 12, 1945.

Lippmann, Walter. "Germany After Yalta." *Boston Daily Globe*. February 17, 1945.

"Lt. J. P. Kennedy Jr., Gets Navy Cross Posthumously." *Boston Daily Globe*. February 16, 1945.

McKinnon, George E. "A Telegram with Two Blue Stars Comes to an American Family." *Boston Sunday Globe*. February 11, 1945.

McManus, Geo. "Bringing Up Father." *Atlanta Constitution*. March 4, 1945.

"Meat." *Boston Sunday Globe*. February 11, 1945.

"Navy Smashes at Tokyo: Warships Shell Iwo; US Landing Possible." *Boston Daily Globe*. February 16, 1945.

"Nazi War Refugees Perish by Hundreds Fleeing Red Armies." *Boston Daily Globe*. February 16, 1945.

"Plenty of Cigarettes!!!!" *Boston Daily Globe*. February 12, 1945.

Reynolds, Lewis. "Home of Alpaca: Peru's Andean Animals Give Soft, Warm Wool for Aviator's Jackets: Most Comes to US Now: In Peacetime It Is Mixed with Worsted for Overcoats: Delay in Rain Slows Shearing." *Washington Post*. January 2, 1945.

"Southworth's Son Killed as Plane Crashes in NY." *Boston Daily Globe*. February 17, 1945.

"Supply of Cigarettes." *Washington Post*. January 2, 1945.

"The 40s: A Story of a Decade." *New Yorker* (New York: Random House, 2014).

"US Bomber Attacks Aid Russian Drive." *Boston Daily Globe*. February 16, 1945.

"We're in Moral Slump, Asserts Dr. Stafford." *Boston Daily Globe*. February 12, 1945.

PERIODICALS

American Magazine
Arizona Daily Star
Arizona Republic
Atlanta Constitution (GA)

Bakersfield Californian

Baltimore Sun

Beatrice Times (NE)

Berkshire Eagle (Pittsfield, MA)

Billboard

Birmingham News

Boston Daily Globe

Boston Evening Globe

Boston Sunday Globe

Burlington Daily News

Charlotte News (NC)

Charlotte Observer (NC)

Chicago Tribune

Cincinnati Enquirer

Citizen News (CA)

Cleveland Plain Dealer

Courier (Waterloo, IA)

Courier Journal (Louisville, KY)

Crisis

Crowley Post-Signal (LA)

Daily Oklahoman

Daily Times (MD)

Dallas Morning News

Dayton Herald

Decatur Daily

Democrat and Chronicle (NY)

Des Moines Tribune

Detroit Evening Times

Evening Independent (St. Petersburg, FL)

Evening Star (Washington, DC)

Evening Sun (Baltimore, MD)

Evening Times (PA)

Falls City Journal (NE)

Flying

Fort Worth Star-Telegram

Freeport Journal-Standard (IL)

Fresno Bee

Globe-Gazette (IA)
Hanford Morning Journal (CA)
Hawaii Tribune-Herald
Henderson Daily Dispatch (NC)
Honolulu Advertiser
Honolulu Star-Bulletin
Independent Record (MT)
Indianapolis News
Indianapolis Star
Kansas City Star
Kenosha Evening News (WI)
Key West Citizen
Knoxville News-Sentinel (TN)
Life
London Times
Los Angeles Times
Mansfield News-Journal (OH)
Miami Daily News
Miami Herald
Michigan Chronicle
News and Observer (NC)
News-Herald (Franklin, PA)
New York Daily News
New York Times
Nome Nugget (AK)
Pensacola News Journal
Philadelphia Inquirer
Pittsburgh Post-Gazette
Pittsburgh Press
Pittsburgh Sun-Telegraph
Popular Mechanics
Popular Photography
Press and Sun-Bulletin (Binghampton, NY)
Richmond Times-Dispatch (VA)
Salt Lake Tribune
San Francisco Examiner

Scrantonian Tribune (PA)
Spokesman-Review (WA)
Star Tribune (Minneapolis, MN)
St. Louis Post-Dispatch
Sunday Star (Washington, DC)
Tampa Bay Times
Topaz Times (UT)
Tucson Daily Citizen
Volksblatt (OH)
Washington Post
Wilkes-Barre Times Leader, The Evening News

NEWS WIRES

Associated Press
International News Service
United Press International

NEWS BROADCASTING MEDIA

1XE
6XC
8XB
8XK
ABC
CBS
Dumont
KDKA
Mutual Broadcasting System
NBC
WWJ
WWV

ELECTRONIC MEDIA

Patton, George S. *George Smith Patton Diaries, 1910–1945.* (1945 only). Washington, DC: Library of Congress Digital Collections.

Ridgon, William M. *Log of the President's Trip to the Berlin Conference, July 6, 1945–August 7, 1945.* National Archives. https://www.trumanlibrary.gov /library/personal-papers/subject-file-1943-1980/president-trumans -travel-logs-1945?documentid=NA&pagenumber=1.

OTHER MATERIALS

Franklin D. Roosevelt Library. Hyde Park, NY. Select Online Items Pertaining to 1945.

Franklin D. Roosevelt Library. Hyde Park, NY. Selected Digitized Correspondence from the Anna Eleanor Roosevelt Papers, General Correspondence Series, 1945–1947.

Presidential records, Franklin D. Roosevelt Presidential Library and Museum.

Presidential records, Harry S. Truman Library and Museum.

Private Collection, President Roosevelt in Hawaii, Star Bulletin.

Private Collection, Hawaii, as the Camera Sees It, Star Bulletin.

Private Collection, Mauer Archives.

Specialty Publication. Arnn, Larry. *Three Lessons of Statesmanship.* December 2017. Vol. 46, no. 12. Hillsdale College.

Specialty Publication, Lucas, Harold V. *So This Is Hawaii.* Printed in Hawaii by *Hilo Tribune Herald.* First Edition, 2,000 copies, 1928. Second Edition, 5,000 copies, 1935.

Specialty Publication, Personal Scrapbook of Ms. Beatrice Shurfelt. Schenectady, New York.

INDEX

ABOUT THE AUTHOR

Craig Shirley is the author of four critically praised bestsellers about Ronald Reagan: *Reagan's Revolution, Last Act, Reagan Rising,* and *Rendezvous with Destiny,* which was named one of the five best campaign books of all time by the *Wall Street Journal*. His book *December 1941* appeared multiple times on the *New York Times* bestseller list. Shirley is chairman of Shirley & McVicker Public Affairs and is a widely sought-after speaker and commentator. The *London Times* called him "the best of the Reagan biographers." He also wrote the definitive biography of Speaker Newt Gingrich, *Citizen Newt*. The Visiting Reagan Scholar at Eureka College, Shirley is on the Board of Governors of the Reagan Ranch and lectures frequently at the Reagan Library, and he has written extensively for Newsmax, *Washington Post, Washington Examiner, Washington Times, Los Angeles Times, Townhall, Breitbart, National Review, LifeZette, CNS,* and many other publications. Considered one of the foremost public intellectuals on the history of conservatism in America, Shirley also wrote *Mary Ball Washington: The Untold Story of George Washington's Mother,* which won the People's Choice Award from the Library of Virginia. He is now working on *The Search for Reagan* and other books. During the Cold War, he was a contract agent for the CIA. He is the founder of the Ft. Hunt Youth Lacrosse League where, as a coach, he sported a 126-19-4 record. With his wife, Zorine, they divide their time between

Ben Lomond—a three-hundred-year-old foursquare Georgian—and Trickle Down Point on the Corrotoman River in Virginia. Zorine and Craig are the parents of four children—Matthew, Andrew, Taylor, and Mitch—along with their daughter-in-law and Matthew's wife, Brittany. They have a new granddaughter, Eleanor. Craig's mother is Barbara Cone Shirley Eckert, and his sister is Rebecca Sirhal. Both were instrumental in the development of this book. His ancestor Henry Cone was a soldier of the American Revolution and served for seven years under George Washington. In 2021, Shirley addressed the national convention of the Daughters of the American Revolution.